D0875327

Herbert L. Searles, Ph.D. University of Iowa, is Professor of Philosophy, Emeritus, at the University of Southern California, where he has been a faculty member since 1930. Before coming to California he taught at Millikin University and subsequently at San Diego State College. He has been an Associate Editor of *The Personalist,* and has served as Secretary-Treasurer and Vice-president of the Pacific Division of the American Philosophical Association. Dr. Searles has contributed articles to *Philosophy of Science, World Affairs Interpreter, The Personalist,* and other journals.

Logic and Scientific Methods

An Introductory Course

HERBERT L. SEARLES

UNIVERSITY OF SOUTHERN CALIFORNIA

Third Edition

THE RONALD PRESS COMPANY • NEW YORK

Library of Congress Catalog Card Number: 68–13474
PRINTED IN THE UNITED STATES OF AMERICA

To Xan and Herb

Preface

Designed for the introductory course in logic, this textbook has been written not only for students for whom this one course may be definitive but also for those who will be going on to advanced study in logic.

As in previous editions, the exposition proceeds from the familiar and concrete to the abstract. Equal emphasis is given to the logic of deduction and the methods of the sciences. Other significant topics are: the relations of logic to language, embracing semantic problems that arise in the verification and communication of knowledge; the logic of relations and the position it sustains with respect to the classical logic; and statistics and probability theory, as they pertain to scientific methods.

There are a number of significant innovations in this Third Edition, the major one being the addition of an extensive section on symbolic logic—which includes the construction and use of truth tables, the evaluation of truth-functional arguments, and quantification. In addition, the chapter on probability has been amplified to include a comprehensive discussion—with illustrations—of Bayes' theorem. Other changes have moved the chapter on informal semantic and material fallacies to an earlier part of the book (for pedagogical purposes), and added a number of problems and exercises as well as an appendix of formal, semantic, material, and inductive fallacies. The features that have been found useful, such as the glossary of logical terms and the suggested answers to selected problems, have been retained and expanded. Finally, the bibliography has been revised and brought up to date.

I wish to thank students and teachers who have written me both kind and critical commentary about the book. Their criticisms have, as far as possible, been incorporated.

I would also like to mention with appreciation the helpful suggestions of the following persons: Robert L. Caldwell, University of

Arizona; Eugene G. Bugg, Vanderbilt University; Willard O. Eddy, Colorado State University; Milton D. Hunnex, Willamette University; William H. K. Narum, Saint Olaf College; and Sherwood M. Nelson and William S. Snyder, San Diego State College. My gratitude is especially due to my wife, who has again rendered valuable assistance in the preparation of the manuscript.

HERBERT L. SEARLES

Los Angeles, California
  January, 1968

Contents

APPENDIXES

I

LOGIC AND MEANING

1

Introduction: What Is Logic?

I. THE STUDY OF LOGIC

The modern student approaches the study of logic with mixed feelings. He is likely to find a strong appeal and excellent motivation in many of the objectives which he has associated with the study of logic, such as discipline in clear thinking, skill in weighing evidence in support of an argument, and knowledge regarding the methods of the sciences. But on the other hand he is likely to be puzzled by its somewhat technical vocabulary, its seeming complexities, and the abstractness of formal arguments which make it appear quite foreign to the general tenor of his previous educational pursuits, oriented as they are today primarily in the direction of the concrete and the practical.

This strangeness, however, will begin to disappear as soon as he realizes that, during the greater part of his life, in fact ever since he began to meet such unpleasant contradictions as, "You cannot both eat your cake and have it," he has been consciously and unconsciously exposed to the forms and methods of reasoning which logic studies and systematizes.

One of the first questions he is likely to ask is: "Is the study of logic practical?" Now if he means by this, is the study of logic likely to increase his intelligence, make him into an eloquent debater or lawyer, or double his usefulness to his employer in business, and hence his salary, the answer must be in the negative.

But if he means practical in a more inclusive sense, which includes some theory, then the answer is definitely affirmative. Learning how

3

to reason according to the evidence in making judgments of fact, and in evaluating our conclusions according to the principles of valid inference, is practical in the fullest sense of the word. There is nothing in the process of acquiring an education that is more practical. Some of the reasons for studying logic in this broader sense of the practical are listed below. These reasons may not be of equal importance for every student but will serve as a guide and a goal of attainment in the study of logic.

1. Logic may be regarded both as a *science* and as an *art*. If logic is regarded as a *science*, its study should give the student an *understanding* of the nature of the principles and methods of logical inference, both inductive and deductive.

2. Considered as an *art*, the study of logic should assist the student to improve his own powers of cogent reasoning so that he may be able to present his conclusions together with the supporting evidence clearly, and to recognize the difference between good and bad evidence for a belief, truth-claim, or conclusion, whether it be his own or that of someone with whom he communicates and argues.

3. It should make the student aware of the difference between persuasion through various psychological means, such as emotional appeal and majority pressures, and rational conviction through evidence and logical reasoning. This should put him on his guard against propaganda and enable him to evaluate and resist ballyhoo.

4. It should enable the student to develop a critical attitude toward the assumptions and presuppositions which form the background of his own and many others' arguments in such fields as politics, economics, race relations, and other social sciences, where the facts are not fully verified but contain elements of tradition, preference, and evaluation.

5. It should familiarize the student with the vocabulary of logical terminology. Such words as "inference," "logical," "fallacy," "proposition," "evidence," "contradiction," and "imply," permeate our entire literature—not only of philosophy and science, but of all writing of the kind that is designed to appeal to the intellect or convey knowledge. The exact meaning of these terms is best acquired in connection with the study of the processes for which they stand.

6. It should make the student conscious of the ambiguity of words and the various functions of language, and should encourage him to be more exact and hence more effective in his use of linguistic symbols.

7. It should serve as an introduction to the main principles and

methods of scientific procedure, such as care in observation, inductive inference, and the use and verification of hypotheses. While it is granted that these processes cannot be fully mastered until put into practice in scientific experiments, they can be studied with great profit to the student, and can be used to some extent in the solution of simple problems.

8. For the student of philosophy, especially, the study of logic is important, since it is basic to everything else he will study. Because it is difficult to be a critic much less a creator in a growing field without knowing something of the tradition which is to be superseded, one who wishes to go beyond present developments in logic must master that tradition.

II. A DEFINITION OF LOGIC

The word "logic" is derived from the Greek word *logos,* which means word, reason, or discourse. It occurs as the suffix in the names of most of the sciences, such as geo-logy, bio-logy, and psycho-logy, and suggests the systematic search for universal laws and principles, in accordance with sound rational criteria and experimental procedures, modified to best serve the ends of the particular science. But underlying all of the sciences, as well as the ordinary thinking of daily life, are some general logical principles common to all thought.

In the broadest sense, logic is the science of evidence. Deductive logic is the science of the norms and principles of valid inference. More simply stated, it is the method of correct reasoning from a premise or premises to a conclusion, or of supporting conclusions by a premise or premises which imply them. This is *the method of demonstration* or *formal proof.* Inductive logic, known as *the method of discovery,* may be defined as the process of arriving at general conclusions of varying degrees of probability on the basis of observation and empirical or factual evidence.

These two logical methods, *deduction* and *induction,* are in no sense antagonistic to each other, in spite of the fact that partisans of each method have carried on extensive controversies to the disparagement of the other. In fact, both in daily life and in the sciences the two methods are complementary, and it is often difficult to know where one leaves off and the other begins. When Sherlock Holmes takes out his magnifying glass and scrutinizes the carpet of the room where a murder has been committed, and exclaims, "Aha! The murderer is over six feet tall!" he may be reasoning deductively from the premises: Any man whose footprints are fourteen inches long is over six feet tall, and these footprints are over fourteen inches. Or he may be reasoning inductively and this observation is just another case of large footprints which in the past in his experience have been associated with tall men.

In science, the inductive and observational approach to the materials provides the starting point and groundwork for the making of hypotheses, and deductions draw out and explore the logical consequences or implications of these hypotheses in order to eliminate those that are inconsistent with the observed facts, while induction again contributes to the verification of the remaining hypothesis.

III. LOGIC IN EVERYDAY LIFE

Every time we seek to solve a problem either practical or theoretical, or take part in debate or argumentation, we engage, in varying degrees, in a mental activity we call logical reasoning. The psychological activities of sense awareness, perception, and conception are presuppositions of the more complex processes involving judgment and inference. Much of our knowledge is direct and *immediate*, of the kind that can be verified by direct observation. Logical inference goes beyond simple observation and is *mediated* through something previously known or granted. Suppose you open the door of your new electric refrigerator and notice that a light bulb flashes on. If someone were so skeptical as to ask you how you know the light is on, you would doubtless point to it and exclaim impatiently, "Can't you see?" But suppose your questioner persisted and asked you how you know whether or not the light goes off when you close the door, you are no longer able to answer from direct sense experience. Your conclusion would have to be arrived at indirectly, or mediated through some other accepted fact or hypothesis such as, "Whenever I press the button with my finger the light goes off, and when I close the door it presses the button; therefore, whenever I close the door the light goes off." Thus you have arrived at a logical conclusion not on the basis of seeing alone, but as the result of an *inference*. Often because the solution of a problem comes "as quick as thought," we do not realize that we are doing anything that can be dignified by the name *logical reasoning*. The steps in the process, however, may be brought into clear outline whenever we are asked why we believe some of the things we do, or how we have reached such and such a conclusion. Notice that we usually begin to answer by saying "because," and this is followed up by stating the reasons, evidence, logical grounds, or *premises* of our argument. When these premises and the *conclusion implied by them* are clearly formulated, we have what in the technical language of logic is called a *syllogism*. The word "premise" is from the Latin *praemittere*, which means to put first, and constitutes the data or grounds or evidence for a conclusion.

Most of our logical reasoning in daily life, however, is of the *elliptical* kind; that is, not all of the premises of the argument are explicitly stated because the people with whom we associate and communicate from day to day have the same general background as ourselves, and to be too explicit would be to sound pedantic. For example, while I am working in my front yard on a very hot day, the sun gets higher and higher until I finally give up with the exclamation, "It is too hot to work today." Now, no one in my general locality would be so unfamiliar with the reasons as to ask why, because the conditions governing the relation of excessive heat to the human organism are generally understood. These general laws and principles constitute my major premise, which has been purposely suppressed because it is assumed to be taken for granted. However, if some persistent logician insisted on my complete argument, it would run as follows:

> Whenever the temperature reaches 100 degrees,
>   it is too hot for me to work.
> The temperature today has reached 100 degrees.
> Therefore, it is too hot for me to work today.

Or again, if I have been so careless as to have left my car standing at a curb that is painted red, and return to find a traffic officer making out a ticket, I suspect that the officer, without any very involved process of reasoning on his part, has come to the conclusion that I have committed an illegal act. If I know my logic and my Vehicle Code, I do not argue with him, for I know that the major premise, or general rule of law, is written in the Code, to wit, "All parking on red zones is illegal." The present occurrence of red-zone parking is the case applied to the rule and is the minor premise, and the conclusion is that this is an illegal act. The complete form of the argument runs:

> Rule: All cases of red-zone parking are illegal.
> Case: This act is a case of red-zone parking.
> Conclusion: This act is illegal.

This illustration, however, provides an excellent example of one of the pitfalls for which the student must always be on his guard. Are

we sure that our terms such as "parking" are unambiguous? Is this
an actual case of parking? What actually constitutes a case of parking? If in your Vehicle Code there are various definitions of "parking," "stopping," and "standing," you might be inclined to argue the
point with the officer, hoping to save yourself a trip to the courthouse.
It is obvious that if the word "parking" is too loosely defined, or has
different meanings, the conclusion would not follow, and you might go
scot free. But when you have defined "parking" as any case of stopping your car and leaving the wheel unattended, then it is clear that
this case comes under the general rule and the conclusion logically
follows.

Most of the problems we meet in daily life, as well as in science, call
for both inductive and deductive reasoning. In meeting some problems, deduction is sufficient and is a great timesaver. The method
employed must depend upon the kind of problem to be solved or the
kind of supporting evidence sought. Suppose you are asked by your
prospective employer for proof of your birth. Legally it is not sufficient evidence, at least in most States, to present him with the following deduction:

> All persons now alive were born.
> I am now alive.
> Therefore, I was born.

While your premises may be entirely true, and your conclusion
validly drawn, your employer would not be satisfied with your evidence. He might argue that you have told him nothing that he did
not already know, that the argument is too formal and abstract and
could apply to anyone; that what he wants is specific evidence of
your particular birth as to time and place to be placed on file for both
the company's and the government's future information. This, of
course, would call for documentary evidence such as that of a birth
certificate, which, provided its authenticity is empirically established,
requires nothing more than simple identification to be admitted as
proof. If no record of your birth has been kept, there is still another
inductive approach by means of an affidavit of a physician, nurse, or
hospital staff member. If all of the avenues of objective proof from
documentary or testimonial evidence fail, however, we are left with
only the purely formal deduction as given above.

These familiar examples will serve to show that we all use both
inductive and deductive logic in everyday matters of problem solving
and casual discussion. We use induction whenever we make ob-

servations of particular instances and arrive at generalized conclusions. We use deduction whenever we try to give reasons for our beliefs and conclusions by appeal to evidence which may be already accepted by both parties to the discussion, and which logically supports or implies the conclusion.

IV. VALIDITY AND TRUTH

In the above examples we have been concerned mainly with the question of *validity*, and the word *truth* has been mentioned only incidentally. Both terms are in need of clarification. The word "valid" comes from the Latin *valere*, meaning to be of worth or to be strong. A valid argument is, then, a strong or sound argument. Validity has to do with the question of whether or not a conclusion is correctly inferred from premises, or whether or not the premises imply the conclusion. This is the central problem of deductive logic. The term *inference* may be applied either to the logical act of drawing the conclusion implied by the premises, or to the conclusion so drawn. *Implication* is the relation between propositions whereby given one or more propositions another logically follows.

The term *truth* refers not to arguments and inferences but to propositions. A proposition is *empirically (or factually) true or false* by reason of some state of affairs or condition which could be used as evidence to verify or falsify it. "All magnets attract iron" and "The orbits of the planets are ellipses" are examples of propositions which are empirically true or false. The question of empirical truth involves a discussion of induction, hypotheses, probability, and confirmation, and must await a more extensive and adequate treatment of scientific methods in later chapters.

A proposition is *logically (or analytically) true or false* not with reference to any empirical or factual state of affairs but because of its meaning and form or structure. "No unmarried man is married" and "Whales are either mammals or not mammals" are examples. These are called *analytical* propositions, as contrasted with *synthetical* propositions, which are based upon experience.

It should be noted, however, that the truth or falsity of the premises does not affect the logical relation of implication, and that consequently conclusions may be validly inferred from premises whether true or false. The importance of this will become clear later when it is observed that in science it is just as important to be able to make deductions from false hypotheses as from true, in order to test their consequences empirically.   These nine arguments and the table which follows will show the various relations between validity and truth.

1. All Communists are Russians, and all Socialists are Communists; therefore, all Socialists are Russians.
2. All African countries are sovereign states, and all members of the United Nations are Africans; therefore, all members of the United Nations are sovereign states.
3. All Americans are Californians, and F.D.R. was not a Californian; therefore, F.D.R. was not an American.
4. All animals are mammals, and all whales are animals; therefore, all whales are mammals.
5. All superstitious people are human beings, and no civilized people are human beings; therefore, no superstitious people are civilized.
6. All men are mortal, and all animals are men; therefore, all animals are mortal.
7. All animals are organisms, and all lions are animals; therefore, all lions are organisms.
8. No men are angels, and all men are mortal; therefore, all mortals are angels.
9. All animals are organisms, and all dogs are organisms; therefore, all dogs are animals.

Argument Number	First Premise	Second Premise	Conclusion	Validity
1	False	False	False	Valid
2	False	False	True	Valid
3	False	True	False	Valid
4	False	True	True	Valid
5	True	False	False	Valid
6	True	False	True	Valid
7	True	True	True	Valid
8	True	True	False	Invalid
9	True	True	True	Invalid

The following points regarding the relation of validity and truth are illustrated here:

1. That an argument may be valid regardless of the truth or falsity of the premises (numbers 1–6).
2. That if the premises are true and the argument is valid the conclusion will be necessarily true (number 7)
3. That if the premises are true and the conclusion false the argument will necessarily be invalid (number 8)
4. That both premises and conclusion may be true and the argument invalid (number 9)

The methods of establishing the validity of arguments will be postponed to a later chapter.

V. FORM AND MATTER OR CONTENT IN LOGIC

The distinction between *form* and *matter* or *content* in a work of art was familiar to the Greeks long before the development of the Aristotelian Formal Logic. If you look at a Greek vase you will agree that it is the form or structure that makes for its perfection as compared with other similar objects. Yet it could not have this particular structure without a certain kind of raw material which is capable of being so formed. In a physical object like a work of art, it is impossible for us to imagine the form and matter existing independently, yet in most cases the form or structure is of more importance to art than the matter. Now thought as expressed in proposition and argument also has its subject matter or content, and its structure or form, although this distinction is perhaps not so easy to grasp as it is when the object can be seen with the eye. What we have already said about validity and truth will help us to understand the difference between form and matter or content in logic. The form of a proposition or sentence is the arrangement or syntax of the words in such a manner as to convey meaning. The form of an argument is the arrangement of the constituent parts of the argument. For example, in the above arguments, many of the propositions have the same logical form, but the subject matter is different in all. In the argument

> All Communists are Russians.
> All Socialists are Communists.
> Hence, all Socialists are Russians.

all three propositions are in the Universal Affirmative form, i.e., something is affirmed universally (of every member) of the subject class, but the content, or what is asserted, is different in all three. From the viewpoint of purely formal arguments it does not matter what the content is. This is beautifully illustrated in simple arithmetic where 2 plus 2 equals 4, without reference to content. So in logic, if we choose, we may abstract our attention from the particular materials or subject matter asserted or denied by logical propositions and center it upon the form. In other words, the relation of logical implication between premises and conclusion is abstract and formal and does not depend upon the matter-of-fact truth of the premises. Words are abstract linguistic symbols for the concrete objects and processes of our experience, and in logic it serves our purpose to use symbols of an even higher level of abstraction. For the linguistic symbols "Communists," "Socialists," and "Russians" in the above argument, we may substitute the more abstract symbols X, Y, and Z, respectively. Thus we can draw the inference:

> All X's are Z's.
> All Y's are X's.
> _____
> Hence, All Y's are Z's.

Thus the form of the argument is made to stand out clearly and it is more easily seen that the inference is formally valid no matter what the particular content of X, Y, and Z may be, and independently of whether or not they have any content.

VI. LOGIC AND PSYCHOLOGY

The types of mental activity involved in concept formation, inductive reasoning, judgment, and deductive inference presuppose the more elementary psychological processes, such as sensation, perception, imagination, and emotion as foundational. Psychology as a science studies all of the aspects of mental behavior both in their conscious and subconscious aspects, and also in their relation to instinctive drives, volitions, emotions, imagination, and the motor and physiological behavior of the organism.

An important distinction, then, between logic and psychology is that psychology has a much broader field and wider interest in the mental life than does logic. The interests of logic and psychology overlap only with respect to the mental activity we call thinking or reasoning. Psychology may describe the facts of certain types of mental activity and formulate the laws of its behavior, but it is not especially concerned with the problem of truth or falsity of propositions, or the logical validity of arguments as such. Psychology, of course, uses logic as an important part of its methodology. Logic, on the other hand, is concerned with thinking and reasoning only with respect to its consistency and formal validity, and its conformity to standards of truth and falsity.

Pragmatic logicians, however, have emphasized the close relation between psychology and logical reasoning on the grounds that most of our thinking has a practical purpose, that judgments of fact are at least somewhat determined by our selective interests, and that concepts must be understood in terms of the purpose of the one using the concepts. The position is well stated by Schiller:

Every judgment originates in the matrix of some mind . . . consciously or unconsciously it is the product of selection from among alternatives which existed for its maker or for others, and so to some extent "arbitrary" or volitional. Every principle similarly is in the end a postulate, i.e. a demand, and not a "law" descriptive of the course of nature. Without principles (postulates), hypotheses (questions), ideals (purposes), and interests (motives), no science can arise or prosper. In short, the nature and course of thinking cannot be understood without taking into account this "psychological" side of judgment.[1]

If we think of psychology not as the science of psychology, but in the broader sense of "psychology of daily life," not only must we recognize this close relation between psychological and logical factors in thinking, but we should also recognize that psychological factors of an emotional and volitional character often interfere with and hinder the attainment of objectivity in judgment and disinterestedness in science. The daily routine of the average individual is not a logically or rationally thought out pattern, but largely the result of habit, or in response to unconscious drives and urges to activity and attitudes for the satisfaction of fundamental needs, colored by emotional prejudices for or against certain objects, causes, and beliefs. Jastrow says:

Thinking colored by emotional inclination is the rule, even among the more intellectually inclined; and thinking warped by desire and emotional bias is the even more common rule for the far more numerous nonintellectual classes.[2]

Freudian psychology would go even further and assert that much of what we call thinking or reasoning is *wishful thinking or rationalization*. In wishful thinking the desire to have our hopes and dreams realized is so strong that we are prevented from distinguishing between hoped-for possibilities and real probabilities. In rationalization we use arguments and reasons to justify what we have done or believed, or want to do and believe, in response to deep-seated urges and drives within us.

On the other hand, formal logicians have emphasized the fact that reasoning has a formal structure. For them the field of logic is the form of thought expressed in terms of propositions stated in linguistic or other symbols, their meaning, their truth and falsity, and the logical relations between them which permit of inferences. They regard it as a great human advantage that the mind has the capacity for abstraction, since in the interests of achieving greater generality it is possible to center the attention upon the form of propositions and the logical relation of implication between them. This relation is logical and not psychological. In this respect logic approaches the ab-

---

[1] F. C. S. Schiller, *Formal Logic* (New York: The Macmillan Co., 1912), p. 96. By permission of The Macmillan Company.

[2] Joseph Jastrow, *The Psychology of Conviction* (Boston: Houghton Mifflin Co., 1918), pp. 302, 303.

stractness of mathematics and as such has very little or nothing to do with psychology. The position of the formal logicians has been well stated by Cohen and Nagel:

The logical distinction between valid and invalid inference does not refer to the way we think—the process going on in someone's mind. The weight of evidence is not itself a temporal event, but a relation of implication between certain classes or types of propositions. Whether, for instance, it necessarily follows from Euclid's axioms and postulates that the area of no square can be exactly equal to that of a circle is a question of what is necessarily involved in what is asserted by our propositions; and how anyone actually thinks is irrelevant to it. Of course thought (and not mere sense perception) is necessary to apprehend such implications. But thought is likewise necessary to apprehend that the propositions of any science are true. That, however, does not make physics a branch of psychology—unless we deny that these sciences have different subject matters, in other words, unless we deny that physical objects and our apprehension of them are distinguishable and not identical. Similarly, our apprehension of the logical implications on which our inferences are based may be studied as a psychological event, but the relation directly apprehended is not itself a psychological event at all. It is a relation between the forms of propositions and indirectly one between the classes of possible objects asserted by them.[3]

We may sum up this discussion of the relation of logic and psychology by saying that there is an area of our total mental life which is the exclusive field of psychology and which is presupposed by logic. There is an area belonging to the field of abstract and formal logic with which psychology has little to do. Third, there is a much larger area where the two overlap and where the relation of psychology in the broadest sense and logic is very close. Within this area logical reasoning is conditioned by psychological factors which may adversely affect clear thinking, as in the case of biases and prejudices. On the other hand, psychological factors, such as those upon which learning and motivation are based, aid in the development and discipline of native intelligence, and emotional, volitional, and imaginative factors give drive and direction to creative and reflective thinking.

PROBLEMS

I

Hand in for class discussion a specific example of an argument you regard as logical, and one you regard as illogical, and formulate in your own words the reason for your choice.

[3] Cohen and Nagel, *An Introduction to Logic and Scientific Method* (New York: Harcourt, Brace & Co., 1934), pp. 18, 19.

II

1. Show by what logical procedure you would support your belief that when you close the door of your electric refrigerator the light bulb, which is burning when the door is opened, actually goes off.

2. If there are 1,000 girls in the university all wearing nylon stockings, and only 400 different makes of nylon stockings are available, show that more than 2 girls are wearing the same kind of stockings.

3. If you see smoke and infer that fire is present, what is the complete form of your inference?

4. A plaintiff arguing before the small claims court charged the defendant with having spotted the collar of a borrowed dress with dye from her hair. The judge asked, "Do you know that she dyed her hair?" The plaintiff said, "No." "Then," said the judge, "you only inferred it." How sound an inference do you think this is? What is the difference between this inference and numbers 2 and 3 above?

5. A newsboy collector passed by Mrs. Smith's house without calling, for, he said, "Whenever she is at home, her car is always standing outside, and it is not there today." If you did not want to accept that conclusion, what would be the reason for your doubt?

III

The following problems and brain twisters are offered for the purpose of stimulating thought and discussion and involve both logical and psychological factors for their solution. Certain sample solutions are given in the Appendix.

1. What are two different numbers between (and not including) 1 and 10 the product of which equals twice their sum?

2. A state trooper, while driving on a highway, suddenly came upon the scene of an accident. He found two cars headed in opposite directions and parked opposite each other on the sides of the road. Between them lay a man who had been struck and killed a few minutes before by one of them. Each driver said that the other had struck the man. Mr. A said that he, for the past two or three hours, had been examining the inscriptions in a cemetery which was near by, and that he had just returned, to find the scene of the accident as the trooper discovered it. Mr. B claimed that, as he approached the spot, he had seen Mr. A's car strike the man, and that he had consequently stopped in order to render assistance. There were no other witnesses; furthermore, the trooper could learn nothing from marks on the ground or the position of the body. After a brief investigation, however, he definitely proved that Mr. B was guilty. How did he do it?

3. Imagine four horizontal lines an inch apart and directly under one another. Then imagine four vertical lines also an inch apart,

each cutting all four of the horizontal lines. How many squares do these lines form?

4. Mary is twice as old as Ann was when Mary was as old as Ann is now. Mary is twenty-four. How old is Ann?

5. A hungry hunter leaves his camp on an expedition in search of food. He trudges three miles due south, at which point he spies a fine bear. He takes careful aim, shoots, and the prize is his. Leaving his kill where it has fallen, he marches on five miles due east in quest of further game. At this point he finds that he is only three miles from where he first started. What was the color of the bear?

6. A train is operated by three men: Smith, Robinson, and Jones. They are fireman, engineer, and brakeman, but not respectively. On the train are three businessmen: Mr. Smith, Mr. Robinson, and Mr. Jones. Consider the following data about all concerned:

(1) Mr. Robinson lives in Detroit.
(2) The brakeman lives halfway between Chicago and Detroit.
(3) Mr. Jones earns exactly $6,000 per year.
(4) Smith beat the fireman at billiards.
(5) The brakeman's nearest neighbor, one of the passengers, earns exactly three times as much a year as the brakeman, who earns $3,000 per year.
(6) The passenger whose name is the same as the brakeman's lives in Chicago.

Who is the engineer?

7. Visualize one wooden three-inch cube, painted black.

(1) How many cuts would it require to divide the cube into one-inch cubes?
(2) How many cubes would you then have?
(3) How many cubes have four black sides?
(4) How many cubes have three black sides?
(5) How many cubes have two black sides?
(6) How many cubes have one black side?
(7) How many cubes are unpainted?

8. There are seven amoebae in a bowl. They multiply by dividing in two every minute. At the end of 40 minutes the bowl is completely filled. How long did it take to get the bowl half filled?

9. In a certain town there are huntsmen and noblemen. A huntsman is incapable of telling the truth. A nobleman is incapable of a lie. There were three men, either noblemen or huntsmen, walking along the street. The man on the right turned to the man in the middle and said, "I am a ———." The man in the middle turned to the man on the left and said, "He says he's a nobleman." The man on the left turned to the man in the middle and said, "He's not a nobleman, he's a huntsman." How many noblemen were there, and how many huntsmen? Which was which?

10. Three men came to a hotel and rented a suite of rooms which cost $60. Each man paid $20. Later the hotel clerk discovered that the suite cost only $50, so he gave $10 to the bellboy to be returned to the three guests. The bellboy kept $4 for himself and gave $2 to each of the three men. Thus, each man actually paid $18. This made a total of $54 for the suite, and the $4 which the bellboy kept for himself made a sum total of $58. What happened to the other $2?

11. A worm eats through two books standing side by side. Each book is an inch thick, and each cover is ¼ inch thick. The worm starts at the first page of the second volume and eats through to the first page of the first volume. How far did he eat?

12. A barber in a certain village shaves all of those, and only those, who do not shave themselves. Does he shave himself?

13. A man owed $3.00. He had a $2.00 bill, which he pawned for $1.50, and then sold the pawn ticket to another man for $1.50, who redeemed the $2.00 bill. Who lost?

2

Logic and Language

I. LANGUAGE

Language is a highly specialized tool for the expression and communication of thought, feeling, and purpose. It is a marvelously flexible tool and, together with gestures and facial expressions, is capable of communicating the most delicate shades of meaning. There are various theories of the origin of language with which we are not here concerned. It is sufficient to note that its origin lies far back in the infancy of the race, and that it served the many functions of biological and social adaptation and survival long before it became a tool for discriminating and disciplined thought. It is natural, therefore, that it should bear the marks of its origin and long development, and that there should be a specialization of functions even though with some degree of overlapping, and even conflict, among them. The development, refinement, and specialization of language has in some measure kept pace with the demands made upon it for clarity and precision of meaning, logical consistency, and objectivity, but no natural or ordinary language is yet a perfect tool either for communicating meanings in everyday life or for formulating the concepts and propositions of the sciences and philosophy.

Language is made up of words and syntax. Words are linguistic symbols and may symbolize objects, qualities, quantities, events, processes, and relations, as in the sentence, "The high, majestic mountain eroded and raised the adjacent valley floor." Syntax is the manner in which words are arranged in the sentence to express significant meanings. Sentences are of five kinds: declarative, interrogative, imperative, exclamatory, and optative. Declarative sentences set forth affirmation or denial; interrogative sentences pose questions; imperative sentences formulate commands; exclamatory sentences express surprise and pleasure; optative sentences desire or wish. Since only declarative sentences make affirmations and denials, they alone may be true or false and hence are of utmost significance for logic. They will be discussed in more detail in Chapter 6.

This richness and diversity of language presents many problems for logic, since language is the tool for symbolizing, expressing, and communicating so much more than strict formal or factual judgments. Problems connected with the origin and growth, use and functions of symbols have been a concern of linguists, philologists, and philosophers since earliest times, resulting in the development of a special discipline, which, since the latter part of the nineteenth century has been variously called "semantics," "semasiology," and more recently "semiotic," the last term being now used in the most inclusive sense. All of these words are derived from the Greek *sēma,* meaning sign. Semantics in its elementary form has to do with the question of the relation of signs and symbols to the things for which they stand, and the relation of both objects and symbols to meanings. Related to these are questions regarding the symbolic nature and various functions of language, and the avoidance of ambiguity and vagueness of words by care in definition of terms.

II. THE FUNCTIONS OF LANGUAGE

1. The Expressive or Poetic Function. If we adopt the genetic approach, which studies the functions of language in terms of its origin and development, it will be natural to suppose that the expressive function of language developed early in the process of evolution and has always been closely associated with the life of imagination and emotion. The expressive function of language, sometimes called the emotive and poetic, may be seen in its purest form in the spontaneous outpouring of feelings of awe and wonder in primitive hymns, psalms, and religious ritual. From ancient Egypt comes the following Hymn to Aton:

> Thy dawning is beautiful in the horizon of the heaven,
> O Living Aton, Beginning of Life!
> When thou risest in the horizon of the east
> Thou fillest all lands with Thy splendour;
> Fair-shining art Thou and great and radiant
> Exalted above the earth.[1]

[1] Grace H. Turnbull, *Tongues of Fire* (New York: The Macmillan Co., 1929), p. 62.

The expressive function is illustrated in certain kinds of lyric poetry where the main purpose is to give vent to the inner emotion of the poet and to evoke similar feelings in others through rhythmic sounds and carefully chosen images making use of the flight of fancy or the play of imagination. The following lines from Walt Whitman are an example:

> O powerful western fallen star!
> O shades of night—O moody, tearful night!
> O great star disappeared—O the black murk that hides the star!
> O cruel hands that hold me powerless—O helpless soul of me!
> O harsh surrounding cloud that will not free my soul.[2]

Other examples in lyric poetry, where the primary purpose is to give aesthetic pleasure, may approach the effective and informational uses by moving the reader or hearer to some kind of vision, knowledge, or comprehension. This is not knowledge in the ordinary factual or logical sense, but the recreating of experiences that are so vital that they arouse thought and reflection of the reader upon his own experience and may thus contribute to self-knowledge as well as insight into human nature in general. Shelley's *Adonais*, an elegy on the death of Keats, is an example from which this stanza is quoted:

> Or go to Rome, which is the sepulchre,
> Oh, not of him, but of our joy; 'tis nought
> That ages, empires, and religions there
> Lie buried in the ravage they have wrought;
> For such as he can lend,—they borrow not
> Glory from those who made the world their prey;
> And he is gathered to the kings of thought
> Who waged contention with their time's decay,
> And of the past are all that cannot pass away.[3]

Sacred lyric poetry, psalms, and hymns illustrate the expressive function, provided the teaching of a moral, or the expectation of a reward from the Deity is not the dominating theme. Whenever language through rhythmic sounds and emotive words and imagery stimulates the imagination thus producing enjoyment and eliciting response on the part of the hearer or reader, its function becomes effective and evocative. The expressive function is further illustrated by spontaneous outbursts such as "Whoopee!" "Hurrah!" and "Eureka!" and by slang expressions, exaggerated name-calling giving vent

[2] Harry H. Clark (ed.), *Walt Whitman* (New York: American Book Co., 1934), p. 232.
[3] John N. Manly (ed.), *English Prose and Poetry* (New York: Ginn & Co., 1916), p. 472.

to feelings of approval or disapproval, and expletives in the form of oaths to relieve pent-up emotions.

2. The Effective or Practical Function. One of the primary functions of language is to produce a psychological effect upon others, and as a result to influence them in the direction of some desired activity or attitude. Whereas the expressive function may be largely individualistic, the effective or persuasive function is primarily social. There is no estimating its importance to the safety and solidarity of the primitive tribe, even as in a modern civilized community or nation where cooperation in political and governmental action is essential. Unlike the expressive function, it is purely utilitarian, but is similar in that it is grounded in emotional factors and may depend largely upon emotional responses for fulfillment. Eloquent oratorical literature contains many examples. In his "Everlasting Yea" Carlyle exhorts;

On the roaring billows of Time, thou are not engulfed, but borne aloft into the azure of Eternity. Love not Pleasure; love God. This is the Everlasting Yea, wherein all contradiction is solved: wherein whoso walks and works, it is well with him.[4]

The most obvious example of the effective function of language is propaganda, where the question of the truth or falsity of what is asserted is not of primary importance. All that counts is that the truth-claims be accepted and acted upon. The extreme faith in this function of language was expressed by Hitler, the master propagandist, in *Mein Kampf:* "By propaganda, with permanent and clever application, even Heaven can be palmed off on a people as Hell, and the other way round, the most wretched life as Paradise."

In its most direct form, the practical function is expressed in the imperative sentence, such as a command to perform an action: "Hand me the book." "Please pass the butter." Appeals to loyalty, tradition, and patriotism are more indirect: "We must all sacrifice for national defense." "The life you save may be your own." The most indirect form is subtle suggestion such as is used in advertising: "Keep that schoolgirl complexion." "The beauty soap for the skin you love to touch."

3. The Ceremonial Function. The ceremonial function of language serves several purposes in a complex society. One purpose is that of facilitating social intercourse by the use of familiar conventional stock phrases for the purpose of small talk and chitchat to break the ice and

---

[4] Thomas Carlyle, *Sartor Resartus,* Everyman's Library Edition (New York: E. P. Dutton & Co., 1913), p. 145.

put people at their ease. It is quite different from the logical or informational function in that the statements, although made in the declarative form, are not supposed to be taken too seriously and their truth or falsity is in general regarded as irrelevant. "You must come and see us soon," "It was a lovely party," "What a charming dress you are wearing!" "How is the family?" and "Happy to make your acquaintance" are not said because they are meant or taken literally, but they do serve to make human relations more pleasant and relieve the embarrassment or stiffness which would prevail if one were always expected to say something quite witty and original. To ignore the purely ceremonial nature of such usages would be to become "the kind of bore who, when asked how he is, tells you."

Another form of ceremonial language is found in religious ritual and liturgy. The repetition of well-chosen words and phrases which carry emotional significance for the devotee tends to create a feeling of oneness and establishes a community of interest and feeling among those who participate, at the same time giving expression to and celebrating the common spirit of the group. It fulfills its purpose even when not literally understood, since its function is not logical and informational. The reading of the liturgy in the Church of Our Lady at Guadalupe, Mexico, is carried on in a sing-song chant throughout the day, while the church is thronged with tourists who pay no attention and are intent on their own interests. It is meaningful only for those who are affected by it.

4. The Logical and Informative Function. The logical and informative function of language is to formulate and record knowledge and to communicate it to others by means of declarative sentences. There are many degrees of complexity and reliability in such knowledge, from the simplest assertions based on direct testimony of immediate sense perception to statements of traditional beliefs and opinions, from the more or less vague formulations of the tested wisdom of mankind based upon extensive accumulated experience to the precisely asserted findings of theoretical and experimental science. Examples of the logical and informational function of language may be drawn from the areas of daily social and business intercourse: "The speed limit here is 35 miles per hour." "This suit costs $75.00." From the area of informative literature, scholarship, and research about the physical world, man, and society: "Jet planes now travel faster than sound." "Some Congressmen are opposed to federal aid to education." "Uranium has the atomic weight of 238.07." "Light is both waves and particles." "The Piltdown Man is a hoax." Perhaps the purest example of this function of language is that of theoretical and experimental science, where findings are constantly being subjected to criticism and modification by fellow scientists, where knowledge is sought for its own sake, and noninformational uses of language are strictly excluded.

5. Mixed Functions of Language. It is not always possible to discriminate clearly, as we have just tried to do, between the various functions of language. In fact, many people never realize until it is called to their attention that language has any function other than just to talk, that is, to communicate, and they unconsciously assume that they have always been using language to communicate "facts." This is because the various functions of language overlap and the differences are more of degree than of kind. For example, the practical function of language may be served through language that is primarily logical and informational, when as a result of a purely technical and scientific lecture, the hearers are stimulated to go back to their research in order to beat a competitor in the market. Conversely a merely practical demonstration and exhortation to the staff to work harder might convey the information that a competitor is farther advanced in research. If one gives expression to his deep conviction about modern warfare in the sentence "Because of the disastrous consequences, atomic warfare must be shunned at all costs," he is using language primarily for *practical* or effective purposes by calling attention to the gravity of the consequences, which everybody should be made to realize, in the hope that it may arouse a responding sentiment in others and thus dissuade nations from atomic warfare. In a secondary way, his language is expressive of his own deep conviction and sense of foreboding about the possible consequences of future atomic warfare. In the third place, the informational function is undoubtedly present in that the sentence purports to contain information that there are dire consequences to atomic warfare. Since these consequences are future and not present the information is of course hypothetical.

The opening paragraph of *The Crisis,* by Tom Paine, is an example of the mixed functions of language:

These are the times that try men's souls. The summer soldier and the sunshine patriot will, in this crisis, shrink from the service of their country; but he that stands it *now,* deserves the love and thanks of man and woman. Tyranny, like Hell, is not easily conquered; yet we have this consolation with us, that the harder the conflict, the more glorious the triumph. What we obtain too cheap, we esteem too lightly; it is dearness only that gives every thing its value. Heaven knows how to put a proper price upon its goods; and it would be strange indeed if so celestial an article as *freedom* should not be highly rated.[5]

III. SYMBOLISM, ITS USES AND ABUSES

For both animals and men the world is full of sights and sounds which function as signs or signals calling attention to or indicating things and events. A humming motor outside in the garage may be taken as a sign by both the family collie and human auditors that the master of the house has just driven in. When his master enters the house and calls out with great enthusiasm, "We won! We won!" these *signs*, together with gestures and facial expressions, are for the collie only *indicators* of his master's mood, signals for joyful response; but for humans they are *symbols* of a rich complex of meanings which may evoke pleasure in some and at the same time displeasure in others who wanted the other side to win. As far as we know, man is the only species that has developed the capacity for using symbols which refer to or represent objects and events which are not present to immediate experience. Man has been defined as the symbolizing animal. This power of using symbols is without doubt the secret of his mastery over his environment. With the lower animals signs can be learned and responded to directly, but if something unusual occurs to interrupt the habitual "signal reaction" they are unable to adjust themselves to the novel situation.

Signs are either *natural* or *conventional*. The falling of leaves and a cold wind are natural signs of approaching autumn. A semaphore on a railroad track is an artificial or conventional sign which indicates stop, go, or proceed with caution. *Symbols* are artificial or conventional signs and may be either *linguistic* or *nonlinguistic*. Such concrete symbols as the cross, the flag, the swastika, and the hammer and sickle are nonlinguistic. Language and various kinds of mathematical and musical notation are abstract symbols conventionally agreed upon by humans for the purposes of communication and the preservation of knowledge and the arts. The distinction between sign and symbol is well expressed by Langer as follows:

The logical relation between a sign and its object is a very simple one: they are *associated*, somehow *to form a pair;* . . . To each sign there corresponds one definite item which is its object, the thing (or event, or condition) signified.[6]

[5] *Selections from the Writings of Thomas Paine*, Modern Library Edition, p. 41.

[6] Reprinted by permission of the publishers from Susanne K. Langer, *Philosophy in a New Key* (Cambridge, Mass.: The Harvard University Press, 1942), p. 57.

Symbols are not proxy for their objects, but are *vehicles for the conception of objects*. To conceive a thing or a situation is not the same thing as to "react toward it" overtly, or to be aware of its presence. In talking about things we have conceptions of them, not the things themselves; and it is the conceptions, not the things, that symbols directly "mean." . . . The fundamental difference between signs and symbols is this difference of association, and consequently of their use by the third party to the meaning function, the subject; signs announce their objects to him, whereas symbols lead him to conceive their objects.[7]

The first part of this quotation tells us that the relation between a sign (No. 1) and what it stands for (No. 2) is simple and direct, i.e., it is a *two-term relation*, as for example, between a dog's customary red dish and his dinner, the classroom bell and class being dismissed, the stop signal and the brakes applied. The relation may be illustrated by a straight line:

1. Sign————————2. What is signified.

The second part of the quotation tells us that symbols (words) are vehicles which enable us to conceive objects when they are not immediately present to perception. There are in every symbolic situation the word or *symbol* (No. 1), what it stands for, the object or *referent* (No. 2), and the conception, reference, or *meaning* (No. 3). This is a *three-term relation*, best illustrated by a triangle.

The diagram on page 26, first used by Ogden and Richards,[8] will serve to illustrate the symbolic situation with the relations between symbols, referents, and meanings.

The first important thing to notice about the triangle is that the line representing the relation between the symbol and the referent at the base of the triangle is a broken line, unlike the other two, and the relation is called "an imputed relation." By this the authors mean that it is not a necessary or causal relation, but rather arbitrary and manmade. For example, if the referent were a piece of chalk, the symbol or word could be "chalk," "crayon," "white marker," "X," or anything else we wish to call it. The reason we call it "chalk" is that we have inherited this name and it has become the conventional one. It is the relative obscurity and strangeness of the semantic relation between words or symbols and things, and both of these to meanings which has given rise to the errors and misconceptions that have marked the history of man's use and study of language.

One of these common errors is to assume that the relation between words and things (illustrated by the base line of the triangle) has some

[7] *Ibid.*, pp. 60, 61.

[8] Adapted from C. K. Ogden and I. A. Richards, *The Meaning of Meaning* (New York: Harcourt, Brace & Co., 1923), p. 14.

kind of objective necessity, that is, that these things must have certain names and no other. Such *identification* occurs when words are believed to be inescapably associated with certain characteristics of things. In its extreme form (hypostatization), words themselves are treated as if they had the characteristics of things. This is to forget that names and words are only symbols and that the unique and arbitrary relation of "standing for" or "denoting" is their only connection with real or objective states of affairs. So widespread is the

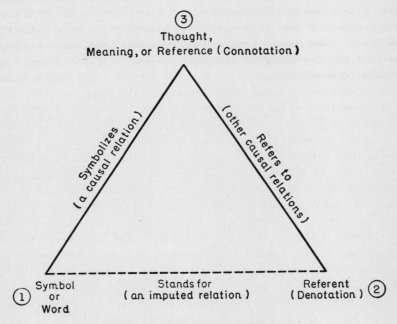

Figure 1. The Symbolic Triangle

public inability to distinguish names of things from the qualities and characteristics of the things named, that business firms and advertisers must be restrained by the Federal Trade Commission from such activities as "passing off domestic products as imported" and "misrepresenting source." Examples of these practices are found in the July 18, 1941, report of the Commission ordering manufacturers to "cease and desist" from "using the words 'Khandah,' 'Aristan,' 'Calcutta,' 'Chinese,' or any other words . . . suggestive of the Orient, to designate rugs made elsewhere than in the Orient and not possessing the essential characteristics of rugs made therein." Also prohibited is "using the term 'Havana' or any other terms suggestive of Cuba, unless accompanied by the words 'Blended with Havana' or words of similar import, in immediate conjunction therewith and in type equally as conspicuous, to designate cigars composed of Cuban tobacco in substantial part only."[9]

The purpose of the Federal Trade Commission in these cases is to protect consumers who may not realize that names do not necessarily accurately describe materially what they are only meant to symbolize.

A common form of semantic error occurs when gossip about somebody is believed on the grounds that "Where there is smoke there is fire," suggesting that since there is gossip there must be something behind it. Aside from the obvious circularity of this as an argument there is the psychological mistake of identifying the natural sign relation between smoke and fire with the arbitrary and fallible human association between people's statements and the facts.

Another form of the misunderstanding of the nature of symbols is the belief of primitive peoples that words and names have some kind of magical power in them for good or evil over persons and objects, just as they believe that hair and nails and other parts of the material body have. It was believed that one's enemy could be slain by incantations and that a knowledge of their names gave one power over them. In many primitive tribes the names of the chieftains and kings were kept secret to prevent enemies from doing them harm. Among the ancient Hebrews the name "Adonai" was substituted for the sacred name of "Yahweh," which was forbidden because it had acquired such sacredness that it was unlawful for men to utter it. Modern counterparts of these ancient identifications are found in certain mental patients for whom the subjective connotations of special words are so potent that the mere mention of them arouses fears, hatreds, and anxieties until they come to believe that words can actually hurt like knives and bullets.

Another semantic error is the belief that names are somehow natural rather than arbitrary and conventional. Plato's dialogue *Cratylus* deals with this question of whether names belong to things by nature or by convention. The speaker who defends the natural view in his discussion with Socrates says: "I think the truest account of these matters is this, Socrates, that some power greater than human laid down the first names for things, so that they must inevitably be the right ones." The same position is illustrated in the story of the woman who asked an astronomer (after having admitted that she

[9] Federal Trade Commission *Bulletin,* July 18, 1941.

marveled at their ability to discover the names of the planets), "How for instance did you ever manage to find out that the red planet named Mars is really Mars?"

Another corollary of the above error is the belief that if you know words and names you know facts; by analyzing words you are penetrating beneath them to the facts, and by manipulating and changing words you are also manipulating and changing facts. In the *Cratylus* the speaker says: "It seems to me quite simple. The man who knows the names knows the things." Some such similar view lies behind the excessive use of euphemisms, that is, when something which has an unsavory or unpopular name is given a better sounding name on the naive assumption that we have thereby mellowed the facts. The famous Judge Landis used to admonish his attendants and associates when dealing with mentally disturbed people in his court and in the hospital not to use the words "disease" and "insanity" but to substitute for both the word "illness." In this case, of course, it was because of the psychological effect upon the patients.

There is another group of semantic errors resulting from completely neglecting the referent in the right corner of the triangle and emphasizing only the abstract symbols and the syntactical relations between them. Now if these symbols have merely subjective connotations due to some highly personal experience, bias, or evaluation, or if they are abstract and ideal, referring to general attributes such as beauty, goodness, and truth, or to concepts such as liberty, justice, freedom, they lose all contact with any definite empirical content and hence are not very successful as instruments of communication. The indiscriminate use of such words opens the way for the charge of excessive abstraction.

Overemphasis upon abstractions may lead to the belief that a system of esoteric truth resides in or behind every set of symbols, and that truths are deducible from symbols alone. Because the abstract symbols are "clear and distinct" there sometimes arises a tendency to believe that they symbolize a realm of reality deeper than empirical facts and signify operations more potent than merely the manipulation of definitions and deductions.

Equally at fault, however, and at the opposite extreme, probably as a reaction against this excessive abstraction, are many popular treatises in the field of semantics which disparage any kind of abstract thinking and the use of symbols without concrete referents. In their eagerness to attain perfect clarity in communication they stress the "extensional" or "denotative orientation" (i.e., concrete referents) and condemn the "intensional" or "connotative orientation" (i.e., abstract conceptual meanings). This advice must not be taken so seriously by the student of logic and language that he will conclude that he cannot speak significantly of anything to which he cannot point as a referent. To be confined to such concrete referents would be to revert to the limitations of primitive pictorial and gesture language.

Overemphasis upon the close relation of words and referents is a natural result of the fact that children think in terms of objects. Because they have not yet learned to think in abstractions, children can best be taught meanings by the use of concrete referents, and in this way it is assured that the speaker and hearer are talking about the same thing. Since the ability to think abstractly emerges gradually in the mental development of children, they become wedded to concrete ways of thinking and as a result may find it difficult to learn to think abstractly. Overemphasis upon the concrete aspect of communication has led to the misleading advice, "Think things not words," and the erroneous doctrine that "Every word should have a concrete referent."

The tremendous advantage of the development of symbolism over primitive forms of pictorial representation is too great to be overestimated. In primitive picture language, communication is limited to the concrete material which can be pointed to or graphically portrayed. Symbolism enables us to communicate abstract ideas. But it also confronts us with the symbolic problem. Logicians ever since Leibniz (1646–1716) have dreamed of a completely abstract universal language which would avoid the ambiguities of linguistic symbols. He says:

Telescopes and microscopes have not been so useful to the eye as this instrument would be in adding to the capacity of thought. . . . If we had it, we should be able to reason in metaphysics and morals in much the same way as geometry and analysis. . . . If controversies were to arise, there would be no more need of disputation between two philosophers than between two accountants. For it would suffice to take their pencils in their hands, to sit down to their slates, and to say to each other (with a friend as witness, if they like), "Let us calculate."[10]

Modern symbolic logic (and electronic calculating machines) have grown out of this dream, but it is now more clearly recognized that the great strength and certainty of mathematical and symbolic logic lies in the fact that these sciences assert nothing and are therefore free from the limitations of the physical world; that is, they have no

---

[10] Quoted by Bertrand Russell in *The Philosophy of Leibnitz* (London: Cambridge University Press, 1900), pp. 169, 170.

concrete referents but deal only with the realm of possibility by the use of symbols constructed for clear and definite purposes. Even where the informational function is paramount, such constructs must then be regarded as legitimate abstraction so long as they obey logical rules and are consistent both with each other and the facts of experience.

The solution to semantic problems lies not in altogether disparaging abstractions, but rather in training ourselves to handle them with greater precision, and in discriminating between their proper uses and their abuses.

There is another semantic error which should be mentioned, arising out of the confusion of the various functions of language. Under the discussion of that topic we gave examples of these various functions, and also of discourse where the functions are mixed. It was admitted that in many types of discourse it is impossible to separate these functions. The breakdown in communication comes when symbols are used for the primary function of arousing emotions and stimulating action, and at the same time the hearer is led to the perhaps unwarranted belief that he is also being given facts about actual referents. This confusion is best illustrated in the field of political and economic discussion, debate, and propaganda, where symbols such as "liberty," "democracy," "*égalité*," "imperialism," "*Lebensraum*" (living space), and "free enterprise" are used variously to perform four distinct functions. Not only is it assumed that they symbolize actual referents, but they are also used to express and arouse emotion as well as to produce practical action and to communicate supposed facts. Because of the many ways such words are used and understood, it is a mistake to assume that they have any referent that is definite and concrete enough to anchor clear meanings. Semantic pitfalls such as occur when ambiguous language is used without sufficient context to establish its meaning, or when vagueness results from excessive abstraction, become doubly dangerous when their seeming or pseudo-meaningfulness pave the way for false propaganda and demagoguery.

IV. CLASSIFICATION OF TERMS

In ordinary discourse "words" and "terms" are synonymous, but in classical logic there is a distinction. Terms are the objects of thought as distinguished from the words that express them. Terms perform the logical function of conveying meaning. A term is so called because it comes at the end of a logical proposition (from the

Latin *terminus*), that is, either the subject end or the predicate end. Both the logical subject and predicate may be expressed in one or more words. For example, in the proposition "(Man) is (mortal)" the subject and predicate consist of only one word each. In the proposition "(All of the people present) are (American citizens)," all of the words that come before the verb "are" constitute the logical subject term and those which follow constitute the predicate term.

1. Singular, General, and Collective Terms. *Singular terms* are those which denote a single object, thing, or person. Examples are: the man on the flying trapeze, the first day of the month, the joy of living, a Roman holiday, and all proper names.

General terms designate class names and are also applicable to individual members of the class distributively. Such terms as man, horse, airplane, battleship, planet, metal, etc., connote qualities belonging to the class of objects named and also denote any one of an indefinite number of individual members of the class. Thus, for example, the term "planet" designates a class of heavenly bodies which revolve about the Sun and is applicable to individual members of the class, such as Earth, Mars, and Jupiter.

Collective terms have traditionally been distinguished from general terms on the ground that they name a number of things when grouped together as a whole collectively, but which are not applicable in the same sense to each member of the class distributively. Examples are: army, flock, crew, herd, regiment, etc. Thus, the collective term "army" applies to the whole group of soldiers and officers making up the army when taken as a unit, but cannot correctly be applied to the individuals composing it. But it is obvious that this distinction between general and collective terms is relative to context and use. For example, the collective term "army" may be used in a general sense as a class name for a whole group of fighting forces consisting of the First, Second, Third, and Fourth Armies, or the armies of the United States, Canada, and Great Britain. Thus, the same term may be both general and collective depending on how it is used in the sentence. Likewise, collective terms may be used in a singular sense in certain contexts. For example, the Library of Congress, the United Nations, and the High Sierras are used as singular names since they refer to classes having only one member, but are also collective terms since they refer to a group of entities taken together as a unit.

2. Concrete and Abstract Terms. *Concrete terms* are names of things given in perception, or of any thing possessing attributes, as contrasted with what is an attribute of something. For example, a *tree* has the attribute of greenness, and *man* has the attribute of humanity.

Abstract terms are names of qualities, attributes, or characteristics of things which are objects of thought. Greenness is an attribute of a tree, humanity of man, beauty of a house, and spaciousness of a park. The word "abstract" is from the Latin *abstrahere* (to draw away from) and signifies that the quality abstracted is thought of in isolation from other qualities which may belong to the object named.

3. Relative and Absolute Terms. *Relative terms* are terms which name objects as standing in certain relations to something else, and which have their meaning through this relationship, such as father, mother, brother, disciple, follower, debtor. The other term to which they are related, as debtor to creditor, is called the correlative term.

Absolute terms refer to an object apart from and independent of its relations. Examples are all proper names, such as Mary, Anne, Elizabeth; terms that name relations (as distinct from the things related), such as brotherhood, discipleship, motherhood; qualities such as green, bright, brilliant, gregarious; and so on.

4. Positive, Negative, and Infinite Terms. *Positive terms* are those which express the existence of a quality. Examples are: animate, intelligent, potent, strong, active.

Negative terms express the absence of positive qualities. For the purposes of grammar, negative terms are indicated by such prefixes as *im, un, in, ir,* and *dis,* as in the words im-possible, un-canny, in-definite, ir-responsible, dis-honest. But, because they often suggest positive qualities in spite of their negative form, for the purposes of logic it is better to express the negative in the form of the logical contradictory, so that there is no middle ground between a term and its negative. The logical contradictory is expressed by the prefix "non." Thus the contradictory negative of responsible is non-responsible, of honest is non-honest, of good is non-good, of man is non-man.

Infinite terms are the contradictory negatives of the above positive terms. Any term with the prefix "non" is applicable to an infinite number of objects that are excluded from the positive term. Thus the term non-animal is applicable to automobiles, airplanes, submarines, houses, chairs, tables, and so on indefinitely.

PROBLEMS

1. What is a sign, a symbol, a referent, a reference, and what are the relations between them?

2. Classify the items in the first list under either natural or conventional signs, and those in the second list under linguistic or non-linguistic symbols:

clouds	the stars and stripes
a stop signal	justice
birds flying south	penicillin
a green light	the cross
left arm extended	humanity
a shrug of the shoulders	success
smoke	a triangle
a barking dog	a woman holding a balance

3. What are some of the semantic errors resulting from a misunderstanding of the relation of words to their referents?

4. State a proposition illustrative of each of the functions of language; logical and informational, expressive or emotive, effective or practical, and ceremonial.

5. Select an example of the legitimate use of abstractions. Give several instances of the misuse of abstractions.

6. Give an example of literature corresponding to each of the four functions of language.

7. What language function is the most prominent in the following quotations? What other functions are present if any?

Is life so dear or peace so sweet as to be purchased at the price of chains and slavery? Forbid it, Almighty God! I know not what course others may take, but as for me, give me liberty, or give me death!—PATRICK HENRY

But mathematics is not to be identified with any of its applications however important and impressive, nor indeed with all its applications, whether actual or only potential . . . for mathematics itself, as we are going to see, is not at all concerned with any kind of subject-matter whatever.[11]

Fear not torture, for therein lies the crown of martyrdom. The way is short, the struggle brief, the reward everlasting. Yea, I speak now with the voice of the prophet, 'Arm thyself, O mighty one!' Take up your arms, valiant sons, and go. Better fall in battle than live to see the sorrow of your people and the desecration of your holy places.—From a speech of POPE URBAN II[12]

Hail to Thee, mighty Lord, the world's Creator, Supporter and Destroyer, three in one! Unmeasured and unmeasurable, yet Thou measurest the world; desireless, yet fulfilling all desire; unconquered and a conqueror, unmanifested, yet manifesting; uniformly one, yet ever multiform.
—"Hymn to Vishnu"[13]

[11] C. J. Keyser, *Mathematics as a Culture Clue* (New York: Scripta Mathematica, 1947), p. 2.
[12] Harold Lamb, *The Crusades* (New York: Doubleday & Co., Inc., 1930), p. 42.
[13] Turnbull, *op. cit.*, pp. 54–55.

8. Classify the following terms under one or more heads: singular, general, concrete, abstract, or collective.

swarm
President Johnson
library
blueness
rationality
forest
the Great Lakes

seaplane
beauty
the Pacific Ocean
metal
the red house
United Nations
battalion

9. Classify the following terms under one or more heads: absolute, relative, positive, negative, or infinite.

organic
uncle
optimistic
non-metallic
atoms

teacher
intelligible
unreliable
non-negotiable
studio

3

Meaning and Definition

I. MEANING

In our discussion of the relation of language to logic we have seen that one of the major functions of language is that of the communication of thought and information by means of words arranged in sentences according to linguistic rules. Successful communication between speaker and hearer, writer and reader, requires that words have the same meaning for both, and refer to the same referent. Also, it is obvious that if we wish to test statements as to their truth or falsity, or use them in arguments, the meaning must be clear. Now the term "meaning" itself presents us with a problem, for it has many meanings. Rather than attempt to define the word "meaning" we shall exhibit its use in a number of different contexts as follows:[1]

1. "The professor *means* that we should hand in the assignment." "What do you *mean?*" "I *mean* you." In these examples it is a *person* who means or intends.
2. "The bell *means* dinner." "The blossoms *mean* a good crop." Here it is the *things* that mean. The bell is a sign or signal for dinner, and the blossoms are a sign of a good crop.
3. "The project *means* a great deal to me." "If you do that, it *means* trouble." "What does the proposed legislation *mean?*" "What is the *meaning* of Existence?" Here it is the *situation, process,* or *event* that means. In the first sentence it is *emotional or personal significance;* in the second, the situation has *causal* meaning; in the third the reference is to *social purpose;* in the fourth the reference is to *cosmic purpose.*
4. "This triangle is equilateral *means* that it is equiangular." The meaning is that of implication, one proposition *implies* another.

[1] This discussion has been influenced by Heinrich Gomperz, "The Meanings of 'Meaning,'" *Philosophy of Science,* VIII (1941), No. 2.

5. "The word 'horse' *means Equus caballus.*" The word "horse" means or *connotes* qualities or properties which constitute the intension of the term, and *denotes* members of the class which constitutes its extension.

6. "The proposition 'Some kittens are playful' has *meaning.*" The *sentence* or *proposition* means in the sense that it *expresses a complete act of thought* and *refers to* an actual or possible *state of affairs.*

In this chapter we shall be concerned with "meaning" in the sense of 1, that is, meaning as personal, and in the descriptive or referential senses illustrated under numbers 5 and 6, that is, with words, terms, and sentences in their cognitive or logical significance.

II. AMBIGUITY AND VAGUENESS

The previous discussion of the various functions of language, the complexity of the symbolic situation, and the various meanings of "meaning" has prepared us for understanding the notorious ambiguity of linguistic symbols. If we recall, in addition, the diverse origin of our words from many languages, the process of transferring meanings from the original objects to others through analogy, association, or special usage, and even by accidental confusion of different words, it is not surprising that we do not understand each other perfectly on all subjects on all occasions. The fact that words change their meanings with time and usage makes it impossible for us to depend entirely on the etymology of words, although tracing the origin of words is both educational and exciting. Time and usage have so completely changed many words that the original meaning has been lost. For example, the word "atom" meant originally an indivisible particle, which is no longer an adequate definition. The word "Sophist" originally meant a wise man, but has come to mean a captious and fallacious reasoner. The word "disease," which meant originally merely lack of ease, has been generalized to cover any departure from the state of health which displays certain symptoms. The original meaning of such words as "luminiferous ether" and "phlogiston" has become obsolescent.

The word "ambiguity" comes from the Latin word *amb,* meaning about or around, and *agere,* meaning to drive, and carries the significance of driving our thought about in different directions instead of leading it directly to the goal. More simply, ambiguous words are those which have more meanings than one in a given context. Ambiguous *sentences,* arising from the way words are arranged in the sentence, are called *amphibolous.*

Fortunately for us, much of the language of ordinary everyday communication is not seriously handicapped by ambiguity because the context is so familiar, and because we purposely or habitually choose words in popular use. But whenever the discussion turns to matters slightly beyond popular speech, where the referents are unfamiliar, where the terminology is technical or abstract, or where we give words an emotional coloring through personal associations, the bugaboo of ambiguity arises.

It is not ambiguity itself but the failure to recognize it or interpret it properly that is dangerous. If we did not have words with many meanings, we would have to invent new words to denote each of the many things to which we wish to refer, and to express different shades of meaning. Metaphor, for example, is a special technique of extending the use of words beyond their literal meaning so as to amplify the language and give it expressive flexibility. Ambiguity is especially useful in poetry, in humor, and in imaginative writing, where the author wishes to combine meanings into pregnant images or to be purposely unprecise so that the reader may be free to use his own imagination in his interpretation of the writer's thought. On the other hand, for the purpose of successful communication, logic and science find it necessary that we become aware of the dangers of ambiguity and learn how to avoid them. The habit of looking up words in an unabridged dictionary and noting their various contextual meanings is the first step toward avoiding these dangers. What words in an unabridged dictionary are most ambiguous? Here are a few:

Light

1. Give me a light   (fire)
2. Put a light in the window.   (illumination)
3. Light is both waves and particles.   (radiant energy)
4. He is a light, vain person.   (frivolous)
5. Can you throw any light on the subject?   (information)
6. You have put me in a false light.   (perspective)
7. We are traveling light.   (unimpeded)
8. It is a light fault.   (unimportant)
9. The bird is going to light.   (settle)
10. As I pondered, all at once light dawned.   (understanding)

Think

1. What do you think of the new teacher?   (esteem)
2. Think of others!   (consider)
3. Think the problem through.   (reason)
4. I think it is going to rain.   (opinion)
5. I will think up several routes.   (plan)
6. I am sad as I think of the past.   (recollect)
7. How far do you think it is to town?   (judge)
8. One cannot think Infinity.   (conceive)
9. Just think! I may get the position.   (imagine)
10. Leave me alone, I want to think.   (reflect)

Logical

1. He arrived at a logical conclusion from his premises.   (sound deduction)
2. Mr. X seems the logical candidate for the office.   (best fitted)
3. It is logical to suppose that Germany will be united.   (highly probable)
4. I pointed out to him the logical meaning of the word.   (proper)
5. He reached a logical generalization on the basis of the facts.   (correct inference)
6. The man seemed sane, for when I spoke to him he gave a perfectly logical answer.   (rational)
7. He considered all makes of cars, and made a logical decision.   (best possible)
8. It is logical to suppose that one will do better in an examination for which one is prepared.   (reasonable)
9. On the basis of past events the columnist concluded logically what would happen.   (accurate prediction)
10. The logical thing for the candidate to do is to withdraw.   (expedient)

Vagueness is somewhat different from ambiguity. It derives from the Latin *vagus,* meaning wandering. Terms are vague when their meaning shades off into other meanings with no precise delimiting of their boundary lines, and hence they have no precise application. To some extent this is unavoidable because the referents, qualities, and characteristics in nature to which words refer exist not only in kinds but in degrees. When is a man "honest" or "dishonest"? When is a government "democratic"? What degree of "freedom of speech" may be tolerated in time of international tension? When is a man "famous," or a "security risk"? How few hairs must a man have on his head to be defined as "bald-headed"? In the *Mishna* there is a section governing the sacrifice of the "red heifer." There is a prohibition against the sacrificing of a "red heifer." But, how is a "red heifer" to be defined. Five rabbinical schools of thought arose, and as a result a "red heifer" was defined in the following five ways:

1. A heifer is red when every hair on its body is red.
2. A heifer is red when it is almost all red.
3. A heifer is red when the majority of its hairs are red.
4. A heifer is red when a considerable number of its hairs are red.
5. A heifer is red when one hair is red.

It is obvious that a similar dispute might arise if the quality of "redness" and the different shades of red were the point at issue, and an entirely different technique would need to be adopted for the removal of this vagueness, which might not yield any more conclusive or successful results.

Thus we see that both ambiguity and vagueness present us with handicaps to clarity of meaning and successful communication. The simple question "what do you mean?" is always legitimate, and although it can be asked in an insulting manner, should never be considered an insult. Many disputes would end much earlier if it could be determined exactly what the dispute is about. We may characterize some issues as *verbal issues* in contrast to *real issues*. Real issues are those in which genuine differences of opinion regarding matters of fact or value are involved. Verbal issues are those in which the parties to the dispute believe they are disagreeing over real issues, when actually the words they use do not denote the same referent. It is obvious that the distinction between real issues and verbal issues will be more easily made with respect to some problems than it will with others.

William James tells the following story to illustrate the method of Pragmatism in settling philosophical disputes,[2] which incidentally illustrates the nature of a verbal issue. A large tree is standing in a forest clearing before his camp, with a squirrel clinging to its trunk and going round and round the tree, keeping out of sight of a man who is walking around the tree vainly trying to catch sight of it. The question now is: does the man *go around* the squirrel? The question is very puzzling. Some members of the party say yes, and others say no. When the question is put to him, James replies by saying that it

[2] William James, *Pragmatism* (New York: Longmans, Green & Co., 1931), pp. 43, 44.

depends upon what you mean by *going around* the squirrel. The difficulty is resolved the minute the ambiguity of the words *go around* is recognized and removed. If the question is: does the man pass from the north to the east, then to the south, then to the west, and then to the north again, the answer is *yes*. But if the question means: does the man go around the squirrel in the sense that he is first in front of the squirrel, then on his right, then behind him, then on his left, and finally in front again, the answer is *no*, for the squirrel keeps his belly turned toward the man all the time and his back turned away. Both parties to the dispute are right, and both are wrong, depending on how they interpret the words *go around*.

James MacKaye suggests the following standard form for the avoidance of ambiguity. He uses, among many examples, one which every student of philosophy has debated, namely: "Does the fall of a tree in an uninhabited wilderness cause a sound?" By throwing the issue into the standardized form we have:

1. Does a tree falling in an uninhabited wilderness cause a sound?
2. "Sound" is ambiguous.
3. "Sound" means, according to a dictionary definition, "Noise or acoustic phenomena" (but is still ambiguous).
4. "Sound" (a) means "an audible sensation."
   "Sound" (b) means "a series of waves in the air which are capable of causing sound (a) when they impinge on the human ear."
5. Does a tree falling in an uninhabited wilderness cause a sound (a)? Answer: No. Does a tree falling in an uninhabited wilderness cause a sound (b)? Answer: Yes.

Thus it is entirely true that the nature of sound (a) is that it shall be heard, but it is not true of the nature of sound (b).[3]

III. CONNOTATION AND DENOTATION

1. Conventional Connotation. In previous sections we have used the rather technical terms "intension" or "connotation," and "extension" or denotation." We must now refer to them again in order to clarify their function in the meaning situation. All common nouns and class terms such as "man," "horse," "dog," "tree," etc., have both connotative and denotative meaning. The *denotation* of a term is all *actual things* to which the term applies; the class of such things constitute its extension. For example, the term "dog" denotes all mem-

[3] James MacKaye, *The Logic of Language* (Hanover, N. H.: Dartmouth Publications, 1939), p. 136.

bers of the class which come under the term, such as Rover, Napoleon, and Fido, and these objects constitute the extension of the term "dog."

The *connotation* of a term is that *set of characteristics,* attributes, or qualities common to the members of the class and by which a criterion is provided for judging when the term is correctly applied. Such essential or defining characteristics are the term's intensional meaning. For example, the connotation of "dog" is domesticated carnivorous mammal belonging to the family Canidae, and any existing thing possessing these characteristics would be called by that name. *Conventional connotation* refers to those characteristics commonly or conventionally accepted as essential to its adequate definition.

2. Subjective Connotation. The subjective connotations of words are more psychological than logical. They are the meanings which are peculiar to an individual's state of mind when a symbol is used or interpreted as an instrument of communication. Thus subjective connotations are of little value for logic and science, but are of great significance for literature and art. This characteristic of language enables the poet to call up imagery, and to arouse emotions which may differ for each reader, by his careful choice of words and of contexts. A person may have acquired a particular association with a word through some emotional experience or in a highly personal context, and thereafter mistakenly thinks of it as having only this one meaning. Sometimes words are used to conceal as well as to reveal meaning, and we are often left to our own subjective interpretation of what is meant by a speaker. If a notoriously feline woman taking leave of her hostess says, "Darling, you'll never know how pleasant this has been!" one is led to suspect some unwelcome connotation in the remark.

3. Objective Connotation, or Comprehension. The class of objects denoted by a term has an almost infinite number of common qualities and attributes beyond those we know and name. *Objective connotation,* or *comprehension,* includes all of those attributes which are possessed in common by all of the individual objects to which the word applies, whether anybody knows about them or not. Since most of these attributes are irrelevant to the meaning of a term, they may for the practical purpose of definition be neglected.

We have said that common nouns and class terms possess both connotation and denotation. That is, they perform the double function of applying to instances and implying attributes or qualities. Now it is interesting to ask whether or not proper names have both connotation and denotation. It is customary in traditional logic to hold that such proper names as Tom, Dick, and Harry have denotation, or specific application to individual persons. They do not have connotation, or if so it is, at the most, subjective connotation. Also it is generally agreed that there are certain terms which have connotation but no denotation. Such names as "centaur" and "hippogriph," and descriptive phrases like "circle squarers" and "intelligent morons" have a meaning but we cannot point to examples. Finally, there are merely functional words, such as conjunctions and interjections, which have neither connotation nor denotation.

It will be observed that when a series of terms is arranged in the order of subordination, as the intension increases the extension decreases; or in other words, intension and extension vary inversely. Thus, if we arrange the following terms in the order of subordination, "ship," "sea-going ship," "war vessel," "submarine," atomic-powered submarine," we find that each successive class includes less members, that is, has a decreasing extension. At the same time we find that each successive class has a larger number of attributes and properties, that is, the intension is increased. For example, the intension of the class "submarine" includes the intension of "war vessel" and "sea-going ship," but not conversely. Since many series of terms may be arranged in this way, the principle involved has been stated as the "law of inverse variation," namely, that when a series of terms is arranged in the order of subordination, the extension and intension vary inversely.

This principle, however, does not apply in any mathematically exact sense, and it does not apply to every series, for in some cases the addition of carefully chosen attributes increasing the intension does not decrease the extension. For example, if we increase the intension of "sea-going ship," by adding "with steering apparatus," "power-propelled," "incapable of 1,000 miles per hour," we have not changed the extension. Exceptions such as this have led to the modification of the above principle so as to state that as intension increases the extension will either decrease or remain the same.

IV. KINDS OF DEFINITION

The main purpose of definition is to state the meaning of a term. Any process which seeks to clarify and fix a meaning to a term is a defining process. In the long history of definition-making and criticism of the process of defining, logicians have proposed different ways of defining and have classified them under certain heads. In this process there has been some confusion and difference of opinion. Certain problems have arisen and different ways of solving these problems have been advocated. One question is, exactly what are we defining: words, things, or concepts? Those who say we are defining words only will hold that all definition is *nominal*, that is, having to do only with the relations of names and symbols to each other and their referents. Those who say we are defining things or essential realities hold to what they call *real* definition. There are a few conceptualists, but their view is not widely proclaimed. The great majority of contemporary logicians hold the view that definitions pertain to symbols and not to things. If definitions are of words or symbols only, then the question as to whether a definition is true or false has little meaning. Rather we would ask whether it is adequate or correct, or if it fulfills its function. Again, if definitions are of words and symbols only, we are led to ask the question—are we entirely free to stipulate meanings as we please, since from the beginning of time names have been arbitrarily stipulated before becoming conventional by general acceptance.

In his discussion of definition, John Stuart Mill assessed the defining process as follows:

The simplest and most correct notion of a definition is, a proposition declaratory of the meaning of a word; namely, either the meaning which it bears in common acceptance, or that which the speaker or writer, for the particular purpose of his discourse, intends to annex to it.[4]

In this quotation we find mention of two distinct types of definition.

1. Lexical or Conventional Definition. Mill says that a definition is the "meaning which it [a word] bears in common acceptance." Lexical or conventional definitions are reports of how words are actually used at a given time by a certain class of people who speak, write, and read a given language. When children or learners of a language ask the meaning of a word we give them the definition in use or in common acceptance. Dictionaries are records of conventional or lexical definitions along with other more specialized meanings, and when we wish to know the accepted meanings we look them up in a dictionary. For example, "automobile" means a self-propelled vehicle for use on streets and roadways. An "airplane" is a self-propelled heavier-than-air flying craft.

[4] John Stuart Mill, *A System of Logic* (New York: Harper & Bros., 1887), p. 105.

2. Stipulative Definition. Mill also refers to meanings "which the speaker or writer, for the particular purpose of his discourse, intends to annex to it." These are stipulative definitions, and are relative to a purpose. They express a decision that a word shall have such and such a meaning in a given context. Thus a stipulative definition cannot be true or false. It is particularly convenient in fields such as aesthetics and art, where words are ambiguous and agreement cannot be secured by critics for such terms as "beauty," "aesthetic quality," "style," etc., but where the meanings of these terms can be stipulated for limited contexts and for definite purposes. Freedom of stipulation is also very important in science, when new words must be invented because no adequate word exists or where familiar words do not adequately express the purpose intended. Thus when Alexander Fleming wanted to avoid the awkward phase "mold broth filtrate" he stipulated, "Let us for convenience use the name 'penicillin.'" If we adopt the view that all words are arbitrary we must hold that at one time all meanings were stipulated and when generally accepted became customary or conventional. There is nothing to prevent us from stipulating meanings, but it is highly desirable that when meanings are stipulated they be used consistently throughout the discourse.

3. Synonymous Definition. Synonymous definitions are given by relating two words together in such a way as to show that their meanings are the same. This method of definition is useful as a means of teaching the meanings of words to those who may be supposed to already know one meaning and wish to increase their vocabulary. Thus an "abridged" dictionary means a "shortened" dictionary, "courage" means "valor," a "decision" means a "resolution," and "synonymous" means "alike or nearly alike in meaning." Synonymous definition is the method employed in learning the meanings of words in a foreign language, and in the making of interlinguistic dictionaries such as German-English or German-French. The limitations of this method of definition are of course quite obvious since its purpose is confined to learning a new vocabulary either in one's own or in another language, or for variety in expression.

4. Ostensive or Demonstrative Definition. Ostensive or demonstrative definition refers to examples by means of some gesture such as pointing and, strictly speaking, is not definition at all. This method has mainly pedagogical significance and is fruitfully employed in teaching children the meaning of words and names of objects in their environment. For example, a child learns the words "cat," "dog," and "kitten" by repeated use of the words over a period of time accompanied by pointing to the objects named, or by pointing to many concrete examples at one time, such as when he learns the word "book" by the demonstration that this, and this, and this are books.

5. Denotative Definition. Denotative definition exhibits a part of the denotation of a term by referring verbally to individual cases or examples. Socrates may be regarded as the first of the logicians to pay a great deal of attention to the use as well as the criticism of this kind of definition. Plato's dialogue *Euthyphro* tells how Socrates meets the young Euthyphro who is about to accuse his father of murder. Socrates raises the question as to whether thus accusing his father, guilty though he was, is a pious act. This leads to a progressive definition of "piety," passing through various stages. We quote the most significant passages:

SOCRATES. But just at present I would rather hear from you a more precise answer, which you have not as yet given, my friend, to the question, What is 'piety'? When asked, you only replied, Doing as you do, charging your father with murder.

EUTHYPHRO. And what I said was true, Socrates.

SOCRATES. No doubt, Euthyphro; but you would admit that there are many other pious acts?

EUTHYPHRO. There are.

SOCRATES. Remember that I did not ask you to give me two or three examples of piety, but to explain the *general idea* which makes all pious things to be pious. Do you not recollect that there was one idea which made the impious impious, and the pious pious? . . . Tell me what is the nature of this idea, and then I shall have a standard to which I may look, and by which I may measure actions, whether yours or those of anyone else, and then I shall be able to say that such and such an action is pious, such another impious.

EUTHYPHRO. I will tell you, if you like.

SOCRATES. I should very much like.

EUTHYPHRO. Piety, then, is that which is dear to the gods, and impiety is that which is not dear to them.

SOCRATES. Very good, Euthyphro; you have now given me the sort of answer which I wanted. But whether what you say is true or not I cannot as yet tell, although I make no doubt that you will prove the truth of your words.[5]

The point we wish to illustrate by this example is not the perfection of the final definition of "piety," but rather the fact that the first attempt on the part of Euthyphro was not a definition in the Socratic sense, but a mere example. It was definition by denoting or

[5] *The Dialogues of Plato,* trans. Benjamin Jowett (New York: The Oxford University Press, 1892), "Euthyphro" (6b–7a).

pointing out verbally a specific case of piety, namely, doing what I
am doing, accusing my father of murder. Thus we may denotatively
define "citrus fruit" as fruit such as oranges, lemons, limes, and grape-
fruit; or "fairy story" as a story such as *Cinderella, Little Snow-White,*
and *Sleeping Beauty.* The disadvantages of this kind of definition
are obvious since it is possible to enumerate only a small part of the
denotation of any term, which leaves us guessing as to the other related objects to which it might possibly apply. On the other hand,
it has obvious advantages when we wish to convey the meaning of a
word in teaching, writing, and speaking, and when owing to the vagueness or ambiguity of the word, or because of the limited knowledge
of the hearer or reader, specific examples convey the meaning better
than any other method. If denotative ambiguity exists, that is, when
a term may denote several of the many members of a class although
it is supposed to denote only one, the ambiguity may be removed by
narrowing the denotation. Thus, "the man who was here last week"
may be made less ambiguous by specifying "the Fuller brush man,"
"with the gold teeth," or "with the red mustache" until all ambiguity
is removed.

6. Connotative or Analytical Definition. Connotative definition states
the essential characteristics or attributes of that which is defined.
The essential characteristics or attributes have traditionally meant
the nearest *genus,* plus the *differentia.* "Genus" is the term used
to designate a class of anything that may be divided into subordinate
classes called "species." The "differentia" is the characteristic attribute of the species which differentiates it from all other species
in the same genus. In placing a term under its genus in order to
define it, the nearest genus should be picked. When we play the
game of "animal, vegetable, or mineral" and place objects under one
or another of these genera, and then differentiate them from other
objects of the same genus, we are defining by connotation. For example, *gold* is a mineral or metal (genus), very malleable and of a
yellow color (differentia). A *triangle* is a closed rectilinear figure
(genus) with three sides (differentia). A *satellite* is a heavenly body
(genus) which rotates in an orbit around a planet (differentia).

We should notice that connotative definition, which is the Aristotelian type, undertakes to give us the essential qualities of the thing
being defined and hence always uses the verb "is" rather than the
verb "means." J. S. Mill, who was a critic of Aristotelian or real
definition and a defender of nominal definition, held that if the verb
"means" can be substituted for "is" then nothing but a nominal

definition is involved, that is, an explanation of the use and application of a word. But if this substitution cannot be made, as in the above example, "A triangle is a closed rectilinear figure with three sides," then the sentence includes *two* propositions, namely, "There may exist a figure bounded by three straight lines," which is a *postulate*, and "This figure may be termed a triangle," which is a nominal definition. We might also note that some terms such as "space," "time," "relation," etc., have no superior genus in the sense that we can place them under a higher class.

7. Other Ways of Defining. Traditional definition was supposed to give us the essential nature of the thing defined. This was possible within limits in a simple static world, but in a world of process is no longer possible. We are not so sure today that we know what the essence of a thing is, and would be inclined to argue that what is essential for one purpose would not be essential for another. Therefore we resort to other ways of defining. *Systematic* definition gives the meaning of a term by relating it to a system in terms of laws; for example, "water" is H_2O. *Genetic* definition refers to the method of production or origin of that which is being defined; for example, a "stalagmite" is a deposit formed on the floor of a cave by dripping water containing calcium bicarbonate. Other definitions are in terms of *purpose* or use; for example, "chalk" denotes a soft limestone used for writing on blackboards. *Operational* definitions are given by performing certain operations. Thus "length" is defined by performing (or describing) the operation of placing a standard measuring stick along any space to be measured. In physics, an "electron" is a certain effect that can be observed when certain operations are performed in the Wilson Cloud Chamber.

V. RULES OF DEFINITION

The following rules, which apply mainly to connotative definition, have, with some modifications, come down to us from Aristotle and will serve as standards or criteria by which we may check the clarity and adequacy of our own definitions, and analyze and evaluate the definitions of others.

1. A definition should state the *essential attributes* of that which is being defined, that is, its *nearest genus* and *essential differences*. By essential attributes is meant the qualities and characteristics which necessarily belong to the class being defined. This is done by de-

termining under what larger class or genus it falls, and then differentiating it from other members of that genus. Zoological and botanical definitions of animals and plants are of this type. For example, the definition of "horse" is *Equus caballus*. *Equus* is the genus which includes other similar animals such as the ass and zebra, and *caballus* is the differentia which distinguishes the horse from other members of the genus. To give as a definition some nonessential or accidental quality would be inadequate definition; for example, a "horse" is a grass eater.

2. A definition (*definiens*) should be exactly equivalent to the class of objects defined (*definiendum*); that is, it should be neither too broad nor too narrow. To define a table as "an article of furniture" is too broad, or to define a chair as "the thing I am now sitting on" is too narrow. There is a legend to the effect that Diogenes was listening to Plato one day in the Academy while he was trying to define *man*. At the end of the session the point had been reached where those present were willing tentatively to agree on the definition, "Man is a featherless biped." Next morning, according to the story, Diogenes appeared at the Academy with a cock in his hand which he had plucked. Presenting this to the teacher he said, "Plato, here is your man." It then became apparent to all that the definition was too broad, and further discussion led to the addition of the differentiating characteristic "with broad nails." The definition of man was then "Man is a featherless biped with broad nails," which was a slight improvement.

3. A definition should not contain the name of the thing or concept being defined. When this rule is not observed we have circular definition. Examples of the violation of this rule would be to define "intelligence" as that which intelligence tests measure, or an "infinite series" as a series which is infinitely divisible. These attempts at definition are not enlightening since anyone who does not understand the *definiendum* would not understand the *definiens;* that is, they make no progress in clarifying the meaning of a term. Violation of this rule is often unnoticed because the *definiens* is stated in words which have the same etymological origin as the *definiendum* but in a different language. For example, "Intoxication is the result of imbibing poison" and "A sleeping powder is a substance having soporific qualities."

4. A definition should not be negative when it can be affirmative. Since the purpose of definition is to make clear what a term means, or what a thing is, and not what it does not mean, or what it is not, this

rule has some importance. What we want in a definition is the positive characteristics which can be understood as constituting the meaning of the term, and not a list of the infinity of qualities falling outside or not belonging to its essential nature. The violation of this rule would yield the following: We might define a "football" as not a baseball, not a tennis ball, not a basket ball, and so on indefinitely. A "horse" is not a ruminant, does not have a cloven hoof, is not a biped, etc., but since these negative characteristics are infinite this is a very cumbersome method. It is true, however, that there are some terms the essential meaning of which consists in the absence of something. "Blind" is well defined as being without sight. A "spinster" is an unmarried woman. "Parallel lines" are lines that do not intersect in a plane. We might define "academic freedom" positively as being that condition of speaking and writing characterized by independence of thought and freedom of speech. But it would also be adequately defined negatively as not being under restrictive influences when speaking and writing. A definition of "property" as something of which there is not enough to go around, violates this rule as well as rule 2.

5. A definition should not be expressed in ambiguous, obscure, or figurative language. Since the purpose of definition is to clarify meanings and remove ambiguity, the introduction of ambiguous language defeats this purpose. Obscurity, however, is relative to the hearer or reader. Laymen are often irritated at technical books and journals because a terminology is used not familiar to them, but which, relative to the purpose of the writer, is quite legitimate and highly necessary. Herbert Spencer's definition of evolution as "An integration of matter and concomitant dissipation of motion, during which the matter passes from an indefinite, incoherent homogeneity to a definite, coherent heterogeneity, and during which the retained motion undergoes a parallel transformation" is not necessarily a poor definition for the highly abstract conception of evolution he was elaborating. Nevertheless it is somewhat obscure for ordinary purposes.

Ambrose Bierce's definition of "eat" is a good example of unnecessary obscurity. "To 'eat' is to perform successively (and successfully) the functions of mastication, humectation, and deglutition." Figurative language belongs more to the area of literature than to logic or science. In literature figurative language such as metaphors, similies, and analogies is legitimate since it helps convey the writer's thought and suggests subjective connotations to the reader, but because of this very fact it destroys precision of meaning. Examples are: "Time is the moving image of eternity" and "Paradox is the passion of thought."

PROBLEMS

1. Distinguish between denotation, or extension, and connotation, or intension. Make a series of five or more terms, and arrange them in the order of increasing intension. Examine them to see whether or not the intension and extension vary inversely.

2. Use the "standard form for the avoidance of ambiguity" of James MacKaye to remove the ambiguity from the italicized words in the following sentences:

(1) Is it *possible* to build a bridge across the Atlantic?
(2) Is the law of gravity a *certainty?*
(3) In the story about William James's squirrel, does the man *go around* the squirrel?
(4) Do we have a *great* army?
(5) Is the United States a *democracy?*
(6) Is man a *rational* animal?

3. Which term has the wider extension, "man" or "American citizen," and what is the reason for your answer?

4. A man and a horse are crossing a stream. How does a knowledge of connotation help you to determine whether the man was on the horse's back or the horse on the man's back?

5. Distinguish between ambiguity and vagueness. Are the following terms vague or ambiguous or both? Explain how the ambiguity or vagueness can be removed.

explanation	heap of sand
circumstantial	real
in the long run	organic
approximately	insane
security risk	neurotic
famous	normal
bald-headed	humanism
welfare state	free enterprise

6. Show which words in the following sentences render the sentence ambiguous.

(1) What a life!
(2) Eversharp pencils are guaranteed forever.
(3) I have lost my dog.
(4) Throw the searchlight on the shore.
(5) He is the most disinterested scientist I know.
(6) The bullfight ended in a grand flourish of horns.
(7) If the United States and Russia go to war, a great nation will be destroyed.

7. Which of the following are good connotative definitions? Criticize the others from the standpoint of the rules.

(1) "Man" is a featherless biped.
(2) " 'Prejudice' is being down on what you are not up on."
(3) "Glass" is something you can see through.
(4) " 'It' [life] is a tale
    Told by an idiot, full of sound and fury,
    Signifying nothing."
(5) "Biology" is the science of life.
(6) A "professor" is a student who forgot to graduate.
(7) A "sponge" is like what you wash the car with.
(8) "Water" is a transparent, tasteless, colorless liquid which normally boils at 212°F. and freezes at 32°F.
(9) "Discontent" is want of self-reliance.
(10) A "lion" is a dangerous catlike animal, not a leopard, not a cheeta, not a tiger, and not an ocelot.
(11) " 'Metaphysics' is the finding of bad reasons for what we believe on instinct."
(12) Any group is "autonomous" if it is permitted autonomy in making essential decisions.
(13) An "ocelot" is a large American spotted animal, *Felis pardalis.*

8. Classify the following definitions as conventional, stipulative, synonymous, ostensive, denotative, or connotative. If any is more than one, so indicate.

(1) Let the word "rectangle" mean a right-angled quadrilateral.
(2) "Mathematics" is the science that deals with pure order or form regardless of any content.
(3) "Beauty" is the quality displayed by nature in the north country in the autumn.
(4) An "elevator" is a lift.
(5) "Majority" is plurality.
(6) That object [accompanied by a gesture] is a television set.

9. A newspaper story referred to a member of a recent investigation in Washington as "the famous Private X." A reader objected and protested the use of the word "famous" as applied to the Private. The newspaper, in printing the letter, defended the use of the word and commented, "More millions have looked at Private X (on television) than at any man in the ranks in history." Comment on this definition of the word "famous."

10. Are the following disagreements over verbal or real issues? If real, what are the issues as to matters of fact? If merely verbal, locate and remove the ambiguity of the offending words or phrases.

She: Please close the front window of the car; it's cold in the back seat.
He: The window isn't open.
She: It is open; there's a wind back here.

He: It's more closed than open.
She: If it's open at all, it's open.
He: If it's more closed than open, it isn't open.
She: If it's capable of being closed, it's open.

He: Professor Jones believes in free speech both in and out of the classroom.
She: Not he. He charges $100 for every lecture he gives in my hometown.

He: I'm tired of all this talk about police brutality. There are always people who are looking for some way to discredit the police, and so they exaggerate the cases where police must use force in their normal function of suppressing violence.
She: No! I don't agree with you. We read every day in the papers both in the North and the South about the police pushing people around, even including the use of firearms against unarmed citizens.

He: The people in the Far East are being stirred up by the threat of "Yankee imperialism" in that area.
She: The Americans are not a threat in the Far East. On the contrary, several Asian countries are the source of military expansionism. There is no such thing as Yankee imperialism; we don't want an inch of foreign soil.

She: I am in favor of a greater amount of authority being exercised by administrations over college students. They are immature and need strict supervision and a strong hand.
He: Oh, you don't want them to think for themselves; you want them to do what they are told, to conform and take everything on the authority of the administration and the professors! That's not the way to get an education.

4

Logical Division and Classification

I. LOGICAL DIVISION

In our discussion of definition in Chapter 3, we saw that one important kind of definition consisted in stating the essential or defining characteristics of that which is defined by placing it under the nearest genus to which it belongs and adding appropriate differentiae which mark it off from other species of the genus. The process of logical division now to be discussed is closely related to this type of definition; in fact, one may be said to be an aspect of the other.

The terms *genus* and *species* are relative to one another. For example, we may start with the genus "man" and divide it into the various races of man, such as "Caucasian," "Mongolian," "Ethiopian," etc. Then we may take any one of these species as genus and divide it into its subaltern species and so on.

Logical division is the process of breaking down a genus, concept, or class into its logically constituent species until the lowest species is reached. The process of division goes forward as we distinguish subaltern species as belonging under a genus, and as we recognize the differentia peculiar to that species. *Differentiae* are those properties or characteristics which mark one species off as entirely different from another. Now this process of division is essentially the same as connotative definition, for to know whether or not a class of objects belongs in a certain subdivision its essential qualities must be known; that is, it must be defined. Logical division is also closely related to classification. Ideally, one is the inverse of the other. In actual

53

practice, the main difference is that in logical division we are dealing with concepts, universals, or classes, and the process is logical, rational, and formal and can be relatively complete; while in classification we are dealing with objects in nature which belong to dynamic systems, hence classification can never be comprehensive or conclusive.

There are a number of somewhat technical terms with which we must be familiar in order to understand fully the nature of logical division. The genus with which the division begins is known as the *summum genus;* the species with which the division ends is the *infima species;* the intermediate species are known as *subaltern genera.* The *proximum genus* of a species is that genus next above it in the series. *Coordinate species* of a genus are those which stand on the same level and go to make up the *constituent species* of the genus. The *fundamentum divisionis* is the principle or basis on which the division is made. An example will illustrate the method and these various terms:

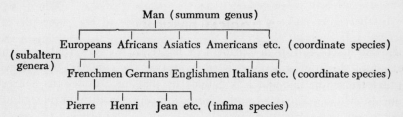

There are certain rules for the guidance of an ideal logical division which we will now state and illustrate:

1. A logical division *must be exhaustive;* that is, the constituent species when added must equal the genus. Failure to observe this rule results in the simple and obvious error of *incomplete division.* Thus in the above illustration where we have divided *man* into Europeans, Africans, Asiatics, and Americans, the "etc." was made to represent inhabitants of geographical areas which for the sake of brevity were omitted. To be a complete logical division of the genus "man" on the basis of geography, all geographical areas would have to be included.

2. The constituent species of the genus must be *mutually exclusive.* Neglect of this rule would result in the fallacy of *overlapping of species.* The error results from making a species or class coordinate with another when it should be subordinate. For example, if we divide a group of public buildings on the basis of architectural style

into classical revival, Gothic revival, eclecticism, functionalism, and modernism, this error would appear in the overlapping of functionalism and modernism, since functionalism should be made subordinate to modernism. Another example would be to divide a residential property consisting of house and grounds into house, garage, lawns, driveway, walks, cultivated ground, and vegetable garden.

3. A logical division must proceed *according to a single principle*, or, as it is called, *fundamentum divisionis*, throughout any one class of coordinate species. Any principle of division may be chosen with reference to the purpose of the division, but once having been chosen it should not be changed or supplemented throughout the process on any one level. Suppose we are sent out by our employer to make a survey of the buildings in a given city block. We would need to know before we begin the survey what the principle of division is to be, that is, the purpose of the survey.

It may be architectural style, materials in use, function, financial value, size, or any other practical or theoretical purpose. Now if we are instructed to make the division on the basis of the principle of *function* and proceed to divide the buildings into the subclasses of residences, business houses, museums, schools, churches, etc., we must not on this level of coordinate species also use the principle of architectural style and include such subdivisions as classical, Gothic, etc. To do so is to commit the fallacy of *cross division*. Since the primary purpose of logical division is to create an ordered division, we have here introduced disorder by reason of creating classes that cross over one another. However, having made our first division on the basis of the principle of function, we may then if we choose, or are so instructed, further divide the subaltern species or genera, such as churches, on the basis of architectural style, or the business houses on the basis of financial value; but if we do so, we must stick to the principle with which we start throughout that class of coordinate species.

It will be observed that a division which uses a single principle and conforms to the third rule will likewise always conform to the second. To disregard the third rule will usually involve the violation of the second. However, this is not always the case, since it is not impossible to conceive of cases of mutually exclusive divisions when more than one principle of division is used. For example, we may divide the human population of North America on the basis of more than one principle into three mutually exclusive classes: those who live in frigid zones, those who eat meat, fruit, and vegetables as a major staple in their diets, and those who are strict vegetarians.

II. LOGICAL DIVISION BY DICHOTOMY

Division by *dichotomy* (a cutting in two) is based upon the logical law of excluded middle, which by its very nature (everything must be either A or not-A) provides an exhaustive division into two mutually exclusive classes. It consists of taking a genus and making a subdivision into two exclusive classes on the basis of a chosen differentia. The positive member of this dichotomy is again divided into another positive class and its contradictory, and so on until the infima species is reached, while the negative members of the dichotomy are ignored. The popular song which runs, "Accentuate the positive, eliminate the negative, don't fool with Mr. In-between," is a perfect illustration of dichotomous division. The method of dichotomy was illustrated by Porphyry, the third century A.D. logician, in his "Tree of Porphyry," which follows:

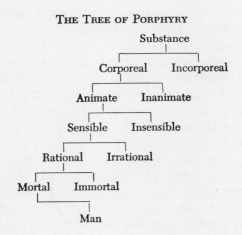

THE TREE OF PORPHYRY

This method of division has the merits of simplicity and logical rigor. It may be regarded also as a good method of developing a definition of a term. Thus the definition of *man* the infima species, consists of an enumeration of the various differentiae: "Man is a mortal, rational, sensitive, animate, corporeal substance." On the other hand the method is limited in that the negative items of the dichotomy may be null (empty), and even if they do have members, since they are not further divided, no information is conveyed about them.

III. CLASSIFICATION

Whereas logical division begins with the *summum genus* and moves by a logical process down to smaller and smaller classes until the lowest species is reached, classification moves in the opposite direction from individual things, events, facts, or processes in nature in their rich variety, toward systematic order as dictated by their common properties and differences, until the highest genus is reached. As previously suggested, division is more closely related to the purely formal process of following logical principles, while classification is more empirical and inductive and belongs to the logic of scientific methodology. As such it will be treated later in Chapter 14. Classification, like division, is intimately related to definition, in that a clear understanding of the meaning of a term is essential in order to know whether or not a given object falls under the term, belongs in a border-line or intermediate position, or falls under some other term or class. To know what a term, thing, class, or concept is, which is the essential nature of definition, is to be able to classify it systematically in relation to other objects, terms, or concepts.

The three rules governing logical division, listed on pages 54 and 55, are also applicable to classification, although they cannot be so rigidly followed. Adherence to the rule that there should be a *single principle of classification* assures a logical structure and prevents *cross classification*. The rule that a classification should be *exhaustive* is an ideal which may be only partially achieved in a growing field such as the social sciences, or in a dynamic science such as biology, botany, or zoology. *Incomplete classification*, which results then, is not a serious defect until the science has become quite systematic and coherent and the laws governing the evolutionary process are known. The third rule which asserts that the *constituent species of a classification must exclude one another* is an ideal which can be achieved only in so far as the properties of the species, and hence the constituent members of the various species, are known. Only then can *overlapping classification* be overcome.

The importance of classification as an elementary way of ordering or pigeonholing objects, facts, and experiences in the early stages of knowledge, whether of the race, the individual, or of a science, is obvious. Some sciences are still in their classificatory stage and others have passed through it. In its initial stages, all science was primarily classificatory, and some sciences have remained at that level, while in others, as accumulated bodies of reliable knowledge began to reveal systematic order, classification was supplemented by hypotheses and experimental methods. It is evident that with the development of the evolutionary theory, which replaced the idea of the fixity of species, greater complexity was introduced into the process of biological classification. This called for more adequate methods of ordering and investigating nature, now conceived of as a continuous process of change.

Classification is guided both by the nature of the materials to be classified and by the purpose of the classifier. This two-fold aspect may serve to introduce us to the distinction which is usually made between *natural* and *artificial* classification. Natural classification ideally is dictated by the discoverable natural structures, properties, and attributes of the materials under investigation. Artificial classification, on the other hand, is dictated by some practical human purpose, such as convenience in handling and the saving of time and energy. Thus, an example of natural classification of plants would be one based upon a phylogenetic system, or order of common descent, while an example of artificial classification would be the listing of the names of plants alphabetically in an index, manual, or catalogue.

Somewhere between these two extremes is an intermediate form of classification, neither wholly natural nor wholly artificial, of the exploratory type likely to be found in a new or partially developed field such as the social sciences. This intermediate type has been called *diagnostic* classification.

For example, a police officer may classify the cases of misdemeanor encountered on his beat merely in terms of time, place, persons involved, and nature of offense, to be filed in the local police office index for future reference. In so far as this classification is guided by the purpose of convenience, it is *artificial*. However, a social case worker might seek to classify the same cases in terms of partially known and suspected causal factors such as psychological and social maladjustments, to be alleviated by the modification or correction of the causal conditions. Because it is exploratory and unfinished, this classification should perhaps be regarded as *diagnostic*. If, however, extensive research on the cases involved were carried forward by expert criminologists and anthropologists to the extent of classifying the cases according to body type, blood type, head shape, cranial capacity, and other structural traits, we should be justified in regarding this as *natural* classification.

PROBLEMS

1. Divide by dichotomy the following concepts or classes into at least six subdivisions: "Organic," "Sports," "Beauty," "Vehicles."

2. Divide by logical division a city lot containing a house, garden, etc., into its various parts by using first the principle of function or use, and second the principle of ground covering such as vegetation, etc.

3. Criticize the following division of instruments in a concert orchestra from the viewpoint of the three rules given in the text: strings, brasses, winds, and cymbals. What principle of division is used?

4. Illustrate the fallacies of cross division, incomplete division, and overlapping species by dividing the class term "army" into its constituent species.

5. Classify the books on one of the library shelves according to both natural and artificial classification.

6. Make a division of the sciences under the heads of physical, mental, social, and formal. Then begin at the other end with a catalogue of individual sciences, classify them, and compare the results of the two operations.

7. Classify the objects in your bedroom, kitchen, or living room, using both natural and artificial classification. Include at least fifteen articles and use subclasses as well as major divisions.

8. A farm of 1,000 acres is surveyed and subdivided as follows: 500 acres grassland, 100 acres gardens, 150 acres grain, 100 acres woods, 50 acres buildings, 40 acres lake, 50 acres rocky waste, and 10 acres roads and walks. What principle of division has been used here?

9. Use Problem 8 to illustrate how the three rules of division may be broken.

10. Distinguish and illustrate by example natural, artificial, and diagnostic classification.

11. Which of the following subclasses are irrelevant according to the rules of logical division?

(1) Religions:	(2) Trees:	(3) Buildings:
Christianity	Maple	Churches
Monotheism	Beech	Wholesale
Mohammedanism	Fruit-bearing	Museums
Buddhism	Birch	Libraries
Judaism	Spruce	Theaters
Oriental	Deciduous	Mercantile

5

Semantic and Material Fallacies

I. FALLACIES

A fallacy may be defined as any process of reasoning or arguing which fails to satisfy the requirements of logical validity, whether formal, semantic, or material. In later chapters, we shall study the positive rules for validity in formal reasoning and their corresponding fallacies. However, there are other common fallacies of informal discourse and argumentation having to do with inattention to language, inattention to the subject matter, and inattention to the argument, rather than to the formal structure of the argument itself. Since fallacies of this nature are more likely to be encountered in the discussions, debates, and disputes of daily communication, they will be treated in some detail here.

No classification of fallacies that has been made by logicians has been entirely satisfactory or complete. As De Morgan says: "There is no such thing as a classification of the ways in which men may arrive at error; it is much to be doubted whether there can ever be."[1]

II. FALLACIES OF AMBIGUITY, OR SEMANTIC FALLACIES

1. Fallacy of Equivocation. Equivocation is the fallacy of assuming that words are always used in the same sense when in fact they are

[1] A. De Morgan, *Formal Logic* (La Salle, Ill.: The Open Court Publishing Co.), p. 237.

ambiguous, and of using ambiguous terms intentionally in order to win an argument. Ambiguity has already been dealt with in Chapter 3, and the fallacy of ambiguous middle, or four terms, where the ambiguity is unintentional, is found in the treatment of the syllogism in Chapter 8. As we shall see there, the soundness of an argument depends upon, among other things, the meaning of the terms remaining the same throughout the argument. When one or more of the terms or phrases shifts its meaning in the course of the argument, the conclusion does not follow. This fallacy is easily detected and would not be serious in short arguments such as the following: "The sick man is well, for men who have recovered are well, and the sick man has recovered." The equivocation rests upon the confusion between the past and present tense of the verb "to be." "The sick man" in one part of the argument refers to the man who *was* sick, and in the other it refers to the man who *is* sick. Likewise, the following equivocal argument rests upon the failure to take account of time: "All able men are consistent with themselves. Any man who changes his opinions is not consistent with himself. Hence, he who changes his opinions is not an able man." In the first premise "consistent with themselves" means consistent with themselves at any given time. But in the second premise the meaning has shifted and suggests that a man cannot over a period of time change his opinions and still be "consistent with himself." The conclusion therefore does not follow because of this equivocation. The dangers of equivocation are greater in long-drawn-out arguments where many words may have intervened between the equivocal terms, and hence the equivocation is not so easily detected. For example, an orator advocating "free enterprise" traced the history of the *laissez-faire* concept of economy and showed that our economy has gained freedom from arbitrary interference with the operation of competition. After many illustrations of these operations he concluded that modern business has acquired freedom to do as it pleases in the competitive market. The equivocation resulting from the shifting of the meaning in the two kinds of freedom, *freedom from* and *freedom to do,* may easily pass unnoticed.

2. Fallacy of Amphiboly. Amphiboly refers to ambiguity in the structure of the sentence or proposition. The mystery surrounding the deliverances of the oracle of Delphi was due to their ambiguity. For example, the oracle delivered to Pyrrhus by Apollo: "Pyrrhus the Romans can, I say, subdue." A modern counterpart might be: "If the United States and Russia should go to war, a mighty nation would be destroyed." Sports fans who wish to be on the safe side, as well as loyal to the home team, may wager with a high degree of confidence that, unless there is a tie, "The home team, the opponents will subdue." Newspaper advertisements present many humorous examples, such as, "Wanted: Three bedrooms for girls with private bath and north side entrance."

3. Fallacy of Composition. The fallacy of composition may be interpreted in two ways. The oldest form of this fallacy consisted in using words and terms *distributively* in one part of an argument which in another part are used *compositely* (from which the name composition is derived) or *collectively,* resulting in the fallacy of arguing from *each* to *all.* A term is called distributive when it denotes each member of the class individually, as for example in the proposition *"All* (each) of the angles of a triangle are less than two right angles." A term is used collectively when it denotes all of the members of a class when taken collectively, for example, "All (taken together) of the angles of a triangle are equal to two right angles."

If a real estate salesman were to describe a piece of property he was trying to sell us as consisting of a block in which "All of the buildings cover a space of 600 square feet, and all of the buildings consist of a house, a barn, and a garage," and allow us to draw the conclusion that "All of the buildings cover only 600 square feet," we would regard him as a poor salesman. What he actually would mean is that each of the buildings covers 600 square feet and that all of them taken together cover 1,800 square feet. The fallacy is due to the fact that in the first premise the word *all* is meant *distributively* in the sense of *each,* whereas in the second premise and the conclusion it means *all* of the buildings taken together or *collectively.*

In later times the fallacy of composition has been extended so that it is now regarded as a material fallacy and takes the form of the claim that what is true of the parts of any class is true of the whole class. If we were to argue that because five individual basketball players chosen from five different teams were all expert players, that therefore they would constitute an expert team when brought together without practice, we would commit the fallacy of composition.

This fallacy may also be explained as due to a confusion between class inclusion and class membership. For example, in the proposition "Horses are quadrupeds," the class of horses is *included in* the class of quadrupeds, but, in the proposition "Dobbin is a horse," the individual Dobbin is a *member* of the class of horses. As will be explained more fully in a later chapter, class inclusion is *transitive,* and class membership is not. When we say that class inclusion is transitive, we mean that, if A is included in B, and B is included in C, it follows that A is included in C. But, if we say that A is a member of B, and B is a member of C, it does not follow that A is a member of C, since class membership is not transitive. In the argument "Units of uranium consist of atoms, and atoms are innumerable; hence, units of uranium are innumerable," the conclusion does not follow, and the fallacy of composition occurs, because in the first premise the relation between the terms is that of class inclusion, but in the second premise and conclusion the relation between terms is that of class membership.

4. Fallacy of Division. The fallacy of division is the converse of the fallacy of composition, and results from using a term or concept in a *collective* sense in one premise, and a *distributive* sense in the conclusion, resulting in arguing that what is true of *all* is true of *each*. This may be illustrated by the example from Whatley: "All the angles of a triangle are equal to two right angles; ABC is an angle of a triangle; therefore, ABC is equal to two right angles."

This fallacy is also interpreted as a material fallacy consisting of affirming that what is true of a whole class may be affirmed of the parts when taken separately or individually. Thus, to argue that because a constitution, legislative enactment, or philosophical system is coherent and adequate when taken as a whole, each individual part in its specific content and application is equally adequate, coherent, and free from defects is a case in point. Or again, "All inhabitants of the city consist of men, women, and children, and the members of the student body are all inhabitants of the city; therefore, the members of the student body consist of men, women, and children."

The fallacy of division may also be the result of a confusion of class inclusion with class membership. An example would be: "Dogs are widely distributed over the country, and any collie is a dog; therefore, any collie is widely distributed over the country." Here it is argued that because the class of dogs is a member of the class of classes widely distributed over the country, and any collie is included in the class of dogs, that any collie is a member of the class of classes widely distributed over the country. The fallacy results from the fact that class membership is nontransitive.

5. Fallacy of Accent. The fallacy of accent originally referred to ambiguity of a word which had different meanings when accented differently. It has come to mean, however, the fallacy of drawing a conclusion with a certain accent from a premise with a different accent.

Consider the statement "Woman without her man would be lost." As it stands, unpunctuated and unaccented, it is not clear what is asserted. If someone claimed that it has only one meaning and that it should be accented "Woman, without *her*, man would be lost," and someone else claimed that it has only one meaning and that it should be accented "Woman, without her *man*, would be lost," they would be equally guilty of the fallacy of accent. If we were to accept the conclusion that the accent on the word "neighbor" in the commandment "Thou shalt not bear false witness against thy *neighbor*" releases us from the obligation of fair dealing where those who are not our neighbors are concerned, we would have committed the fallacy of accent. Children are often puzzled by the words of the minister administering the Eucharist, "Drink *ye all* of it," and would draw an entirely erroneous conclusion if it were accented, "Drink ye *all of it*."

III. MATERIAL OR NONVERBAL FALLACIES

Material fallacies are distinguished from formal fallacies which result from inattention to the formal structure of the argument as in the syllogism, and from verbal or semantic fallacies which result from inattention to language. Material fallacies are so called because they result from inattention to the subject matter or content of arguments.

1. Fallacy of Accident. The fallacy of accident consists in claiming that what is true in *essence* of a thing is also true in its *accidents*. Any given subject has essential characteristics which constitute its real nature, and also many other accidental qualities. Now what is assertable of a subject in essence may or may not be assertable of the accidents, and vice versa. We might argue fallaciously that "In a democracy all matters of public interest should be publicly debated and decided by a majority vote or according to the Gallup Poll, and that therefore, since matters pertaining to strategy in war are matters of public interest, all matters pertaining to strategy in war should likewise be debated and decided."

It is notably the fallacy of the doctrinaire, or those who have become wedded to certain dogmas, ideologies, or abstract principles which under normal conditions may be essentially sound but which fail to take into account special or accidental conditions.

2. Converse Fallacy of Accident. The converse fallacy of accident consists of arguing that what is true of a thing under *accidental conditions* can also be asserted of it in its *essential nature*.

This method may be used to trick an opponent by getting his assent to a statement with such qualifications as "other things being equal" or "under ordinary conditions" understood, and then arguing as though the proposition has been granted without these qualifications. For example, if we were to argue that under ordinary conditions it may be granted that "An intoxicated man is irrational (accidentally), and this person is intoxicated; hence, this person is (essentially) irrational," we would commit this fallacy.

It may be regarded as the special fallacy of the uncritical mind which is too readily influenced by a specific case and reaches a conclusion without realizing that the case may not be typical. This fallacy would be committed if a committee sent to study the administration of a prison or reform school, under investigation for known inefficiency, were to find everything in perfect order and running smoothly, and further, were to accept the testimony of other visitors to the effect that they found similar conditions, and were to conclude that therefore this administration is essentially sound and efficient.

3. Fallacies of Irrelevancy. Traditionally these fallacies have been known as *ignoratio elenchi,* which literally means *ignorance of confutation.* They result from a failure to pay attention to the conclusion required, by allowing a substitution for the proposition requiring to be proved. Sometimes this substitution is made deliberately by sophistically inclined disputants. Getting a laugh, or arousing some emotion to turn attention away from the point at issue, are some of the techniques employed.

(a) *Argumentum ad hominem. Argumentum ad hominem* means, literally, an argument directed "to the man." It may be interpreted in two ways. The usual interpretation is illustrated by the prosecuting attorney who abandons the evidence bearing directly on the defendant's guilt or innocence and attacks the record or character of the man, hoping thereby to discredit his testimony in this case. Now this material may be relevant to the case or it may not be. When it is not relevant, the fallacy has been committed. The other interpretation of this fallacy is that the argument is directed *to this man,* and that he is obliged to accept a certain conclusion in view of the circumstances relating to himself, that is, his conduct, beliefs, and admissions, but which may not be a sound conclusion when judged objectively on its premises. For example: "You admit that you are a member of the Klan, and that they believe in race discrimination; hence, you are guilty of these atrocities."

(*b*) *Argumentum ad populum*. *Argumentum ad populum* is the common fallacy of the propagandist and the demagogue, and is involved whenever the passions and prejudices of the audience are appealed to instead of reason, through evidence.

Antony's address over the body of Caesar is a notable example.

> But yesterday the word of Caesar might
> Have stood against the world: now lies he there,
> And none so poor to do him reverence.
> O masters, if I were disposed to stir
> Your hearts and minds to mutiny and rage,
> I should do Brutus wrong, and Cassius wrong,
> Who, you all know, are honorable men:
> I will not do them wrong; I rather choose
> To wrong the dead, to wrong myself and you,
> Than I will wrong such honorable men.
>
> But here's a parchment with the seal of Caesar,
> I found it in his closet; 'tis his will:
> Let but the commons hear this testament—
> Which, pardon me, I do not mean to read—
> And they would go and kiss dead Caesar's wounds
> And dip their napkins in his sacred blood,
> Yea, beg a hair of him for memory,
> And, dying, mention it within their wills,
> Bequeathing it as a rich legacy
> Unto their issue.

(*c*) *Argumentum ad misericordiam*. *Argumentum ad misericordiam* is known as the appeal to pity, and may be regarded as a species of *ad hominem*. It is committed whenever the evidence bearing on the case is ignored or put aside and the argument is centered upon the circumstances of the accused which might arouse pity and sympathy. In the *Apology*, Socrates hints that this was a common practice in the courts of his day, but refused to resort to it himself, as indicated in the following passage:

Yet a word more. Perhaps there may be some one who is offended at me, when he calls to mind how he himself on a similar, or even a less serious occasion, prayed and entreated the judges with many tears, and how he produced his children in court, which was a moving spectacle, together with a host of relations and friends; whereas I, who am probably in danger of my life, will do none of these things. The contrast may occur to his mind, and he may be set against me, and vote in anger because he is displeased at me on this account. Now if there be such a person among you,—mind, I do not say that there is,—to him I may fairly reply: My friend, I am a man, and like other men, a creature of flesh and blood, and not 'of wood or stone,' as

Homer says; and I have a family, yes, and sons, O Athenians, three in number, one almost a man, and two others who are still young; and yet I will not bring any of them hither in order to petition you for an acquittal.[2]

In spite of Socrates' asserted refusal to employ this device, the cited example may in fact be held to be a subtle employment of it.

(d) *Argumentum ad verecundiam.* *Argumentum ad verecundiam* means the appeal to reverence or authority and is committed whenever advantage is taken of the feeling of reverence and respect people have for the authority of great names, for the purpose of silencing objections and winning assent.

This does not mean that it is necessarily a fallacy to appeal legitimately to authority. An example of the fallacy would be to appeal to the opinions of Darwin, who is an authority in biology and evolution, or to the writings of Einstein, who is an authority in mathematical physics, as authoritative in the field of religion. The weakness of this kind of argument is more apparent when we realize that in these days of specialization a thorough knowledge of one's own field often restricts the possibility of authoritative knowledge in many other fields.

(e) *Argumentum ad ignorantiam.* *Argumentum ad ignoratiam* is the argument from ignorance. The fallacy is committed whenever a disputant attempts to place the burden of disproof upon an opponent, and then argues that his ignorance or inability to disprove the contention is itself proof of its truth. It is usually committed in connection with such matters as psychic phenomena, immortality, telepathy, etc., where evidence is lacking either for or against the beliefs.

(f) *Argumentum ad baculum.* *Argumentum ad baculum* is the appeal to force. It is resorted to when evidence and rational arguments fail, and thus is irrelevant to any process of reason, and hence goes beyond the realm of logic. Strong-arm methods used in coercing and intimidating political opponents in nondemocratic political struggles provide numerous contemporary examples.

(g) *Non sequitur.* *Non sequitur* means literally "it does not follow." *Non sequitur* is any fallacy in which the conclusion affirms or denies what cannot be validly inferred from the premises. According to this definition all formal fallacies would be regarded as examples of *non sequitur*, and some logicians interpret it in this sense. But since these fallacies have their own characteristic names, *non sequitur*

---

[2] *The Dialogues of Plato,* trans. Benjamin Jowett (New York: Oxford University Press, 1892), "Apology" (34b).

is reserved for the nonsyllogistic fallacy in which there is a complete lack of necessary logical relation between the premises posited and the conclusion drawn. The deceptive nature of the argument may be concealed by much verbiage and because some of the same terms appear in premises and conclusion, and it may be arranged in what may appear to be a logical order, but nevertheless fails as far as proof is concerned. An element of emotion is usually present lending a form of irrationality to the argument. It would be a *non sequitur* if an employee argued that he did not see why he had been fired from his job, because in addition to taking a course on how to make a good impression on his employer, he had read several books on how to operate his department. If we were to argue that since we all have the greatest respect for the sanctity of marriage and the purity of women that the Kinsey report should never have been published, we would commit the fallacy of *non sequitur*.

4. Fallacies of Unwarranted Assumption.   (a) *Begging the question, or petitio principii.* This is the fallacy of seeking to prove a conclusion by assuming it in the premises in order to prove it, without admitting that it is assumed. Since nothing new is established the argument is fruitless and does not constitute proof. One form of begging the question is to assume the point at issue and repeat the conclusion to be proved in the premises, sometimes in a different form or in synonyms which may have a different etymological origin, and thus have the show of making progress in the argument. To argue that "This treaty is out of date because it is an anachronism" is a case in point. Whatley gives the following illustration: "To allow every man an unbounded freedom of speech must always be, on the whole, advantageous to the state: for it is highly conducive to the interests of the community, that each individual should enjoy a liberty, perfectly unlimited, of expressing his sentiments."

(b) *Arguing in a circle.* Another form of begging the question is arguing in a circle. This fallacy is to assume a universal premise which if true would establish the desired conclusion, but which could be established only through the particular case that goes to make up the universal principle. For example, we may try to prove that any particular body gravitates because of the universal law that "All bodies gravitate." If, however, we ask how do we know that all bodies gravitate, we may answer by showing that this, and this, and this body does, and conclude from this that "All bodies gravitate."

But in this induction we have used the fact that this body gravitates to prove the universal law by which we then prove that this body obeys the law of gravity. Another example would be to argue that the Koran is infallible because it was composed by the prophet of Allah, and we know this to be true because the Koran says so.

(c) *Question-begging epithets.* This is a form of name-calling which assumes that the epithet used correctly designates the character or policy of the opponent when this is the very point to be proved and is a matter of evidence. It is particularly prominent in the rough and tumble of partisan politics, labor relations, and economic competition, and in international, educational, and religious controversies. When the Taft-Hartley Law was enacted it was called "the slave labor law." Theodore Roosevelt referred to a New York newspaper as "a sheet of voluble scurrility and versatile mendacity." Supporters of UNESCO have been described as "those internationalists who want to sabotage the American constitution through corrupting the minds of our youth" and as "a band of spies and traitors." The teachings of the organization have been branded as "palpable and evident treason," "lying propaganda and palpable untruths," "monstrous poison" and "an infamous plot."

(d) *False cause.* This fallacy is sometimes confused with the inductive fallacy of *post hoc ergo propter hoc,* which means, "after this therefore as a consequence of this." In the inductive fallacy the word "cause" is used in the material sense rather than in the logical sense of "reason for," and the fallacy occurs whenever we assume because one event immediately precedes or follows another event in time, that these events are therefore causally related. This fallacy and others relating to cause and effect are discussed under inductive fallacies in Chapter 19.

In the traditional sense the fallacy of false cause occurs when it is argued that as a result of an absurd conclusion, a certain premise must be rejected as false, when in fact it is the other premise from which the absurd conclusion follows, although it may appear to follow from the one in question.

Joseph gives the following illustration: "It is ridiculous to suppose that the world can be flat; for a flat world would be infinite, and an infinite world could not be circumnavigated as this has been."[3] If

---

[3] H. W. B. Joseph, *An Introduction to Logic* (Oxford: The Clarendon Press, 1906), p. 594.

we arrange the premises and conclusion in proper order, we have the following syllogism:

> A flat world would be infinite.
> An infinite world could not be circumnavigated (as this has been).
> Hence, the world is not flat (i.e., it is ridiculous to suppose that the world can be flat).

In order to fully appreciate the nature of this fallacious argument, we might place ourselves in imagination at a time when it was not yet an accepted fact that the world is round, and suppose that one party to the dispute is trying to prove that the world is flat and another that it is not.   But does either advocate succeed in proving his conclusion on these premises?   The minor premise, "An infinite world could not be circumnavigated as this has been," asserts that the world is finite, and implies neither roundness nor flatness.   It simply disproves the claim of the major premise; that is, this world has been circumnavigated, and hence, whether round or flat, it is not infinite. The fallacy of *false cause*, then, is illustrated by the conclusion that to hold that the world is flat is ridiculous, and the absurdity is supposed to be due to the minor premise, which is a simple statement of fact, when actually it is due to the false assumption in the major premise that "A flat world would be infinite."   In order to see the fallacious argument more clearly, we may put it in hypothetical form and notice that the minor premise correctly denies the consequent and the conclusion denies the antecedent.   But the conclusion does not follow truthfully from these premises, since the major premise is false.

> If the world were flat, it would be infinite.
> But this world is not infinite.
> Hence, this world is not flat.

(e) *Complex question or many questions.*   This fallacy consists in putting a question in such a way that a single answer involves a double admission, one or both parts of which the person being questioned would not make if the question were plain and explicit.   Complex questions are often used to great advantage by attorneys in cross-examination for the purpose of eliciting from witnesses admissions that are damaging because of the assumptions involved in them.   If the prosecutor asks a witness, "Why did you wipe the fingerprints from the gun?" the question is called complex because it involves two questions: "Did you? and "Why did you do so?"   The question assumes that the witness did so, and he is asked for his reasons for so doing, but the original question, which is legitimate—"Did you wipe the fingerprints from the gun?"—has not been put to him. The first and legitimate question would need to be asked and answered before the *reasons* why he did so could become relevant.

If a witness is required to answer "yes" or "no" to such questions, he will be placed in a difficult position. Suppose a witness is asked, "Have you given up stealing from your employer? Answer "yes" or "no." If he answers "no," he is likely to be understood as admitting that at one time he indulged in this practice and that he has not reformed. If he answers "yes," he is admitting that he at one time stole from his employer. But, if neither is true, and he wants to say that he has never been guilty of such an act, the right question is not being asked, namely, the one which could be answered by a straightforward denial.

Other examples of the fallacy of complex questions are "Why did you hide the gun when you arrived at the scene of the crime?" "Where have you been since I last saw you in jail?" "Why does a live fish placed in a bowl already full of water not cause it to overflow, whereas a dead fish does?" The only way to avoid becoming a victim of complex questions is to break them down into their elements and examine the constituent propositions singly.

PROBLEMS

I

Select from newspapers, magazines, and/or political-social commentary several illustrations of one or more of the semantic, and/or material fallacies discussed in this chapter. Analyze the arguments; locate the fallacies; and hand them in for class discussion.

II

Examine each of the following quotations. If it is an argument, locate the conclusion and the reasons for the conclusion. If it is not possible to classify them under the various fallacies discussed in this chapter, state in your own words why you accept or reject the conclusion.

Marking his return to University life, Arthur M. Schlesinger Jr. defended the rule of men of ideas in the affairs of state as he delivered his first public lecture as Albert Schweitzer Professor of Humanities at the City University yesterday.

"If intellectuals do take part in public affairs, are they to be permitted by their fellows any role save that of intransigent opposition? If they accept political responsibility must they be chastised by intellectual excommunication?" asked the historian, who during the time he served in the White House as a special adviser to President Kennedy, was frequently chided as a defector from the academic world.

". . . Despite the recurrent view in our society that the proper position for intellectuals is detachment, the recognition of political realities does not implacably mean the relinquishment of political principles," Mr. Schlesinger declared. "It is entirely possible to deal with practical realities without yielding inner convictions; it is entirely possible to compromise in program and action without compromising in ideas and values."—From *The New York Times,* October 26, 1966, © 1966 by The New York Times Company. Reprinted by permission.

Dr. John F. Cuber, preaching a philosophy of giving youth straight information, spoke on "Realistic Teaching about Family Relations." Dr. Cuber, Professor of Sociology and Anthropology at Ohio State University, addressed a luncheon at the Hotel Sheraton-Cleveland.

"Everyone is for realistic teaching about family relations," Dr. Cuber said, "but the community really does not want you to be realistic." He said the teacher of family relations must use information which is "dreadfully inaccurate, biased, and not scientifically based." The teacher must be conscious of an atmosphere of hypocrisy and pretence among parents, and there is always the problem of "small powerful pressure groups that will use things you say in the classroom to attack you," he said.

—From *Cleveland Plain Dealer,* November 5, 1966

There is one all-important lesson to be learned from the recent election: The time has come for the public to look behind the slogan. The time has also come for Congress to limit the millions of dollars spent to spread slogans and create images.

Electing a governor or a senator has now become a question of selling a candidate with the same Madison Avenue techniques as you sell underarm deodorants.

The secret of political success is not in letting the public know what a candidate stands for, but in hiring the right public relations firm. And that PR firm may decide that the easiest road to victory is to hide what a candidate stands for, not advertise it.—DREW PEARSON, from *Los Angeles Times,* November 14, 1966. Reprinted by permission of Bell-McClure Syndicate.

Jerome B. Wiesner, who served as President Kennedy's science adviser, likened society to the scientific laboratory, and compared attempts to solve society's problems to scientific experiments. The comparison is apt. There are complicated problems aplenty, and the best way to find solutions is by trial and error. Yet the social experimenters in Washington refuse to adopt the humility necessary for a true scientist. Dr. Wiesner puts it this way: "Today any failure of a social experiment to come out entirely as predicted is regarded as a personal failure by those who initiated it. Politicians thus defend these initiatives long after they have proved ineffective."

—From *The National Observer,* December 5, 1966

New hope for the American university is generated by the decision of the University of Pennsylvania to do no more "classified" research for the government. This means that the university will not take government contracts that require secrecy; the results of all future studies must be freely publishable.

The university is abolishing its Institute of Cooperative Research which has coordinated scientific investigations done under contract with the Department of Defense.

Only a few months age the university accepted two large Defense Department contracts for classified research on weapons systems, including guided missiles. It has also contracted in the past to work on the most distasteful of all Defense Department projects, chemical-biological warfare, that is, how to poison people.

The decision to get out of this kind of business shows that the idea of a university is not dead. The essence of that idea is community. An intellectual community cannot exist if the members of it are required to conceal what they are doing from one another.

—ROBERT M. HUTCHINS, from *Los Angeles Times*, November 14, 1966

The Supreme Court has again restricted the police in their efforts to protect the public in the matter of obtaining evidence that will convict wrong-doers. Even though a suspect is known to have committed a crime, the police are severely restricted in the matter of obtaining evidence that will convict him. As a result, known murderers, robbers, and rapists are allowed to continue in their crimes against innocent people. We are told that it is better for a hundred guilty men to go unpunished than for one innocent man to suffer for a crime he did not commit. Nothing is said about the innocent victims of the crimes that are committed by the one hundred guilty men who go unpunished. Our soft society seems more determined to protect the criminal than his victim.

—DR. HOWARD E. KERSHNER, from *Christian Economics*, October 18, 1966

Can the United States maintain the freedom of the press and assure fair trials too? The point is hotly debated by jurists and journalists, and earlier this month a panel of the American Bar Association proposed a controversial range of tight new reins on court reporting. One would prohibit pretrial information on prospective witnesses, their testimony and credibility.

Ironically, it was just such information last week that provided convincing evidence that front-page headlines need not always work against the accused. In the aftermath of last summer's racial violence Ernest Gallashaw, a 17-year-old Negro from Brooklyn's East New York ghetto, stood accused of killing another Negro boy, 11-year-old Eric Dean—a friend of his—while aiming a pistol at police during a riot. The shooting had aggravated racial tensions, but the arrest of a Negro cooled the tempers of those who had blamed local white roughnecks. Then an unusual decision to free Gallashaw on bail threw the arrest into question, and drew suspicious reporters into the street.

A New York Times team scoured the ghetto and found the Gallishaw murder indictment rested upon tales told by an emotionally disturbed 14-year-old and an 11-year-old later adjudged incompetent to testify under oath. Both were Negroes and they repudiated their signed statements while talking to the Times. The reporters also discovered that police had chosen to ignore another young Negro who swore he had seen a white boy fire the fatal shot. Daily stories that would be banned by the Bar Association prompted the prosecution to an early trial. After listening to the testimony—much of it inconsistent, even from prosecution witnesses—the jury deliberated for six and a half hours, spurned the government's confidence in the children's changing stories and voted Gallishaw not guilty.

—From *Newsweek*, October 24, 1966. Copyright 1966, Newsweek, Inc.

It is dangerous to have two cultures which can't or don't communicate. In a time when science is determining much of our destiny, that is, whether we live or die, it is dangerous in the most practical terms. Scientists can give bad advice and decision-makers can't know whether it is good or bad. On the other hand, scientists in a divided culture provide a knowledge of some potentialities which is theirs alone. All this makes the political process more complex, and in some ways more dangerous, than we should be prepared to tolerate for long, either for the purposes of avoiding disasters, or for fulfilling—what is waiting as a challenge to our conscience and goodwill—a definable social hope.[4]

III

Examine the following arguments, and state whether valid or invalid. If invalid, explain the defects in the argument and name the fallacy.

1. The Gallup Poll expresses a conservative view on public matters, and my friend was a member of the last Gallup Poll; hence, my friend expressed a conservative view on the question submitted to him.

2. No cat has nine tails. Any cat has one more tail than no cat. Therefore, any cat has ten tails.

3. I could not live in a world which was not controlled by a loving, divine power; hence, this power must exist.

4. Why do boys resemble their maternal uncles more than their paternal uncles?

5. The testimony of the defendant accused of contributory negligence in this accident should have no weight, because there is evidence that he once served a term in the state penitentiary.

6. The Book of Mormon is true because it is the word of God, and we know it is the word of God because it tells us so.

7. Human nature is changing, because otherwise how would progress be possible?

8. All of the angles of a triangle are less than two right angles. *A, B,* and *C* are all angles of this triangle. Therefore *A, B,* and *C* are less than two right angles.

9. All of the angles of a triangle are equal to two right angles. *A* is an angle of this triangle. Hence, *A* equals two right angles.

10. He did not make a mistake in his computation of his income tax, for he never makes a mistake.

[4] C. P. Snow, *The Two Cultures: And a Second Look* (London: Cambridge University Press, 1963), p. 98. Reprinted by permission of the publishers.

11. Progress must be a fact; otherwise, all the activities of schools, churches, and universities are in vain and a waste of time.

12. Since George Washington warned us against all entangling alliances, and Monroe established the Monroe Doctrine, we should take no part in international movements.

13. The law of supply and demand does not hold in Russia, Germany, or Italy (under price regulation); hence, the law of supply and demand has been annulled.

14. You can trust the majority to do what is right in the long run, and, since Mr. X is a member of the majority, he can be trusted to do what is right in the long run.

15. I will not do this act, because it is unjust. I know that it is unjust because my conscience tells me so, and my conscience tells me so because the act is wrong.

16. Metals are common. Platinum is a metal. Hence, platinum is common.

17. Interference with another man's business is a breach of business ethics. Underselling interferes with another man's business. Hence, underselling is a breach of business ethics.

18. A high protective tariff is excellent for the wheat growers, the meat industry, and the dairy industry; hence, a high tariff is excellent for the economy of the whole country.

19. Iron bars are made of atoms. Atoms are innumerable. Hence, iron bars are innumerable.

20. Sioux Indians are inhabitants of America. The inhabitants of America are numerous. Hence, the Sioux Indians are numerous.

21. Libraries are widely distributed throughout the country. Any large collection of books is a library. Hence, any large collection of books is distributed throughout the country.

22. All able men are consistent with themselves. He who changes his opinions is not consistent with himself. Therefore, he who changes his opinion is not an able man.

23. Water boils at 212 degrees Fahrenheit at sea level and will boil an egg in five minutes; hence, boiling water on top of a mountain will cook an egg in five minutes.

24. I have a right to vote a straight party ticket at the coming election. What is right for me to do I ought to do. Therefore, I ought to vote the straight party ticket.

25. The argument for evolution is supported by evidence from the "survival of the fittest." If we are asked how we know what the fittest species are, we reply, "because they survive."

26. Forty million Frenchmen can't be wrong. Pierre is a Frenchman. Hence, Pierre can't be wrong.

27. A foundation is investigating the presence of fear and hysteria in the teaching profession. We may conclude from this that a great deal of fear and hysteria exists in educational institutions.

28. A public figure knows that his living depends on pleasing his constituents; hence, a good teacher will never say anything to his classes that will offend anyone.

29. You can tell that he is a disreputable person by the character of his associates. The kind of people who go around with people like him are the lowest type.

30. My congressman says that Wall Street has ruined the economy of the country, and what he says on this subject is true. How do I know this? Because he tells us so in his book on economics.

31. Nietzsche argued that the moral law is a mere man-made convention. But Nietzsche was a sickly, self-tormented, disloyal little man who spent the last years of his life in an insane asylum. His conclusion is, thus, clearly seen to be false.

32. There are more churches in New York City than in any other city in the United States, and more crimes are committed in New York than anywhere else. This makes it clear that to eliminate the criminal we must abolish the church.

33. The doctrine of free will must be true, for its acceptance is a necessary presupposition of every person who deliberates and decides what action he should take. Everyone accepts the doctrine in fact, consciously or unconsciously.

34. There must be something to psychical research, since such famous physicists and astronomers as Lodge, Jeans, and Eddington took it seriously.

35. A customer returned a shipment of goods and asked for his money back, calling attention to the guaranty: "Money refunded if not entirely satisfactory." The shipper replied, "Your money is entirely satisfactory."

II

TRADITIONAL LOGIC

6

Propositions

I. JUDGMENT, PROPOSITION, SENTENCE

In ordinary usage the word *judgment* is ambiguous, for it may mean anything from a simple act of discrimination within perceptual experience, such as "This is a red color," "My seatmate is pretty," "My professor is getting bald," to the most profound critical opinion on the quantum theory or a decision of the Supreme Court. Logically, it usually refers to the affirmation or denial of some kind of relation between the subject and one or more other terms. The ambiguity of the word is further seen in its use to refer either to the mental act of judging, or to that which is judged and stated in verbal or other symbols. Psychologically, "judgment" refers to the simplest unit of significant expression of opinion, taste, or knowledge. It is the mental act of accepting or rejecting, affirming or denying. Although some logicians use the word "judgment" for both, the distinction between judgment as mental act and the *proposition* as the logical unit enables us to avoid this ambiguity. The proposition is that which is judged or asserted; it is the object of thought, the objective meaning. A proposition is still a proposition whether it be true or false, possible or impossible, believed or disbelieved. Propositions should be distinguished both from the act of judging and from the "facts" or states of affairs existing in time and space to which they refer.

Summarizing the above distinction we may then say: A proposition is a statement in the form of verbal or other symbols which must be either true or false, whereas a judgment is the mental activity involved in affirming or denying the proposition. The proposition may be further understood when distinguished from the *sentence*. The sentence is the grammatical or linguistic unit, and is made up of words in syntactical arrangement to express a complete thought. Propositions are usually expressed in sentence form, but not every sentence is a proposition. Aristotle states this clearly.[1]

"Every sentence has a meaning . . . yet every sentence is not a proposition; only such are propositions as have in them either truth or falsity. Thus a prayer is a sentence, but is neither true nor false." Consider the following sentences:

> The female of the species is more deadly than the male.
> Where are you going?
> Bring me an ice-cream cone.
> What a man!
> Would that I had the gift of tongues!

Of the five kinds of sentences, listed in the order of declarative, interrogative, imperative, exclamatory, and optative, only the declarative expresses a proposition. The other four as they stand do not express propositions explicitly, since they are neither true nor false. It may be said, however, that they do contain implicit propositions about the speaker's subjective state of mind, namely, the interrogative that I want to know where you are going, the imperative that I want an ice-cream cone, the exclamatory that there is something unusual about the man in question, and the optative that I wish that I had the gift of tongues.

The same proposition may be expressed in different sentences, and in different languages. For example, all three languages express the same proposition:

> He is an honest man.
> *Er ist ein ehrlicher Mann.*
> *C'est un homme honnête.*

In other words, the proposition is the objective meaning, which is not changed in translation.

II. KINDS OF PROPOSITIONS

Let us examine the following set of propositions:

1. The present winter is not a good winter for fruit in California.
2. All humanitarian impulses are worthy.
3. Some of the students present are not Orientals.
4. If a man is wise, he will not fear death.
5. If we desire peace, we must pay the price.
6. It is a cold winter in California, *and* it is not a good winter for fruit.
7. Some propositions are called atomic *and* others molecular.

[1] *The Works of Aristotle* (New York: Oxford University Press, 1928), "De Interpretatione," 17a, I.

8. Either we have universal military training or we do not.
9. He is either a student or a clerk.
10. It is not possible that the orbits of the planets are both circles and ellipses.

The first three are *simple categorical propositions* either affirming or denying unconditionally something of something. Numbers 4 and 5 are not simple but *compound*[2] in that they have as constituents two simple categorical propositions arranged in the form of a conditional, the first constituent stating a condition, and the second a consequent. Propositions of this type are called *hypothetical propositions*. Numbers 6 and 7 have two categorical propositions as constituents and are joined by the conjunction "and," and are known as *conjunctive propositions*. Numbers 8 and 9 are made up of two categorical propositions placed in the form of alternatives indicated by the word "either." The alternatives in Number 8 are seen to be exclusive of one another, while in Number 9 they are not. Propositions of this type are known as *alternative propositions*. Number 10 is also made up of two categorical propositions and states and disjunction between the two constituents more sharply than in Number 9. It states that it is not the case that both constituents can be true. Propositions of this kind are known as *disjunctive propositions*.[3]

The discussion of the relations between compound propositions will be postponed to a later chapter. We shall now turn to the analysis of simple categorical propositions.

III. CATEGORICAL PROPOSITIONS

1. The Parts of a Categorical Proposition. The categorical proposition is a simple form of assertion or denial, and consists of (1) a *quantifier*, in the form of "some," "all," "no," or "none"; (2) *a subject term*, about which something is asserted or denied; (3) a *copula*, which is some form of the verb "to be," e.g., "is," "am," or "are"; and (4) a *predicate term*, that which is asserted or denied of the subject. The categorical proposition may be symbolized "S is P."

The relations between terms in categorical propositions expressed by the verb "to be" may be interpreted in various ways, giving rise to different forms of categorical propositions.

[2] Some writers call compound propositions "molecular" in that they are made up of simpler "atomic" components.

[3] Many authors use "disjunctive" to apply to what are here called "alternative" propositions, thus eliminating any separate discussion of "not both . . . and" propositions. Such reduction does not lead to clarity in ordinary language, and is a compromise even in symbolic notation.

2. Forms of Categorical Propositions.   (*a*) *Predication or attribution*. In the proposition "The house is beautiful," the attribute of "beauty" is asserted or predicated of the subject, "house."   This is the *connotative* or *intensional* interpretation, that is, the predicate asserts qualities, properties, or attributes of the subject.

(*b*) *Class inclusion*.   In the proposition "All animals are organic," the subject, "animals," is regarded as a class which is included in the larger class of "organic" beings.   Here we adopt the *denotative* or *extensional* analysis, and are not referring to attributes but to individuals constituting a class.   Propositions of this kind are also called general propositions and may be taken to assert, "If anything is an animal, then it belongs to the class of organic beings"; that is, the class of animals falls within the class of organic beings.

(*c*) *Class membership*.   In the proposition "John is a good student," we are asserting that the subject, "John," is related to the predicate, "good student," by way of class membership.   John is a member of the class of good students.

(*d*) *Identity*.   In this class of categorical propositions, the subject term is said to be identical with the predicate; for example, "All circles are closed plane curves such that all their points are equidistant from the center."

(*e*) *Relational propositions*.   Modern logic goes beyond the traditional subject-predicate propositions by recognizing relations other than those of inclusion and exclusion of classes.   Relational propositions consist of two or more terms and a relation between them, such as mathematical, spatial, and temporal relations, etc.   Certain transitive verbs, such as love, hate, and kill, also express relations.   Examples of relational propositions are: "Mary is taller than John" and "Mary loves John."   These can be reduced to the traditional form, "S is P," so that they become: "Mary is one who is taller than John" and "Mary is one who loves John."   There are, however, many propositions of this type that cannot be so reduced without doing violence to their meaning.   The importance of the distinction between class inclusion and class membership will be noted later.

IV. THE STANDARD FORMS OF CATEGORICAL PROPOSITIONS

Categorical propositions may be classified according to their *quantity* and *quality*.   Quantity refers to the range of generality of the proposition and may be either (1) universal, (2) particular, or

(3) singular. If the proposition refers to all of the members of the class signified by the subject term, the quantity of the proposition as a whole is *universal,* and this is indicated by such quantifiers as "all," "any," "every," "no," and "none." For example, "All men are bipeds," "No men are quadrupeds." If only a part of the subject class is denoted, its quantity is *particular* and is indicated by such quantifiers as "some," "few," etc. For example, "Most of the regiment returned alive," "Some students are ambitious." If an individual person or thing is denoted, as in the propositions "Socrates was a philosopher," "This man is a genius," the proposition is *singular.* Since singular terms when treated as classes have only one member, the whole of the class is denoted; hence, they can be treated exactly like universals.

In addition to quantity, propositions have another characteristic whereby they are either (1) affirmative or (2) negative, and this is called their *quality.* In affirmative propositions the copula affirms the predicate of the subject, e.g., "All men are mortal"; and in the negative propositions it denies something of the subject, or excludes the subject class (or member) from the predicate class, e.g., "Some men are not wise."

Thus we have the four standard forms of categorical propositions:

A. Universal affirmative   All S is P.
A. Universal affirmative (singular)   This S is P.

E. Universal negative   No S is P.
E. Universal negative (singular)   This S is not P.

I. Particular affirmative   Some S is P.

O. Particular negative   Some S is not P.

The symbols A and I are used to designate the universal affirmative and the particular affirmative, respectively, and are taken from the first two vowels of the Latin word *affirmo,* I affirm. The symbols E and O designating the universal negative and the particular negative, respectively, are taken from the vowels of the Latin word *nego,* I deny.

V. THE DISTRIBUTION OF TERMS

The full meaning of *distribution* of terms in categorical propositions will become clear as we proceed to combine propositions in deductive arguments, but at present it will be of assistance in understanding the nature of distribution if we illustrate in advance how it works. In order to know what our propositions mean, and imply, we need to know whether the copula affirms or denies the predicate of the subject universally or only in part. If it affirms or denies something universally of a term or a class, we are logically justified in affirming or denying the same of any member of the class, and if it does not, we are not so justified. For example, if we take the proposition "Women are attractive," it is important to know whether it means "All women are attractive" or merely "Some women are attractive," since from the first we are able to infer the second and a good deal besides, but from the second we are not able to infer the first, and in fact very little. A term of a categorical proposition is *distributed* if the proposition refers to all members of the class signified by that term. The term is *undistributed* if the proposition refers to only a part of the class.

The universal affirmative proposition A takes the following form:

A. All birds are vertebrates.

In this proposition the subject term is *distributed* since it refers to all members of the class of birds, which as a whole is said to be included in the class of vertebrates, but it makes no assertion about all vertebrates. The class of birds is only a small part of the larger class of vertebrates, which includes men, horses, etc. The predicate term, vertebrates, is not used in its widest possible extension, and hence is *undistributed*.

The universal negative proposition E takes the following form:

E. No dictators are modest people.

This proposition asserts universally that the subject class, dictators, is excluded from the entire predicate class of modest people, and hence also asserts universally that the class of modest people is excluded from the entire class of dictators. Both terms are used in the widest possible extension and both subject and predicate are *distributed*.

The particular affirmative proposition I has the following form:

I. Some birds are vertebrates.

This proposition asserts nothing universally about either birds or vertebrates. Neither class is said to be wholly included in or excluded from the other. Both terms are limited in extension and refer only to an indefinite part of the class. Both subject and predicate terms are therefore *undistributed*.

The particular negative proposition O has the following form:

O. Some dictators are not modest.

It will be obvious from what has been said about the I proposition above that the subject term here is also *undistributed*, since "some" always refers to part of a class. But in an O proposition the predicate is *distributed*. The proposition says of the subject, some dictators, that they are excluded from the entire class denoted by the predicate term, the class of modest people; we have denied the attribute modesty in its entire extension of some dictators. A more concrete illustration will help to clarify this. Suppose you are playing tennis and lose some of your tennis balls. You suspect they are in a nearby field. In order to convince yourself that they are *not in the field,* what part of the field would have to be covered in order to be able to assert, "Some of my tennis balls are not in the field"? It is obvious that the whole field would have to be covered.

The above discussion of the distribution of terms in categorical propositions is summarized in the following diagram:

		PREDICATE	
		Undistributed	Distributed
SUBJECT	Distributed	A	E
	Undistributed	I	O

Letting D stand for distributed and U for undistributed, we may further simplify:

A.   All S (D)   is   P (U)
E.   No S (D)   is   P (D)
I. Some S (U)   is   P (U)
O. Some S (U) is not P (D)

1. Distribution Illustrated by the Euler Diagrams. Euler, an eighteenth-century logician, worked out a diagrammatic method (see p. 86) for illustrating distribution by letting circles stand for terms or classes, including or excluding each other either in whole or in part. The circles which are *whole* represent *distributed terms;* those circles *which are occupied by or overlap with other circles are undistributed.*

A. All S is P.

    All squares are equilateral parallelograms having four right angles. All of the class S is identical with the class P.

IDENTITY

A. All S is P.

    All birds are vertebrates. All of the class S is included in the larger class P.

CLASS
INCLUSION

A. This S is P.

    This person (John) is a good student. S (John) is a member of the class of good students, P.

CLASS
MEMBERSHIP
INCLUSION

E. No S is P.

    No dictators are modest. The subject class S is entirely excluded from the predicate class P.

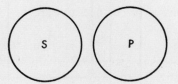

CLASS
EXCLUSION

E. This S is not P.

    This person (Tom) is not a good student. None of this person, S (Tom), is a member of the class of good students, P.

CLASS
MEMBERSHIP
EXCLUSION

I. Some S is P.

    Some birds are vertebrates. The two classes overlap. Some S is included in the class P.

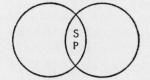

PARTIAL
INCLUSION

O. Some S is not P.

    Some dictators are not modest. The predicate class, P, is denied universally of the class S, or some S is excluded from every part of the class P.

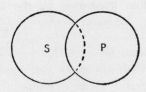

PARTIAL
EXCLUSION

2. Venn Diagrams. John Venn, a nineteenth-century logician, proposed another way of diagraming class relations which has certain advantages over the Eulerian. If we take any two classes such as we have in the proposition "Men are fallible beings" and together with their negatives consider all possible combinations we have:

Classes	Symbols
Men who are fallible beings	SP
Men who are not fallible beings	$S\bar{P}$
Beings that are not men and are fallible	$\bar{S}P$
Beings that are neither men nor fallible	$\bar{S}\bar{P}$

By drawing a rectangle representing the universe of discourse, or subject matter under discussion, and two overlapping circles we obtain four compartments, one for each of the four logical possibilities above. In ordinary A, E, I, and O propositions not all of these compartments are referred to, and if not they may be disregarded.

In the following diagrams a shaded compartment signifies that it has no members, and an x will indicate that it has at least one member. The symbol $\neq$ is the negative of $=$. The zero symbol, "0," signifies an empty class.

The A proposition, "All men are fallible," asserts that all members of the class S are members of the class P, that is, that there are no members of the class S that are not members of the class P, or in other words that the S that is not P is empty. $S\bar{P} = 0$.

A
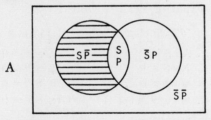

The E proposition, "No men are fallible," asserts that no members of the class S are members of the class P, that is, there are no things that belong to both classes. The S that is P is empty. $SP = 0$.

E
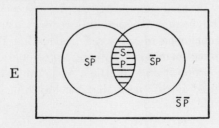

The I proposition, "Some men are fallible," asserts that at least one member of the class S is also a member of the class P, or the class of S that is P is not empty. SP ≠ 0.

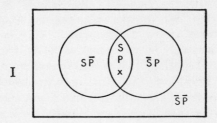

I

The O proposition, "Some men are not fallible," asserts that at least one member of the class S is not a member of the class P, or the class of S that is not P is not empty. SP̄ ≠ 0.

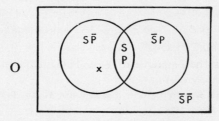

O

We shall utilize the Venn Diagrams for testing syllogisms in Chapter 8. By way of summary the relation between the traditional symbolism of propositions and that of Venn is shown:

Traditional	*Venn*
A. All S is P	A. $S\overline{P} = 0$
E. No S is P	E. $SP = 0$
I. Some S is P	I. $SP \neq 0$
O. Some S is not P	O. $S\overline{P} \neq 0$

VI. EXISTENTIAL IMPORT OF CATEGORICAL PROPOSITIONS

The Venn Diagrams have introduced us to the concept of the *null* or *empty* class. In traditional logic it is assumed that universal propositions of the form "All animals are organisms" are asserting something about existence in time and space, that the classes represented by terms have members. In contrast, modern logic adopts the convention that propositions of this type are hypothetical. The proposition just cited asserts only that "If anything has the property

of being an animal, then it has the property of being an organism";
but it does not assert the existence of any individuals. This makes it
possible to assert universal propositions as hypotheses in different
contexts. It is extremely important logically to be able to assert
such propositions as "All future wars will be fought with atomic
weapons" where there are no future wars; "All Centaurs have four
legs" where there are no Centaurs; and scientific hypotheses such as
Newton's first law of motion, "All bodies free of impressed forces will
persevere in their states of rest or of uniform motion in a straight
line forever," where there are no bodies free of impressed forces.

This matter can be made more clear through the concept of *propositional function*. We have already defined a proposition as an assertion that is capable of being either true or false. Such a statement as
"*x* is organic" is, however, neither true nor false, and therefore is not
a proposition. An expression containing one or more *variables* is
called by Russell a propositional function, and becomes a proposition
when the same value is substituted for *x* which in principle can be
verified as either true or false.

A. "All animals are organisms" means: For all *x*'s, if *x* is an animal,
then *x* is an organism.

E. "No animals are organisms" means: For all *x*'s, if *x* is an animal, then
x is not an organism.

I. "Some animals are organisms" means: There *is* an *x* such that *x* is
an animal *and x* is an organism.

O. "Some animals are not organisms" means: There *is* an *x* such that *x*
is an animal *and x* is not an organism.

A and E do not imply existence, while I and O do.

The problem of existential import of categorical propositions may
be summed up by referring once more to the Venn Diagrams of A, E,
I, and O propositions in the previous section. There we saw that A
propositions, such as "All animals are organisms," assert that the class
of animals which are not organisms does not exist. The E proposition,
"No animals are organisms," asserts that the class of animals which
are organisms does not exist. In other words, universal propositions
simply deny that classes have members, and affirm nothing. On the
other hand, the I proposition, "Some animals are organisms," asserts
that the class of animals which *are* organisms does have members.
The O proposition, "Some animals are not organisms," asserts that the
class of animals which *are not* organisms does have members. Thus
we see that particular propositions do affirm existence. The application of this convention respecting existence will be noted when we

come to the discussion of the Square of Opposition and the syllogism in Chapters 7 and 8.

VII. REDUCING IRREGULAR PROPOSITIONS TO STRICT LOGICAL FORM

The language of everyday life is not always expressed in the neat form of class inclusion and exclusion and class membership propositions we have just studied. In a previous section we noticed the need of the logical analysis of language in the interest of clarity. It is necessary to know exactly what is meant by propositions, what is affirmed or denied by them, and what they imply; for tests of logical validity begin where the analysis and clarification of meaning leave off. When sentences can without distortion be put within the pattern of the traditional A, E, I, and O propositional forms, affirming class inclusion or exclusion, and class membership or nonmembership, there is no simpler way of expressing what is meant. It will be remembered that when a proposition is in strict logical form we have (1) the quantifier, "all," "no," "none," or "some"; (2) the subject; (3) the copula, expressing nothing more than the relation of inclusion or exclusion; and (4) the predicate. The subject and predicate must be substantive class names (no matter how awkward they may appear stylistically).

The following are some of the most important cases of irregular sentences requiring reduction to logical form:

(1) Some sentences are stated without quantifiers, such as "Women love to talk," "Labor leaders helped to win the election," "Magnets attract iron." What must be done in these cases is to determine as nearly as possible what is meant in the given context, and supply the proper quantifier. Perhaps we mean to say "Most women love to talk." "Most" does not mean "all," but only "some"; therefore "Some women love to talk," "Some labor leaders helped to win the election," "All magnets attract iron."

(2) Some sentences have a syntactical construction such that it is not clear which is the logical subject and which the predicate; hence they must be translated into logical form. Examples are: "That man is happy who finds his chief interest in intellectual pursuits," which becomes "All those who find their chief interest in intellectual pursuits are happy persons"; "The blinds are always closed when our neighbor is away," which becomes "All cases of our neighbor being away are cases of closed blinds."

(3) Some sentences are not supplied with a copula in the form of "is," "are," or "am." The purpose of supplying the copula is to designate clearly which is the subject and which the predicate. Examples: "No political states tolerate disloyalty" becomes "No political states *are* states which tolerate disloyalty"; "Our friends went to the movies" becomes "Our friends *are* people who went to the movies." Relational propositions also can be treated in this way by placing the relation between the terms in the predicate; e.g., "John is *older than* Mary" becomes "John *is* one who is older than Mary."

(4) Many sentences are expressed in such a way that the predicate is an adjective and not a noun representing a class, and therefore need an added substantive. In the proposition "All airplanes are heavier than air," the subject, "airplanes," is a class which has members, but "heavier than air" is only an adjective. When, however, we add the complement "craft" or "machines" it becomes a class: "All airplanes are heavier-than-air craft." In "The portrait is beautiful," "beautiful" needs the complement so that it becomes "The portrait is a beautiful painting."

(5) Many sentences are of the form "Only faculty members may park here," "Only the brave deserve the fair," "None but ticket holders will be admitted," "Man alone uses symbols." These are called *exclusive* propositions since the language is so chosen and arranged that an indefinite number of members is excluded from the subject class. All of the above can be interpreted as A propositions only when the positions of the subject and predicate are reversed; for example, they become: "All who may park here are faculty members," "All those who deserve the fair are the brave," "All those who are admitted are ticket holders," and "All symbol users are men." They may also be reduced to E propositions by negating the subject terms in each case, for example, "No non-faculty members may park here," "No non-brave deserve the fair," "No non-ticket holders will be admitted," and "No non-man uses symbols."

(6) In addition to exclusive propositions there are some which are called *exceptive*. For example: "All but minors are admitted," "All of the books except those on the shelf are fiction," "All students are admitted unless they are broke." These contain in their meaning *two different* propositions, an A and an E. "All but minors are admitted" becomes A, "All non-minors are admitted," and E, "No minors are admitted." "All of the books except those on the shelf are fiction" becomes A, "All of the books not on the shelf are fiction," and E, "None of the books on the shelf are fiction." "All students

are admitted unless they are broke" becomes A, "All students who are not broke are admitted," and E, "No students who are broke are admitted."

(7) Propositions such as "All of the students are not present" are sometimes taken to be asserting "None of the students are present," which is obviously not what is meant. The context must determine the meaning, and it will usually be found that "All are not" means "not all" and "not all" means "some," which yields an O proposition, "Some of the students are not present." "All is not gold that glitters" means "Some things that glitter are not gold"; "All France is not Paris" means "Some (i.e., most) of France is not Paris."

(8) The quantifier "some" which belongs to the indefinite subject of particular propositions is quite vague, covering as it does anything from plus one to one less than universality. Other words which are synonyms are "several," "most," "many," and "a few," all of which take the logical quantifier "some." "Few" and "hardly any," as in the proposition "Few of the regiment returned alive," have the force of a negative, O, "Some (most) of the regiment did not return alive." Finally, there are numerical particulars, such as "75 persons are in the auditorium" and "25 per cent of the class did not pass the examination," which are much more specific and yield more precise information than propositions with the vague quantifier "some," yet, since they are less than universal, belong in the standard forms of I and O respectively.

PROBLEMS

1. What are the parts of a categorical proposition?

2. What is the difference between a judgment, a proposition, and a sentence?

3. Distinguish between simple and compound propositions; between universal and particular, affirmative and negative propositions.

4. Distinguish between a singular and a general proposition. Give several examples of each.

5. Classify the following propositions under A, E, I, or O:

(1) Nero was a Roman emperor.
(2) Any horse is herbivorous.
(3) Most kittens are playful.
(4) Fifty per cent of the voters are democratic.
(5) Some of the students are not present.
(6) This man is not eligible.
(7) Man is a rational animal.

6. What is meant by the distribution of terms, and upon what logical principle is it based? What terms are and are not distributed in A, E, I, and O propositions?

7. Reduce the following to as many strict logical forms of A, E, I, or O as possible. Do not go beyond the meaning of the original:

(1) Only athletes are allowed on the field.
(2) Few of the regiment returned alive.
(3) All of the officers are not present.
(4) None but employees may enter.
(5) The honest alone are respected.
(6) None know the brave are timid but the brave.
(7) All students except graduates are eligible.
(8) Hardly any escaped the draft.
(9) "Except ye be born again ye cannot enter the Kingdom of Heaven."
(10) Man alone is a symbol user.

8. Classify the following propositions as A, E, I, or O, and indicate the distribution of subject and predicate terms:

(1) All musicians are versatile.
(2) Some artistic people are imaginative.
(3) No profiteers are patriotic.
(4) Some dictators are not democratic.
(5) Socrates was not a Spartan.
(6) This horse is a prize winner.

9. Reduce the following sentences to standard propositional form of A, E, I, or O, supplying the copula when necessary, and adding a complement to the predicate when necessary to constitute it a class.

(1) All airplanes are heavier than air.
(2) The house stands on the hillside.
(3) All dentists are dreaded by children.
(4) None of the party arrived in time for dinner.
(5) Some propositions are not categorical.

10. What is the problem of "existential import" of categorical propositions?

11. Reduce the following ambiguous sentences to strict standard form. Identify and label the subject and predicate terms and the copula.

(1) All but children are admitted.
(2) All that glitters is not gold.
(3) Parking by permit only.
(4) "He jests at scars who never felt a wound."
(5) Few men have ever swum the Channel.
(6) Most candidates have no chance for election.
(7) A curious man is not easily satisfied.
(8) The door is always closed when the owners are away.
(9) All cigarettes are not alike.
(10) Happy indeed is the man who knows his own limitations.

7

Relations Between Propositions

I. LOGICAL RELATIONS BETWEEN CATEGORICAL PROPOSITIONS

Propositions may be related to one another in many ways, or they may be entirely independent of one another. The logical relations between propositions enable us to draw inferences concerning the truth or falsity of propositions when the truth or falsity of other propositions is known or asserted. It is of the utmost importance for clarity and logical consistency in debate, discussion, and reasoning to know when one proposition logically implies another, is incompatible with it, or independent of it. The possible logical relations between any two propositions may be classified as follows:

1. Contradiction
2. Contrariety
3. Subcontrariety
4. Superimplication
5. Subimplication
6. Equivalence
7. Independence

II. THE TRADITIONAL LAWS OF THOUGHT[1]

Some of the above relations are based upon the three fundamental logical principles known as *The Laws (or Principles) of Thought*

[1] Although it is generally conceded that these principles are so general in nature as to be less fruitful in application than Aristotle thought them to be,

94

which have come down to us from Aristotle, and are:

1. *The Law of Identity*

    For entities: Every entity is what it is.

    For logic: If a proposition is true then it is true. *"p* implies *p"* is always true. Such a statement is called a *tautology.*

2. *The Law of Noncontradiction*

    For entities: An entity cannot both be and not be at the same time and place.

    For logic: No proposition can be both true and false when the circumstances and definitions of terms are the same.

3. *The Law of Excluded Middle*

    For entities: An entity either is or is not at the same time and place.

    For logic: Every proposition is either true or false when the circumstances and definitions of terms are the same. "Either *p* or not-*p"* is tautologically true.

III. IMMEDIATE INFERENCE

Inference made with the help or "mediation" of a middle term contained in two premises is known as *mediate* inference (see Chapter 8). An example is found in the syllogism: "All S is M; all M is P; therefore, all S is P." Inference drawn directly from a single premise is known as *immediate* inference. The first to be considered is known as *opposition,* which is concerned with inference from a given proposition to another with the same subject and predicate. It will involve the relations of contradiction, contrariety, subcontrariety, superimplication, and subimplication. For example, the contradictory of "All S is P" is "Some S is not P," a completely different proposition.

The second kind of immediate inference is based upon the relation of equivalence and is sometimes called *eduction* (a leading out), in which the inferred proposition is the logical equivalent or a limited form of the original. It may be produced by the operations of conversion, obversion, contraposition, and inversion. For example, "No S is P" is logically equivalent to the converse form of the same proposition, "No P is S."

---

they are innocent of many of the misconceived charges leveled against them by such people as the Marxists and "General Semanticists." If the meanings of terms are precise and fully explicit, then no amount of change in the history or character of an object can alter the truth of a statement made about it at any particular time. No tension or conflict within the nature of an object or situation can make contradictory statements about it both true, but they may make contrary statements about it both false.

IV. IMMEDIATE INFERENCE BY OPPOSITION

Opposition is a technical term that traditionally means that two propositions with the same terms as subject and predicate differ in quality or quantity or both. The accompanying diagram, known as the Square of Opposition (see Fig. 2), is an ancient device for schematizing the relations between A, E, I, and O propositions. By its aid, the student will be able to start with any simple categorical proposition, whether true or false, and, with a few exceptions which are indeterminate, infer the truth or falsity of the rest.

First, however, it is necessary to define more clearly the various relationships exhibited in the Square of Opposition.

1. Contradiction. A and O propositions, which are contradictory, differ in both quality and quantity. The same is true of the E and I. Two propositions are contradictory when if one, p, is true the other, q, is false, and if p is false q is true. For example, if "All Quakers are peacemakers" is true, then "Some Quakers are not peacemakers" must be false, and vice versa.

If p is true, q is false.
If p is false, q is true.

2. Contrariety. A and E propositions differ in quality and are contraries. Two propositions are contraries when, if p is true q must be false, and if q is true p must be false; that is, *both cannot be true, but both may be false*. Thus, if "All students are ambitious" is true, then "No students are ambitious" is false, but both may be false. If either is known to be false then it is undetermined whether the other is true or false.

If p is true, q is false.
If p is false, q is undetermined.

3. Subcontrariety. I and O propositions differ in quality and are subcontraries. In subcontraries if p is false q is true, and if q is false p is true; that is, both cannot be false, but both may be true. Thus, if "Some men are wise" is false, then "Some men are not wise" must be true; but, if "Some men are wise" is true, then "Some men are not wise" may or may not be true—that is, it is undetermined.

If p is true, q is undetermined.
If p is false, q is true.

4. Superimplication. A propositions stand in the relation of super-implication to I propositions, and E's to O's. A proposition p stands in this relation to q when from the truth of p the truth of q follows, although from the falsity of p nothing can be inferred regarding the truth or falsity of q. Thus if "All encyclopedias are educational" (superimplicant) is true, it follows that "Some encyclopedias are educational" (superimplicate) is also true; but, if the first is false, nothing can be inferred regarding the truth value of the second. The same holds true for the relation between E and O in the Square of Opposition.

If p is true, q is true.
If p is false, q is undetermined.

5. Subimplication. I and O propositions are in the relation of sub-implication to the universals A and E standing above them. A proposition p stands in the relation of subimplication to q when from the truth of p nothing can be inferred regarding the truth value of q,

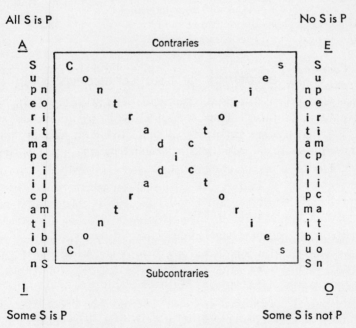

Figure 2. The Square of Opposition[2]

[2] The traditional Square of Opposition assumes that the subject class in A, E, I, and O propositions has members.

but if p is false q is also false. Thus, if it is true that "Some men are happy" (subimplicant), we cannot infer that "All men are happy" (subimplicate); but, if it is false that "Some men are happy," then it is false that "All men are happy." The same relation holds between O and E in the Square of Opposition.

If p is true, q is undetermined.
If p is false, q is false.

6. Summary of the Opposition Relations. The following table states in summary form the various relationships within the Square of Opposition, and the inferences which may be drawn when the truth or falsity of any proposition is known.

If A is true, E is false, I true, O false.
If E is true, A is false, O true, I false.
If I is true, E is false, A and O undetermined.
If O is true, A is false, E and I undetermined.
If A is false, O is true, E and I undetermined.
If E is false, I is true, A and O undetermined.
If I is false, A is false, E true, O true.
If 0 is false, E is false, I true, A true.

V. THE OPPOSITION OF SINGULAR PROPOSITIONS

The Square of Opposition, because it expresses only the purely formal relations among A, E, I, and O propositions, does not cover such cases as the contradictory and contrary of singular propositions, such as "Plato was a philosopher" or "The President is a good politician." However, it is obvious that such propositions do have a contradictory; that is, there is a proposition which cannot be true if the original is true, and which must be true if the original is false. Thus, the contradictory of "The President is a good politician" is "The President is not a good politician."

The contrary of a singular proposition is one which has a contrary predicate term. Contrary terms express degrees of opposition within a given universe of discourse. For example, in the field of aesthetics, "beautiful" and "ugly" are extreme contraries, but there may be degrees between them. In the field of politics the extreme contraries are "radical" and "conservative," but there are degrees between them. Value judgments in any field may assert the extreme contraries of good and bad, but may also have intermediate degrees such as fair, mediocre, and poor. Thus, the contrary of "The President is a *good* politician" may be any one of several: "The President is a *fair* (or *mediocre,* or *poor*) politician."

VI. SOME PROBLEMS IN THE APPLICATION OF OPPOSITION

A knowledge of the formal relations between propositions in the Square of Opposition and of the formal principles of contradiction and excluded middle is of great practical use, but when formal principles are applied to situations for which they were never intended they lead to great confusion. One of these confusions often results from the failure to distinguish between contradictory and contrary. If, for example, in a controversy we are able to produce evidence which *contradicts* our opponent's view, then we have also established our own. If, however, we are able to assert only that a *contrary* position is false we may mistakenly think we have refuted him, when as a matter of fact we have not, since both may be false or the truth may lie between the two.

Since there are many concrete situations in nature, in social conventions, and in practical life where there are only two sides to the questions, we are often led mistakenly to a two-valued orientation toward every situation and assume that there are only two sides to all questions. For example, in nature, on the observational level at least, two bodies cannot occupy the same place at the same time. Hence, if one occupies a place, another cannot occupy it. In law, if a man is found not guilty, then he is not held to be guilty. In traffic laws governing speed, an arbitrary point must be agreed upon below which it is not illegal to travel, and above which it is. In football, a referee must decide whether the ball is or is not across the line. In elections in democratic communities, if one party wins by a majority the other loses. In business, a date must be set before which bills are not overdue and after which they are. A train either starts on time or it does not, and we either catch it or we do not.

Since these conventions work so well to settle disputes and to regulate the practical functioning of society, there are many psychological reasons why we try to apply them where they do not apply. In controversy over political, moral, economic, and social questions, issues are sharpened and emotions are aroused by assuming that there are only two sides and that "He who is not for us is against us." This tends to a placing of people and classes in watertight compartments and to a labeling of them as "honest" or "dishonest," "interventionist" or "isolationist," "capitalist" or "collectivist," "fascist" or "democrat," and as favoring a "soft" peace or a "hard" peace.

If this labeling be regarded as merely a convenient technique of classification for handling by means of symbols diverse elements in a complex field, it is harmless (provided sufficient caution is exercised) and even necessary. But it too often leads to the fallacy of assuming that because one group, policy, or program does not succeed, its opposite will. It is often assumed, for example, that because "isolationism" failed to keep us out of war, "interventionism" will; that because a "soft" peace did not, a "hard" peace will; that because one political party failed to bring about universal prosperity, another will succeed in bringing it about.

Psychologically we are more impressed by extremes than by middle-of-the-road policies. Bold and dogmatic assertions are more readily accepted by the many than a careful weighing of arguments, first on the one hand and then on the other, which is considered rather dull. Satirists use the device of caricature and produce exaggerated and grotesque effects in order to stimulate the imagination and give pleasure. Political orators and propagandists present extreme alternatives in order to arouse fears and produce action.

Psychologically considered, this is simply an indication of the complex nature of human personality, consisting as it does of rational, irrational, emotional, volitional, and imaginative elements. Sociologically, it is symptomatic of the fact that all social and communal life is a form of cultural and social striving. The student of logic should be able to discriminate between various kinds of truth claims, and know when a "two-valued" logic is applicable and when not. By "two-valued" is meant that the two values true and false alone exhaust the possibilities, whereas in many cases of a controversial nature the evidence may be sufficient to justify a judgment to a limited degree only, or the issue may be obscure and need further clarification.

VII. IMMEDIATE INFERENCE—EQUIVALENCE

As already indicated there is a type of immediate inference in which the inferred proposition may have a different subject and predicate from the original proposition, the two being logically equivalent. Equivalence, which was listed in our table of relations, has not yet been discussed. To be logically equivalent means to have the same truth value. Aside from the reasons already given for being concerned with the many logical relations between propositions, it is interesting even as a mere matter of curiosity to observe the many ways in which it is possible to state the same proposition, i.e., affirmatively and negatively by means of the four operations of conversion, obversion, contraposition, and inversion. Practically, an understanding of eductions is an aid in interpreting legal and other documents, which for the sake of greater precision often use the double negative, as well as certain literary works which seek variety in sentence structure for stylistic effects. That the technique is not without pitfalls may be illustrated by the college paper editorial which declared: "We challenge our critics to *deny* that the facts in this paragraph are *not true.*"

We shall now proceed to explain the various eductions and give an example of each:

1. Conversion. (*a*) *Conversion in terms of class inclusion and exclusion.* In conversion we reverse the position of subject and predicate, with the retention as far as possible of the logical equivalent, that is, the original meaning. It will be noted that in one instance this is impossible. There are two rules governing conversion which will be helpful as guides:

1. The quality of the original proposition must remain the same; i.e., affirmatives remain affirmatives and negatives remain negatives.

2. No term may be distributed in the converse which was not distributed in the original. The reason for this will be clear if we recall that a distributed term denotes the whole of a class, while an undistributed term denotes only a part of a class, and it is impossible to infer a whole from a part.

Let us take some examples:

A. All (universities) are (educational institutions).
I. Some (educational institutions) are (universities).
E. No (lions) are (invertebrates).
E. No (invertebrates) are (lions).
I. Some (poets) are (engineers).
I. Some (engineers) are (poets).
O. Some (poets) are not (engineers).
[Has no converse.]

Starting with the above A proposition, "All universities are educational institutions," and following the above rules, we find that we cannot infer that "All educational institutions are universities" since the predicate in our original proposition is undistributed, while in the converse it is now the subject and would have to be distributed. The most we can infer from the original proposition is that "Some educational institutions are universities." This is called *conversion by limitation*.

The E proposition is converted *simply*. If we assert that "No lions are invertebrates," we have denied that the class of lions belongs to the class of invertebrates. By conversion we have changed the position of S and P and asserted that "No invertebrates are lions," or denied that the class of invertebrates belongs to the class of lions. Both terms are distributed in the original and both are distributed in the converse.

The above I proposition, "Some poets are engineers," asserts that some of the class of poets belongs to the class of engineers, and its converse is "Some engineers are poets." Neither term is distributed in the original and neither is distributed in the converse.

The O proposition cannot be converted for the reason that its subject is undistributed while its predicate is distributed. From the proposition "Some poets are not engineers" we cannot infer that "Some engineers are not poets," since by conversion the subject "poets" would become the negative predicate "not poets," which would break the above rule.

(*b*) *Conversion in terms of relations other than class inclusion, or conversion by converse relations*. In a previous section we referred to propositions in terms of relations other than those of class inclusion and class membership, such as, "Mary is taller than John." These relations have certain properties only the simplest of which will be mentioned here. *Symmetrical* relations are those that, if they hold between *a* and *b*, hold also between *b* and *a*; that is, they are convertible. Examples are: equals, relative of, identical with, married to, etc. *Asymmetrical* relations are those that, if they hold between *a* and *b*, do not hold between *b* and *a*. Examples are: greater than, father of, east of, older than. When a proposition containing asymmetrical relations is converted, the relation must be changed. Examples of conversion by converse relation where the relation is *symmetrical* are as follows:

1. Original: He is a relative of mine.
   Converse: I am a relative of his.
2. Original: Napoleon was married to Josephine.
   Converse: Josephine was married to Napoleon.
3. Original: Mary's achievement was equal to John's.
   Converse: John's achievement was equal to Mary's.

Examples of conversion by converse relation where the relation is *asymmetrical* are as follows: Notice that the relation has been changed.

    1. Original: Hitler's army was larger than Mussolini's.
       Converse: Mussolini's army was smaller than Hitler's.
    2. Original: Philip was the father of Alexander.
       Converse: Alexander was the son of Philip.
    3. Original: New York is east of Chicago.
       Converse: Chicago is west of New York.

2. Obversion. A second method of immediate inference from any proposition to its equivalent is known as obversion. The following rules may be used as a guide:

    1. Change the quality of the proposition from affirmative to negative, or from negative to affirmative.
    2. Negate the predicate of the original proposition.

Examples: Notice that the double negative equals an affirmative.

    1. Original: A. All (winning teams) are (well-coached teams).
       Obverse: E. No (winning teams) are (non-well-coached teams).
    2. Original: E. No (elements) are (compounds).
       Obverse: A. All (elements) are (non-compounds).
    3. Original: I. Some (fattening foods) are (delicious).
       Obverse: O. Some (fattening foods) are not (non-delicious).
    4. Original: O. Some (planets) are not (self-luminous).
       Obverse: I. Some (planets) are (non-self-luminous).

It is important in negating the predicate to place the negative sign in the proper place. The goal is to produce the logical equivalent in the obverse. For example

            A. All (planets) are (bodies which move through space).
Incorrect: E. No (planets) are (non-bodies which move through space).
Correct: E. No (planets) are (bodies which do not move through space).

3. Contrapositive. If the above operations of conversion and obversion are well understood, inferring the contrapositive equivalent is easy. Simply follow three steps: *Obvert* the original, convert the result, and then *obvert* the result. The first two steps yield the *partial contrapositive,* and the final step yields the *full contrapositive.*

Examples:

1. Original: A. All (dentists) are (people dreaded by children).
   Obversion: E. No (dentists) are (people non-dreaded by children).
   Conversion: E. No (people non-dreaded by children) are (dentists). [Partial contrapositive]
   Obversion: A. All (people non-dreaded by children) are (non-dentists). [Full contrapositive]
2. Original: E. No (frogs) are (poetical creatures).
   Obversion: A. All (frogs) are (non-poetical creatures).
   Conversion: I. Some (non-poetical creatures) are (frogs).
   Obversion: O. Some (non-poetical creatures) are not (non-frogs).
3. Original: O. Some (swans) are not (white birds).
   Obversion: I. Some (swans) are (non-white birds).
   Conversion: I. Some (non-white birds) are (swans).
   Obversion: O. Some (non-white birds) are not (non-swans).

It will be observed that the I proposition has no contrapositive, since the first step, obversion, yields an O, and an O cannot be converted.

4. Inversion. Only the A and E propositions yield inverse inferences. The I and O have no inverse because of the rule regarding the nonconversion of an O proposition. In inverting an A proposition, alternately *obvert* and *convert* until the process can be carried no further. Notice that the full inverse of the A proposition comes a step before the partial inverse. In inverting the E proposition, begin by *converting;* then alternately *obvert* and *convert* until the process can be carried no further. Notice that the step next to the last yields the partial inverse and the last step the full inverse.

1. Original: A. All (gold bricks) are (valuable objects).
   Obversion: E. No (gold bricks) are (non-valuable objects).
   Conversion: E. No (non-valuable objects) are (gold bricks).
   Obversion: A. All (non-valuable objects) are (non-gold bricks).
   Conversion: I. Some (non-gold bricks) are (non-valuable objects). [Full inverse]
   Obversion: O. Some (non-gold bricks) are not (valuable objects). [Partial inverse]
2. Original: E. No (babies) are (logical creatures).
   Conversion: E. No (logical creatures) are (babies).
   Obversion: A. All (logical creatures) are (non-babies).
   Conversion: I. Some (non-babies) are (logical creatures). [Partial inverse]
   Obversion: O. Some (non-babies) are not (non-logical creatures). [Full inverse]

Table I will enable the student to check every one of the above processes. A word of explanation may be needed in interpreting the table. Unlike the various steps under contraposition and inversion which proceed by converting or obverting the immediately preceding proposition, the operations listed in the left-hand column of the table revert to the original proposition at every step. For example, the obverse of the original S a P is S e $\overline{P}$; the converse of the original S a P is P i S; etc.

Table 1
Table of Immediate Inferences*

	A All S is P	E No S is P	I Some S is P	O Some S is not P
Original proposition	S a P	S e P	S i P	S o P
Obverse	S e $\overline{P}$	S a $\overline{P}$	S o $\overline{P}$	S i $\overline{P}$
Converse	P i S	P e S	P i S	
Obverted converse	P o $\overline{S}$	P a $\overline{S}$	P o $\overline{S}$	
Partial contrapositive	$\overline{P}$ e S	$\overline{P}$ i S		$\overline{P}$ i S
Full contrapositive	$\overline{P}$ a $\overline{S}$	$\overline{P}$ o $\overline{S}$		$\overline{P}$ o $\overline{S}$
Partial inverse	$\overline{S}$ o P	$\overline{S}$ i P		
Full inverse	$\overline{S}$ i $\overline{P}$	$\overline{S}$ o $\overline{P}$		

* $\overline{S}$ and $\overline{P}$ indicate non-S and non-P. The lower-case letters a, e, i, and o symbolize A, E, I, and O propositions, respectively.

The remarks made under the discussion of the Square of Opposition regarding the nonexistential or hypothetical nature of universal propositions are also applicable here. If universal propositions have null classes as terms, and particular propositions assert existence, then converting an A proposition such as "All (animals) are (organisms)" into "Some (organisms) are (animals)" is invalid since they are not logically equivalent. Likewise, inverting the universal negative proposition "No (mathematicians) are (those who can square a circle)" into "Some (non-mathematicians) are (those who cannot non-square a circle)" or more simply "Some (non-mathematicians) are (those who can square a circle)" is invalid, since they are not logically equivalent.

VIII. EQUIVALENCE OF COMPOUND PROPOSITIONS

In Chapter 6 the distinction between simple and compound propositions was pointed out and illustrated. Compound propositions have simple propositions as components and are of four kinds: *hypothetical* (or *implicative*), *alternative, conjunctive,* and *disjunctive.* The hypothetical proposition is of the form "If . . . , then . . ." For example, "If it is a cold winter, it will not be a good winter for fruit." The first part, "it is a cold winter," is the *antecedant,* and the second part, "it will not be a good winter for fruit," is the *consequent.* What the hypothetical proposition asserts is that the truth of the antecedent implies the truth of the consequent; i.e., the antecedent cannot be true and the consequent false. The *alternative* proposition is of the form "Either . . . or . . ." and is made up of two simple propositions called *alternates* placed in the position of alternation. "He is either a liar or a thief" has as constituents "He is a liar" and "He is a thief," and when stated in the above alternative form means to assert that at least one of the alternates is true. The *conjunctive* proposition is made up of two simple propositions united by the conjunctive "and." The *disjunctive* proposition is of the form "Not both . . . and . . ." and is made up of two simple propositions called *disjuncts;* for example, "It is not the case that he is both a parson and a lawyer." It means to assert that at least one of the disjuncts must be false.

It is of great interest and logical significance to note that the same proposition can be stated in any of the above forms except the conjunctive, and since they are logically equivalent one can be inferred from the other.

Consider the following equivalent propositions:

Categorical: All diamonds are hard substances.
Hypothetical: If anything is a diamond, then it is a hard substance.
Hypothetical: If anything is not a hard substance, then it is not a diamond.   [Contrapositive]
Alternative: Either something is not a diamond or it is a hard substance.
Disjunctive: It is not the case that something is both a diamond and not a hard substance.

Or we may take a negative categorical proposition and show equivalence of the various forms:

Categorical: No octogenarian is less than eighty years old.
Hypothetical: If anyone is an octogenarian, then he is not less than eighty years old.

Hypothetical: If anyone is less than eighty years old, then he is not an octogenarian. [Contrapositive]

Alternative: Either someone is not an octogenarian or he is not less than eighty years old.

Disjunctive: It is not the case that someone is both an octogenarian and is less than eighty years old.

In Chapters 9, 10, and 11 symbols will be substituted for the language of the various propositional forms so that the equivalence may be exhibited more compactly and hence more clearly.

PROBLEMS

1. Given as true "All nylon stockings are fragile," are the following true, false or undetermined?

(1) Some nylon stockings are not fragile.
(2) No nylon stockings are fragile.
(3) Some nylon stockings are fragile.
(4) Few nylon stockings are not fragile.

2. Begin with a true E proposition and demonstrate what can be known of the other corners of the Square of Opposition.   Do the same for a false E proposition, a true O, and a false I.

3. State the contradictory of each of the following:

(1) No thieves are honest.
(2) All bores are dreaded.
(3) Some merchants are not bankrupt.
(4) Some boys are not anxious to learn.
(5) The train failed to whistle.

4. Give the simplest proposition that will disprove the following propositions:

(1) All politicians are opportunists.
(2) Some poets are engineers.
(3) No lions are invertebrates.
(4) Some tigers are not gentle.

5. Show by means of the contradictory relation that the subcontrary propositions, I and O, cannot both be false.

6. If subcontrary propositions cannot both be false, show that contrary propositions cannot both be true.

7. By what process do we pass from the original proposition "All animals are irritable" to each of the following:

(1) No animals are non-irritable.
(2) Some irritable things are animals.
(3) Some non-animals are not irritable.

(4) All non-irritable things are non-animals.
(5) Some non-animals are non-irritable.
(6) No non-irritable things are animals.

8. Convert and obvert the following.

(1) All bootleggers are criminals.
(2) No rash man is a good general.
(3) No compounds are elements.
(4) Some men are snobs.
(5) All of those who are guilty must be punished.

9. Assuming that the proposition "All college professors are kind" is true, which of the following are true and which false? Why?

(1) All kind people are college professors.
(2) Some kind people are college professors.
(3) No kind people are college professors.
(4) No non-kind people are college professors.
(5) Some college professors are kind.
(6) All college professors are non-kind.
(7) All non-kind people are non-college professors.

10. Show the converse of the following propositions by converse relations:

(1) The word is mightier than the sword.
(2) California is greater in area than Washington.
(3) The king loves the dairymaid.
(4) The president sat on the right of the speaker.
(5) X is an ancestor of Y.

11. Show the relation of each of the following propositions to the one immediately preceding it:

(1) All mammals are vertebrates.
(2) No mammals are vertebrates.
(3) All mammals are non-vertebrates.
(4) Some mammals are not non-vertebrates.
(5) No mammals are non-vertebrates.
(6) All mammals are non-vertebrates.

12. Contrapose:

(1) No parsons are lawyers.
(2) All sailors are swimmers.
(3) Only students are eligible.
(4) No lovers of truth are Sophists.
(5) Good people alone are to be trusted.

8

The Categorical Syllogism

I. A DEFINITION OF THE SYLLOGISM

In Chapter 1, Section III, we discussed in a preliminary way the manner in which we support our beliefs, conclusions, and theses by means of one or more premises constituting the evidence for those conclusions. We are now ready to outline in some detail the structure of deductive reasoning, and to examine the logical principles and rules which must be observed if valid conclusions are to be inferred from premises and our conclusions are to be adequately supported by evidence. At the same time we shall examine and illustrate the fallacies which result from the disregard of these logical principles.

The word *syllogism* comes from the Greek words *syn*, meaning "together," and *logizesthai*, meaning "to reason" or "to reckon." It was defined by Aristotle as "discourse in which certain things being posited, something else than what is posited necessarily follows merely from them."

In more familiar language, a categorical syllogism is an argument containing three categorical propositions, two of which are premises and one the conclusion, and having *three and only three terms,* in which from the relation of major and minor terms to the middle term there follows logically the conclusion.

It is often argued that we do not use syllogisms in ordinary discourse and casual communication. This is quite true if it is meant that we always go from premises to conclusion. The world would be a dreary and unimaginative place if everybody were to confine his language to "scientific" terms and order his discourse in the monotonous form of stereotyped premises followed by valid conclusions. Nothing would be left to interpretation, to the imagination, and the play of wit, irony, and humor. But even ordinary conversation often uses syllogistic reasoning in reverse when we revert from our conclusions to our premises by making an assertion (conclusion) and seeking to follow it up with justifying premises. Suppose that two fans are arguing about the probable outcome of the baseball season. A states his conclusion to B, "I believe the Dodgers will win this season." But when challenged by B with an opposing opinion, A brings forth his reasons or premises as supporting evidence in some such language as this: "Any team which has such and such a record, and has players X, Y, and Z, will win; and the Dodgers have these qualifications." It will be found on analysis that whenever any such discussion is clearly formulated it will fall into the form of an argument with a conclusion supported by a premise or premises offered as the evidence for the conclusion.

II. THE PARTS OF THE CATEGORICAL SYLLOGISM.

Let us have before us an example of a valid categorical syllogism for analysis so that we can visualize its structure and learn to perform the various operations necessary to prove validity, or to detect a possible fallacy:

> A. *All airplanes* are *heavier-than-air craft*.
>   middle (M)   major (P)
>
> A. *All helicopters* are *airplanes*.
>   minor (S)   middle (M)

Hence:

> A. *All helicopters* are *heavier-than-air craft*.
>   minor (S)   major (P)

It will be observed that this syllogism is made up of three universal affirmative categorical propositions. The various combinations of A, E, I, and O propositions are known as the *moods* of the syllogism (see page 127). This one is mood AAA.

A categorical syllogism consists of: (1) A major premise, consisting of a categorical proposition containing two terms, namely, the major term and the middle term; (2) a minor premise, consisting of a categorical proposition containing two terms, namely, the minor term and the middle term; (3) a conclusion consisting of a categorical proposition containing two terms, namely, the minor and major terms.

In the standard form above we have used the symbol S for the minor term, P for the major, and M for the middle, each of which occurs twice. In analyzing a syllogism into its parts in order to test its validity, it is necessary first to find and identify the various terms. *This is done by beginning with the conclusion.* The *subject* of the conclusion is always the *minor term* (S), and will always occur both in the conclusion and in the minor premise. The *major term* (P) is always the *predicate* of the conclusion, and also occurs in the major premise. It follows that the *middle term* (M) must be *the one remaining,* there being only three terms in the syllogism. The middle term may occur in any of four different positions in the premises. The position of the middle term determines what is known as the *figures* of the syllogism (see page 126). It is well for the beginner to practice identifying the major, minor, and middle terms, labeling them as above.

The Aristotelian syllogism of the first figure is based upon the so-called *dictum de omni et nullo,* which is: Whatever is asserted or denied of a whole class may be asserted or denied of any member of that class. Thus, in the above example, the class of airplanes, M, is included in the larger class of heavier-than-air craft, P; and the class of helicopters, S, is included in the class of airplanes, M. Hence, the conclusion follows logically that the class of helicopters, S, is included in the class of heavier-than-air craft, P, which is what the conclusion asserts: All S is P. The Euler diagrams may be used to test the validity of all such arguments by letting a circle represent each class or term, S, P, and M, first diagraming the major premise and then the minor. If the conclusion corresponds to the diagram the argument is *valid,* and if it does not it is *invalid.*

III. TESTING SYLLOGISMS BY DIAGRAMS

1. Euler Diagrams.

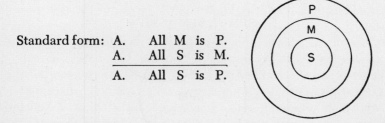

Standard form: A.   All M is P.
               A.   All S is M.
               _____
               A.   All S is P.

Let us take another valid syllogism and illustrate it by an Euler Diagram.

E. No chessplayers are athletes.
        M   P

A. All intellectuals are chessplayers.
        S   M

E. No intellectuals are athletes.
        S   P

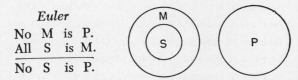

Euler

No M is P.
All S   is M.
————————
No S   is P.

Since the following syllogisms which we are to test by both the Euler and Venn Diagrams contain various combinations of A, E, I, and O propositions, we repeat here the two interpretations of each propositional form. The symbol $\neq$ is the negative of $=$.

Euler	*Venn*	
A. All S is P.	A. $S\overline{P} = 0$	The S that is not P = zero.
E. No S is P.	E. $SP = 0$	The S that is P = zero.
I. Some S is P.	I. $SP \neq 0$	The S that is P $\neq$ zero.
O. Some S is not P.	O. $S\overline{P} \neq 0$	The S that is not P $\neq$ zero.

2. Venn Diagrams. In Chapter 6 we illustrated the way in which two circles are used to diagram the relations between two terms, S and P, resulting in four classes. Now in the syllogism we have introduced a third term, M, which requires the use of a third circle intersecting the other two. Each circle represents one of the three classes, S, P, and M, and together they yield eight combinations.

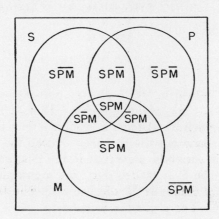

Letting S stand for the class of students, P for the class of physicists, and M for the class of males, we find that the compartments correspond to the following combinations, which are exhaustive of the *universe of discourse*. The universe of discourse is the totality of all classes and subclasses under discussion.

1. SPM The class of students who are physicists and males.
2. S$\overline{\text{P}}$M The class of students who are not physicists and are males.
3. $\overline{\text{S}}$PM The class of male physicists who are not students.
4. SP$\overline{\text{M}}$ The class of students who are physicists and are not males.
5. S$\overline{\text{PM}}$ The class of students who are not physicists and not males.
6. $\overline{\text{S}}\overline{\text{P}}$M The class of males who are not students and not physicists.
7. $\overline{\text{S}}$P$\overline{\text{M}}$ The class of physicists who are not students and are not males.
8. $\overline{\text{SPM}}$ The class of people who are not students, nor physicists, nor males.

In using the Venn Diagrams to test syllogisms we need concern ourselves only with those classes or compartments about which membership is affirmed or denied in the constituent propositions of the syllogism we happen to be using. By convention a null or empty class or compartment is shaded out, and in a compartment which has members we place an "x." For example, the syllogism:

A. All airplanes are heavier-than-air craft.
A. All helicopters are airplanes.
A. Hence, all helicopters are heavier-than-air craft.

is translated into the Venn notation as follows:

$$M\overline{P} = 0$$
$$S\overline{M} = 0$$
$$\overline{S\overline{P} = 0}$$

To diagram this syllogism, we begin by drawing three overlapping circles (page 114). The major premise, $M\overline{P} = 0$, requires that we shade out the M which is outside the P. The minor premise, $S\overline{M} = 0$, requires that we shade out the S that is outside the M. If the conclusion, $S\overline{P} = 0$, is correctly portrayed in the diagram (that is, if the S that is outside the P is shaded out), the argument is *valid*, and if not it is *invalid*. A glance at the diagram will show that the condition has been fulfilled. The argument is *valid*.

$$M\overline{P} = 0$$
$$S\overline{M} = 0$$
$$\overline{S\overline{P} = 0}$$

$$S\overline{P} = 0$$

IV. THE RULES OF THE SYLLOGISM: FALLACIES

1. A Syllogism Must Contain Three and Only Three Terms. *Fallacy:* The breach of this rule yields the *fallacy of four terms* or *ambiguous middle*.

It is held by some logicians that, since this rule is part of the definition of the syllogism, i.e., that it must contain three and only three terms, the rule is unnecessary. It is, however, included here because it is the source of much confused reasoning. A most obvious example of four terms would be an attempt to draw a conclusion from two unrelated class membership propositions such as

> Logic is a branch of philosophy.
> William James was a Pragmatist.

It is obvious that no conclusion can be drawn from these premises, since there is no middle term common to both through which the conclusion can be mediated. There is, however, a subtle and less easily detected form of this fallacy which often in the heat of argument may pass as valid. As we have seen earlier, ambiguity means that words and terms have double meanings. Every syllogism must be examined to determine whether or not the terms are ambiguous. Take the example

> All criminal actions are punishable by law.
> Prosecution for theft is a criminal action.
> Hence, prosecution for theft is punishable by law.

If merely the form of the argument is examined without attention to meanings of the terms, it might be held valid. But, on examination, it is obvious that the term "criminal action" is ambiguous. In the major premise it means acts of crime committed in breach of law. In the minor premise it has a technical legal meaning, referring to the filing and prosecuting of a suit in court.   The reason for naming such arguments "four terms" is now clear, since two terms plus the ambiguous term equals four terms.   Many humorous examples of the fallacy could be cited from the traditional logic textbooks.   Students have universally been interested in this one:

> Nothing is better than a good lesson.
> A poor lesson is better than nothing.
> Hence, a poor lesson is better than a good lesson.

2. The Middle Term Must Be Distributed in at Least One of the Premises.   *Fallacy: Undistributed middle.*

In our previous discussion of distribution of terms we saw that a term is said to be distributed if the proposition refers to all members of the class signified by that term, and is undistributed when the proposition refers only to an indefinite part of the class.   Since the middle term is the term which mediates between premises and conclusion, if it is not distributed in either premise it cannot so mediate between them, since then the major and the minor (which appear in the premises) are related to only an indefinite part of the middle, and we have no evidence that they are related to the same part.   Hence, we have no logical right to relate them to each other in the conclusion. If we argue that

> A. All of the company's cars are Fords.
>   P   M
>
> A. All of the cars in the garage are Fords.
>   S   M
>
> A. Hence, all of the cars in the garage are the company's cars.
>   S   P

we have committed this fallacy, since in each premise we are told about only a part of the class of Fords (this term being in both cases the predicate of an A proposition).   In other words, the middle terms, "Fords," is undistributed in both cases.

Let us take another example and illustrate the fallacy of undistributed middle by means of the diagrams.

> A. All Communists are believers in heavy taxes.
>   P   M
>
> A. Senator Jones is a believer in heavy taxes.
>   S   M
>
> A. Hence, Senator Jones is a Communist.
>   S   P

Starting with the conclusion we label the subject of the conclusion the minor, S, and the predicate of the conclusion the major, P. We then label the same terms in the premises in the same way. The term still remaining is the middle, M, which occurs in both premises. Examining the middle term, we see that it is the predicate of two A propositions, both of which are undistributed. Hence, the fallacy of *undistributed middle*.

Euler Diagram	*Venn Diagram*
A. All P is M.	$P\overline{M} = 0$
A. All S is M.	$S\overline{M} = 0$
A. All S is P.	$S\overline{P} = 0$

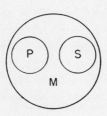
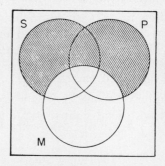

One of the most famous cases of this fallacy is illustrated dramatically in the book of Job, where the friends of Job argue,

> All sinners suffer affliction.
> Job is suffering affliction.
> Hence, Job is a sinner.

Fortunately for literature, Job was not able to point directly to the logical fallacy but delivered many long eloquent speeches to convince his friends that, though he was suffering afflictions, he was not a sinner. To insist on a too literal application of the old saw that "a man is known by the company he keeps" would be to commit this fallacy. For example, if we know that gangsters hang out at Tony's Restaurant and one day we see a respected friend patronizing Tony's Restaurant, we must not conclude without further evidence that our friend is a gangster.

3. No Term May Be Distributed in the Conclusion Which Is Not Distributed in the Premises. *Fallacies: Illicit major* and *illicit minor*.

If the major term is the one which is distributed in the conclusion and not in the premises, the fallacy is that of *illicit major;* and if the minor term is the one distributed in the conclusion and not in the premises, the fallacy is that of *illicit minor.* If the meaning of distribution is kept clearly in mind, it will be at once recognized that the breach of the above rule is an attempt to affirm or deny something universally (or in its widest extension) in the conclusion, which was affirmed or denied only partially or in an indefinite sense in the premises. In other words, it is an effort to get a whole out of a part, or to infer more than the premises warrant. Let us examine the fallacy of *illicit major.*

This fallacy is often committed in the heat of controversy, of political debate and oratory, where the speaker may not realize that he is committing a fallacy, and where the hearer finds it difficult to separate the conclusion from the premises. If an orator should argue, "Everybody knows that all those who believe in subversive doctrines are radicals, but no one would accuse me of being a radical because I repudiate any such beliefs," he would be committing the fallacy of illicit major.

If we arrange this argument in logical order we have the following:

A. All who believe in subversive doctrines are radicals.
               M   P

E. I am not a believer in subversive doctrines.
    S   M

E. Hence, I am not a radical.
        S   P

Euler Diagram	*Venn Diagram*
A. All M is P.	$M\overline{P} = 0$
E. No S is M.	$SM = 0$
E. No S is P.	$SP = 0$

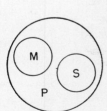

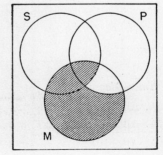

It will be observed that the major term in the conclusion is the predicate of an E proposition and is distributed, whereas in the premise the major term is the predicate of an A proposition and is undistributed. The conclusion makes a universal assertion about radicals, whereas the premises make no such universal assertion. Hence, the fallacy of *illicit major*. We may accept both of his premises and not accept his conclusion since it is not implied by the premises.

Next let us examine the second violation of the above rule resulting in the fallacy of *illicit minor*.

If an orator should declare, "Everyone interested in progress is interested in national defense, because all good citizens are interested in progress, and all good citizens are interested in national defense," we might be inclined to accept his conclusion until we had time to formulate and analyze it and discover the fallacy. Putting it in the standard form we see that his conclusion is stated first, then the supporting premises are introduced by the word "because." The way to put such an argument into syllogistic form is to write down the conclusion in the third place (see below), then arrange the premises in correct order with the premise containing the major term (the predicate of the conclusion) coming first:

A. All good citizens are interested in national defense.
    M   P

A. All good citizens are interested in progress.
    M   S

A. Hence, everyone interested in progress is interested in national defense.
           S   P

It will be readily seen that the rule is broken, that the minor term, S, is distributed in the conclusion and not in the premises; that is, the conclusion makes an assertion about the whole class of those interested in progress, whereas the premise makes an assertion about only a part of the class—hence, the fallacy of *illicit minor*.

Euler Diagram	*Venn Diagram*
A. All M is P.	$M\overline{P} = 0$
A. All M is S.	$M\overline{S} = 0$
A. All S is P.	$S\overline{P} = 0$

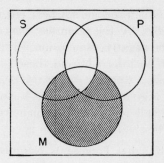

4. From Two Negative Premises No Conclusion Can Be Inferred.
Fallacy: The violation of this rule is known as the fallacy of *negative premises.*

The relation between terms in negative propositions is that of "excluded from." Thus when the minor S and the major P are excluded from the middle M, which is supposed to mediate the conclusion, there are no logical grounds in terms of class relations which enable us to draw an inference. For example:

E. A rainy day is not a good day for a picnic.
    M   P

E. Today is not a rainy day.
    S   M

A. Hence, today is a good day for a picnic.
    S   P

Euler Diagram	*Venn Diagram*
E. No M is P.	$MP = 0$
E. No S is M.	$SM = 0$
A. All S is P.	$S\overline{P} = 0$

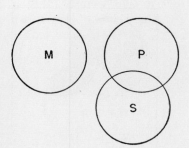

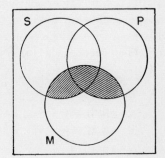

The diagrams do not bear out in the conclusion the logical situation demanded by the premises; hence, the fallacy. It is equally obvious that the negative conclusion, E, "Today is not a good day for a picnic," cannot be inferred from these premises. In the Euler Diagram this conclusion would call for the S and P circles to be entirely separate, which they are not. In the Venn Diagram such a negative conclusion would call for SP = 0, which would require that all of the S inside the P be shaded out, which is not the case.

5. If Either Premise Is Negative, the Conclusion Must Be Negative. *Fallacy: Affirmative conclusion from a negative premise.*
Example:

> E. No bill of attainder shall be passed by Congress.
>   P   M
>
> A. This bill was passed by Congress.
>   S   M
>
> A. Hence, this bill is a bill of attainder.
>   S   P

Since the universal negative major premise excludes the class P from the class M, and the minor premise includes the minor term, S, in the middle, M, we have no logical reason for asserting the inclusion of the minor, S, in the major, P, in the conclusion. It is obvious that to be valid our conclusion should be the negative, E. "This bill is not a bill of attainder." The fallacy is illustrated as follows:

Euler Diagram	*Venn Diagram*
E. No P is M.	PM = 0
A. This S is M.	$S\overline{M} = 0$
A. This S is P.	$S\overline{P} = 0$

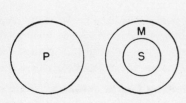 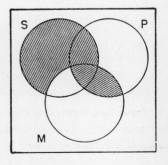

6. If the Conclusion Is Negative, One Premise Must Be Negative.
Fallacy: Negative conclusion from two affirmative premises.

This fallacy follows from the fact that affirmative propositions include the subject in the predicate wholly or partially, and negative propositions exclude the subject from the predicate wholly or partially. A negative conclusion, either E or O, would then exclude wholly or partially the minor, S, from the major, P; but in order for this to be possible, there would need to be in one of the premises an exclusion of the S or P from the M; that is, one of the premises would have to be negative. Example:

> A. All gentlemen are polite.
>   M   P
>
> I. Some gamblers are gentlemen.
>   S   M
>
> O. Hence, some gamblers are not polite.
>   S   P

Euler Diagram	*Venn Diagram*
A. All M is P.	$M\overline{P} = 0$
I. Some S is M.	$SM \neq 0$
O. Some S is not P.	$S\overline{P} \neq 0$

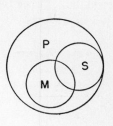
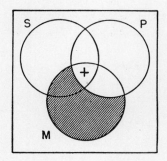

In the Venn Diagram, the conclusion called for is $S\overline{P} \neq 0$; that is, the S compartment outside the P should have members, indicated by an "x." But it does not, and the syllogism is invalid. Examination will show that this argument also contains the fallacy of illicit major.

7. From Two Particular Premises Nothing Can Be Inferred. *Fallacies:* The breach of this rule leads either to the fallacy of *undistributed middle, illicit major,* or *two negative premises.*

The possibilities of combining particular premises are as follows:

1. II. This combination does not distribute the middle term and therefore yields the fallacy of *undistributed middle*.

2. OO. This combination yields the fallacy of *two negative premises*.

3. IO. According to Rule 5, the conclusion must always be negative if one premise is negative. The major term, then, would be distributed in the conclusion and not in the major premise; hence, the fallacy of *illicit major*. In case the middle term is the subject of the minor premise, O, we would have the fallacy of *undistributed middle*.

4. OI. Likewise, according to Rule 5, the conclusion of this combination must be negative. If the major term is the subject of the major premise, O, we would have the fallacy of *illicit major*. If it is the predicate, the fallacy of *undistributed middle* would result.

Let us use as an example of the above fallacy the following syllogism:

I. Some interesting things are instructive.
M   P

I. Some speakers are interesting.
S   M

I. Hence, some speakers are instructive.
S   P

Euler Diagram	*Venn Diagram*
I. Some M is P.	MP $\neq$ 0
I. Some S is M.	SM $\neq$ 0
I. Some S is P.	SP $\neq$ 0

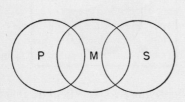

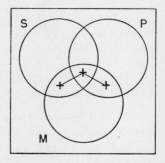

In diagraming particular propositions with the Venn Diagrams, we must note carefully how the "x's" are placed in the compartments. Since some of the compartments contain only two classes, and some three, any conclusion reached from such premises would be equivocal and hence invalid. Let us follow the steps carefully. The major premise calls for an "x" in compartment MP. But because MP is made up of two parts, we do not know which part is meant; so we place an "x" in both and connect them with a line. The minor premise calls for an "x" in the SM compartment, but because it is also made up of two parts we place an "x" in both and connect them with a line. The conclusion calls for an "x" to be in SP, but SP is made up of two compartments, the SP exclusively and SP that is also M. Because of this equivocal nature of the partial class inclusion no certain conclusion can be drawn; hence, the fallacy of *two particular premises*.

8. If Either Premise Is Particular, the Conclusion Must Be Particular.
Fallacies: Undistributed middle, illicit major, illicit minor.
If one premise is particular we have three possibilities:

1. AI and IA. Since we are prohibited from drawing a negative conclusion (Rule 6), the only universal conclusion would be the universal affirmative, A, which distributes the subject or minor term. If the middle term were the predicate of the A premise, we would have the fallacy of *undistributed middle,* and if it were the subject, we would have the fallacy of *illicit minor.*
2. EO and OE. These combinations are ruled out by Rule 4.
3. AO, OA, EI, and IE. Fallacies resulting from these combinations: *undistributed middle, illicit major, illicit minor.* Accordng to Rule 5, the conclusion from any of these combinations would have to be negative, hence the only universal conclusion possible is the universal negative, E. In AOE and OAE combinations, if the middle term were the subject of the O and predicate of the A we would have the fallacy of *undistributed middle.* If the minor were the subject of the O or predicate of the A, we would have *illicit minor.* If the major were the subject of the O or predicate of the A we would get an *illicit major.* In the EIE combination, since the minor premise, I, contains the minor term and is undistributed, there appears the fallacy of *illicit minor.* In the IEE combination, since the major premise, I, contains the major term and is undistributed, there appears the fallacy of *illicit major.*

Let us take the following example of the attempt to draw a universal conclusion when one premise is particular:

I. Some nationalists are aggressive.
      M   P

A. All nationalists are patriots.
      M   S

A. Hence, all patriots are aggressive.
      S   P

In diagraming syllogisms with the Venn Diagrams, when one premise is particular and the other universal, always diagram the universal premise first, since universal compartments are always shaded (empty). This enables us to place the "x" in the exact compartment which contains members.

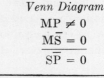

Euler Diagram	*Venn Diagram*
I. Some M is P.	MP $\neq$ 0
A. All M is S.	M$\bar{S}$ = 0
A. All S is P.	$\bar{S}$P = 0

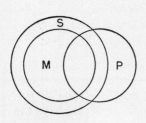 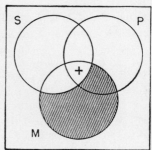

It will be observed that as a result of the failure to draw a particular conclusion, the argument results in the fallacy of *illicit minor*.

9. If the Conclusion Is Particular One Premise Must Be Particular. *Fallacy: The existential fallacy.*

In an earlier discussion of *existential import of propositions* it was pointed out that in traditional logic both universal and particular propositions imply existence of members of subject and predicate classes, but that in modern logic the convention is adopted that universal propositions are hypothetical and do not imply existence. If existence is to be assumed, then it must be stated in a separate proposition; for example, "All animals are organisms" means "For all x's, if x is an animal (and animals exist), then x is an organism." In the traditional interpretation, syllogisms such as the following are valid, with weakened conclusions; that is, they assert less than is implied by the premises.

A. All swift runners are in the marathon race.
  P   M

E. No Centaurs are in the marathon race.
  S   M

O. Hence, some Centaurs are not swift runners.
  S   P

It will be observed that by the traditional interpretation it would be possible also to draw the stronger universal conclusion, "No Centaurs are swift runners," from these premises. But by the convention of nonexistence of members of universal classes this syllogism is invalid, since its premises contain empty classes. Its conclusion asserts that there are Centaurs, whereas the premises have made no such assertion. We have inferred what is not implied. It may be proved valid on the traditional assumption by the Euler Diagram, and invalid on the assumption of nonexistence by the Venn Diagram.

Euler Diagram	*Venn Diagram*
A. All P is M.	$P\overline{M} = 0$
E. No S is M.	$SM = 0$
O. Some S is not P.	$S\overline{P} \neq 0$

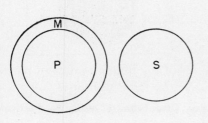

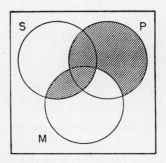

Let us now classify the rules of the syllogism under appropriate heads, placing opposite each the name of the corresponding fallacy:

Rules	*Fallacies*
I. The Rule of Ambiguity:	
(1) A syllogism must contain three and only three terms.	(1) Four terms, or ambiguous middle.
II. Rules of Quantity (Distribution):	
(2) The middle term must be distributed in at least one premise.	(2) Undistributed middle.
(3) No term may be distributed in the conclusion which is not distributed in the premises.	(3) a. Illicit major. b. Illicit minor.
III. Rules of Quality (Affirmative-Negative):	
(4) From two negative premises no conclusion can be inferred.	(4) Negative premises.

Rules	*Fallacies*
(5) If either premise is negative, the conclusion must be negative.	(5) Affirmative conclusion from a negative premise.
(6) If the conclusion is negative, one premise must be negative.	(6) Negative conclusion from two affirmative premises.
IV. Rules of Particulars:	
(7) From two particular premises nothing can be inferred.	(7) See 2, 3, and 5 above.
(8) If either premise is particular, the conclusion must be particular.	(8) See 2, 3, and 4 above.
(9) If the conclusion is particular, one premise must be particular (existential rule).	(9) The existential fallacy.

V. THE FIGURES AND MOODS OF THE SYLLOGISM

1. The Figures of the Syllogism. We have already had some experience in reducing the propositions, sentences, statements, and assertions which go to make up the complex and varied life of thought, judgment, and inference to logical form. Now the student may well ask on his first introduction to formal syllogisms, "Do you mean to tell me that any kind of argument about anything can be put into the form of a syllogism?" We have already seen that modern logic has gone beyond the classical logic in introducing relational arguments, but our present purpose is to reveal the great variety of logical forms possible under the traditional system, thus answering to some extent the above query. An examination of the syllogism will reveal the fact that each of the three terms, major, minor, and middle, occurs twice. Since the middle term is all important, the various positions of this term in the syllogism determine what are known as the *figures* of the syllogism. Letting S symbolize the minor, P the major, and M the middle, we find that four arrangements of the middle term are possible, known as Figures I, II, III, and IV.

Figures of the Syllogism

Figure I	Figure II	Figure III	Figure IV
M – P	P – M	M – P	P – M
S – M	S – M	M – S	M – S
S – P	S – P	S – P	S – P

Each of the four figures may be illustrated by an appropriate syllogism. Note especially the position of the middle term.

Figure I

A.	All men are organisms.	M – P
A.	All Greeks are men.	S – M
A.	Hence, all Greeks are organisms.	S – P

Figure II

E.	No Fascists are Democrats.	P – M
A.	All Laborites are Democrats.	S – M
E.	No Laborites are Fascists.	S – P

Figure III

A.	All mus·cians are versatile.	M – P
A.	All musicians are artistic.	M – S
I.	Hence, some artistic people are versatile.	S – P

Figure IV

A.	All patriots are good citizens.	P – M
E.	No good citizens are profiteers.	M – S
E.	Hence, no profiteers are patriots.	S – P

2. The Moods of the Syllogism. But our analysis of the multiplicity of the forms of the syllogism has just begun. We have already learned to recognize A, E, I, and O propositions. Here is a little mathematical problem: How many combinations of A, E, I, and O propositions in groups of three are possible? The answer is sixty-four, but in order to be perfectly clear let us list them.

Moods of the Syllogism

AAA	AEA	AIA	AOA	EAA	EEA	EIA	EOA
AAE	AEE	AIE	AOE	EAE	EEE	EIE	EOE
AAI	AEI	AII	AOI	EAI	EEI	EII	EOI
AAO	AEO	AIO	AOO	EAO	EEO	EIO	EOO
IAA	IEA	IIA	IOA	OAA	OEA	OIA	OOA
IAE	IEE	IIE	IOE	OAE	OEE	OIE	OOE
IAI	IEI	III	IOI	OAI	OEI	OII	OOI
IAO	IEO	IIO	IOO	OAO	OEO	OIO	OOO

These are called *moods*, as distinguished from the *figures*, which are determined by the position of the middle term.

If we now work out the mathematical possibilities of a combination of both figures and moods, we see that it is possible to state arguments in 256 different forms within the framework of classical logic. Fortunately for us, most of these forms are invalid, as will be readily seen as soon as the rules of the syllogism are familiar. Rule 4 prohibits us from drawing a conclusion from two negative premises, thus eliminating all of the EE, EO, OE, and OO premises. Applying Rule 7, that no conclusion can be drawn from two particular premises, we eliminate all of the II, IO, and OI premises (OO has already been eliminated). The application of the other rules to the various moods will eliminate all but the eleven underscored above.

But some of the underscored moods will be found to be valid in more than one figure, and when these are included we have the following twenty-four valid moods, five of which have so-called "weakened" conclusions (in parentheses below) ; that is, they assert less than can be logically inferred from the premises.[1] If these are omitted, we have left nineteen valid moods in the four figures. If we further omit those which are eliminated by Rule 9, the existential rule, namely, AAI and EAO in the third figure, and AAI and EAO in the fourth figure, underscored below, we have left fifteen valid moods.

Figure I	Figure II	Figure III	Figure IV
AAA	EAE	AAI	AAI
EAE	AEE	IAI	AEE
AII	EIO	AII	IAI
EIO	AOO	EAO	EAO
(AAI)	(EAO)	OAO	EIO
(EAO)	(AEO)	EIO	(AEO)

VI. REDUCTION TO THE FIRST FIGURE

Aristotle regarded the first figure as the perfect figure, and the second and third as imperfect. The fourth was not recognized by him. Since the first figure best exemplifies the *dictum de omni et nullo,* there are certain advantages, when validity is in doubt, in reducing the other figures to the first. The following mnemonic verse was developed by the medieval scholars for this purpose:

Barbara, Celarent, Darii, Ferioque, *prioris;*
Cesare, Camestres, Festino, Baroko, *secundae;*
Tertia, Darapti, Disamis, Datisi, Felapton,
Bokardo, Ferison, *habet; quarta in super addit*
Bramantip, Camenes, Dimaris, Fesapo, Fresison.

The Latin words *prioris, secundae, tertia,* and *quarta* stand for the four figures. "Barbara," "Celarent," etc., are the names of the

[1] There are also so-called "strengthened" moods, i.e., the universal premise could be replaced with a particular and still yield the same conclusion.

various moods. The three vowels in each name stand for the propositions in the correct order of the valid mood. For example, "Baroko" stands for mood AOO in the second figure. The capital initial letter of each name indicates the mood of the first figure to which any valid mood of any other figure may be reduced; for example, "Cesare" of the second figure would be reduced to "Celarent" of the first figure. An "s" indicates that the proposition represented by the vowel preceding the "s" is to be converted *simply*. A "p" stands for conversion *per accidens,* or by limitation. An "m" stands for "metathesis" or transposition of the premises. A "k" (sometimes a "c") indicates that the reduction is by indirect proof involving *reductio ad absurdum* (the "c" or "k" being the initial letter of *contradictionem*). Brief examples of both direct and indirect reduction will now be given:

1. Direct Reduction. Beginning with a valid syllogism in Camestres, i.e., AEE, we note that since the name of the mood to be reduced begins with a capital "C," we are to reduce it to Celarent, or EAE of the first figure. For example:

A. All members of the alumni association are college graduates.   All P – M
E. None of our employees are college graduates.   No S – M
E. Hence, none of our employees are members of the alumni association.   No S – P

The "m" in Camestres indicates that the A premise preceding it should be transposed with the second premise. The first "s" tells us that the E premise should be converted simply. The final "s" tells us that the conclusion, E, should also be converted simply.

The result is a valid syllogism in mood EAE, first figure.

E. No college graduates are our employees.   No M – P
A. All members of the alumni association are college graduates.   All S – M
E. Hence, no members of the alumni association are our employees.   No S – P

The above instructions are sufficient to guide the student in the reduction of any valid mood in Figures II, III, and IV to the first, except Baroko (AOO) and Bokardo (OAO), which, it will be noted, both contain the letter "k," indicating that they should be reduced indirectly.

2. Indirect Reduction by *Reductio ad Absurdum*. Indirect reduction assumes a principle which we have already noticed, namely, that if the conclusion of a valid syllogism is false, one of the premises must be false. It is a method of showing that a contradiction results unless the syllogism in question is valid. Let us take a valid syllogism in the second figure, mood AOO. It is assumed that the premises are true leading to a true conclusion.

A. All corporations are monopolistic.	All P – M
O. Some business houses are not monopolistic.	Some S – not M
O. Hence, some business houses are not corporations.	Some S – not P

Now for the purpose of testing this syllogism by reduction to the first figure let us assume that the conclusion is false, i.e., that its contradictory "All business houses are corporations" is true. We then combine this assumed proposition with our original major premise and construct a valid syllogism in the first figure:

A. All corporations are monopolistic.	All M – P
A. All business houses are corporations. [Contradictory of original conclusion]	All S – M
A. Hence, all business houses are monopolistic. [Contradictory of original minor]	All S – P

This is a valid syllogism in mood AAA, first figure. But its conclusion contradicts the original minor premise, "Some business houses are not monopolistic," which by hypothesis was true; hence, it must be false. Now if it is false, one of the premises must be false. But since it is not the major (by hypothesis), it must be the minor, "All business houses are corporations"; hence, its contradictory, the conclusion of the original syllogism, cannot be false, and the validity of the original syllogism has been proved indirectly.

PROBLEMS

1. Supply premises for the following conclusions:

(1) The President of the United States cannot perform miracles.
(2) I shall die some day.
(3) He deserved to be expelled from school.
(4) Parking here is illegal.
(5) Senator Jones must be at least thirty years old.

2. Test the validity of the following formal arguments by constructing a Venn diagram for each:

(1) AAA first figure
(2) EIO second figure
(3) AAE first figure

(4) IAI fourth figure

(5) AIA third figure

3. State the following arguments in standard form; test them by the rules of the syllogism; and, if a fallacy is present, name it.

(1) Only churches have cross-crowned spires; this building has a cross-crowned spire and, therefore, must be a church.

(2) No sensible man despises friendships; Bill is not a sensible man and, therefore, does not despise friendships.

(3) Every citizen of the United States is eligible for election to this office; he is a citizen of the United States and, therefore, is eligible for election.

(4) All professors are in need of physical relaxation; no people in need of physical relaxation are athletes; therefore, no professors are athletes.

(5) My father's friends deserve my protection; and since he is not my father's friend, he does not deserve my protection.

(6) The power of recognizing important resemblances is the work of genius; the power of making a good metaphor is the power of recognizing important resemblances; hence, genuine metaphor is the work of genius.

(7) Whoever obeys laws submits himself to a governing will; Nature obeys laws, and hence Nature submits herself to a governing will.

(8) All true hypotheses have been confirmed by many experiments; this hypothesis has been confirmed by many experiments and, hence, is true.

(9) All Laborites are Democrats; no Fascists are Laborites; hence, no Democrats are Fascists.

(10) All Communists are believers in heavy taxes, and all my opponents are believers in heavy taxes; therefore, all my opponents are Communists.

(11) Many handsome men marry for money, and John Doe married Mary Roe for her money; therefore, John Doe must be very handsome.

(12) Sherlock Holmes had impeccable honesty, and the highest character is possessed only by men of impeccable honesty; therefore, Sherlock Holmes was a man of highest character.

4. Determine the mood and figure of the following arguments, and test their validity by means of the Venn diagrams:

(1) The fallacy of undistributed middle is what any good logic student can detect, and Jones can detect the fallacy of undistributed middle; therefore, Jones is a good logic student.

(2) Most great literature is not written in syllogistic form, and Shakespeare's writings are great literature; therefore, his writings were not written in syllogistic form.

(3) Some visitors to Spain are converted to Fascism, and some professors at the University have visited Spain; hence, some professors at the University are converted to Fascism.

(4) All missionaries are morally reputable. Among the visitors at this resort are missionaries; therefore, the visitors here must be morally reputable.

(5) Only upperclassmen are eligible for admission. These boys have rightly been denied admission; accordingly, these boys cannot be upperclassmen.

(6) Unless the weather clears, we will postpone the picnic, and, unless we postpone the picnic, we shall miss the concert; therefore, unless the weather clears, we will miss the concert.

(7) Some atomic scientists are spies; some atomic scientists are members of AAAS; therefore, all AAAS members are spies.

(8) All those present at the meeting were members of the association, and only members of the association were applicants; therefore, all those present at the meeting were applicants.

(9) No good sailor gets seasick, and Nelson was a good sailor; hence, Nelson did not get seasick.

5. State the following arguments in syllogistic form; rearrange the position of premises and conclusion when necessary; and test them for validity by the rules of the syllogism and the Venn diagrams:

(1) Everyone who believes this is a heretic; so you are no heretic, since you do not believe this.

(2) Gold is not a compound substance; for it is a metal, and none of the metals are compounds.

(3) An early scientist discovered by experiment that all the known metals are conductors of electricity, and he knew that the atmosphere is not a metal. Could he have deduced without further experiment that the atmosphere would not conduct electricity?

(4) Only those who are social and economic misfits take any stock in Communism; but this man cannot be that sort of misfit, for he repudiates the doctrines of Communism.

(5) Only ambitious people succeed in life; so poor Smith did not succeed for he was not ambitious.

(6) Our neighbor must be away; for the blinds are closed, and the blinds are always closed when he is away.

(7) He is not a member of the association; for he has not paid his dues, and all those who have paid their dues are members.

(8) Some dilemmas are not fallacious, because no syllogisms are dilemmas, and some fallacious arguments are syllogisms.

(9) Bill can run the mile in ten seconds flat, because he is a track man and only track men can run that fast.

(10) This team is not well coached, because all winning teams are well coached, and this team is not a winning team.

(11) Some New Deal supporters are Communists, because no conservative is a Communist and some New Deal supporters are not conservatives.

(12) All flying saucers are amoeba-like bodies, because all flying saucers are rotating discs and some amoeba-like bodies are rotating discs.

(13) None of these people may enter, because all but children may enter and these people are not children.

(14) The owners must be away, because the gate is locked, and whenever the owners are away the gate is locked.

(15) We can have a prosperous economy without war, because a prosperous economy depends upon production, distribution, and consumption in constructive pursuits, and few of these activities are possible in war time.

(16) Destroyers are really cruisers, for cruisers are light, fast warships, and so are destroyers.

(17) Americans admire all who are successful; they must, therefore, admire some who are politically dangerous, for surely some successful people are politically dangerous.

(18) Knowledge of the King's English is desirable, and knowledge of slang is not knowledge of the King's English; therefore, knowledge of slang is not desirable.

(19) It cannot be that intolerant nations are progressive, since civilized nations are progressive, and all nations which are not civilized are intolerant.

6. The following arguments are from Lewis Carroll's *Symbolic Logic*.[2] Test the validity of the conclusions by the rules of the syllogism.

(1) All pale people are phlegmatic. No one looks poetical unless he is pale. Therefore, no one looks poetical unless he is phlegmatic.

(2) Nothing intelligible ever puzzles me. Logic puzzles me. Therefore, logic is unintelligible.

(3) All philosophers are logical. An illogical man is always obstinate. Therefore, some obstinate persons are not philosophers.

(4) Nothing that is nice need be shunned. Some kinds of jam are nice. Therefore, some kinds of jam need not be shunned.

(5) Unpleasant experiences are not eagerly desired. No nightmare is pleasant. Therefore, no nightmare is eagerly desired.

(6) Nothing that waddles is graceful. All ducks waddle. Therefore, all ducks are ungraceful.

(7) No Frenchmen like plum pudding. All Englishmen like plum pudding. Therefore, Englishmen are not Frenchmen.

(8) Pigs cannot fly. Pigs are greedy. Therefore, some greedy creatures cannot fly.

(9) All ignorant people are vain. No professors are ignorant. Therefore, no professors are vain.

(19) Improbable stories are not easily believed. None of his stories are probable. Therefore, none of his stories are easily believed.

(11) A prudent man shuns hyenas. No banker is imprudent. Therefore, no banker fails to shun hyenas.

7. Reduce the following arguments to syllogistic form, and test their validity:

(1) You can get an education in college if you try. But you must bring three things with you: A certain minimum intellectual equipment,

[2] By permission of The Macmillan Company. New York: The Macmillan Co., 1934.

habits of work, and an interest in getting an education. Without them you can still get into college and stay there for four years. You can have a good time; you can keep out of trouble; you can get a degree and become a full-fledged alumnus with a proprietary interest in all subsequent football scores; but you cannot get an education.—R. M. HUTCHINS

(2) We may sum up this discussion in a few words. Science has not given men more self-control, more kindliness, or more power of discounting their passions in deciding upon a course of action. It has given communities more power to indulge their collective passions, but, by making society more organic, it has diminished the part played by private passions. Men's collective passions are mainly evil; far the strongest of them are hatred and rivalry directed towards other groups. Therefore at present all that gives men power to indulge their collective passions is bad. That is why science threatens to cause the destruction of our civilization.[3]

(3) If criticism of drama is regarded as an administration of justice, then the people who are to be criticized should be prepared to receive inequity, because justice depends on knowledge of all the facts of the case and these facts the critic, coming fresh to it all at 8 or 8:30 p.m. on a certain evening, cannot even begin to imagine or comprehend . . . . So the dramatic critic who sets up to be a justicer must bear in mind that, strictly speaking, dramatic criticism is impossible.—IVOR BROWN

(4) Surely also there is something strange in representing the man of perfect blessedness as a solitary or a recluse. Nobody would deliberately choose to have all the good things in the world, if there was a condition that he was to have them all by himself. Man is a social animal, and the need for company is in his blood. Therefore the happy man must have company, for he has everything that is naturally good, and it will not be denied that it is better to associate with friends than with strangers, with men of virtue than with the ordinary run of persons. We conclude then that the happy man needs friends.—ARISTOTLE, *Ethics*

(5) I no longer believe those who say that a poor politician could be a good President, "if he could only be appointed to the job." Without the qualities required of a successful candidate—without the ability to rally support, to understand the public, to express its aspirations—without the organizational talent, the personal charm, and the physical stamina required to survive the primaries, the convention, and the election—no man would make a great President, however wise in other ways he might be.[4]

[3] Bertrand Russell, *Icarus, or the Future of Science* (New York: E. P. Dutton & Co., Inc., 1924), pp. 62–63.

[4] Theodore G. Sorensen, *Decision-Making in the White House* (New York: Columbia University Press, 1964), pp. 50–51.

III

SYMBOLIC LOGIC

9

Truth-functional Propositions—Truth Tables

I. COMPOUND PROPOSITIONS

In the last several chapters, we have been concerned with simple categorical propositions and the various types of inferences in which they function as parts. Simple propositions are made up of terms related in various ways, whereas compound propositions have simple propositions as components joined by connectives such as "if . . . then," "either . . . or," "and," and "not both." These connectives are also known as *logical constants*. As previously indicated, compound propositions are of the four following types:

1. Hypothetical or conditional: "*If* the house is on fire, *then* the occupants are in danger."
2. Alternative: "*Either* the resolution will be passed *or* he will resign from the committee."
3. Conjunctive: "The weather is cloudy, *and* the visibility is zero."
4. Disjunctive: "It is *not* the case that he can be *both* a bribe taker *and* a statesman."

II. TRUTH TABLES

1. The Purpose of Truth Tables. A truth table is a technique in symbolic logic for exhibiting the truth values of compound propositions

137

through an exhaustive portrayal of all of the possible truth values of their simple components. By "truth values" are meant the two values *true* and *false*.

2. Some Definitions. (*a*) *Truth-functional propositions.* In mathematics, a *function* is defined as a "measurable variable whose value is determined by one or more other variables." Similarly, a proposition is *truth-functional* if its truth values are dependent upon (i.e., are a function of) some other proposition. For example, the proposition "He is a good swimmer" is not truth-functional, for the truth or falsehood of this proposition is to be asserted merely on the basis of the externally determined facts in the case. But the compound alternative proposition "Either he is a good swimmer or he will be drowned" is truth-functional, for its truth value depends upon the values assigned to the component propositions.

(*b*) *Variables.* *Variables* (usually symbolized by letters near the end of the alphabet—*p, q, r, s*) represent the various values or propositions which may be substituted to give them content or meaning in particular cases. For example, "*p*" may stand for "Spinach is distasteful," "Astronauts are athletic," "Cats are whimsical," or whatever else we may choose to make it.

(*c*) *Logical constants.* *Logical constants* are symbols which have a fixed and constant meaning and are represented by the symbols for negation, "—"; alternation, "V"; implication, "⊃," or "→"; conjunction, " . "; and equivalence, "≡." These are also called "truth-functional connectives." They enable us to combine simple propositions to form truth-functional compounds, to construct truth tables which define the symbols, to determine truth-functional equivalences of propositions, to define tautology and contradiction, and to test inferences. In summary they are:

	Symbol
1. Negation: "not" (we shall use the symbol " — " for negation)	"$-p$"
2. Conjunction: "*p* and *q*"	"$p \cdot q$"
3. Alternation: "either *p* or *q*"	"$p \vee q$"
4. Implication: "if *p*, then *q*"	"$p \supset q$"
5. Equivalence: "*p* is equivalent to *q*"	"$p \equiv q$"

3. Construction and Interpretation of Truth Tables. In the construction and interpretation of truth tables, it is assumed that every clear and meaningful proposition is either true or false, that if a proposition is true its negation is false, and if it is false its negation is true, and that the truth values of compound propositions are determined by the truth values of their components.

(*a*) *Negation,* "—p." This is to be read, "*p* is false" or "non-*p* is true." A simple proposition such as "Today is Saturday" can be negated by stating, "It is false that today is Saturday" or "It is not the case that today is Saturday." When the negation symbol is placed before a proposition, whether simple or compound, the whole proposition is negated; for example, "$-(p \supset q)$" means that the proposition "*p* implies *q*" is false. The truth table which defines negation is very simply constructed:

p	$-p$
T	F
F	T

If *p* is true, —*p* is false, and, if *p* is false, —*p* is true, and vice versa.

(*b*) *Conjunction,* "p . q." This is read, "*p* is true, and *q* is true." "The grass is green, and the flowers bloom" are asserted to be jointly true.

This truth table is constructed by forming two reference columns on the left, by alternating the T and F under *p*, then by alternating TT and FF under *q*. This yields all possible truth values of *p* and *q*. On the right, list the truth values of the compound proposition "*p* . *q*," which is a function of the truth values of the simple propositions of which it is composed:

p	q	$p \cdot q$
T	T	T
F	T	F
T	F	F
F	F	F

It will be observed that the conjunction, "*p* . *q*," is true only if both *p* and *q* separately are true, as in the top row. If either *p* or *q* is false, the conjunction as a whole is false. This also defines conjunction; that is, any conjunctive proposition is false if either component proposition is false separately or if both are false, and it is true only if both are true.

(*c*) *Alternation,* "p ∨ q." In English, "either . . . or" is ambiguous. When it is used in the weak or *inclusive* sense, it may mean at least one alternate or perhaps both are true, as in "He is either sick or tired." The strong or *exclusive* sense of "either . . . or" means at least one but not both, e.g., "Today is either Monday or Tuesday."

Here it will be used in the weak or inclusive sense of "either . . . or"; that is, the compound proposition "$p \vee q$" is accepted as true if either or both of its constituents are true. The definition of weak alternation is given in the following truth table:

p	q	$p \vee q$
T	T	T
F	T	T
T	F	T
F	F	F

We note in the table that the compound "$p \vee q$" is true in all cases but the one in which both alternatives, p and q, are false. If "He is sick" is false, and if "He is tired" is false, then "He is either sick or tired" is false.

(d) *Implication,* "p ⊃ q." This is read, "p implies q," or "If p is true, q is true." Here p is the antecedent and q is the consequent.

The concept of implication is ambiguous. We shall distinguish here at least four meanings.

1. Causal: In the proposition "If the house is on fire, then the occupants are in danger," the antecedent is a causal condition, and the consequent is a causal consequent, and the proposition as a whole is based upon empirical observation.
2. Definitional: In the proposition "If this is a mammal, then it is warm-blooded," the consequent follows from the antecedent by reason of the definition of the terms "mammal" and "warm-blooded." This form of implication is sometimes called *entailment.*
3. Logical necessity: "If A equals B, and B equals C, then A equals C."
4. Material implication: Material implication defines "$p \supset q$" as equivalent to "either p is false or q is true," "$-p \vee q$." "If you drive recklessly, you will have an accident," is equivalent to "Either you do not drive recklessly, or you will have an accident," "$p \supset q \equiv -p \vee q$." The following truth table defines material implication:

p	q	$p \supset q$
T	T	T
F	T	T
T	F	F
F	F	T

The compound "$p \supset q$" is true if both p and q are true, if p is false and q is true, and if both p and q are false. *In row 3, only when* p, *the antecedent, is true and* q, *the consequent, false is the implication* "p ⊃ q" *false.*

(*e*) *Equivalence*, "p ≡ q." This is read, "*p* is true if, and only if, *q* is true." For example, "If, and only if, he pays his bills will he preserve his credit." If "he pays his bills" is true, "he will preserve his credit" is true, and vice versa. The truth table defining equivalence is:

p	q	$p \equiv q$
T	T	T
F	T	F
T	F	F
F	F	T

The equivalence "$p \equiv q$" is true only if both p and q are either jointly true or jointly false, otherwise it is false.

The above truth-functional patterns will now be summarized under their various heads for future reference.

Negation

p	$-p$
T	F
F	T

Conjunction

p	q	$p \cdot q$
T	T	T
F	T	F
T	F	F
F	F	F

Alternation

p	q	$p \vee q$
T	T	T
F	T	T
T	F	T
F	F	F

Implication

p	q	$p \supset q$
T	T	T
F	T	T
T	F	F
F	F	T

Equivalence

p	q	$p \equiv q$
T	T	T
F	T	F
T	F	F
F	F	T

III. TRUTH-FUNCTIONAL EQUIVALENCES

To say that two compound propositions are truth-functionally equivalent means that they have the same truth value by reason of their truth-functional form. Consequently one may be validly inferred from the other; that is, they are interchangeable in any logical formula.

The simplest example of equivalence is that of double negation. A truth table illustrates:

p	$-p$	$-(-p)$
T	F	T
F	T	F

It will be observed that p and its double negation, $-(-p)$, have the same truth value.

Another simple example:

p	q	$p \supset q$	$-p \lor q$
T	T	T	T
F	T	T	T
T	F	F	F
F	F	T	T

In the first column after the reference columns, we record the truth values for material implication, TTFT. Then we fill in the second column, which is read, "either p is false or q is true," from the reference columns. The result is TTFT. Since the truth values in the two columns are identical, the two formulas are equivalent.

Let us take a more complex example which will illustrate the fact that certain compound propositions are equivalent and others are not.

p	q	$p \lor q$	$-(p \lor q)$	$-p \cdot -q$	$-p \lor -q$
T	T	T	F	F	F
F	T	T	F	F	T
T	F	T	F	F	T
F	F	F	T	T	T

The first column after the reference columns, "Either p is true or q is true," is derived from the reference columns directly. The second column is the negation of the first and results in the truth values' being reversed. The third column, which reads "p is false and q is false," is derived directly from the reference columns. The fourth column, "either p is false or q is false," may also be derived directly from the reference columns.

It will be observed that columns 2 and 3, "$-(p \lor q)$" and "$-p \cdot -q$," are equivalent, while columns 1 and 4, "$p \lor q$" and "$-p \lor -q$," are not equivalent.

IV. TESTING VALIDITY OF ARGUMENTS BY MEANS OF TRUTH TABLES

1. The Mixed Hypothetical Argument. The *mixed hypothetical argument* contains for its major premise a hypothetical proposition, and for its minor a categorical, which together imply a categorical conclusion.

The hypothetical major premise is made up of two component parts, the first being the *antecedent* and the second the *consequent*. We shall, for brevity, symbolize it as "$p \supset q$." What is affirmed in a hypothetical proposition is that, if the antecedent is true, then the consequent is true, or that the antecedent cannot be true and the consequent false. In other words, whenever we assert a hypothetical proposition and then affirm the truth of the antecedent, we are logically required to affirm the truth of the consequent. Likewise, whenever we assert a hypothetical proposition and then deny the truth of the consequent, we are logically required to deny the truth of the antecedent. But it is obvious that we may also deny the antecedent, which may superficially seem to lead to the denial of the consequent, and affirm the consequent, which may seem to lead to the affirmation of the antecedent. The latter, however, will be found invalid. These four "modes" may be summarized as follows:

1. Affirming the antecedent in the minor and affirming the consequent in the conclusion   (Valid)
2. Denying the consequent in the minor and denying the antecedent in the conclusion   (Valid)
3. Denying the antecedent in the minor and denying the consequent in the conclusion   (Invalid)
4. Affirming the consequent in the minor and affirming the antecedent in the conclusion   (Invalid)

(a) *Affirming the antecedent* $(p \supset q . p) \supset q$.

Example: If Jones is efficient, then he should be promoted.
         Jones is very efficient.
         Hence, he should be promoted.

p	q	$p \supset q$ (premise)	p (premise)	q (conclusion)
T	T	T	T	T
F	T	T	F	T
T	F	F	T	F
F	F	T	F	F

We construct a truth table, using, as usual, reference columns at the left. From the table under "implication" above, we know that the truth values for the first premise, "$p \supset q$," are TTFT. From the reference columns, we also know the truth values for p, which is the second premise, to be TFTF, and the values for q to be TTFF for the conclusion. On examination, we find no instances of true premises and a false conclusion, hence the argument is *valid*.

(b) *Denying the consequent* $(p \supset q . -q) \supset -p$.

Example: If the house is on fire, the occupants are in danger.
         The occupants are not in danger.
         Hence, the house is not on fire.

We proceed as above and fill in the columns for premises and conclusion.

p	q	$p \supset q$ (premise)	$-q$ (premise)	$-p$ (conclusion)
T	T	T	F	F
F	T	T	F	T
T	F	F	T	F
F	F	T	T	T

Examination will show that there are no instances where the premises are true and the conclusion false. The argument is *valid*.

(c) *Affirming the consequent* $(p \supset q . q) \supset p$.

> Example: If a conservative party is elected, tariffs will remain high.
> Tariffs remain high.
> Hence, a conservative party has been elected.

When a truth table is constructed following the above pattern and making the proper substitutions, affirming the consequent will be found *invalid,* since there will appear an instance in which the premises are true and the conclusion false.

(d) *Denying the antecedent* $(p \supset q . -p) \supset -q$.

> Example: If it is a warm winter, it will be a good season for fruit.
> It is not a warm winter.
> Hence, it is not a good season for fruit.

Similarly, when a table is constructed for the denial of the antecedent an instance will appear in which the premises are true and the conclusion false, hence the argument is *invalid*.

2. The Pure Hypothetical Argument.

(a) *The chain argument (fourth figure)* $[(p \supset q) . (q \supset r)] \supset (p \supset r)$.

> Example: If you eat your spinach, you may go to the store.
> If you go to the store, you may buy some candy.
> Hence, if you eat your spinach, you may buy some candy.

Since the pure hypothetical argument contains three variables, p, q, and r, we need to construct our truth table with three variables in the reference columns. The columns under p and q are filled in as before and extended to eight rows by allowing for all possible truth values of r for each combination of truth values for p and q.

p	q	r	$p \supset q$ (premise)	$q \supset r$ (premise)	$p \supset r$ (conclusion)
T	T	T	T	T	T
F	T	T	T	T	T
T	F	T	F	T	T
F	F	T	T	T	T
T	T	F	T	F	F
F	T	F	T	F	T
T	F	F	F	T	F
F	F	F	T	T	T

Bearing in mind our rule that a proposition of material implication is false only when its antecedent is true and its consequent false, we fill in the column under the first premise by referring back to the reference columns, under p and q. Then we fill in under the second premise by referring to the q and r in the reference columns. Next we fill in the conclusion by referring back to the p and r in the reference columns. We notice that the premises are true in rows 1, 2, 4, and 8, and, in all these, the conclusions are also true, which establishes the *validity* of the argument.

(*b*) *The pure hypothetical argument (first figure)* [(p $\supset$ q) . (r $\supset$ p)] $\supset$ (r $\supset$ q).

Example: If you care for your lawn properly, the grass will flourish.
If you hire my gardener, you will care for your lawn properly.
Hence, if you hire my gardener, the grass will flourish.

p	q	r	$p \supset q$ (premise)	$r \supset p$ (premise)	$r \supset q$ (conclusion)
T	T	T	T	T	T
F	T	T	T	F	T
T	F	T	F	T	F
F	F	T	T	F	F
T	T	F	T	T	T
F	T	F	T	T	T
T	F	F	F	T	T
F	F	F	T	T	T

No case appears in which the premises are true and the conclusion false; hence, the *validity* of this form is established.

(*c*) *Invalid forms of the pure hypothetical argument may likewise be demonstrated by truth tables.*

Example: [(*p* $\supset$ *q*) . (*p* $\supset$ *r*)] $\supset$ (*q* $\supset$ *r*)
If we go to war, taxes will increase.
If we go to war, prices will rise.
Hence, if taxes increase, prices will rise.

Example: $[(p \supset q) . (r \supset q)] \supset (p \supset r)$
> If a student is brilliant, his teachers are happy.
> If a student is ambitious, his teachers are happy.
> Hence, if a student is brilliant, he is ambitious.

3. Alternative Arguments (Inclusive or Weak Alternation; Either or Both). An alternative argument contains an alternative proposition as the major premise, a categorical minor premise, and a categorical conclusion. Alternative propositions assert the relation of alternation between the simple propositions which are its constituents, e.g., "Either (today is sultry) or (today is cloudy)." In an alternative proposition, at least one of the alternatives must be true, and both may be true. This calls attention to the ambiguity of "either . . . or." In ordinary discourse, if our friend invites us to lunch and asks us to meet him at either the cafeteria or the hotel, he probably means *either but not both*. If we say, "The orbits of the planets are either circles or ellipses," there is no doubt that we mean *either but not both*. This meaning of the alternative is called *exclusive,* or *strong, alternation.* Alternative arguments which contain a major premise with strong alternation will yield a valid conclusion whether the minor premise affirms or denies either of the alternatives. This is because strong alternation means *"p or q, but not both,"* or, in other words, *one and only one* can be true. For example:

> The orbits of the planets are either circles or ellipses.
> They are circles; therefore, they are not ellipses.   (Valid)
> They are ellipses; therefore, they are not circles.   (Valid)
> They are not circles; therefore, they are ellipses.   (Valid)
> They are not ellipses; therefore, they are circles.   (Valid)

However, when the alternatives offered in the major premise of an argument are not exclusive, that is, when we have weak alternation, and we deny one of these alternatives in the minor premise, we may validly affirm the other in the conclusion.

(a) *Denying one alternative* $[(p \vee q) . -p] \supset q$, *or* $[(p \vee q) . -q] \supset p$.

> Example: Either the resolution will be passed, or he will resign from the committee.
> The resolution will not be passed.
> Hence, he will resign from the committee.

p	q	$p \lor q$ (premise)	$-p$ (premise)	q (conclusion)
T	T	T	F	T
F	T	T	T	T
T	F	T	F	F
F	F	F	T	F

In no case are the premises true and the conclusion false, hence the argument is *valid*. Another truth table may be constructed to prove the argument *valid* when the other alternative is denied, $[(p \lor q) \cdot -q] \supset p$.

(b) *Affirming one alternative* $[(p \lor q) \cdot p] \supset -q$ *or* $[(p \lor q) \cdot q] \supset -p$.

Example: You will either wash the dishes or do your homework.
You will wash the dishes.
Hence, you will not do your homework.

p	q	$p \lor q$ (premise)	p (premise)	$-q$ (conclusion)
T	T	T	T	F
F	T	T	F	F
T	F	T	T	T
F	F	F	F	T

We note that in the first row the premises are true and the conclusion false; hence, the argument is *invalid*.

4. Disjunctive Arguments. A disjunctive argument is made up of a disjunctive major premise, a categorical minor premise, and a categorical conclusion. It has the advantage of stating clearly that the major premise is a true disjunctive, of the form "not both p and q," which is assumed but left unexpressed in the strong form of alternation. But it should be noted that it asserts only that one of the disjuncts cannot be true, *but it does not deny that both may be false*. Hence, if one disjunct is affirmed, the other may validly be denied.

(a) *Affirming the first disjunct* $[-(p \cdot q) \cdot p] \supset -q$.

Example: It is not the case that it is both a rainy day *and* a good day for the game.
It is a rainy day.
Hence, it is not a good day for the game.

p	q	$p \cdot q$	$-(p \cdot q)$ (premise)	p (premise)	$-q$ (conclusion)
T	T	T	F	T	F
F	T	F	T	F	F
T	F	F	T	T	T
F	F	F	T	F	T

In no case are the premises true and the conclusion false; hence the argument is *valid*.

(*b*) *Affirming the second disjunct* [−(p . q) . q] ⊃ −p. With proper substitutions, a truth table may be worked out for proving the *validity* of affirming the second disjunct.

(*c*) *The two fallacies* (*1*) *Denying the first disjunct and* (*2*) *Denying the second disjunct*. These may likewise be demonstrated by truth tables. The fallacies appear since the major premise "−(*p . q*)" means "not both" but does not rule out the possibility that both may be false; hence, when one disjunct is denied, the other cannot logically be affirmed.

> Example: [−(*p . q*) −*p*] ⊃ *q*
>> It is not the case that it is both a good product and a low price.
>> It is not a good product.
>> Hence, it is a low price.

One truth table will be sufficient for illustration:

p	*q*	*p . q*	−(*p . q*) (premise)	−*p* (premise)	*q* (conclusion)
T	T	T	F	F	T
F	T	F	T	T	T
T	F	F	T	F	F
F	F	F	T	T	F

In the last row, it appears that the premises are true and the conclusion false; hence, the argument is *invalid*.

5. The Dilemma. No new logical principles are involved in the dilemma. It is, however, somewhat more complex than those arguments we have so far considered. The dilemma has, in the past, been used mainly as a rhetorical device for placing an opponent in an embarrassing position and thus scoring a point in debate. In debate and controversy, we are in a dilemma when we are forced by the premises into a choice between two conclusions, neither of which we want to accept. Practically, we are in a dilemma when we have before us, two or more alternative ways of acting, no one of which is desired. The high school graduate pondering over his prospects for the future thinks to himself, "If I go to college, I must postpone earning an income, and, if I do not go to college, I will not get the kind of education I desire." In the United States Congress, a debate once raged over universal military training. The arguments were very convincing on both sides of the controversial question. After listening to the debate for many days, a commentator summed it up in the form of a national dilemma: "If the nation adopts universal military training, it is preparing for war; and if it does not, we are inviting invasion by an aggressor. But either we adopt universal military training or we do not; therefore, we are either preparing for war or inviting invasion by an aggressor."

From the strictly logical point of view, the dilemma is a compound argument, the major premise of which contains two hypothetical propositions conjunctively affirmed, and the minor of which is an alternative proposition either affirming the antecedents or denying the consequents of the major premise. That is, the rules that apply to valid hypothetical arguments also apply here. The conclusion may be either categorical or alternative. There are four kinds of dilemmas, examples of which will be given.

(a) *Simple constructive dilemma.*

Major premise: Two different antecedents and two identical consequents (two identical consequents mark it as *simple*).

Minor premise: Affirms alternately the antecedents of the major (affirming marks it as *constructive*).

Conclusion: Affirms the single consequent.

> Example: If I work in the back yard, I will get sunburned, and, if I work in the front yard, I will get sunburned.
> But I must work either in the back yard or in the front yard
> Hence, I will get sunburned.

In symbols: $[(p \supset q) . (r \supset q) . (p \vee r)] \supset q$

(b) *Simple destructive dilemma.*

Major premise: Two identical antecedents and two different consequents (two identical antecedents mark it as *simple*).

Minor premise: Denies alternately the consequents of the major (denying marks it as *destructive*).

Conclusion: Denies the single antecedent.

> Example: If Jones enters the university, he will have to work hard, and, if he enters the university, he will have to pay a high tuition.
> But either Jones will not work hard or he will not pay a high tuition.
> Hence, Jones will not enter the university.

In symbols: $[(p \supset q) . (p \supset r) . (-q \vee -r)] \supset -p$

(c) Complex constructive dilemma.

Major premise: Two different antecedents and two different consequents (two antecedents and two consequents mark it as *complex*).

Minor premise: Affirms alternately the antecedents of the major (affirming marks it as *constructive*).

Conclusion: Affirms alternately the consequents.

> Example: If Smith takes out insurance, he will provide for his old age, and, if he invests in stocks, he will risk heavy losses.
> But Smith either takes out insurance or invests in stocks.
> Hence, Smith either provides for his old age or risks heavy losses.

In symbols: $[(p \supset q) . (r \supset s) . (p \lor r)] \supset q \lor s$

(d) Complex destructive dilemma.

Major premise: Two different antecedents and two different consequents (two antecedents and two consequents mark it as *complex*).

Minor premise: Denies alternately the consequents of the major (denying marks it as *destructive*).

Conclusion: Denies alternately the antecedents.

> Example: If farm prices are to remain high, there must be government control of farm surpluses, and, if general prosperity is to exist, we must encourage greater farm production.
> But either there is not government control of farm surpluses or we do not encourage greater farm production.
> Hence, either farm prices do not remain high or general prosperity does not exist.

In symbols: $[(p \supset q) . (r \supset s) . (-q \lor -s)] \supset (-p \lor -r)$

(e) Truth table for a dilemma. We shall construct a truth table for the *complex constructive* dilemma, which is of the form $[(p \supset q) . (r \supset s) . (p \lor r)] \supset (q \lor s)$. Since the dilemma involves four variables, p, q, r, and s, we need four columns for reference. The first column alternates T and F; the second, TT and FF; the third, TTTT and FFFF; and the fourth, TTTT TTTT and FFFF FFFF, resulting in a reference column of sixteen rows.

						(premise)	(premise)	(conclusion)
p	q	r	s	$(p \supset q)$	$(r \supset s)$	$(p \supset q) . (r \supset s)$	$(p \lor r)$	$(q \lor s)$
T	T	T	T	T	T	T	T	T
F	T	T	T	T	T	T	T	T
T	F	T	T	F	T	F	T	T
F	F	T	T	T	T	T	T	T
T	T	F	T	T	T	T	T	T
F	T	F	T	T	T	T	F	T
T	F	F	T	F	T	F	T	T
F	F	F	T	T	T	T	F	T
T	T	T	F	T	F	F	T	T
F	T	T	F	T	F	F	T	T
T	F	T	F	F	F	F	T	F
F	F	T	F	T	F	F	T	F
T	T	F	F	T	T	T	T	T
F	T	F	F	T	T	T	F	T
T	F	F	F	F	T	F	T	F
F	F	F	F	T	T	T	F	F

1. We fill in column 1 after the reference columns by repeating the pattern of implication, TTFT.
2. Column 2 is filled in with reference to the r and s of the reference columns, bearing in mind that material implication means that only if the antecedent is true and the consequent false is the implication false; otherwise it is true.
3. Column 3 is filled in with reference to columns 1 and 2. The conjunction is true only when both of the conjuncts are true; otherwise it is false.
4. Column 4 is filled in from the p and r of the reference columns. The alternative "$p \lor r$" is true if at least one of the alternatives is true; otherwise it is false.
5. Column 5 is filled in from the q and s of the reference columns. The alternative "$q \lor s$" is true if at least one alternative is true; otherwise it is false.

Examination will show that no row appears in which the premises are true and the conclusion false. The argument is *valid*.

V. ESCAPING FROM A DILEMMA

In order to be valid, dilemmas must conform to the formal rules which we have observed for hypothetical arguments; that is, they must *affirm alternately the antecedents of the major premise or deny alternately the consequents of the major*. In addition, in order to be materially sound, the major premise must be true in the sense that the consequents must follow from the antecedents, and the alternatives of the minor premise must be exhaustive. Finally, the argument must be of such a nature that it cannot be rebutted by a counterdilemma. The above examples have been carefully constructed and, therefore, seem to be real dilemmas, providing the premises are granted.

For each of the above material requirements there is a method of attack upon the premises and thus of escape from the dilemma. These are traditionally known by the picturesque names of "taking the dilemma by the horns," "escaping between the horns," and "rebuttal." We are supposed to imagine the bull ring and the matador facing the charging bull. The word "horns" refers to the alternatives forced upon us by the premises and on which we are to be "impaled."

1. Taking the Dilemma by the Horns. This method of escape consists of challenging the material truth of either or both of the hypothetical propositions which make up the major premise, that is, of showing that the consequents do not in fact follow from the antecedents. For example,

> If a nation adopts universal military training, it is preparing for war, and, if it does not, it is inviting invason by an aggressor.
> But ether a nation adopts universal military training or it does not.
> Hence, a nation either is preparing for war or is inviting attack by an aggressor.

The dilemma may be taken by the horns by attacking the material truth of the second hypothetical preposition in the major premise. It can be successfully argued that a nation may adopt that policy of military training which is less than universal and yet sufficient to discourage an aggressor.

2. Escaping Between the Horns. This method of escaping from a dilemma is to challenge the material truth of the minor premise by showing that the alternatives are not exhaustive and, therefore, that the conclusion is not inescapable. This is usually not difficult unless the alternatives in the minor premise are contradictories. If they are contraries, escape is possible by showing that there is a third alternative. For example:

> If a nation demands of a defeated enemy a hard peace treaty, it arouses resentment, and, if it offers a soft peace treaty, it generates contempt.
> But a nation must offer a defeated enemy either a hard peace or a soft peace.
> Hence, a peace treaty either arouses resentment or generates contempt.

This may appear to be an inescapable conclusion because the minor premise contains the words "hard" and "soft," which are often considered to be contradictories. However, the contradictory of "hard" is "not hard" and that of "soft" is "not soft," and it is obvious that there is no middle ground between these contradictories. If it can be shown that there is a middle ground between the extremes of a *hard* peace treaty and a *soft* peace treaty, such as moderate, equitable, just, or hard in some respects and soft in others, the dilemma can be escaped.

3. Rebuttal by Counterdilemma. The third method of escaping a dilemma is by constructing a counterdilemma which leads to a different or contrary and sometimes contradictory conclusion. This means not that the rebuttal is a sounder argument than the original but simply that the situation has been viewed from a different frame of reference, and that the opposition is capable of placing his opponent in an equally embarrassing position from his own point of view.

Examples: An attorney, on being asked to defend a client on an unpopular issue, is placed in this dilemma:

> If I defend this client, I will be opposed by powerful interests, and, if I do not defend him, I will be despised by his friends.
> But I must either defend this client or not defend him.
> Hence, I will be either opposed by powerful interests or despised by his friends.

The prospective client, wishing to persuade the attorney, offers this rebuttal:

> If you accept me as a client, you will not be despised by my friends, and, if you do not accept me as a client, you will not be opposed by powerful interests.
> But you must either accept me as a client or not accept me as a client.
> Hence, either you will not be despised by my friends or you will not be opposed by powerful interests.

It should be carefully noted that the conclusion of the rebuttal does not contradict the original conclusion, although it may appear to do so. In fact, it is not even inconsistent with it, since one of the undesirable alternatives still remains. What the client would like to have shown is that "Both you will not be despised by my friends *and* you will not be opposed by powerful interests." Rebuttal consists in transposing the consequents of the major premise and contradicting them, as follows:

Original: $[(p \supset q) \cdot (-p \supset r) \cdot (p \vee -p)] \supset q \vee r$

Rebuttal: $[(p \supset -r) \cdot (-p \supset -q) \cdot (p \vee -p)] \supset -r \vee -q$

Finally, we shall use as an example the now famous story of the Sophist Protagoras and his student Euathlus. Protagoras had agreed with Euathlus to teach him rhetoric for a fee, of which half was to be paid at the conclusion of the instruction and the remainder when Euathlus won his first case in court. Observing that Euathlus delayed practicing, Protagoras thought that he was evading payment, and hence brought suit himself for the payment of the second half of his fee. He then presented the following argument to the judge:

> If Euathlus loses this case, he ought to pay by the judgment of the court, and, if he wins it, he ought to pay by his own agreement.
> But he must either win it or lose it.
> Hence, in either case he ought to pay.

Euathlus *rebutted* with a *counterargument*:

> If I win this case, I ought not to pay by the judgment of the court, and, if I lose it, I ought not to pay by my own agreement.
> But I must either win it or lose it.
> Therefore, in either case I ought not to pay.

If you were the judge, how would you rule in this case?

VI. TAUTOLOGY AND CONTRADICTION

Tautologies are propositions which are true for all possible values of their constituents, or, in other words, which by reason of their truth-functional form are necessarily true.

A truth table for the principle of excluded middle illustrates its tautological nature. The principle states that every proposition is either true or false. "Either the sea is salt or it is not salt," $(p \lor -p)$.

p	$-p$	$p \lor -p$
T	F	T
F	T	T

We note that the column under the main connective consists of T's. This indicates that the propositional expression "$p \lor -p$" is true under all conditions, or necessarily true.

Similarly, the principle of contradiction states that a proposition cannot be both true and false. "It is not the case that the sea is salt and not salt," $-(p . -p)$.

p	$-p$	$p . -p$	$-(p . -p)$
T	F	F	T
F	T	F	T

Again the main column consists of T's, and indicates that the propositional expression $-(p \cdot -p)$ is true under all conditions, or necessarily true.

Contradictory, or *contravalid*, propositions are always false by reason of their truth-functional form, as the following truth table for the propositional expression $(p \cdot -p)$ will show:

p	$-p$	$p \cdot -p$
T	F	F
F	T	F

The appearance of F under the formula in every case shows that it is false under all conditions, or necessarily false. This truth table will be sufficient to illustrate all propositional expressions of this class.

Complex or extended arguments may be tested by the truth tables, but this sometimes gets to be cumbersome. It is often easier to make explicit the elementary components of an argument, each of which can be tested for validity as step by step it leads validly to a more complex form.

An argument is formally proved if each step follows validly from premises that have already been formally proved. Elementary arguments are proved if they can be substituted for, or are logically equivalent to, one of the valid argument forms (as defined by truth tables and associated definitions).

PROBLEMS

1. Symbolize the following logical equivalences. Prove by a truth table that they are equivalent.

(1) If this creature is an animal, then it is an organism.
(2) Either this creature is not an animal or it is an organism.
(3) It is not the case that this creature is an animal and not an organism.
(4) If this creature is not an organism, then it is not an animal.

2. Translate the following propositional forms into English sentences.

(1) $p \supset q \equiv -p \lor q$
(2) $p \supset q \equiv -(p \cdot -q)$
(3) $-(p \cdot q) \equiv -p \lor -q$
(4) $-(p \lor q) \equiv -p \cdot -q$

3. Construct truth tables to test each of the equivalences in the preceding problem.

4. Construct examples in English and give the truth-value matrix for each of the following functions:

(1) Negation
(2) Equivalence
(3) Conjunction
(4) Implication
(5) Alternation
(6) Disjunction

5. Use truth tables to test the validity of the following propositional forms.

(1) $p \supset q$ (2) $-(p \cdot q)$ (3) $p \supset q$ (4) $-(p \cdot q)$
          q $-p$ $-p$ $-q$
     $\therefore p$ $\therefore q$ $\therefore -q$ $\therefore p$
(5) $p \supset q$ (6) $p \supset q$ (7) $[(p \supset q) \cdot (r \supset q) \cdot (p \lor r)] \supset q$
          p $-q$
     $\therefore q$ $\therefore -p$
(8) $[(p \supset q) \cdot (r \supset s) \cdot (-q \lor -s)] \supset (-p \lor -r)$
(9) $[(p \supset q) \cdot (p \supset r)] \supset (q \supset r)$ (10) $[(p \supset q) \cdot (r \supset q)] \supset (p \supset r)$

6. Which of the following are tautologies, and which are contradictions? Test them by truth tables.

(1) $(p \cdot p) \supset p$ (2) $p \lor -p$ (3) $-(p \lor -p)$ (4) $p \cdot -p$
(5) $-(p \cdot -p)$ (6) $p \supset p$ (7) $[(p \supset q) \cdot p] \supset q$

7. Employing the methods of hypothetical arguments, solve the following problem:

A businessman is seeking a secretary and selects from a number of applicants three promising candidates. The following test is carried out to eliminate all but one. The three candidates are placed seated in the form of a triangle facing each other. They are then blindfolded and given the following instructions: "A mark will be placed on your foreheads with a crayon in either black or white. When the blindfold is removed each of you will look at both of the others in the group, and if you see a black mark, begin tapping with your pencil on the arm of your chair, and keep on tapping until you have deduced what kind of mark is on your forehead, either black or white. When you have decided, stand up and tell the group, and give your reasons for the decision." When the blindfolds were removed, each girl saw a black mark on each of the other foreheads and all began tapping. After some time one girl arose and said that the mark on her forehead was black. How did she arrive at this conclusion?

8. Examine the following hypothetical arguments. Point out and name the specific fallacy, if any, and/or test them by truth tables.

(1) If this man is guilty, he was in the garden at the time of the crime. But he was not in the garden at the time of the crime. Therefore, he is not guilty.

(2) If we are arrested for picketing, there must be an antipicketing ordinance in this city. We were arrested for picketing. Therefore, there must be an antipicketing ordinance.

(3) If you believe this, you are a heretic. You are a heretic. Therefore, you believe this.

(4) If you favor either the Republicans or the Democrats, you will be accused of bias. You favor the Republicans. Therefore, you will be accused of bias.

(5) If he gets a good grade, he must have studied his lessons. He did study his lessons. Therefore, he must have got a good grade.

(6) If a policeman catches me, I will get a ticket. The policeman will not catch me. Therefore I will not get a ticket.

(7) If it does not rain immediately, the crops will be ruined. The crops will not be ruined. Therefore, it will rain immediately.

(8) If a man can give trustworthy testimony, he has access to the facts. If a man is incompetent, he does not have access to the facts. Therefore, if a man is incompetent, he cannot give trustworthy testimony.

(9) If he is opposed to war, he is a humanitarian. If he is a militarist, he is not opposed to war. Therefore, if he is a militarist, he is not a humanitarian.

(10) If Mr. A. does not have his paper finished, he is either lazy or sick. But he does have his paper finished. Therefore, he is neither lazy nor sick.

(11) If you stole the money, you are either a thief or a liar. But you are neither a thief nor a liar. Therefore, you did not steal the money.

9. Examine the following alternative arguments. Point out and name the fallacy, if any, and/or test them by truth tables.

(1) Either the dog will bark, or he will wag his tail. The dog will bark. Therefore, he will not wag his tail.

(2) Either I will prepare a written statement, or I will appear in person at the meeting. I will prepare a written statement. Therefore, I will not appear in person at the meeting.

(3) Either the secretary is in the office, or the office is closed. The secretary is not in the office. Therefore, the office is closed.

(4) Either the people are enlightened, or they are not amused. The people are not enlightened. Therefore, they are not amused.

(5) Either the war will end soon, or civilization will be destroyed. The war will end soon. Therefore, civilization will not be destroyed.

(6) Either the watch was not on time, or the train was late. The train was late. Therefore, the watch was on time.

(7) Either prices will be pegged or there will be an inflation. There will be no inflation. Therefore, prices will be pegged.

(8) The light in the sky is either a space ship, an airplane, a reflection from a searchlight, or a natural phenomenon. It is not a space ship, an airplane, or a reflection from a searchlight. Therefore, it is a natural phenomenon.

10. Examine for any fallacy the following disjunctive arguments, and/or test them by truth tables.

(1) Mr. Jones cannot be both critical and appreciative with respect to this question. Mr. Jones is not critical with respect to this question. Therefore, Mr. Jones is appreciative.

(2) It is not the case that it is both wise to enter the war and prudent to strengthen the enemy. It is prudent to strengthen the enemy. Therefore, it is not wise to enter the war.

(3) It is not the case that there is both good visibility and a low fog. There is good visibility. Therefore, there is not a low fog.

(4) A man cannot both be honest and be a member of this organization. This man is a member of this organization. Therefore, he is not honest.

(5) A man cannot be both a statesman and a bribe taker. This man is not a bribe taker. Therefore, he is a statesman.

(6) It is not the case that there is both a desire for war and a desire for peace at any price. There is no desire for peace at any price. Therefore, there is a desire for war.

11. How would you escape, if possible, from the conclusion in the following dilemmas?

(1) "If a thing moves it cannot move in the place where it is, and if it moves it cannot move in the place where it is not. But it must move either in the place where it is or in the place where it is not. Therefore, in either case it cannot move."

(2) "If you tell the truth men will hate you, and if you tell lies the gods will hate you. But you must either tell the truth or tell lies. Hence, in either case you will be hated."

(3) If this candidate were wise, he would not speak lightly of the common people in jest, and, if he were a good politician, he would not do so in earnest. But he does it either in jest or in earnest. Therefore, he is either not wise or not a good politician.

(4) If the Senate cannot get information from public officials regarding corruption, it cannot protect the nation, and, if it does, confidence in the integrity of public officials will decline. But the Senate either does or does not get such information. Therefore, either the nation will not be protected from corruption, or confidence in public officials will decline.

(5) If we do not raise the living standards of the farmer, agriculture will decline, and, if we do, the consumer will pay higher prices. But we either do raise the living standards of the farmer or we do not. Therefore, either agriculture will decline or the consumer will pay higher prices.

(6) If we become too much involved in the Far East, Europe will be lost to Communism, and, if we devote all our resources to Europe, the Far East will be lost to Communism. But we must either devote attention to the Far East or to Europe. Therefore, either Europe will be lost to Communism or the Far East will be lost to Communism.

(7) "If the charges candidates make against each other are true, then it would show glaring deficiencies in men already in high office and running for still higher office; but if they are not right in their estimation of each other, then what they speak is not the truth, and this fact diminishes their stature. But they are either speaking the truth or not speaking the truth. Hence, there are either glaring deficiencies in men already in high office, or candidates are guilty of diminishing their stature."—R. L. C.

(8) If we go by the valley route, it will take us too long, and, if we go by the mountain route, we will endanger our lives. But we must go either by the valley route or by the mountain route. Hence, we will either take too long or endanger our lives.

10

Evaluating Truth-functional Arguments

In the last chapter, we studied truth tables and the way in which they may be used in testing the validity of simple arguments. It becomes obvious that this method is somewhat cumbersome when as many as four variables are involved, as illustrated in our example of the truth table for the complex constructive dilemma (page 151). The method of evaluating truth-functional arguments now to be considered involves the breaking up of long arguments into their simpler elements, each of which can be examined for validity until the final conclusion is reached. The method involves the use of certain valid argument forms, rules of inference, axioms, and logical principles which have become standard in symbolic logic.

I. VALID ARGUMENT FORMS AND RULES OF INFERENCE

1. *Modus Ponens* (M.P.[1]): $[(p \supset q) \cdot p] \supset q$
2. *Modus Tollens* (M.T.): $[(p \supset q) \cdot -q] \supset -p$
3. Hypothetical Syllogism (H.S.): $[(p \supset q) \cdot (q \supset r)] \supset (p \supset r)$
4. Alternative Argument (A.A.): $[(p \lor q) \cdot -p] \supset q$ or
   $[(p \lor q) \cdot -q] \supset p$
5. Disjunctive Argument (D.A.): $[-(p \cdot q) \cdot p] \supset -q$ or
   $[-(p \cdot q) \cdot q] \supset -p$

[1] For convenience, the abbreviations indicated can be used later for reference when analyzing a proof.

6. Conjunction (Conj.): $p, q \supset p \cdot q$
7. Complex Constructive Dilemma (C.C.D.):
   $[(p \supset q) \cdot (r \supset s) \cdot (p \vee r)] \supset q \vee s$
8. Complex Destructive Dilemma (C.D.D.):
   $[(p \supset q) \cdot (r \supset s) \cdot (-q \vee -s)] \supset (-p \vee -r)$
9. Simplification (Simp.): $(p \cdot q) \supset p \ (p \cdot q) \supset q$
10. Addition (Add.): $p \supset (p \vee q)$

The following logically equivalent expressions may be substituted for each other:

11. Association (Assoc.): $[p \vee (q \vee r)] \equiv [(p \vee q) \vee r]$
    $$[p \cdot (q \cdot r)] \equiv [(p \cdot q) \cdot r]$$
12. Contraposition (Cont.): $(p \supset q) \equiv (-q \supset -p)$
13. Commutation (Comm.): $(p \vee q) \equiv (q \vee p) \ (p \cdot q) \equiv (q \cdot p)$
14. De Morgan's Theorems (De M.): $-(p \cdot q) \equiv (-p \vee -q)$
    $$-(p \vee q) \equiv (-p \cdot -q)$$
15. Distribution (Dist.): $[p \cdot (q \vee r)] \equiv [(p \cdot q) \vee (p \cdot r)]$
    $$[p \vee (q \cdot r)] \equiv [(p \vee q) \cdot (p \vee r)]$$
16. Double Negation (D.N.): $p \equiv - -p$
17. Definition of Material Implication (Impl.): $(p \supset q) \equiv (-p \vee q)$
    $$(p \vee q) \equiv (-p \supset q)$$
18. Definition of Material Equivalence (Equiv.):
    $$(p \equiv q) \equiv [(p \supset q) \cdot (q \supset p)]$$
    $$(p \equiv q) \equiv [(p \cdot q) \vee (-p \cdot -q)]$$
19. Exportation (Exp.): $[(p \cdot q) \supset r] \equiv [p \supset (q \supset r)]$
20. Tautology (Taut.): $p \equiv (p \vee p)$
    $$p \equiv (p \cdot p)$$

Some additional equivalences:

$$p \supset q \ \equiv -(p \cdot -q)$$
$$p \vee q \ \equiv -(-p \cdot -q)$$
$$-(p \vee q) \equiv -p \cdot -q$$
$$-(p \cdot q) \equiv -p \vee -q$$
$$-(p \cdot q) \equiv -p \cdot -q$$
$$p \equiv q \ \equiv (p \supset q) \equiv (q \supset p)$$
$$-(p \cdot -q) \equiv -(q \cdot -p)$$

II. METHODS OF PROVING VALIDITY OF TRUTH-FUNCTIONAL ARGUMENTS

Let us choose a simple example which may seem to be intuitively valid and follow through the steps of the argument from premises to conclusion, justifying each step by using a valid argument form or rule of inference, resulting in a formal proof.

Consider the following example:

> Jones bought either a Jaguar or a Mercedes.
> If he bought a Jaguar, he pleased his son, and, if he bought
> a Mercedes, he pleased his wife.
> But he didn't please his son.
> Hence, he pleased his wife.

Let us symbolize the various parts of the argument as follows (J, M, S, W):

> J—Jones bought a Jaguar.
> M—Jones bought a Mercedes.
> S—Jones pleased his Son.
> W—Jones pleased his Wife.

We begin on the left by numbering the premises, and continue numbering the steps until we reach the conclusion. On the right, we indicate the number of the premises from which we are deriving the deduction, followed by the justification in terms of our elementary valid argument forms and rules of inference. The conclusion should be placed to the right, after the last premise. For example:

1. $J \vee M$ Pr.
2. $J \supset S$ Pr.
3. $M \supset W$ Pr.
4. $-S$ Pr. $/ \therefore W$

Justification

5. $-J$ (1) From 2, 4, by *modus tollens* (M.T.)
6. M (2) From 1, 5, by alternative syllogism (Alt. Syl.)
7. W (Conclusion)   (3) From 3, 6, by *modus ponens* (M.P.)

Premises 2 and 4, by the valid argument form of *modus tollens*, yield number 5. Numbers 1 and 5 yield number 6, by alternative syllogism. Finally, 3 and 6 yield number 7, the conclusion, by *modus ponens*.

Another example:

> If Roger the funnyman is a successful comedian, then he is in
> great demand.
> If he is in great demand, then he must be very clever.
> Either he is a successful comedian or the reports are exaggerated.
> He is not very clever.
> Hence, the reports are exaggerated. [Symbols: S, D, C, E]

1. $S \supset D$ Pr.
2. $D \supset C$ Pr.
3. $S \vee E$ Pr.
4. $-C$ Pr. $/ \therefore E$

Justification

5.	$S \supset C$	(1) 1, 2, by hypothetical syllogism (H.S.)
6.	$-S$	(2) 5, 4, by *modus tollens* (M.T.)
7.	E (Conclusion)	(3) 3, 6, by alternative syllogism (Alt.)

Lines 1 and 2 yield line 5, by hypothetical syllogism. Lines 5 and 4, by *modus tollens,* yield line 6. Lines 3 and 6, by alternative syllogism, yield E, the conclusion.

Now let us introduce an argument which brings into play a still larger number of rules of inference, as follows:

> Tom will not both safari in Africa and climb the Alps this summer, unless his father pays his expenses.
> His father will not pay his expenses unless the stock market improves.
> Tom is already climbing the Alps, and the stock market will not improve.
> Hence, Tom will not safari in Africa. [Symbols: S, A, E, M]

1.	$(S . A) \supset E$	Pr.
2.	$E \supset M$	Pr.
3.	$A . -M$	Pr. $/ \therefore \; -S$

Justification

4.	$-M$	(1) 3, by simplification (Simp.)
5.	$-E$	(2) 2, 4, by *modus tollens* (M.T.)
6.	$-(S . A)$	(3) 1, 5, by *modus tollens* (M.T.)
7.	A	(4) 3, by simplification (Simp.)
8.	$-S$ (Conclusion)	(5) 6, 7, by disjunctive argument (Dis.)

Finding the right combination for a deduction is much like puzzle solving, and you may start anywhere that promises progress. Some logicians suggest starting with the conclusion and working backward. Examining the premises and searching for a starting point, we observe that premise 3 can be divided by the principle of simplification to yield $-M$ for line 4, leaving the A on line 3. We can then use the $-M$ of line 4 to combine with line 2 to form a deduction by means of *modus tollens* to yield line 5 or $-E$. Next, from lines 1 and 5, we are able, by means of *modus tollens* again, to produce line 6. Line 3, by simplification, yields A for line 7. Finally, by a disjunctive argument, lines 6 and 7 yield the conclusion $-S$.

Since some of the rules of inference have not yet been put to use, we shall explain them in some detail as we proceed step by step in context, using an illustration of an argument that involves more of them. Consider the argument on the next page.

If Simpkins takes the case to court, then, if he wins, he will
either pay or give a promissory note.
If he pays, he will have discharged his obligation.
If he gives a promissory note, he will default.
He goes to court, and he wins.
He will not default.
Hence, he has discharged his obligation. [Symbols: C, W, P,
N, O, D]

1.	$C \supset (W \supset (P \lor N))$	Pr.
2.	$P \supset O$	Pr.
3.	$N \supset D$	Pr.
4.	$C \cdot W$	Pr.
5.	$-D$	Pr. $/ \therefore O$

Justification

6. C (1) 4, by simplification (Simp.)

When we look around for a starting point, we note that number 4,
$C \cdot W$, is a conjunction. The principle of simplification holds that a
conjunction implies either of the atomic propositions conjoined, e.g.,
$(p \cdot q) \supset p$ or $(p \cdot q) \supset q$. So, since we can use the C in combination
with the first premise, we separate it from the W for line 6.

7. $W \supset (P \lor N)$ (2) 1, 6, by *modus ponens* (M.P.)
8. W (3) 4, by simplification (Simp.)

Since we are able to use the remaining conjunct, W, by the same rule
of simplification, we place it on line 8.

9. $P \lor N$ (4) 7, 8, by *modus ponens* (M.P.)

Premise 3 is then contraposed. In contraposing a hypothetical proposition, we interchange antecedent and consequent, and negate both.
This gives us line 10.

10. $-D \supset -N$ (5) 3, by contraposition (Cont.)
11. $-N$ (6) 5, 10, by *modus ponens* (M.P.)
12. $N \lor P$ (7) 9, by commutation (Comm.)

The commutative rule holds that the order of an alternative such as
we have under 9, $P \lor N$, is immaterial; hence, we arbitrarily choose,
for our purpose, to make it $N \lor P$ under 12.

13. $-N \supset P$ (8) 12, by material implication (M.I.)

By definition, material implication is to the effect that $(p \lor q)$ is
equivalent to $(-p \supset q)$, and, since we are looking for something to

enable us to make progress in our deduction, we substitute $-N \supset P$ for $N \vee P$ on line 13.

14. P (9) 11, 13, by *modus ponens* (M.P.)
15. O (Conclusion)   (10) 2, 14, by *modus ponens* (M.P.)

III. PROOF OF INVALIDITY

We have suggested two methods of proving validity of truth-functional arguments, viz., truth tables, studied in the last chapter, in which we saw that, if in the truth table no instance can be found of a row in which the premises are true and the conclusion false, the argument is valid. The second method, which we have just examined and illustrated, consists of performing a number of deductions from premises to conclusion and justifying each step by substituting previously authenticated argument forms according to established logical principles and rules of inference.

But suppose we wish to avoid the longer truth table method and cannot easily succeed in showing by the second method that an argument is valid or invalid. We may suspect that it is invalid, which is to say that the premises are true and the conclusion false. If we can find a method of assigning values of truth and falsity to the parts of the argument so that the premises will be true and the conclusion false, we have demonstrated the invalidity of the argument.

Let us take the following example:

> If the college plays a tough schedule, then it will have to recruit football players.
> If it is primarily a football college, then it will recruit football players.
> Hence, if the college plays a tough schedule, then it must be primarily a football college.

We symbolize the argument as (S, R, F):

1. $S \supset R$ Pr.
2. $F \supset R$ Pr. $/ \therefore S \supset F$

This argument is obviously invalid by the rules of the hypothetical syllogism, but there is another method of demonstration. We recall that an implicative proposition is false only when its antecedent is true and its consequent false. If we wish to make the conclusion $S \supset F$ false, we do so by giving the value "true" to S, the antecedent, and "false" to F, the consequent. Now we wish to assign values to the premises so as to make them both "true." On the grounds of the principle that an implicative proposition is always true when its consequent is true, we assign the value "true" to both consequents—the R of both premises. This gives us true premises and a false conclusion, thus proving the argument invalid.

This can be set forth as follows:

S	R	F	$S \supset R$	$F \supset R$	$S \supset F$
True	True	False	True	True	False

PROBLEMS

I

Provide the justification for each step. For this set of problems, use only the first ten rules of inference.

1. (1) $A \supset B$ Pr.
   (2) $B \supset C$ Pr. $/ \therefore A \supset C$

2. (1) $M \supset I$ Pr.
   (2) $M \lor P$ Pr.
   (3) $-I$ Pr.
   (4) $-M$ Pr. $/ \therefore P$

3. (1) $M \supset H$ Pr.
   (2) $H \supset S$ Pr.
   (3) $M \lor E$ Pr.
   (4) $-S$ Pr.
   (5) $M \supset S$
   (6) $-M$ $/ \therefore E$

4. (1) $W \supset M$ Pr.
   (2) $M \supset D$ Pr.
   (3) $W \lor C$ Pr.
   (4) $-D$ Pr.
   (5) $W \supset D$
   (6) $-W$ $/ \therefore C$

5. (1) $G \supset (S \supset U)$ Pr.
   (2) G Pr.
   (3) $-U$ Pr.
   (4) $S \supset U$ $/ \therefore -S$

6. (1) $G \supset C$ Pr.
   (2) $-C$ Pr. $/ \therefore -G$

7. (1) $-(W . P)$ Pr.
   (2) P Pr. $/ \therefore -W$

8. (1) $-(A . B)$ Pr.
   (2) B Pr.
   (3) $C \supset A$ Pr.
   (4) $-A$ Pr. $/ \therefore -C$

9. (1) $P \lor S$ Pr.
  (2) $P \supset M$ Pr.
  (3) $S \supset W$ Pr.
  (4) $-M$ Pr.
  (5) $-P$
  (6) S $/ \therefore W$

10. (1) $A \supset B$ Pr.
  (2) $B \supset C$ Pr.
  (3) $-C$ Pr.
  (4) $A \supset C$ Pr. $/ \therefore -A$

II

Using the suggested symbols, construct a proof of validity for each of the following, and provide justification for each step which is not a premise. Any of the rules of inference may be used.

1. Either Pete was not at home or he was asleep.
   If he was asleep, he was hard to waken.
   Pete was at home.
   Hence, he was hard to waken. [H, A, W]

2. Either Harry was not informed of the meeting or he is busy elsewhere.
   If he was busy elsewhere, he would have called the conference room.
   John says he was informed of the meeting.
   Hence, he will call the conference room. [H, B, C]

3. Either George is sick or both his secretary and his chauffer are absent.
   If George is sick, then he is at the hospital.
   If he is at the hospital, then his secretary is absent.
   Hence, his secretary is absent. [G, S, C, H]

4. If John is at home, his car is in the garage.
   If his car is in the garage, then his mother is at home.
   His mother is not at home.
   Hence, John is not at home. [J, G, M]

5. If the treasurer resigns his position, then it is false that he is both innocent and free from criticism.
   If an examination of his records reveals a balance, then he is innocent.
   If he is innocent, then he is free from criticism.
   An examination of his records reveals a balance.
   Hence, he will not resign his position. [R, I, F, B]

6. If John is out of work and Bill is sick, then there is dire need.
   John is out of work.
   There is not dire need.
   Hence, Bill is not sick. [J, B, N]

7. Either it will not be fair or there will be a game.
   If there is no pitcher, then there will be no game.
   Hence, if it is fair, then there will be a pitcher. [F, G, P]

8. If Goldenhoofs is fast, then he will win the race.
   If he wins the race, then he will earn a valuable purse.
   He will not earn a valuable purse.
   Hence, he is not fast.   [F, R, P]

9. If the paint is of first quality, then it will last for years.
   If it lasts for years, then we can afford to spend more on redecorating.
   If we can afford to spend more on redecorating, then the painter can afford to reduce his rate.
   But the painter says he cannot afford to reduce his rate.
   Either the paint is of first quality or the painter is a sharp operator.
   Hence, the painter is a sharp operator.   [F, Y, M, R, S]

10. If the note was forged, then Spencer was guilty.
    If Spencer was guilty, then he was broke.
    But he was not broke.
    Hence, Spencer was not guilty.   [F, G, B]

11. If today is the day of the clearance sale, then Louise went to town.
    If Louise went to town, then she drove in with Sarah.
    If she drove in with Sarah, then she would have phoned for me to pick her up.
    She did not phone for me to pick her up.
    Either today is the day of the clearance sale or the store has a new policy.
    Hence, the store has a new policy.   [S, T, D, F, N]

12. If Paul committed suicide, then there will be a note.
    If there is a note, then it will be in the house.
    If it is in the house, then a search will reveal it.
    A search failed to reveal the note.
    Either Paul committed suicide or he was murdered.
    Hence, Paul was murdered.   [P, N, H, S, M]

13. If the Chinese intend to attack, then they must assemble their forces.
    If they assemble their forces, then they will use extensive camouflage.
    If they use extensive camouflage, then our special equipment can detect it.
    Our special equipment cannot detect it.
    Either the Chinese intend to attack or they plan a political offensive.
    Hence, the Chinese plan a political offensive.   [C, A, E, D, P]

14. Either Pete was not at home or he was asleep.
    If he was asleep, then there was no one else in the house.
    Pete was at home.
    Hence, there was no one else in the house.   [P, A, N]

15. If Jones gets a diploma, then he will get the job.
    If he doesn't get a diploma, then he will not marry Susan.
    Either Jones is unlucky or he marries Susan.
    Hence, if he is lucky, he gets the job.   [D, J, S, L]

16. If the newspaper is closing its presses, then it is false that it is both influential and progressive.

If it is responsive to public opinion, then it is progressive.
If it is progressive, then it is influential.
It is responsive to public opinion.
Hence, it will not close its presses.   [C, I, P, R]

17. If Sam drives at 60 miles an hour, then he will arrive in one hour.
If his car breaks down, then he will not arrive in one hour.
Hence, if he drives at 60 miles an hour, his car will not breakdown.
[D, A, B]

18. I came to school this morning either by the Hollywood freeway or the Long Beach freeway.
But, since I live in Torrence, I didn't come by the Hollywood freeway.
Hence, I must have come by the Long Beach freeway.   [H, L, T]

19. If Oscar elects economics and either sociology or philosophy, then he will not be able to work part time.
But he intends to work part time and elect sociology.
Hence, he will not elect economics.   [E, S, P, W]

20. If John is a success at farming, then he will stay on the farm.
If he says on the farm, then he will make a good living.
He will not make a good living.
Hence, John is not a success at farming.   [S, F, G]

21. If George is willing, then, if Susan is at home, we can have a conference.
George is willing.
We shall not have a conference.
Hence, Susan is not at home.   [G, S, C]

22. If the museum is famous, then we should make a visit.
If we make a visit, then we should see the modern-art wing.
Either the museum is famous or the advertising is extravagant.
There is no modern-art wing.
Hence, the advertising is extravagant.   [M, V, W, E]

23. If Dr. Proudfoot's invention won the prize, then he must have received a check as well as the honor.
If he received a check, then there is a record of it in the secretary's checkbook.
There is no record of it in the secretary's checkbook.
Hence, Dr. Proudfoot did not receive a check.   [P, C, R]

24. If such a law is in effect, then it was passed by the legislature.
If it was passed by the legislature, then it will be recorded in the *Congressional Record.*
There is no account of it in the *Congressional Record.*
Hence, no such law was passed by the legislature.   [L, P, C]

25. If Johnson signed the note, then he is liable.
If he is liable, then he will need financial assistance.

If he needs financial assistance, then he can get it from either the bank or a mortgage loan.

He cannot get it from the bank.

Hence, he must get it from a mortgage loan. [*J, L, F, B, M*]

26. If it is a good weekly newspaper, then it makes money.
    If it makes money, then it will become a daily.
    Either it is a good weekly newspaper or it should change management.
    It will not become a daily.
    Hence, it should change management. [*W, M, D, C*]

27. If money is scarce, then interest is high.
    Either money is scarce or prices are high.
    Interest is not high.
    Money is not scarce.
    Hence, prices are high. [*M, I, P*]

28. Either Mary is an efficient typist or, if she finished her work, she must have had help.
    It is not the case that Mary is efficient or that she had help.
    Hence, she didn't finish her work. [*E, F, H*]

29. If country X is free, then, if it wishes to do so, it can control its own destiny.
    Country X is free.
    It does not control its destiny.
    Hence, it does not wish to do so. [*F, W, D*]

30. If it is summer, then the weather is hot.
    If it is not summer, then we do not have a vacation.
    Either we do not go on a business trip or we have a vacation.
    Hence, if we go on a business trip, then the weather is hot.

    [*S, H, V, B*]

31. If the Professor drives in by way of the city, then he will be exhausted, and, if he drives by way of the freeway, then he will be scared.
    If he is either exhausted or scared, then he will have a headache.
    But he does not have a headache.
    Hence, he did not drive in by way of the city or by way of the freeway. [*C, E, F, S, H*]

32. If Methuselah lived 969 years, then he must have had hardening of the arteries.
    If he had hardening of the arteries, then he was senile.
    Either Methuselah lived 969 years, or the Bible story is exaggerated.
    Methuselah was not senile.
    Hence, the Bible story is exaggerated. [*M, H, S, E*]

11

Quantification

In an earlier chapter, we saw that the two following arguments reach the same conclusion and deal with the same subject matter:

1. All animals are organisms.
   This creature is an animal.
   Hence, this creature is an organism.

2. If this creature is an animal, then it is an organism.
   This creature is an animal.
   Hence, this creature is an organism.

We can readily see that both arguments are valid. In the second case, we ignore the internal structure of the propositions and formulate the logical skeleton of the argument as a case of *modus ponens:* $[(p \supset q) . p] \supset q$. But we cannot do this with the first argument, since, if we tried to do so, we would have the invalid form of $(p . q) \supset r$.

We must, therefore, go beyond the simple propositional rules to carry out an analysis of such subject-predicate propositions as are exemplified in the first argument and provide a symbolism for subjects, predicates, and quentifier words such as "all," "no," and "some," which occur in these propositions, and provide by quantificational rules a method of testing arguments made up of such propositions.

I. SOME SYMBOLISM

The letters at the end of the alphabet, x, y, z, are used to symbolize individual variables and occur in place of nouns and pronouns. They refer to individual entities, but not to specific individuals. For example, "Some pilot was lost in the raid." "Some x was lost in the raid." The letters at the beginning of the alphabet, a, b, c, through *w,* are used to replace names of individuals or things and are called *individual constants.* The capital letters, *F, G, H,* etc., are used to symbolize predicates, that is, properties or characteristics asserted of entities or relations between entities, and are called *predicate constants.* Capital letters other than *F, G,* and *H* will also be used for predicates, such as *"W"* for warrior, *"O"* for orator, *"S"* for statesman. The predicate symbol is written immediately to the left of the variable. In "Alexander was a Greek warrior," the name "Alexander" is replaced by *"a,"* and the proposition is symbolized as *"Wa."*

II. THE UNIVERSAL QUANTIFIER

The phrase "for every x," symbolized by "(x)," is the *universal quantifier.* If we mean to assert that every individual has such and such an attribute, we express it as "For every x, Fx"; symbolically, "(x) Fx." The operation is called *universal quantification.*

If we wish to symbolize the proposition "All animals are organisms," we have

1. For everything in the universe, if it is an animal, then it is an organism.

Restated:

2. For every x in the universe, if x is an animal, then x is an organism.
3. (x) (x is an animal $\supset$ x is an organism).
4. (x) $(Ax \supset Ox)$, where "A" is animal and "O" is organism.

Synonyms for "all," such as "any," "each," and "every," are symbolized in the same way.

The universal negative "No animals are organisms" may be restated as follows:

1. For everything in the universe, if it is an animal, then it is not an organism.
2. For every x in the universe, if x is an animal, then x is not an organism.
3. (x) (x is an animal $\supset$ x is not an organism).
4. (x) $(Ax \supset -Ox)$. [This is also symbolized as $-(\exists x)$ $(Ax . Ox)$, as we shall see below. Likewise, synonyms, for "no," such as "no one," "nobody," and "none," may be treated in the same way.]

III. THE EXISTENTIAL QUANTIFIER

The symbol of the *existential quantifier* is $(\exists x)$, and corresponds to the words "There exists an x, such that . . . ."

The existential proposition "Some animals are organisms" may be restated as follows:

1. There exists at least one individual such that that individual is an animal and an organism.
2. There exists an x, such that x is an animal and x is an organism.
3. $(\exists x)$ (x is an animal and x is an organism).
4. $(\exists x)$ $(Ax \cdot Ox)$.

The existential quantifier for "some" is also used for synonyms such as "a few," "many," and "most."

Thus, the argument

> All animals are organisms.
> Some groundhogs are animals.
> Hence, some groundhogs are organisms.

is symbolized as follows:

$$(x)\ (Ax \supset Ox)$$
$$(\exists x)\ (Gx \cdot Ax)$$
$$(\exists x)\ (Gx \cdot Ox)$$

The method of proving the validity of such arguments will be treated later.

IV. FREE AND BOUND VARIABLES

A variable that is not governed by a quantifier is called a *free variable*. A *bound variable* is one which is governed by a quantifier. In the expression "(x) $(Fx \supset Gx)$," both the x after the F and the x after the G are quantified and are said to come within the scope of the quantifier, and are, therefore, bound variables. On the other hand, in the expression "(x) $Fx \supset Gx$," the x after the F is within the scope of the quantifier and, therefore, bound, but the x after the G is not and, hence, is said to be free. The *scope* of a quantifier is the quantifier together with the smallest formula immediately following the quantifier. Thus, the proper use of parentheses indicates the scope of the quantifier. In the formula "(y) $(Fy \supset Gx)$," the y is a bound variable and the x is free. In the formula ("$\exists x)$ (x is beautiful) $\lor$ (x is ugly)," the scope of the first quantifier does not extend to the second half of the expression. In the formula "$(\exists x)$ (y opposed x)," the occurrence of y is free, since there is no y in the quantifier, but the occurrences of x are bound because of the $(\exists x)$.

V. THE QUANTIFICATION OF A, E, I, AND O PROPOSITIONS

It will be instructive at this point to examine the traditional A, E, I, and O propositions in terms of symbolic quantification and to point out some implications of the modern analysis for the traditional square of opposition.

A: "All athletes are studious."
"x is an athlete" is symbolized as "Ax."
"x is studious" is symbolized as "Sx."
(1) "For everything in the universe, if x is an athlete, then x is studious."
(2) $(x) (Ax \supset Sx)$
(3) This may also be expressed as follows: "It is not the case that there is an x, such that x is an athlete and is not studious."
(4) Symbolized as follows: $-(\exists x) (Ax . -Sx)$

E: "No athletes are studious."
(1) May be expressed: "For everything in the universe, each x is such that, if x is an athlete, then x is not studious."
(2) $(x) (Ax \supset -Sx)$
(3) Or "It is not the case that there is an x, such that x is an athlete and x is studious."
(4) $-(\exists x) (Ax . Sx)$

I: "Some athletes are studious."
(1) "There exists an x, such that x is an athlete and x is studious."
(2) Something is an athlete *and* is studious.
(3) $(\exists x) (Ax . Sx)$. This should be carefully distinguished from the general implicative proposition "$(\exists x) (Ax \supset Sx)$," which means, "There is an x, such that, if x is an athlete, then x is studious."

O: "Some athletes are not studious."
(1) "There exists an x, such that x is an athlete and x is not studious."
(2) Something is an athlete *and* is not studious.
(3) $(\exists x) (Ax . -Sx)$

In Chapter 6, it was indicated that, in modern logic, the universal propositions A and E do not have "existential import"—that is, they do not imply the existence of their subject—whereas I and O propositions do. We interpreted "All animals are organisms" as hypothetical: "For all x's, if x is an animal, then x is an organism." It will be obvious that, if all of the relations illustrated on the square of opposition were to hold, the existential import of both universal and particular propositions would have to be assumed. If this assumption is not made, the traditional square must be greatly modified, since, in a case where the subject classes of A and E propositions are null, the I and O which do have members could not be inferred from them.

To illustrate the problem further, let us take the propositions "All of the mammalian barracuda we caught are in the net" and the corresponding E, "None of the mammalian barracuda we caught are in the net." Both of these propositions would be true if there existed no mammalian barracuda, and their contradictories, O and I, would then both be false, but all of the other relations in the square of opposition would be annulled. We could not infer the I from the A, nor the O from the E, since and I and O imply existence. There would be no contraries, subcontraries, superimplication, or subimplication. The only relations remaining would be the contradictories and independence. The simplified square of opposition could be represented as follows:

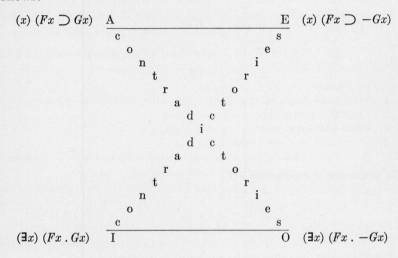

$(x) (Fx \supset Gx)$ A   E $(x) (Fx \supset -Gx)$

$(\exists x) (Fx . Gx)$ I   O $(\exists x) (Fx . -Gx)$

VI. PROVING VALIDITY OF QUANTIFICATIONAL ARGUMENTS

In addition to the rules of inference which have been utilized for truth-functional deductions (pp. 160–61), there is need of several additional rules for quantificational arguments. These will be stated briefly before we proceed to illustrate them by examples. A quantificational argument may contain several kinds of variables—viz., propositional variables, p, q, r; predicate variables, F, G, H; and proper-name variables, a, a_1, a_2, etc. An argument is valid if there is no possible case in which the premises are true and the conclusion false, with respect to every universe of discourse.

1. Universal Generalization—U.G. This is the rule that enables us to replace a singular quantifier with a universal quantifier. For example, the Constitution of the United States provides that a senator must be at least thirty years of age. If John Doe is a United States senator, he must be at least thirty years old. If this qualification applies to *any* senator, it applies to *all* senators, and we argue from any arbitrarily selected member to the universal. Symbolically:

$$\frac{Pa}{\therefore\ (x)\ Px}$$

where *a* denotes any arbitrarily selected individual. This rule excludes names introduced through the use of E.I. (see below).

2. Existential Generalization—E.G. This rule is based upon the assumption that, if in a certain universe of discourse it is true that a given individual which belongs to the universe is such and such, then it must be true that some individual which belongs to the universe is such and such. It enables us to replace a singular by an existential quantifier. For example,

1. Tom Jones is the hero of a book.
2. Davy Jones is lost in the deep.
1. There is someone who is hero of a book.
2. There is someone who is lost in the deep.

$$\frac{Pa}{\therefore\ (\exists x)\ Px}$$

3. Universal Instantiation—U.I. This is a rule which permits substitution instances to be inferred from universal quantifications. It enables us to replace a universal quantifier with a singular quantifier. A proposition true of everything is true of any arbitrarily specified individual. From a universally quantified expression such as $(x)\ Fx$, we can infer any instance of it, such as the following:

$$\frac{(x)\ Fx}{\therefore\ Fa}$$

where *a* is any individual symbol.

4. Existential Instantiation—E.I. This rule means that, from any existential quantification, we may infer any instance of it. It enables us to replace a particular quantifier with a singular quantifier. An existentially quantified formula tells us that "there is at least one individual such that . . . ," so we can select an arbitrary individual (but not a particular individual who can be given a proper name) and identify it by some specific designation such as "*a*," e.g.,

$$\frac{(\exists x)\ Gx}{\therefore\ Ga}$$

where *a* is an individual constant having no prior occurrence in the deduction; that is, for each occurrence of E.I., a different name must be used.

For the purposes of gradually becoming familiar with the procedure of proving validity of quantified arguments, let us begin with some that are very simple:

All animals are organisms.   Symbols: $(x) (Ax \supset Ox)$
All groundhogs are animals. $(x) (Gx \supset Ax)$
Hence, all groundhogs are organisms. ∴ $(x) (Gx \supset Ox)$

1. $(x) (Ax \supset Ox)$ Pr.
2. $(x) (Gx \supset Ax)$ Pr.
3. $Aa \supset Oa$ 1, U.I.
4. $Ga \supset Aa$ 2, U.I.
5. $Ga \supset Oa$ 3, 4, H.S.
6. $(x) (Gx \supset Ox)$ (conclusion)   5, U.G.

Now let us demonstrate one that contains both universal and existential quantifiers:

All animals are organisms.   Symbols: $(x) (Ax \supset Ox)$
Some groundhogs are animals. $(\exists x) (Gx . Ax)$
Hence, some groundhogs are organisms. ∴ $(\exists x) (Gx . Ox)$

Since the rules of E.I., U.I., and E.G. are to be used in the following deduction, the restriction should be noted that the E.I. must be applied to the existential formula before the U.I. may be applied to the universal formula. (The reason for this restriction is that, if in the following example we were to apply U.I. to 1 after line 2 to obtain 4, we should not be able to produce line 3, since E.I. does not allow the use of a name which has previously occurred.)

1. $(x) (Ax \supset Ox)$ Pr.
2. $(\exists x) (Gx . Ax)$ Pr.
3. $Ga . Aa$ 2, E.I.
4. $Aa \supset Oa$ 1, U.I.
5. $Aa . Ga$ 3, Comm.
6. Aa 5, Simp.
7. Oa 4, 6, M.P.
8. Ga 3, Simp.
9. $Ga . Oa$ 8, 7, Conj.
10. $(\exists x) (Gx . Ox)$ (conclusion)   9, E.G.

Let us test for validity another argument in which the E.I. must be applied to the existential formula before the U.I. is applied to the universal:

All pigs are cloven-footed. Symbols: $(x) (Px \supset Cx)$
Some horses are not cloven-footed. $(\exists x) (Hx . -Cx)$
Hence, some horses are not pigs.   ∴ $(\exists x) (Hx . -Px)$

1.	$(x) (Px \supset Cx)$	Pr.
2.	$(\exists x) (Hx . -Cx)$	Pr.
3.	$Ha . -Ca$	2, E.I.
4.	$Pa \supset Ca$	1, U.I.
5.	$-Ca \supset -Pa$	4, Contra.
6.	$-Ca$	3, Simp.
7.	$-Pa$	5, 6, M.P.
8.	Ha	3, Simp.
9.	$Ha . -Pa$	7, 8, Conj.
10.	$(\exists x) (Hx . -Px)$ (conclusion)	9, E.G.

The validation procedure for more complex arguments involving a longer chain of deductions is illustrated by the following:

> Some racers dislike driving.
> Everyone who dislikes driving gets nervous.
> No one who gets nervous is a good driver.
> Some racers are not good drivers.

> Rx = racers
> Dx = dislike driving
> Nx = gets nervous
> Gx = good driver

$$(\exists x) (Rx . Dx)$$
$$(x) (Dx \supset Nx)$$
$$(x) (Nx \supset -Gx)$$
$$\therefore (\exists x) (Rx . -Gx)$$

The proof is as follows:

1.	$(\exists x) (Rx . Dx)$	Pr.	
2.	$(x) (Dx \supset Nx)$	Pr.	
3.	$(x) (Nx \supset -Gx)$	Pr.	$/ \therefore (\exists x) (Rx . -Gx)$
4.	$Ra . Da$	1, E.I.	
5.	$Da \supset Na$	2, U.I.	
6.	$Na \supset -Ga$	3, U.I.	
7.	$Da . Ra$	4, Comm.	
8.	Ra	4, Simp.	
9.	Da	7, Simp.	
10.	Na	5, 9, M.P.	
11.	$-Ga$	6, 10 M.P.	
12.	$Ra . -Ga$	8, 11, Conj.	
13.	$(\exists x) (Rx . -Gx)$ (conclusion)	12, E.G.	

Another example:

Some who will rocket to the moon are experienced astronauts.
Anyone who is an experienced astronaut is a space scientist and technician.

All space scientists and technicians understand mathematics and navigation.
All of those who understand mathematics and navigation are also experienced
pilots.
Hence, some who will rocket to the moon are experienced pilots.

$$Rx = \text{rocket}$$
$$Ax = \text{astronaut}$$
$$Sx = \text{scientist}$$
$$Tx = \text{technician}$$
$$Mx = \text{mathematics}$$
$$Nx = \text{navigation}$$
$$Px = \text{pilots}$$

1. $(\exists x) Rx . Ax$	Pr.	
2. $(x) Ax \supset (Sx . Tx)$	Pr.	
3. $(x) (Sx . Tx) \supset (Mx . Nx)$	Pr.	
4. $(x) (Mx . Nx) \supset Px$	Pr.	$/ \therefore (\exists x) (Rx . Px)$
5. $Ra . Aa$	1, E.I.	
6. $Aa \supset (Sa . Ta)$	2, U.I.	
7. Aa	5, Simp.	
8. $Sa . Ta$	6, 7, M.P.	
9. $(Sa . Ta) \supset (Ma . Na)$	3, U.I.	
10. $Ma . Na$	8, 9, M.P.	
11. $(Ma . Na) \supset Pa$	4, U.I.	
12. Pa	10, 11, M.P.	
13. Ra	5, Simp.	
14. $Ra . Pa$	12, 13, Conj.	
15. $(\exists x) (Rx . Px)$ (conclusion)	14, E.G.	

Finally, let us illustrate a type of argument which does not fit into
the traditional syllogistic schema because of its compound predicate.
For example,

Geniuses are irritable and brilliant. Symbols:	$(x) Gx \supset (Ix . Bx)$
Some musicians are geniuses.	$(\exists x) (Mx . Gx)$
Hence, some brilliant people are musicians.	$\therefore (\exists x) (Bx . Mx)$

1. $(x) Gx \supset (Ix . Bx)$	Pr.	
2. $(\exists x) (Mx . Gx)$	Pr.	$/ \therefore (\exists x) (Bx . Mx)$
3. $Ma . Ga$	2, E.I.	
4. $Ga \supset (Ia . Ba)$	1, U.I.	
5. Ga	3, Simp.	
6. $Ia . Ba$	4, 5, M.P.	
7. Ba	6, Simp.	
8. $Ga . Ma$	3, Comm.	
9. Ma	8, Simp.	
10. $Ba . Ma$	7, 9, Conj.	
11. $(\exists x) (Bx . Mx)$ (conclusion)	10, E.G.	

VII. PROVING INVALIDITY

In the preceding chapter, an illustration was given of a method of proving invalidity by assigning values of truth and falsity to the parts of an argument so that the premises will be true and the conclusion false. Let us use the following example of a quantified argument to show invalidity:

All interns are overworked.	Symbols: $(x)\ (Ix \supset Ox)$
All interns are underpaid.	$(x)\ (Ix \supset Ux)$
Hence, everyone who is overworked is underpaid.	$\therefore\ (x)\ (Ox \supset Ux)$

Assuming a domain of only one member, a, this argument is logically equivalent to

$$Ia\ \text{(False)} \supset Oa\ \text{(True)}$$
$$Ia\ \text{(False)} \supset Ua\ \text{(False)}$$
$$\therefore\ Oa\ \text{(True)} \supset Ua\ \text{(False)}$$

The argument can be proved invalid by assigning the truth value "true" to Oa and the value "false" to Ia and Ua, inasmuch as any conditional with a true antecedent and a false consequent is false.

PROBLEMS

I

Express the following propositions in terms of symbols of quantification:

1. Not all bankers are rich.
2. Unicorns do not exist.
3. What is rare is costly.
4. Sunsets are sometimes beautiful.
5. The majority of the audience are either soldiers or sailors.
6. Few college graduates are unemployed.
7. A philospher is either tender-minded or tough-minded
8. Anyone seeking knowledge is lucky.
9. Only man is a symbolizing animal.
10. If the candidate arrives on time, then, if he speaks, he will win.
11. Some logic texts are not difficult.
12. Lobsters and clams are delicious.
13. Any politician must be prepared for conflict and opposition.
14. If the fire is controlled, then, if the wind dies down, the inmates are safe.
15. All members of the ballet are strong and graceful.
16. No runners are winners unless they are well trained.
17. Something is to be proposed at the meeting if a quorum is present.

18. Some kitchen utensils are both useful and beautiful.
19. Pets are sometimes expensive.
20. Most professional wrestlers are athletes.
21. Television is a waste of time.
22. It is not the case that all coffee comes from Brazil.
23. If he is a gambler, then he is unreliable.
24. Some people are pleasant to nobody.
25. A good driver is able to anticipate the actions of other drivers.
26. John is a pilot and a mechanic.

II

Construct a proof of validity or invalidity for each of the following, using the suggested symbolism:

1. All missionaries are morally reputable, and some visitors to this resort are missionaries; hence, some visitors to this resort are morally reputable. [M, R, V]

2. All things which foretell the future are magical, and some Ouija boards foretell the future; hence, some Ouija boards are magical. [F, M, O]

3. Only upperclassmen are eligible for admission. Tom is not an upperclassman. Hence, Tom has rightfully been denied admission. [U, E, t]

4. No immoral business is respectable; hence, dope peddling cannot be respectable, since certainly it is immoral. [I, R, D]

5. All members of this organization are war veterans, and all supporters of bonus legislation are members of this organization; hence, all supporters of bonus legislation are war veterans. [O, W, B]

6. All those who are expert teachers have the confidence of their students. Joe does not have the confidence of his students. Hence, Joe is not an expert teacher. [E, C, j]

7. All those interested in progress are good citizens, and all good citizens are interested in education; hence, all those interested in progress are interested in education. [P, C, E]

8. No college graduates are members of this club. All members of the alumni association are college graduates. Hence, no members of the alumni association are members of this club. [G, M, A]

9. All civilized nations are progressive, and some nations which are civilized are restless; hence, some restless nations are progressive. [C, P, R]

10. No person who likes to talk is a diplomat, and all fluent writers are persons who like to talk; hence, no diplomats are fluent writers. [T, D, F]

III

Construct a proof of validity or invalidity for each of the following, using the suggested symbolism:

1. Some reactionaries try to destroy organized labor, and everyone who tries to destroy organized labor belongs to the old party. No one who belongs to the old party is in favor of progressive legislation; hence, some reactionaries are not in favor of progressive legislation. [R, D, O, P]

2. All persons who believe in democracy are believers in the dignity of

man, and all those who believe in the dignity of man are also humanists. Some Fascists are believers in the dignity of man; hence, some Fascists are also humanists. [*D, M, H, F*]

3. All gladiators are strong, and strong men make good fighters. Some Romans were gladiators; hence, some Romans were good fighters. [*G, S, F, R*]

4. Some workers are diligent but not skilful, and every worker is willing to be reasonable. Not all workers are diligent, but every housewife is; hence, some who are willing to be reasonable are not housewives. [*W, D, S, R, H*]

5. No one who is skilled at poker will lose if he persists, and anyone who plays in Gardena is skilled at poker. Anyone who does not lose is lucky; hence, if anyone plays in Gardena, he is lucky if he persists. [*S, L, G, P*]

6. All army men will salute when faced by an officer, and every officer will face an army man if he sees him malingering. In base camp, many officers face many malingering soldiers; hence, in base camp, many soldiers are saluting. [*A, S, O, M, B*]

7. Only scientists employ scientific methods, and only humanists are interested in the humanities. None of the scientists or humanists are interested in music, and music is vital to humanity; hence, some scientists and humanists are not interested in things vital to humanity. [*S, M, H, I, M, V*]

8. Many bank accounts have small balances, and every small balance is a risky business. Nothing that is a risky business is a good investment; hence, many bank accounts are not good investments. [*B, S, R, G*]

12

Extrasyllogistic and Relational Arguments

I. ENTHYMEMES

We have already illustrated the prevalence in everyday discourse of elliptical arguments where one premise or the conclusion is unexpressed. This is often done for literary effect, since the suppressed proposition is assumed to be so well understood that it would seem pedantic to state it. Abbreviated arguments of this kind are known as *enthymemes*, literally meaning "to hold in mind," and suggesting that some part of the argument is not expressed. In enthymemes the elliptical expression often hides a fallacy, and as Aristotle has pointed out, enthymemes are better for persuasion than explicit syllogisms. Enthymemes are of three kinds. If it is the major premise that is omitted, the argument is said to be an enthymeme of the *first order;* if the minor premise is omitted, it is of the *second order;* and if the conclusion is not stated, it is of the *third order.*

An example of an enthymeme of the *first order* is found in Antony's oration over the body of Caesar:

> He would not take the crown
> Therefore 'tis certain he was not ambitious.

Other examples:

> Senator Jones is well fitted for the office, because he has shown himself a
> man of sound principles.
> He pays the piper, so he calls the tune.

Examples of the omission of the minor premise, enthymemes of the *second order* are

> None of his family will be flyers, for no one with poor eyesight is able to fly.
> Mr. Jones is a good student, for any student recommended by Professor Brown is a good student.

Examples of the omission of the conclusion, enthymemes of the *third order*, are as follows:

> Any position Professor Jones takes on this issue is a sound one, and this is Professor Jones's position.

Again from Antony's oration:

> But Brutus says he was ambitious
> And Brutus is an honorable man.

Notice that the logical conclusion of this enthymeme does not agree with the conclusion insinuated by Antony. The student should, after supplying the missing premise or conclusion test the above arguments to see if they are valid.

II. POLYSYLLOGISMS

A polysyllogism is a chain of syllogisms in which the conclusion of one syllogism is made a premise of another. It is made up of two parts, a prosyllogism and an episyllogism. A prosyllogism is a syllogism whose conclusion is made a premise of a succeeding syllogism. An episyllogism is a syllogism which takes for its premise the conclusion of a preceding syllogism.

Form:

> All A is B.
> All B is C.
> ∴ All A is C.
> ——————
> All C is D.
> ∴ All A is D.

Example:

Pro-syllo-gism { All building is an expression of architecture.
All expression of architecture is an expression of art.
∴ All building is an expression of art.
All expression of art is an expression of culture. } Epi-syllo-gism
∴ All building is an expression of culture.

It will be observed that in order to make two syllogisms in correct form from these, the premises must be transposed in order to place the major premise in each case in its proper first position.   Thus:

> All expression of architecture is an expression of art.
> All building is an expression of architecture.
> ∴ All building is an expression of art.
> ───
> All expression of art is an expression of culture.
> All building is an expression of art.
> ∴ All building is an expression of culture.

Form:

> All B is C.
> All A is B.
> ∴ All A is C.
> ─────────────
> All C is D.
> All A is C.
> ∴ All A is D.

III. SORITES

The sorites is a polysyllogism in which only the final conclusion is expressed.   Literally, it means *a heap* or a piling up of arguments yielding a conclusion.   The premises must be so arranged that any two successive premises must contain a common or middle term.

The Aristotelian or *progressive* sorites expands the argument from the least inclusive term to the most inclusive.   The subject of the first premise and the predicate of the last premise are united in the conclusion.   The middle term in any two successive premises appears first as the predicate term and then as the subject term.

Form:

> All A is B.
> All B is C.
> All C is D.
> All D is E.
> ─────────────
> ∴ All A is E.

Example:

All merely mechanical labor is tiresome.
All tiresome methods are harmful to initiative.
All methods harmful to initiative are uneconomical.
All uneconomical methods are socially undesirable.
Therefore, all merely mechanical labor is socially undesirable.

This may be illustrated by concentric circles representing classes.

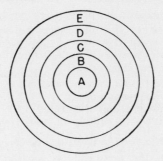

The Goclenian sorites (so called after Goclenius; also called *regressive* sorites) moves from the most inclusive term to the least inclusive and unites the subject of the last premise and the predicate of the first in the conclusion. The middle term in any two successive premises appears first as the subject term and then as the predicate term.

Form:

　　All B is A.
　　All C is B.
　　All D is C.
　　All E is D.
∴ All E is A.

Example:

All uneconomical methods are socially undesirable.
All methods harmful to initiative are uneconomical.
All tiresome methods are harmful to initiative.
All merely mechanical labor is tiresome.
Therefore, all merely mechanical labor is socially undesirable.

This likewise may be illustrated by the following diagram:

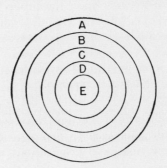

There are certain rules which must be followed in each of the above sorites if fallacies are to be avoided. A careful examination will show why this is so.

Rules for the Aristotelian Sorites

1. Only one premise, the *last,* can be negative; all others must be affirmative.
2. Only one premise, the *first,* can be particular; all others must be universal.

Violation of the first rule involves the fallacy of *illicit major.* Violation of the second involves the fallacy of *undistributed middle.*

Rules for the Goclenian Sorites

1. Only one premise, the *first,* can be negative; all others must be affirmative.
2. Only one premise, the *last,* can be particular; all others must be universal.

Violation of the first rule involves the fallacy of *illicit major,* and violation of the second involves the fallacy of *undistributed middle.*

IV. RELATIONAL ARGUMENTS

In our discussion of forms of categorical propositions in Chapter 6, we saw that the relation between terms expressed by the verb "to be" is interpreted in various ways such as predication, class inclusion, class membership, and identity. But it is obvious that, in addition to propositions of this kind, there are propositions which assert an indefinite number of relations between terms, such as mathematical, space, and time relations, and that these may be so related in an argument that valid deductions may be made because of the properties of the relations. In relational propositions, the emphasis is placed not upon the subject and predicate terms of the proposition, nor upon class inclusion and exclusion, but upon the relations between terms, and the validity of relational arguments depends upon the properties of the relations. Relations are diadic, triadic, tetradic, etc., depending upon the number of terms related. We shall confine our discussion to the simplest diadic relations such as "A is *equal* to B" and "This book is *to the right of* that book." Such relational propositions are symbolized as $R(a, b)$ and are diadic. Triadic relations such as "Niagara is *between* New York and Chicago," are symbolized as $R(a, b, c)$. Some of these relations and their properties were discussed under immediate inference, but it is now necessary to complete the analysis for the purpose of showing how relational propositions may be combined in nonsyllogistic arguments. These are not syllogisms, since they involve four terms. For example:

> X is taller than Y.
> Y is taller than Z.
> ∴ X is taller than Z.

The four terms here are X, taller than Y, Y, and taller than Z.

1. The Analysis of Relational Properties. (*a*) *Symmetry*. Symmetrical relations are such that if they hold between *a* and *b*, they also hold between *b* and *a* (e.g., married to, equal to, identical with, etc.). In symbols, a relation, R, is symmetrical when it is such that if *a* R *b*, then *b* R *a*.

> Example: Peter's grades are equal to Paul's.
> Paul's grades are equal to Peter's.

(*b*) *Asymmetry*. Asymmetrical relations are such that if they hold between *a* and *b*, they cannot hold between *b* and *a* (e.g., father of, greater than, builder of). In symbols, a relation, R, is asymmetrical when it is such that if *a* R *b*, then it is never *b* R *a*.

> Example: George is the father of Henry.
> Henry cannot be the father of George.

(*c*) *Nonsymmetry*. Nonsymmetrical relations are such that if they hold between *a* and *b*, they may or may not hold between *b* and *a* (e.g., friend of, loves, hates). In symbols, a relation, R, is nonsymmetrical when it is such that if *a* R *b*, then *b* may or may not be R *a*.

> Example: Mary loves John.
> John may or may not love Mary.

The above properties characterize relations between any two terms. Those that follow characterize relations between pairs of terms and thus enable us to combine propositions containing a given relation in the form of arguments.

(*d*) *Transitivity*. Relations are called transitive if, when *a* stands in relation to *b* and *b* stands in relation to *c*, then *a* must stand in the same relation to *c* (e.g., greater than, equal to, is included in). In symbols, a relation, R, is transitive when it is such that, if *a* R *b* and *b* R *c*, then *a* R *c*.

> Example: Hitler was younger than Mussolini.
> Mussolini was younger than Roosevelt.
> Hence, Hitler was younger than Roosevelt.

(*e*) *Intransitivity*. Relations are called intransitive if, when *a* stands in a certain relation to *b* and *b* to *c*, then *a* cannot stand in the same relation to *c* (e.g., father of, older by one year.) In symbols, a relation, R, is intransitive when it is such that, if *a* R *b* and *b* R *c*, then it never occurs that *a* R *c*.

Example: George is the father of Henry.
Henry is the father of William.
Hence, George cannot be the father of William.

(*f*) *Nontransitivity*. Relations are called nontransitive if, when *a* stands in a certain relation to *b*, and *b* to *c*, then *a* may or may not stand in the same relation to *c* (e.g., friend of, loves, hates). In symbols, a relation, R, is nontransitive when it is such that, if *a* R *b* and *b* R *c*, then *a* may or may not be R *c*.

Example: Sam is a friend of Dan
Dan is a friend of Bob.
Hence, Sam may or may not be a friend of Bob.

The above six properties of relations may be combined in several ways. The following combinations exhaust the logical possibilities:

(1) Symmetrical transitive
(2) Asymmetrical transitive
(3) Nonsymmetrical transitive
(4) Symmetrical intransitive
(5) Asymmetrical intransitive
(6) Nonsymmetrical intransitive
(7) Symmetrical nontransitive
(8) Asymmetrical nontransitive
(9) Nonsymmetrical nontransitive

2. The Validity of Relational Arguments. Relational propositions can be symbolized, and, by the use of constants, quantifiers, and rules of inference, formal proof of validity or invalidity can be demonstrated, but this would take us beyond an elementary treatment. Whether or not a valid conclusion can be inferred from relational premises depends upon the logical properties of the relation. We shall confine our discussion to examples of relational arguments, both valid and invalid, illustrative of the nine combinations of relational properties above.

Rule governing validity of relational arguments: In all arguments involving premises with transitive relations, the validity of the argument depends upon *the transitivity of the relation*, and the relation must remain the same in premises and conclusion.

(*a*) *Symmetrical transitive arguments.*

Example: The area of lot X is equal to lot Y.
The area of lot Y is equal to lot Z.
Hence, the area of lot X is equal to lot Z.

In our discussion of the various interpretations of the copula, or verb "to be," of the categorical syllogism, we listed that of *identity* as one interpretation. This may also be interpreted as a relation, and it will be recognized as belonging under this head of symmetrical transitive relations and will yield a valid conclusion because of the transitivity of the relation.

Example: Angle A is identical with angle B.
Angle B is identical with angle C.
Hence, angle A is identical with angle C.

(*b*) *Asymmetrical transitive arguments.*

Example: The Amazon River is greater than the St. Lawrence.
The St. Lawrence River is greater than the Hudson.
Hence, the Amazon River is greater than the Hudson.

A *fortiori* arguments (from the Latin, *a fortiori ratione*, "from a stronger reason") are also asymmetrical and transitive and depend upon the property of transitivity for their validity, although not all transitive relations yield *a fortiori* conclusions. Relations such as "greater than," "better than," and "stronger than" are examples.

Example: The evidence for the guilt of B is stronger than that for C.
The evidence for the guilt of A is stronger than that for B.
Hence, the evidence for the guilt of A is stronger than that for C.

(*c*) *Nonsymmetrical transitive arguments.*

Example: An increase in wages implies higher prices.
Higher prices imply an inflation.
Hence, an increase in wages implies an inflation.

In our discussion of the categorical syllogism, we also saw that the verb "to be" may be interpreted as asserting *class inclusion.* Class inclusion when considered as a relation is both nonsymmetrical and transitive, and the validity of the argument depends upon the transitivity of the relation.

Example: All men are included in the class of organisms.
All Caucasians are included in the class of men.
Hence, all Caucasians are included in the class of organisms.

(*d*) *Symmetrical intransitive arguments.* If we adopt the rule given above, that the validity of a relational argument depends upon the transitivity of the relation, the following argument is invalid because the relation "spouse of" is intransitive.

Example: Anne Boleyn was the spouse of Henry VIII.
Henry VIII was the spouse of Catherine of Aragon.
Hence, Anne Boleyn was the spouse of Catherine of Aragon.

(e) *Asymmetrical intransitive arguments.* Asymmetrical intransitive relations yield an invalid conclusion when the relation remains the same in premises and conclusion. But when the relation is changed in the conclusion, the argument will be valid.

Example: George is the father of Henry.
Henry is the father of William.
Hence, George is the grandfather of (or *not the father of*) William.

(f) *Nonsymmetrical intransitive arguments.*

Example: Mary is the closest friend of John.
John is the closest friend of Sally.
Hence, Mary is the closest friend of Sally.

The relation is intransitive and remains the same in premises and conclusion and the conclusion does not follow.

(g) *Symmetrical nontransitive arguments.* In arguments with nontransitive relations *the conclusion may or may not follow,* and whether it does or not must be determined by the context of the argument.

Example: Jones's income is different from Smith's.
Smith's income is different from Brown's.
Hence, Jones's income is different from Brown's.

(h) *Asymmetrical nontransitive arguments.*

Example: Citizen Ford is a benefactor of laborer Smith.
Laborer Smith is a benefactor of the local church.
Hence, Citizen Ford is a benefactor of the local church.

We have still to account for the traditional categorical propositions known as *class membership* propositions of the form "Plato was a Greek philosopher" in terms of relations. The relation of class membership is asymmetrical and nontransitive and yields a doubtful conclusion.

Example: The student is a member of the University.
The University is a member of the Association of American Universities.
Hence, the student is a member of the Association of American Universities.

(*i*) *Nonsymmetrical nontransitive arguments.*

Example: Antony was a lover of Cleopatra.
Cleopatra was a lover of Caesar.
Hence, Antony was a lover of Caesar.

3. Miscellaneous Relational Arguments. (*a*) *Elimination arguments.*
When one premise expresses the transitive relation of *identity* or
inclusion, and the other *denies the relation,* or *is different,* a valid
conclusion follows if the relation of identity or inclusion is *eliminated*
in the conclusion.

Example of identity denied:

The capital of California is identical with Sacramento.
Sacramento is *not identical* with Los Angeles.
Hence, the capital of California is not identical with Los Angeles.

Example of inclusion and a different relation:

Company 80 is included in Battalion 64.
Battalion 64 *is on occupational assignment.*
Hence, Company 80 *is on occupational assignment.*

(*b*) *Fusion arguments.* When the relations in the premises differ,
the relations may be *combined* in the conclusion.

Examples: Jones is a partner of Smith.
Smith is a more industrious man than Brown.
Hence, Jones is a partner of a more industrious man than
Brown.

Wisconsin is north of Illinois.
Minnesota is west of Wisconsin.
Hence, Minnesota is *northwest* of Illinois.

(*c*) *Substitution arguments.*

Example: Peter is the paternal grandfather of Paul.
Paul is the son of Patrick.
Hence, Peter is the father of Patrick.

PROBLEMS

1. Supply the missing premise or conclusion in the enthymemes in
the first section of this chapter, and indicate whether they are valid
or invalid.

2. Construct both an Aristotelian and a Goclenian sorites, and
demonstrate the nature of the fallacies present when each of the rules
of the sorites is broken.

3. Classify the following enthymemes under first, second, or third order, and supply the missing premise or conclusion:

(1) "Only an innocent fool could have remained unaware of the crookedness practiced by the Long gang in that primary, and I shall never contend that Smith is either innocent or a fool."
—WESTBROOK PEGLER

(2) There must be a sadistic streak in this man, for he takes pleasure in punishing his dog.

(3) The football team with the heaviest line should win the game; therefore, our football team should win.

(4) No spoiled children are attractive, since no selfish children are attractive.

(5) The unit price is low; therefore, sales resistance is low.

(6) The events reported must have happened, because I saw the account in the *Manchester Guardian*.

(7) Professor Smith must be an expert in his field, because he occupies an important chair in the university.

(8) Tonight is either Monday, Wednesday, or Friday; hence, we are open tonight.

(9) We are open on Monday, Wednesday, and Friday nights; hence, we are open tonight.

(10) We are open on Monday, Wednesday, and Friday nights, and tonight is Wednesday night.

(11) "If he contend, as sometimes he will contend, that he has defined all his terms and proved all his propositions, then either he is a performer of logical miracles or he is an ass; and as you know, logical miracles are impossible."—C. J. KEYSER

4. State whether the following relations are symmetrical transitive, asymmetrical transitive, nonsymmetrical transitive, symmetrical intransitive, asymmetrical intransitive, nonsymmetrical intransitive, symmetrical nontransitive, asymmetrical nontransitive, or nonsymmetrical nontransitive:

obligated to	confidant of	as old as
superior to	contemporary with	divisible by
known to	tangent to	ancestor of
amused at	genus of	lover of
angry at	contradictory of	cousin of
indebted to	species of	father of
synchronous with	descendant of	to the left of
independent of	incompatible with	east of
congruous with	caused by	spouse of
dependent on	included in	employer of
relative of	presupposed by	after, in time
symmetrical with	generated by	landlord of
adjacent to	murderer of	nearest relative of
offensive to	contrary to	

5. Examine the following relational arguments, and indicate the properties of the relations and whether the arguments are valid or invalid and why.

(1) The toastmaster sat next to the speaker.
The speaker sat next to the guest of honor.
Therefore, the toastmaster sat next to the guest of honor.

(2) The state of Illinois is a member of the United States.
The United States is a member of the United Nations.
Therefore, the state of Illinois is a member of the United Nations.

(3) Pittsburgh is east of Chicago.
Chicago is east of Denver.
Therefore, Pittsburgh is east of Denver.

(4) Mr. X wrapped the package before the messenger arrived.
The messenger arrived before the crime was committed.
Therefore, Mr. X wrapped the package before the crime was committed.

(5) The workers are excluded from the organization.
The organization is excluded from the plant.
Therefore, the workers are excluded from the plant.

(6) Ruth is engaged to Tony.
Tony is wealthier than Mike.
Therefore, Ruth is engaged to a wealthier boy than Mike.

(7) The icebox is colder than the bedroom.
The bedroom is colder than the kitchen.
Therefore, the icebox is colder than the kitchen.

(8) Susan is the daughter of Helen.
Helen is the sister of Marguerite.
Therefore, Susan is the niece of Marguerite.

(9) Smith is a better presiding officer than Jones.
Jones is a better presiding officer than Johnson.
Therefore, Smith is a better presiding officer than Johnson.

(10) The defendant agrees with the evidence presented to the court.
The evidence presented to the court agrees with the court's decision.
Therefore, the defendant agrees with the court's decision.

(11) Senator X offended his political constituents.
His political constituents offended the national party.
Therefore, Senator X offended the national party.

(12) His ability to speak well is irrelevant to his political views.
His political views are irrelevant to his effective service in office.
Therefore, his ability to speak well is irrelevant to his effective service in office.

IV

SCIENTIFIC METHODS

13

The Nature of
Scientific Knowledge

I. INTRODUCTION

In the first part of our study we were concerned with deductive inference, and we learned how to derive valid and necessary conclusions from a premise or premises which implied them. This is known as the process of formal proof in which the truth of the propositions composing the argument was not particularly in the foreground; that is, the propositions were regarded as being purely formal, as asserting hypothetical facts, or as being taken for granted for the sake of the argument. It was assumed in making the distinction between validity and truth that we understood in a general way what is meant by truth, and we saw that if the premises are true and the argument valid the conclusion will be necessarily true. Also, in our treatment of immediate inference, the Square of Opposition, Truth Tables, and the relations between propositions, the values "true" and "false" were used, but no attempt was made to analyze these concepts.

We are now ready to approach the problem directly and to ask how propositions or truth claims are verified or falsified, confirmed or tested. In other words, what are the grounds of rational belief?

It is already obvious that propositions vary greatly with respect to difficulty of confirmation. Consider the following set of propositions:

1. This book is red.
2. There are 100 chairs in this room.
3. This weight is heavier than this one pound of butter.
4. If it rains, the pavements will be slippery.
5. Light travels at the rate of 186,300 miles per second.

6. All bodies gravitate toward the center of the earth.
7. Sunspots are causally related to magnetic phenomena.
8. Every man has the right to the products of his own labor.
9. The oppressed will turn against their oppressors.
10. It is more blessed to give than to receive.
11. Men ought not to kill one another.
12. This painting is very beautiful.
13. God is Love.
14. The empirical ego survives the death of the body.

The first four propositions are on the elementary level of common sense, and their truth or falsity is doubted by no one with normal perception. They have as grounds of their truth claim such data and operations as immediate perception, common sense, counting, measurement, and probability judgments. The next three (5, 6, 7) belong in the area of the most advanced theories and laws of physics and astronomy and have been arrived at by extended and elaborate methods of measurement, hypotheses, and experimental confirmation, and are open to further confirmation or modification. The next two (8, 9) belong to the realm of political and social theory, and their truth claim is based less upon data observed by the senses, and more upon a body of funded knowledge and presuppositions about human nature, and a *norm* of what *ought to be* in the realm of social and political relations. The next three (10, 11, 12) are in the realm of moral and aesthetic values, and are shared by most people in a given cultural tradition. However, if disagreement arises or should exist, the method of settling such disputes is determined less by objective evidence than by norms already accepted. The last two are in the realm of religious value judgments. Here we are concerned not only with the question of the nature of the confirming evidence but also with the possible vagueness and emotive nature of the language. If we do not know with some precision what is meant by the terms employed, we have a corresponding difficulty in settling any dispute which may arise as to the truth value of the propositions, and, hence, resort must be had to our own individual and subjective experience.

Thus, we are introduced by truth claims such as these to the problem of determining what kinds of statements are amenable to verification and scientific treatment. This involves the problems of inductive inference, the relation between induction and deduction, observation and generalization from experience, the use of hypotheses, measurement, indirect methods of testing, calculating degrees of probability, and related problems now generally included under the head of *scientific methods*.

In daily life much of our knowledge is derived from common sense, practical experience, and a funded body of accepted beliefs. Our beliefs, opinions, and knowledge are adhered to with varying degrees of tenacity, depending upon the nature of the materials and evidence involved, upon the degree of attention, critical analysis, and study we have given the problem, and upon our own standards as to what constitutes evidence and proof. In practical life we often must act on evidence which would not be regarded as conclusive if we were engaged in a scientific enterprise where our results might have great practical and theoretical consequences for the future. On the pre-scientific level of daily life, we derive our beliefs from some of the same sources which are used on the scientific level. However, on the latter level they are formulated with more care, with more reference to weight of rational evidence, systematic coherence, generality, and the possibility of empirical verification. Some of the sources of knowledge and belief are: sense experience, perceptual experience, reason, authority, intuition, common sense, mystical experience, and utility.

In discussing *authority* as a source of knowledge we need to make a distinction between a legitimate and necessary appeal to authority, and authoritarianism as a dogma or habit of mind. Since we are all laymen in most areas of knowledge it is obvious that we must depend upon the authorities in those fields in which we are not specialists. This is true even between different specialized departments of science, and has good sanction in the necessity of specialization and the rapid changes taking place in scientific knowledge. On the other hand, *authoritarianism* in the sense of a habit of mind which resorts to authority to settle troublesome doubts on matters of fact, whether the authority be of majority opinion at a given time, or based on age or prestige, is contrary to the scientific attitude. Its weakness is revealed when the question is asked, how did the authority in question become an authority, and some other source of knowledge such as experience or reason is appealed to as evidence.

The term *intuition* is ambiguous, but all varieties claim immediacy and self-evidence. Disregarding for our purpose the many psychological explanations of how and why some people have this gift and others do not, we may note that the term is sometimes used to refer to the quality of the results claimed, and again to the suddenness of the insight, or to both. Many great scientists have claimed suddenness of insight for their discoveries in areas where the materials are structured as in mathematics, or in a laboratory experiment where the materials are homogeneous. The insight is the perception of certain relations which have become clear after a period of vagueness and confusion. Sir William R. Hamilton tells of the discovery of quaternions which came to him in a flash of insight. It is doubtful, however, that the insight would have come suddenly without many years of tension and painstaking conscious thought and unconscious cerebration which preceeded it. As in the case of authority, the weakness of intuition as a special and independent source of knowledge may be shown by asking for a test of the intuition. Usually some other source of knowledge will be appealed to as supporting evidence.

Common sense is a term which may be used in a eulogistic or derogatory sense. When used in a eulogistic sense it usually means the accumulated experience of the race such that in practical affairs and politics the great mass of people may be trusted to know their own interests and to vote for and defend those policies which tend to preserve them. When common sense is used in a derogatory sense it means the opinion of the nonexpert majority, the uncritical unanalyzed deliverances of sensory experience, everyday popular opinions about matters on which it cannot be informed, and lack of critical attitude. In this sense it is contrary to the critical analytical attitude of science.

Mystical experience is to religious knowledge what intuition is to ordinary knowledge. It is an immediate grasping of religious truth or knowledge and may be thought of as the special gift of the mystic or as the result of a high degree of integration of an ordinary person in the special area of religious experience.

Undoubtedly there are areas within the broad range of human experience and the complex interaction of the human knower and his environment where all of these sources of knowledge have been and may be appealed to with some degree of confidence, but within the narrower area of scientific knowledge and scientific methods, which seeks empirically tested and rationally grounded knowledge, authoritarianism, certain kinds of intuition, mystical experience, common sense, and mere utility will be regarded with suspicion. Scientific knowledge is the most general kind of knowledge, hence theoretical and rational, but it is grounded in perceptual experience and must be submitted to the test of experimental verification, and is subject to modification at any time in the light of new empirical evidence.

II. THE AIMS AND SPIRIT OF SCIENCE

1. What Is Science? Etymologically, the word "science" is derived from the Latin *scire*, which means "to know." This does not tell us much, for as we have seen there are many kinds of knowledge which lay claim to recognition. We may carry the definition of science a little further, and say that it is the *most exact, most carefully verified,* and *most general knowledge* available to man. Since ours is an age of technology, and since the practical results of the application of science are so impressive, we are inclined to think almost exclusively of *applied science* when the word "science" is mentioned. This, however, is a serious mistake, for lying behind the applied results of science is the elaborate theoretical work of *pure science,* without which applied science would be impossible. There are many ways of classifying the pure sciences, and whatever scheme is adopted will be mostly a matter of convenience. The following classification will serve as a beginning, since only a few examples can be given and borderline sciences must be neglected:

I. Formal and Abstract Sciences
   (a) Mathematics and Statistics
   (b) Logic
II. Concrete or Descriptive Sciences
   1. Physical Sciences
      (a) Physics (b) Chemistry, etc.
   2. Life Sciences
      (a) Biology (b) Zoology, etc.
   3. Psycho-Physical Sciences
      (a) Psychology (b) Psycho-Physics, etc.
   4. Social Sciences
      (a) Sociology (b) Ethnology (c) History, etc.
III. Normative Sciences
   (a) Aesthetics (b) Ethics, etc.

The terms "descriptive" and "normative" used in this classification are not exclusive but are meant to mark the distinction between those sciences which deal with the concrete materials of the physical, psychophysical, and social world of fact and those which are "normative," such as ethics and aesthetics. While the latter are partly descriptive, they are more concerned with a standard or *norm* of what ought to be, and observed situations and facts are judged as conforming or not conforming to these criteria.

Today, in addition to recognizing its pure and applied aspects, we usually think of science in connection with a laboratory. This is directly in keeping with the nature of advances which have been made in recent science in the direction of experimentation and of improved techniques for increasing our powers of observation and testing. Microscopes, telescopes, and various other measuring, observing, and calculating devices may be thought of as extensions of our eyes, ears, hands, and brains. At the same time, unobserved except to the student of advanced science, there is the corresponding perfection of mathematical and theoretical techniques and knowledge, without which laboratory instruments would be useless.

Scientific knowledge may be thought of as a refinement and extension of common sense, perception, and practical knowledge, or it may be thought of as very different from all other kinds of ordinary knowledge by reason of its systematic character and its rigorous standards of methods and results. Science seeks to comprehend the laws of nature, confirmed by experimental evidence; its aim is material truth of the most general character.

2. Science and Certainty. Some propositions we hold to be true with great certainty, others with varying degrees of probability. When we are challenged by the question "But are you sure?" it is not always clear whether it is the sufficiency of the evidence upon which our judgments are made that is being challenged, or merely the strength of our subjective and psychological convictions. Many "psychological certainties" are due to the fact that in practical life we cannot always pause to consider the evidence, and others are the result of the predominance, in the total mental life, of feelings, emotions, and prejudices of various kinds. These, however, are not the kinds of certainties that have the greatest significance for science. Of the latter kind, there are first of all *sensitive certainties* which are private, immediate, and self-evident, but become publicly available to science through observation statements such as "this is a patch of color," "this is sour," or "this is smooth." There are various explanations as to how these *sense data* are to be explained that will account for not only the knowledge of what is experienced, but also the possibility of error. One view is that the evidence for such propositions does not lie outside of experience, and if anyone challenges the truth of them, we would suspect him of doubting the normality of our sense organs or our veracity in reporting what is experienced, and the only defense we have to offer is to refer him to his own experiences under similar operational conditions. An alternative view is that such *immediate* experiences are psychological events, and when what is experienced is stated in propositional form they are to be regarded as highly probable inferences about what is immediately experienced. It should be emphasized that we are not here defending the view that interpretations, inferences, and judgments made upon the basis of immediate experiences are self-evident—indeed, it is in this area between immediate experiences and their interpretation where the errors in observation and reporting that are notorious in daily life and in the courtroom occur and constitute hazards even to the careful scientist.

In addition, there is another species of certainty which is of interest to science and logic. It may be called *formal certainty*, or formal truth. When the word "truth" is used in this context to refer to propositions expressing these certainties, it is logical (or analytic) truth and not empirical truth about nature that is meant. Such propositions are "true" only in the sense of being self-consistent. There are, first of all, the traditional laws of thought. For example, the law of contradiction states that S cannot be both P and not-P at the same time and place. The law of excluded middle asserts that S must be either P or not-P at the same time and place. These laws hold for propositions which are determinate or have meaning. In our earlier discussion of the formal principles of inference, we also saw that the relation of implication which exists between premises and conclusion is objective and logically certain.

When we come to the question of certainty regarding matters of fact dealt with in the solution of concrete problems, in the reporting and predicting of events in politics, and in the propositions of the empirical sciences which deal with a world in process, the matter is different. Since most questions regarding matters of empirical fact go beyond observed instances, generalizations from experience cannot be certain, and are at best only highly *probable*. Inductions from experience do not give us *certain* knowledge, but merely degrees of probability, by making hypotheses, deducing their consequences, and then submitting them to further confirmation or verification. When the subject matter is homogeneous, probability can approach rational certainty (e.g., "All men are mortal"). The difficulty of predicting what a heterogeneous object, such as an army for instance, will do is intensified by the fact that so much depends upon the interacting decisions of many individuals, which from the viewpoint of the predictor are usually unknown or changing variables. In the social sciences, there is considerably less possibility of certainty in prediction than in the physical sciences. In the changing field of politics, for example, predictions are extremely hazardous; the best that the debater or reporter can do is to argue from trends of the past and present, to compile evidence for this or that possibility, and to predict the course that seems most probable.

3. The Scientific Attitude. Much has been made in the history of science of the *disinterestedness* of the scientific attitude of mind. It is well expressed in Huxley's exhortation to scientists to "sit down before the facts as a little child, and let them lead you where they will." Karl Pearson has put it in still another way:

The classification of facts, the recognition of their sequence and relative significance is the function of science, and the habit of forming a judgment upon these facts, unbiased by personal feeling, is characteristic of what may be termed the scientific frame of mind.[1]

Does this represent an impossible ideal? It is obvious, in the first place, that science had its origin and early development in response to man's needs and not through a purely disinterested attitude toward discovering the laws of nature, although this has now become its primary goal. In the second place, as F. C. S. Schiller has so well shown,[2] science is selective, in a double sense. It is selective in the sense that the scientist is impelled toward the selection of his problem by his own interests; and in the second place he must select his hypothesis from among many rival hypotheses, and this process is influenced by the peculiar nature and training of the scientist. We may seek to reconcile the two seemingly opposed views by saying that as much disinterestedness as possible is an ideal of science. That is, the scientist must be aware of the danger of allowing his own prejudices to distort his findings. On the other hand, it may well be recognized, as the Voluntaristic logic has maintained, that human purpose and interest is inevitably present in all human activity, even including the most objective scientific enterprise. It might be said that human purposes direct and determine the use to which experimental evidence is put, but that it should not constitute or alter the substantive aspect of the discoveries. The scientist's work is *for* his purposes, but not *of* his purposes.

III. FACTS, THEORIES, LAWS

1. Facts. The practical man who has a great reverence for fact often remarks that he wants facts rather than theories, and he will point out with great satisfaction that beautiful theories are often wrecked by one single fact. He does not realize that the number and kinds of facts that we would possess without theories are indeed very limited. This misunderstanding often occurs because the words "fact" and "theory" are notoriously ambiguous. When we say, "Here are

[1] Karl Pearson, *Grammar of Science* (London: A. & C. Black, 1900), p. 6.
[2] F. C. S. Schiller, *Logic for Use* (New York: Harcourt, Brace & Company, Inc., 1929), p. 410.

the facts," we often mean to refer to the actual physical data which may be observed by any competent observer. Or we may mean to refer to the judgment itself, which is made on the basis of the observed data (e.g., "The average of the scores in the test is 75"). Or, finally, by "fact" we may be referring to a scientific law such as Galileo's law of falling bodies or Newton's law of gravitation. In these last cases, the facts were established only after certain theories were set up as hypothetical explanations of the phenomena and tested by numerous experimental observations.

2. Theories. The objective of scientific inquiry is the formulation of systematically coherent and experientially substantiated explanations. These range from *ad hoc* explanations of individual occurrences to broadly ranging theoretical constructs that are beyond the scope of direct observation. These formulations are variously named "hypotheses," "theories," or "laws," according to their scope or degree of generality (which usually is in inverse ratio to the proximity to direct verifiability by experience). The word "theory" is sometimes confused with "hypothesis" and with "law." An *hypothesis* may be regarded as the earliest or lowest in the scale. When supporting evidence has been gathered, the hypothesis may then assume the dignity of a *theory,* and, when it is systematically coherent and capable of explaining every instance it exemplifies, it may be regarded as a scientific *law.* Theories are rational and empirical constructions for the purpose of unifying and explaining the laws of the materials studied. They grow out of hypotheses in various stages of confirmation, and are usually in process of modification by further observations.

Without a theory around which to organize particular facts, the work of the scientist would be endless, since he cannot possibly observe all of the data. This is illustrated by Darwin's careful gathering of material over a period of many years before he could organize it into a fully meaningful whole. He tells us how his work was given direction by a suggestion from Malthus:

In October, 1838, that is, fifteen months after I had begun my systematic inquiry, I happened to read for amusement, Malthus on *Population,* and being well prepared to appreciate the struggle for existence which everywhere goes on, from long-continued observations of the habits of animals and plants, it at once struck me that under these circumstances favorable variations would tend to be preserved, and unfavorable ones destroyed. The result of this would be the formation of new species. *Here then I had at last got a theory by which to work,* but I was so anxious to avoid prejudice that I determined not for some time to write even the briefest sketch of it. In June, 1842, I first allowed myself the satisfaction of writing a brief abstract of my theory in pencil, in thirty-five pages, and this was enlarged during the summer of 1844 into one of 230 pages.[3]

3. Laws. We have remarked from time to time that the purposes of science are to discover, to formulate, and to explain the laws of nature. The nature of *laws* and the relation between them and their relation to theories is an extremely complex matter, and there is wide divergence in the views of philosophers of science and of scientists themselves.

One very helpful distinction is that between laws as *prescriptive* and laws as *descriptive*. Laws passed by a legislature are prescriptive; that is, they are rules which have been adopted by society for the welfare and guidance of the community, and they can be broken. Scientific laws, on the other hand, are descriptive; that is, they are formulas stating the results of empirical observations describing observed sequences and uniformities in some special area of nature and, as such, are never broken in the sense of a civic law, although they may be superseded by later laws. The later laws do not always refute or overthrow the old, but, rather, they go beyond them by fitting in more adequately with established observations and the body of accepted laws and theories. In this way, what is called a "successive approximation" to the truth is continuously in progress. For example, the Einsteinian theory of relativity goes beyond the Newtonian theory of gravity in the sense of providing greater accuracy and wider application to the operations of our solar system, and explains many other scientific facts as well. The use of the term "descriptive" as applied to scientific laws should not be taken to mean that they are not also explanatory. The relation between description and explanation will be discussed later.

When it was suggested above that law stands at the head of a hierarchy of hypothesis, theory, and law, it was an oversimplification. There is a hierarchy among each of these when taken separately. Sometimes theory may stand at the head of the list, and may be capable of comprehending minor laws and theories by reason of greater generality and explanatory power. A famous example is the explanation of Kepler's laws of planetary motion, Galileo's law of falling bodies, and the law of the tides by Newton's theory of gravity. Thus, it is possible to say that science unifies and explains laws by means of theories.

There is a difference of opinion as to whether laws of nature are

[3] Charles Darwin, *Life and Letters of Charles Darwin* (New York: Appleton-Century-Crofts, Inc., 1896), I, 68. (Italics not in original.)

immutable, invariable, and absolute, and once true always true, or subject to change as science advances. When we speak of a law of nature or a scientific law, we are likely to have in mind well-established laws such as the law of gravity, the Mendelian laws of heredity, or the law of the conservation of energy. But there is a sense in which everything which has a structure of its own is "governed," as we say, by laws characteristic of its own nature. Primitive man learned very early that fire burns and boils water, that water drowns animals that are too long submerged, and that it always freezes in winter (in cold climates), that if he lifts a stone that is too heavy it falls on his toes and causes pain. These laws seem to be eternal and immutable and as true today as they ever were. In the other sense of the term *laws*, as we have seen, the history of science bears ample evidence that laws are but successive approximations to the truth as science advances.

In the nineteenth century, laws of nature were generally believed to be based upon the postulate of strict mechanical causality. In the early part of the twentieth century, the view that laws are statistical in certain sciences such as chemistry and physics has gained wide acceptance. The molecular theory of gases provides a good example. A gas is made up of molecules in rapid motion which collide with each other and with the sides of their container. In their doing so, no loss of kinetic energy results. It is impossible to obtain exact measurement of individual molecules in motion. The observed regularity appears as, with increasing numbers, the chance irregularities tend to balance each other so as to enable us to formulate statements about those causal regularities which are not due to chance variation, in accordance with the statistical law of large numbers. Regularity can be seen in the form of statistical averages in the same way as an average value is secured from the tossing of a die many times.

IV. WHAT IS INDUCTION?

1. Induction by Complete Enumeration. In its simplest form, induction may be illustrated by the simple process of counting, and the propositions announcing the result would be merely descriptive. We arrive at a general conclusion about the number of students in a class or a university by enumeration. This procedure is obviously possible only in the most elementary stages of any investigation, and is often regarded by logicians as not an inference at all. Supposing a general proposition is in dispute as to whether or not all of the students in a given group are American citizens. It would be verified or refuted by an enumeration and questioning of each member of the class, and if no exceptions occurred it would be concluded on this evidence that: "All of the students in this group are American citizens."

Since Aristotle regarded the syllogism as the perfect demonstrative form of reasoning, he sought to express the inductive argument in syllogistic form. His own illustration is as follows:

> Man, the horse, the mule are long lived.
> Man, the horse, the mule are bileless.
> Hence, all bileless creatures are long lived.

Now it is obvious that this conclusion follows only if the minor premise is convertible into the proposition "All bileless creatures are man, the horse, the mule," which is another way of saying that the inductive syllogism is a case of enumerating all the instances. Now if universal propositions are established by means of an enumeration of all instances, and these universal propositions are used in deductive syllogisms in order to establish particular conclusions, is not this a case of reasoning in a circle?

2. Intuitive Induction.[4] Aristotle met this problem by means of another conception of induction, which has gone under the name of *intuitive induction*. He made a distinction between the act of sense perception which is of the particular, and the content of sense perception which is universal. Though the principles arise through sense perception, they rest upon universal relations grasped by the mind.

We conclude that these states of knowledge are neither innate in a determinate form, nor developed from other higher states of knowledge, but from sense perception. It is like a rout in battle stopped by first one man making a stand and then another, until the original formation has been restored. The soul is so constituted as to be capable of this process.

. . . When one of a number of logically indiscriminable particulars has made a stand, the earliest universal is present in the soul: for though the act of sense-perception is of the particular, its content is universal—is man, for example, not the man Callias. A fresh stand is made among these rudimentary universals, and the process does not cease until the indivisible concepts, the true universals, are established: e.g., such and such a species of animal is a step towards the genus animal, which by the same process is a step towards a further generalization.

Thus, it is clear that we must get to know the primary premises by induction; for the method by which even sense-perception implants the uni-

---

[4] The word "intuition" is notoriously ambiguous. It is derived from the Latin *intueri* (to look on). All kinds of intuition—mystical, sensitive, intellectual, and moral—have the characteristics of being immediate instead of mediate. With Aristotle, and with Johnson, quoted on pages 208 and 209, intellectual intuition is meant.

versal is inductive. Now of the thinking states by which we grasp truth, some are unfailingly true, others admit of error—opinion, for instance, and calculation, whereas scientific knowledge and intuition are always true: further, no other kind of thought except intuition is more accurate than scientific knowledge, whereas primary premises are more knowable than demonstrations, and all scientific knowledge is discursive. From these considerations it follows that there will be no scientific knowledge of the primary premises, and since except intuition nothing can be truer than scientific knowledge, it will be intuition that apprehends the primary premises—a result that also follows from the fact that demonstration cannot be the originative source of demonstration, nor, consequently, scientific knowledge of scientific knowledge. If, therefore, it is the only other kind of true thinking except scientific knowing, intuition will be the originative source of scientific knowledge. And the originative source of science grasps the original basic premise, while science as a whole is similarly related as originative source to the whole body of fact.[5]

Intuitive induction is for Aristotle, then, a case of recognizing that what is true of one instance is true of all instances of that kind. The mind has the power of grasping the necessary relation existing between the properties of the members of the class. The increasing of the number of instances does not increase the certainty or knowledge of the essential nature of the class.

W. E. Johnson[6] applies the name abstractive or *intuitive induction* to the process of establishing generalizations with felt certainty from particulars. In this form of induction the increase in the number of instances does not affect the result, for it is seen that what is true of one instance will be true of all instances of that form. He gives the following example:

For example, in judging upon a single instance of the impressions red, orange, and yellow, that the qualitative difference between red and yellow is greater than that between red and orange (where abstraction from shape and size is already pre-supposed) this single instantial judgment is implicitly universal; in that what holds of the relation amongst red, orange, and yellow for this single case is seen to hold for all possible presentations of red, orange, and yellow.

3. Induction by Analysis. Although Roger Bacon visualized methods of experimental science for the investigation of the secrets of nature three hundred years before the time of Francis Bacon, the latter has been generally credited with the formulation of the basic theory of induction. According to him, the true nature of science is the dis-

[5] *The Works of Aristotle Translated into English* (New York: Oxford University Press, 1928), *Analytica Posteriori* (99b–100a).
[6] W. E. Johnson, *Logic: Part II* (Cambridge: University Press, 1924), pp. 192, 193.

covery of the *forms* or *laws of nature* which are not accessible to
sense experience, but which are related to properties which are. The
problem is to analyze experience so as to make these relationships
manifest to the understanding as a basis for induction. For this
purpose he proposed to draw up three "tables of comparative instances." Suppose we are seeking the scientific *form* or *law of heat*.
The nature of the tables is briefly suggested as follows:

1. Instances agreeing in the Nature of Heat. Examples are the rays
   of the sun, meteors, flame, etc. (27 instances are listed).
2. Instances in Proximity where the Nature of Heat is Absent. Bacon
   notes that to give a list of negative instances (i.e., where heat is
   absent) would be endless, therefore the negatives are subjoined to
   the foregoing affirmative instances. Examples are the rays of the
   sun in the middle region of the air, quicklime sprinkled with water,
   etc. (32 instances are listed).
3. Table of Degrees or Comparison of Heat. Examples are animal heat
   increased by exercise, fevers, etc. (41 instances are listed).

When these lists are completed the work of induction begins. The
purpose of the tables is to enable us to observe what properties are
invariably related to certain forms. By a process of elimination,
which is the next step, all nonessential conditions not found invariably
related to the form of heat are eliminated. That is, properties which
are not present in some instances where the given nature is present, or
are present in some instances where the given nature is absent, or are
found to increase in some instances when the given nature decreases, or
to decrease when the given nature increases, are eliminated. What is
left after the process of exclusion is an affirmative which he calls the
"First Vintage," which is a summary of results up to date. This
induction is that the form or law, of which heat is a particular case,
appears to be motion; that is, motion is a genus of which heat is a
species.

It is not necessary that we go into details in pointing out the
defects in Bacon's method of induction. One difficulty with the
method is that without some guiding idea or principle of selection of
instances, the tables would have to be so complete and exhaustive that
it would be beyond human capacity to compile them, for the physical
and sensible properties in nature are almost infinite. Again, he had
a negative attitude toward what he called "the anticipation of nature,"
and as a result did not make use of hypotheses which would have lent

direction, order, and meaning to the mass of facts gathered by observation and experiment.

4. Induction Through Generalization. This is sometimes called imperfect induction or *induction proper*, in contrast to complete enumeration or perfect induction. As we have already seen, induction by complete enumeration is not strictly a form of inference. Further, it is obvious that in the most important fields of investigation, complete enumeration is not possible because of the complexity and extent of the materials.

The real nature of induction is found in the process of *reasoning from some observed cases to a universal conclusion regarding all similar cases, some of which are unobserved.* It is the seeking of a general principle in the midst of a diversity of facts. The problem of induction is to arrive at a logical basis for such generalizations when not all of the possible instances have been observed, in other words, to find the logical justification for inference from *some* to *all*.

John Stuart Mill regarded the *principle of the uniformity of nature* and the *law of universal causation* as the foundations of induction. The principle of the uniformity of nature means that "there are such things in nature as parallel cases, that what happens once will, under sufficient degree of similarity of circumstances, happen again."[7] The law of causation "is but the familiar truth that invariability of succession is found by observation to obtain between every fact in nature and some other fact which has preceded it."[8] Mill held that the principle of the uniformity of nature functions as the ultimate major premise in all inductions and stands in the same relation as the major premise of a syllogism stands to the conclusion. The inductive syllogism would appear as follows:

> Whatever is true of John, Peter, etc., characterizes all men.
> Mortality characterizes John, Peter, etc.
> Hence, mortality characterizes all men.

However, it appears that the principle of uniformity does not enable us to judge whether or not in a given case the major premise is true, for in addition to uniformities in nature there are also numerous non-uniformities, and the real problem of induction is to know when these uniformities exhibit invariant causal laws.

[7] John Stuart Mill, *A System of Logic* (New York: Harper & Bros., 1887), p. 223.

[8] *Ibid.*, p. 236.

For example, suppose we have the following argument, which we may for contrast also throw into syllogistic form:

> Whatever is true of John, Peter, etc., is true of all fat people.
> Good natures characterize John, Peter, etc.
> Hence, good natures characterize all fat people.

It is obvious that we do not accept the conclusion of this syllogism, for we do not regard the concurrence of good nature and obesity, which we have observed in a few cases, to be sufficiently uniform to entitle us to draw the universal conclusion that these qualities are invariably related. If, however, we regard the principle of the uniformity of nature as a postulate which lends order and enables us to progress in our understanding of observed sequences, it may be regarded as provisionally acceptable. Mill seemed to regard the second principle mentioned above, that of the law of universal causation, as equally important in induction, and it is upon this principle that he based his so-called experimental methods, which will be considered in some detail later. The phenomena of nature, he said, exist in the relations of simultaneity and succession to one another. Relations of simultaneity enable us to recognize natural kinds or classes. The relations of succession are most important for us, since they enable us to predict. One of the major marks of causation is invariant sequence, but this is not synonymous with causation unless it is also unconditional or necessary. If invariant sequences were enough to enable us to detect causation, we might say that day causes night and night causes day. However, this is a derivative sequence depending upon something else which causes both day and night. Causal laws exhibit regular sequence, but not all cases of regular sequence imply the presence of causal laws. The problem of causality is to determine which antecedents and consequents are merely accidental and which are causal; that is, which are connected by invariable law.

The foregoing discussion serves to indicate that what we need in order to make sound generalizations from *some* to *all* is a knowledge of the nature of the instances which go to make up the universal conclusion. The observed instances are samples of the whole class, and a limited number of samples is sufficient as a basis for generalizations if the material is homogeneous. If we are dealing with instances not known to be homogeneous, we may, on the basis of samples, make a provisional hypothesis, and then by further sampling and the study of further instances confirm, modify, or refute that hypothesis. Inductive generalizations from some observed instances can never be absolute, even though they may be held with a high degree of probability.

For example, suppose I wish to purchase an orange grove of a thousand trees and am told that they are navel oranges. I do not care to count the whole grove, but am content to observe certain groups of a dozen or more in certain *random* areas. Such a procedure of course does not give certainty, for there is nothing in the nature of a law governing the kind of trees originally planted in an orange grove, that is, their grouping may be *heterogeneous*. The excellence of a sample is to be judged not only on its size, but on its *representativeness* of the group. On the other hand, if I go to the drugstore for a gallon of hydrochloric acid, it would seem unreasonable to demand that every cubic centimeter be tested for composition and purity. It would be sufficient to analyze a small sample. This sampling would be regarded as satisfactory, since something is already known of the composition or structure of such *homogeneous* chemicals which enables us to predict that if this sample is of such and such a composition, then the whole is of the same composition.

V. DESCRIPTION AND EXPLANATION IN SCIENCE

Much discussion has been devoted to whether scientific knowledge is merely *descriptive* in nature or whether the ultimate function of science is *explanation*. It is often insisted that it is sufficient for the purposes of science to describe what *is* and *how* it operates, and that it is beyond the purposes of science to undertake explanation as to *why* it is so.

This controversy is partly due to the fact that a certain ambiguity lies in both of the terms "description" and "explanation."

Description, in the narrow sense, is the mere delineation of observed instances, qualities, or properties and their definition and classification as of such and such a nature. It seeks to answer the simple question— *what?* Description as a scientific method in this narrow sense does not provide for the anticipation of nature, and is to that extent limited. In the broader sense, however, description involves generalizations from some observed instances to all, which are stated in the form "All magnets attract iron" and "All heat expands bodies." The laws and theories of which they are the expression answer the question *how?* and are sufficient both for practical and theoretical purposes without involving the larger question as to *why* the instances which they generalize act that way.

The term "explanation" is also ambiguous. Scientific explanation is one thing, and ultimate metaphysical explanation is another. Some sciences limit themselves to description because of the nature of their materials. Others disclaim any pretense at explanation because the term has been associated with metaphysical speculations which involve teleological explanations about final causes and ultimate purposes on the part of nature itself. On the side of philosophy there has been a tendency to restrict science to description because some scientific theories have been based upon mechanistic assumptions which have been generalized to cover not only matter but also life and mind. Since this is in a sense an attempt at ultimate explanation, it is felt that it lies outside the sphere of science. It should be sufficient for the resolution of this conflict if we were to agree that both scientific description and scientific explanation are legitimate functions of science but that ultimate metaphysical explanation is beyond its purpose.

Scientific explanation has been reached when phenomena are made intelligible with reference to their setting in a larger body of systematic and coherent relations. It goes beyond description and explains in the sense that the individual facts are placed in a deductive system. There are of course degrees of explanation. While scientific theories may be sufficient for the understanding of a set of facts by referring them to a law, they do not pretend to be explanatory in the sense of making intelligible why there should be such a law. If we mean by "explanation" in science, answering such questions as "What is the ultimate purpose of nature's behavior?" no science professes to explain in this sense.

Both description and explanation involve hypotheses. Descriptive hypotheses are offered to guide further investigation, and hence are tentative. An hypothesis is explanatory if it is capable of yielding consequences which account for the behavior of individual cases and is confirmed by the experimental operations. We have explained a fact when a true hypothesis can be formulated which implies it or from which it can be deduced. In this sense the laws of thermodynamics explain individual cases of the behavior of heat. The highest kind of scientific explanation then is the establishment of a law.

As in science, so in the ordinary problems of daily life, if there is an element of curiosity present we are not content with descriptions but ask the question *why?* The soldiers I see drilling in the park may be described as to their number, branch of military service, and as to how well or poorly they march according to the rules laid down in the manual of arms, but the explanation as to why they are drilling comes only with the background knowledge of national policy, international affairs, and conscription laws from which the observed facts are inferrable.

PROBLEMS

1. Which of the following propositions do you regard as easiest to verify, and why? How would you go about verifying them? Why are the others difficult to verify?

(1) The boiling point of lewisite gas is 378° F.
(2) Caesar conquered Britain in 55 B.C.
(3) George Washington was born on February 22, 1732.
(4) Honesty is the best policy.
(5) This magnet will attract this iron nail.
(6) Wilson died in 1924.
(7) Heat expands bodies.
(8) This two-pound weight is twice as heavy as this bag of peanuts.
(9) It is more blessed to give than to receive.
(10) There are twenty students in this class.
(11) The laggard and the wastrel will end in poverty.

2. What scientific principle is involved in the old saw "One swallow does not make a summer"?

3. Pick out any simple proposition or assertion that you regard as a fact, and explain why you hold it to be a fact.

4. Give an example of a problem or investigation where the increase in the number of cases studied might increase the probability of the generalization, and one where it would not. Explain.

5. If you were about to purchase an oil field, and the owner showed you that drillings in three or four widely separated places on the field all yielded oil, how many such drillings would satisfy you that the entire field was oil-bearing? Why? What is the difference between this induction and that involved in the random sampling of a shipment of oranges?

6. Codrington the anthropologist gives an interesting account of a belief held by the natives of Melanesia. Natives on the hunt collect smooth round stones and bury them at the foot of their yam plants. The following spring, when the plants bear abundant fruit, they believe that it is because the stones contain a magical property called "mana." Criticize the logical method involved.

7. Point out the central principle in the following quotations:

(1) Why is a single instance, in some cases, sufficient for a complete induction, while in others myriads of concurring instances, without a single exception known or presumed, go such a little way toward establishing an universal proposition? Whoever can answer this question knows more of the philosophy of logic than the wisest of the ancients, and has solved the problem of Induction.—J. S. MILL
(2) For to renounce the assumption of induction would be necessary only

if we knew that the assumption is false. But that is not the case—
we do not know if it is true or false. And that is quite another
matter! Without believing that the assumption is true or false,
we are still justified in defending it in the sense in which we make a
wager. We want to foresee the future, and we can do it if the assumption of induction is justified—and so we wager on this assumption. If it is false, well, then our efforts are in vain; but if we
use the principle of induction, we have at least a chance of success.
                                                    —H. REICHENBACH

(3) "In short, induction cannot be justified. We can only base it on a
more or less plausible sounding assumption . . . We may argue as
to the best way of forming theories, but whatever method we arrive
at, we will know only that the theories agree with past observations,
and we must take on faith that they will hold true in the future.
Only in one sense can we justify induction. While our assumption
must be taken on faith, we can point out that unless some such assumption were true human life would be impossible. If nature
were designed so that plausible inductions invariably turn out to be
wrong, the human race would be wiped out soon. We may not be
able to justify the assumption, but we must have faith in some such
assumption if life is to be possible."[9]

8. How would you reconcile or explain the following divergent viewpoints on the aims of science?

(1) For Science, though it starts from observation of the particular, is
not concerned essentially with the particular, but with the general.[10]

(2) Science can also study the individual for his own sake. Thus the
science of psychology can set itself to study an individual mind and
character, and there are psychologists who do this (novelists), often
with great ability and success.[11]

9. State several nonscientific or prescientific ways of determining
beliefs, and state the advantages claimed for the scientific method.

10. What obstacles and difficulties account for the relative back-
wardness and lack of progress in ethics and the social sciences as
compared with the physical sciences such as physics?

11. What can be learned from the scientific method which can be
applied to individual conduct and social policy?

12. Why are the fields of economics, politics, race relations, religion,
and morals less susceptible to the scientific methods? Secure an example in each of these fields, and segregate the matters of "fact" from
those of "evaluation" and "logical factors."

[9] From J. G. Kemeny's *A Philosopher Looks at Science*. Copyright, 1959
Princeton, N.J.: D. Van Nostrand Co., Inc., p. 121.
[10] Reprinted from *The Scientific Outlook* (pp. 57, 58), by Bertrand Russell, by
permission of W. W. Norton & Co., Inc. Copyright, 1931, by Bertrand Russell.
[11] F. C. S. Schiller, *Logic for Use* (New York: Harcourt, Brace & World, Inc.,
1929), p. 405.

13. Discuss and clarify your own thinking on the issue in the following quotation from Max Planck's *Where Is Science Going?* (1932):

Scientific discovery and scientific knowledge have been achieved only by those who have gone in pursuit of them without any practical purpose whatsoever in view.

14. Discuss the ambiguity of the terms *fact, theory,* and *laws of nature,* and the relations between them in scientific method.

15. Discuss the following quotation from Ackoff, and see if you can think of a concrete example under each of his four points.   Discuss the possibilities and difficulties of constructing a deductive system in an empirical science as compared with a theoretical science.

Perhaps the relationship between theory, law and fact is best grasped in the context of a deductive system.   In a deductive system there are (1) a set of undefined and defined concepts, (2) a set of assumptions (axioms and postulates, or formation and transformation rules), (3) a set of deduced theorems, and (4) instances of the theorems.   The assumptions constitute the theory, the theorems constitute laws, and the instances of the theorems are the facts. In the construction of scientific theories the objective is to construct just such a deductive system.[12]

16. What is induction, and how is it related to observation, enumeration, classification, generalization, sampling, and probability?

17. What is the essential difference between deduction and induction, and what is the relation between them in the solution of a scientific problem?

18. Discuss the statement "Generalizations from experience cannot be certain; they can only be probable."

[12] Russell L. Ackoff, *Scientific Method* (New York: John Wiley & Sons, Inc., 1962), p. 22.

14

The Pattern of
Scientific Inquiry

I. OBSERVATION

The first step in the solution of any problem, whether practical or theoretical, is the preliminary survey of the problem and the observation of the "facts," "data," or "occurrents." In popular parlance, we ask, "What are the facts?" The term *observation*, as used here, does not mean mere immediate sense perception such as that described in the proposition "That is a noise," although it is obvious that observation could not proceed without such simple basic propositions, or "protocol statements," as they are sometimes called. In addition to sense perception, observation usually involves some degree of interpretation and inference. This is what we mean when we ask a man who has been studying a problem, "What are your observations?" We expect him not simply to describe his bare perceptions but, rather, to name objects and events and to interpret meanings, and perhaps to draw inferences.

In ordinary life, observation is likely to be cursory and inexact unless it is directed by the desire to solve some problem or to work ourselves out of some difficulty.[1] On the other hand, when interest is present in the extreme, observation is likely to be notoriously *selective*,

[1] See John Dewey, *How We Think* (5th ed.; Boston: D. C. Heath & Co., 1910), p. 72, for the five steps in problem solving, later called "The Pattern of Inquiry." "(1) a felt difficulty; (2) its location and definition; (3) suggestion of possible solution; (4) development by reasoning of the bearings of the suggestion; (5) further observation and experiment leading to its acceptance or rejection."

as witnessed by the disparity in the reporting of an accident by various participants and eyewitnesses, or by conflicting accounts of competing propaganda agencies in their analyses of the tides of warfare. A poet, a farmer, and a botanist walking through the woods and fields will "observe" totally different things. Scientific observation lies somewhere between the extremes of objectivity and subjectivity—it is inevitably selective to a certain extent, for not all facts are relevant, but it nevertheless seeks to avoid bias. Preliminary observation in a new field may be merely exploratory for the purpose of locating the problem, but beyond this elementary stage it is guided by some elementary theory and is therefore to that extent selective. A careful scientific observer will be guided by the accumulated body of knowledge in his field and therefore will know how to look for what is relevant to the problem. He will be aware of the distinction between observations as such and inferences made from them. He will carefully check observations by means of instruments, and, if the nature of the materials be such that he can do so, will induce repetitions in the nature of elementary experiments for the purpose of verifying his observations. Some of the pitfalls in observation will be noted in the chapter on inductive fallacies.

II. CLASSIFICATION

Closely connected with observation, yet a step beyond it, is the classification of the objects, facts, or occurrents. The ultimate purpose of science is to find *order* in a world of occurrents which exhibits to casual observation some degree of both order and disorder. Classification of objects implies the recognition of an elementary form of order. Objects exist in nature with individual structures, and perform certain characteristic functions. To recognize the properties, structural organization, and functions of objects is preliminary to placing each in its class along with others of the same general kind, and to separating it from others of different kinds. It will be obvious that this process is related to definition, which was treated in Part I, for definition seeks to state the essential qualities of the object and at the same time to differentiate it from all other objects. In more complex problems, such as are presented in the diagnosis of symptoms of disease, in social case work, or in the identification of chemical compounds, the nature of the complex of properties and relations does not lie open to superficial observation but involves interpretation, inference, and experimentation. This means that properties and relations open to inspection are related in various ways to those not open in the same way. These must be brought out by modes of description, definition, investigation, and experimentation appropriate to the various sciences. The excellence of a scientific classification is measured by the discovery of *essential properties,* so that knowledge of the presence of a given property holds implications regarding the presence of other properties, ultimately resulting in a large degree of systematic coherence. Classification in this systematic stage is exemplified in paleontology, where the discovery of a new fossil having certain properties is easily identifiable as belonging to a certain geological period and biological or botanical species. The periodic table in chemistry is a good example of a highly coherent classification, and the knowledge of the properties and structure of elements has simplified the location and identification of new elements as chemical and atomic research has advanced.

In an earlier chapter reference was made to the distinction between *natural, artificial,* and *diagnostic classifications. Natural* classification is dictated more by the nature of the materials classified, such as animate and inanimate natural elements and processes which may belong to some kind of evolutionary or phylogenetic series which it is the business of science to discover and order. The science of botany offers one of the most elaborate illustrations of phylogenetic (descent) classification in which approximately 300,000 kinds of plants are arranged in order of variety, species, genus, family, order, class, and division. The class names are based upon the properties and structures of leaves, flowers, roots, seeds, fruit, and stem. An example of the classification of the White Oak (*Quercus alba*) follows:

Kingdom	Plant
Phylum or Division	Spermatophytes
Class	Angiosperms
Subclass	Dicotyledons or exogens
Series	Primitive dicotyledons
Order	Fagales
Family	Fagaceae
Genus	*Quercus*
Species	*alba*

In contrast with this natural classification, an example of *artificial* classification would be the arrangement of the names of all known plants alphabetically in a botany manual or catalogue; it is based upon the human purpose of convenience and utility. This distinction is, however, relative, since the classifications may differ according to the purpose and scientific curiosity of the classifier. Furthermore, especially in new fields, it is never certain that the most important structural properties have been chosen, or that all of the members of the class have been included. Classifications which are still groping and exploratory, somewhere in a borderline position between natural and artificial, may be called *diagnostic*. Since the purpose of classification is the revelation of systematic order in nature, it should be judged with reference to its success in achieving this goal.

Since the rules governing classification, and the fallacies to be avoided, have been treated in Chapter 4, they will not be repeated here.

III. ANALYSIS AND SYNTHESIS

The operations of *analysis* and *synthesis* are not independent of observation and classification, but are carried on in connection with these whenever a critical attitude is maintained and ingenuity is employed in discovering relationships, similarities, and differences commonly unnoticed or ignored by a careless observer. To anticipate a little, it should also be said that analysis and synthesis are present throughout the operations of framing and testing hypotheses by means of experiments.

Analysis is the examination of any whole, whether of a concept, a problem, or an object, in order to distinguish its elements, component parts, or constituents. A concept may be vague and in need of clarification by analysis. A problem or difficulty, as it stands in its wholeness, may be beyond our grasp, and analysis may be needed to enable us to get hold of some specific and more familiar aspect which will give us a clue to the less-known aspects.

Analysis of objects may be of physical wholes into their component parts, or it may be of their qualities. This difference is relative to our purposes. Analysis into physical parts is illustrated by the long and careful labor which produced the cell theory in biology, the molecular theory of gases, the theory of elements and compounds in chemistry, and analogous modes of simplifying complex data in the other sciences. The other kind of analysis, called qualitative, is related closely to our discussion in Part I of objective connotation and definition. Objects possess numerous qualities and attributes, such as certain sizes, shapes, colors, odors, positions, and relations, which, for ordinary purposes of definition and manipulation, may be safely ignored. In scientific analysis, it is never to be taken for granted that these are not essential to the purpose of complete understanding under certain novel conditions. The practical difference between physical and qualitative analysis may be illustrated by the difference in analytical knowledge necessary in various divisions of chemical warfare. The expert, for example, needs to know the exact chemical composition of the various gases in order to combine the compounds in correct proportions, whereas it is sufficient for the members of the decontamination squad that they be able to detect the qualities of a gas by smell, color, solubility, and physiological effects upon its victim.

Synthesis is the inverse of analysis; that is, it is the combining or reconstruction of separate elements or component parts into wholes. In cases where the structure of the material analyzed is somewhat static, such as that of a machine, putting it together simply reverses the process of taking it apart. However, in cases of problem solving and where invention and novelty are required, synthesis will perform its function best by bringing elements together in novel ways on the basis of what has been learned from the analytical operations.

IV. REASONING BY ANALOGY

Reasoning by *analogy* is very common in any type of communication, argumentation, and investigation where unfamiliar ideas must be made clear. Analogy is a means of explaining the unknown by the better known. Writers whose works abound in metaphor are using this device to suggest likenesses or analogies between things and ideas which are concrete and familiar, and those which are less so. Metaphor falls short of true logical analogy in that it is sufficient if the identity suggested in metaphor serves the purpose of conveying meaning. Logical analogy, however, seeks to point to real resemblances between relations, objects, and ideas, and thus is a very fertile source of hypotheses which may be tested and either confirmed or refuted. It is also a fertile source of error.

When used as a form of argument, an analogy would be formulated as follows:

The well I see in the distance resembles the last well we stopped at, in that it has windlass, rope, and bucket. The last well, in addition to windlass, rope, and bucket, had also plenty of water. Hence, this well will further resemble the last one in that it will have plenty of water.

As an inference, it is obvious that this line of reasoning might easily be fallacious unless it were known on other evidence that the presence of water in the two wells is connected by some law, i.e., that they either are in the same general area with a similar rainfall or are fed by a similar subterranean source. If this is not the case, the presence of a rope, a windlass, and a bucket may be entirely irrelevant to the presence of an amount of water in the well. Whether or not this relation exists must be determined not by analogy, but by methods of observation and experimentation. The soundness of an analogy depends upon whether the resemblances and connections are superficial, or of a fundamental and systematic character enabling us to infer from observed properties, relations, and similarities other hidden properties and relations which are invariable.

It has been argued that there is an analogy with respect to certain properties between the earth and the other planets which might lead to the inference that life also exists on them as it does on the earth. That is, the earth is *positively analogous* to other planets in that the earth revolves about the sun, borrows its light from the sun, rotates on its axis, and is subject to the law of gravity. The other planets likewise revolve about the sun, borrow their light from the sun, and are subject to the law of gravity, and at least some of them revolve on axes; hence, it is argued, they like the earth may support some kind of life.

But there are also differences between the earth and the other planets with respect to other properties. One of the necessary conditions of life, as we know it, is the presence of an atmosphere containing air. Since this is present on the earth, and not so far as we know, on the other planets, this fact constitutes the *negative analogy* and operates to weaken or refute the positive constructive analogy, unless we may assume that there are forms of life which may exist without air.

As previously suggested, the importance of analogies in induction and scientific methods consists in their potency in suggesting possible hypotheses for testing and consequent confirmation or refutation. The ability to suspect and detect possible analogies that may turn out to be real similarities is invaluable in scientific discovery. The history of science records many discoveries where analogies from the familiar may have led to hypotheses about the unfamiliar, such as the wave theory of light by analogy from the wave theory of sound, and Bohr's atom, with its central nucleus about which the electrons revolve, by analogy from the solar system.

V. HYPOTHESES AND DEDUCTIONS

1. What Is a Hypothesis? A hypothesis is a tentative and provisional thesis put forward upon the basis of accumulated knowledge for the guidance of further investigation and research. The word is derived from the Greek *hypo* (under) and *tithenai* (to place), and suggests that when the hypothesis is placed under the evidence as a foundation they lend each other mutual support. It performs this function by providing a proposed explanation which will have certain consequences deducible from it. These consequences may then be confirmed or refuted by further testing or experimentation. Hypotheses *may* be used on the most elementary levels of science, and they *must* be used in making complex inferences. Hypotheses are suggested by the knowledge of the field already possessed by the scientist. The more thorough and extensive the knowledge of the field, the more likely the hypothesis is to be adequate to explain the facts. In addition, imagination and scientific genius in a high degree are essential. To suggest that the scientist use imagination may conflict with the somewhat widespread conception of the scientist as "coldly scientific." We do not mean, of course, by "scientific imagination" the undisciplined fancy of the child, but rather the ability to explore possibilities and anticipate nature in her devious ways. This is but another way of saying that it requires a high degree of scientific ability to propose relevant hypotheses. Almost anyone is capable of making vague guesses as to the possible implications of a body of accumulated facts or regarding the solution of a difficult problem, but only a few are capable of seeing all around the problem in the manner required to formulate an adequate and successful hypothesis.

2. The Use of Hypotheses. In its simplest form a hypothesis is an application of the old saw "Use your head to save your heels." If I were to lose my fountain pen, I might search without any plan over every inch of the house, but I could save time by forming hypotheses as to its possible whereabouts on the basis of what I remembered about last using it, the nature of the house, the family, etc., making rapid deductions and then testing these consequences by observation, and eliminating hypotheses one at a time until a satisfactory one has been found.

An elementary example may be found in the case of an amateur gardener who was disturbed one spring by the appearance of a crop of grass in his year-old lawn quite different from the prevailing blue-grass, which with the help of experts he was able to identify as "crab grass." He recalled that about a month previously he had applied a generous supply of fertilizer which was guaranteed not to contain seeds. But the proximity in time suggested the hypothesis that the fertilizer might have been the source of the new growth. The hypothesis that the fertilizer was the source was capable of being developed deductively by means of an hypothetical argument; that is, certain implications or consequences follow if the hypothesis is true, and others if it be false. For example: "If the fertilizer contains seeds, they will germinate in a box if properly prepared and kept watered." This suggested an experiment actually to verify or refute the hypothesis. While this experiment was in preparation, other rival hypotheses presented themselves. The *original grass seed* might have been a possible source of the undesirable grass, which, because of its seasonal nature and the stimulation of the recently applied fertilizer had begun its cycle at this time. A difficulty however arose, since there was no way of knowing absolutely that one supply of fertilizer or grass seed will be identical with another. Further suggestive hypotheses were, the *original subsoil*, the *original topsoil, carried by winds*, or *by birds*. While it was not likely that the seeds would be in the *city water supply*, this was held as a possibility to be tested indirectly, since it could not be observed directly. Finally, an *adjacent lot* might be the source of the seeds. This hypothesis might have been developed deductively and eliminated:

If the vacant lot is the source, similar vegetation will be found there.
No such vegetation is there.
Hence, the vacant lot is not the source.

Returning to the original hypotheses, that the seeds were brought by either the fertilizer, grass seed, water, winds, or birds, the following experiments were performed. Four boxes of fertilizer, mixed with sterilized soil were prepared for testing. One was protected from outdoor winds and birds and watered with filtered spring water; one was exposed to outdoor winds and birds and watered likewise with filtered water; a third was protected from winds and birds and watered with city water; and a fourth containing bluegrass seeds was protected from winds and birds and watered with filtered water.

After a year the gardener felt satisfied that his experiment with the boxes was complete since no seeds of the grass under study sprouted in any of the boxes, even though some error was possible because the second box which was open to winds and birds was not large enough to expose sufficient area to provide conclusive results. The results for each of the experiments eliminating fertilizer, grass seed, winds, birds, and city water might have been stated deductively after the following pattern:

> If the fertilizer contains the seeds, they will appear in a box if watered.
> No such seeds sprout in a watered box.
> Hence, the fertilizer does not contain the seeds.

After the elimination of these hypotheses there remained the rival hypotheses of the subsoil and topsoil. It occurred to him that he might eliminate one of these by planting another lawn in the back yard. The ground was prepared *without topsoil*, the same guaranteed fertilizer being used, and the same bluegrass planted. At about the same time after planting, crab grass appeared in various places. The consequences of this hypothesis and its confirmation may be stated as follows:

> If the topsoil in the front yard is the sole source, crab grass would not appear in the back yard.
> Crab grass does appear in the back yard.
> Hence, the topsoil is not the sole source.

A further successful experiment, using subsoil only and eliminating all the other alternatives, demonstrated rather convincingly that the subsoil was the culprit, but since the experiment with winds and birds was not regarded as conclusive, the possibility remained that winds and birds were accessories. Therefore the three remaining rival hypotheses were subsoil, winds, and birds. Pending further experimental verification of these, a final deductive argument might have been stated in the form of an eliminative alternative syllogism:

> The source of the crab grass is either fertilizer, subsoil, topsoil, water, winds, birds, or grass seed.
> The source is not the fertilizer, topsoil, water, or grass seed.
> Hence, the source of the crab grass is either the subsoil, winds, or birds.

The conclusion is only moderately probable, since the experiments, to be conclusive, would have to be performed with the utmost care and under perfectly controlled conditions. Actually, from the great variety of our hypotheses regarding the source of the alien seeds, it is highly probable that this was a case of *plurality of causes*, since some of the seeds might have come from one source, and some from another, the most likely sources being, however, *subsoil, winds*, and *birds*, which the improperly controlled experiments failed to eliminate.

3. Galileo's Hypothesis on the Law of Falling Bodies. A classic example of the use of hypotheses in science and the interplay of deductive and inductive inferences is to be found in the work of Galileo on the laws of falling bodies involving the relations between velocity, acceleration, space, and time. Although the ultimate verification of his most famous hypothesis is rightly called inductive and experimental, it is nevertheless interesting to note that the inductive part of his work might never have been possible had it not been for the extensive deductions from hypotheses which prepared the way for the final confirming experiments.

He started with the following definition of accelerated motion: "A motion is said to be uniformly accelerated, when, starting from rest, it acquires, during equal time-intervals, equal increments of speed."[2]

Today, accurate methods have been developed for measuring the velocity and accelerated motion of falling bodies, but in Galileo's time such direct observation was impossible. He might, of course, have measured the relative momentum produced by different velocities by dropping identical weights from different altitudes upon an upright stake and then measuring how far the stake was driven into the ground, but the result would have varied greatly with the hardness of the earth, the angle of the stake, the directness of the blow, and many other uncontrollable factors, so that it would be extremely difficult to claim accuracy for such results.

His first hypothesis then was, "A falling body acquires force in its descent, its velocity increasing in proportion to the *space,* and that the momentum of the falling body is doubled when it falls from a doubled height."[3]

But Galileo believed that this hypothesis involved the contradiction that "motion should be completely instantaneous," and consequently it was rejected.

He then proposed a second hypothesis: that accelerated motion is such that the momentum of the velocity of a falling body goes on increasing after departure from rest, in direct proportion to the time. That is, at the end of two seconds a freely falling body would be going twice as fast as at the end of one, and at the end of the third second it would be going three times as fast as at the end of the first, and so on. Inability to measure accelerated motion directly, however, led to

<hr>

[2] Galileo, *Two New Sciences,* trans. Henry Crew and Alfonso de Salvio (Evanston, Ill.: Northwestern University Press, 1914), p. 162.

[3] *Ibid.,* pp. 167, 168.

the further hypothesis: "The spaces described by a body falling from rest with a uniformly accelerated motion are to each other as the squares of the time-intervals employed in traversing these distances." [4] That is, the distance fallen increases as the square of the time. In 1 second the distance covered is 16×1 or 16 feet, in 2 seconds (2×2) $\times 16$ or 64 feet, in 3 seconds (3×3) $\times 16$, or 144 feet, in 4 seconds (4×4) $\times 16$ or 256 feet, and so on. By means of this deduction he eliminated the necessity of measuring the speed, and instead had to measure only the time and the distance. The next step was to establish this consequence of the hypothesis experimentally. He was able to demonstrate that he could exactly correlate the time of the descent of a ball down an inclined plane with the time of its vertical drop from the top of the plane. Since it was much easier to measure the rolling of the ball down the plane than it would have been to measure the much more rapid and less observable direct vertical drop, this device greatly simplified the work of the experiment.

The actual experiment is best described in Galileo's own words. Note in particular the originality of this ingenious means of verification:

A piece of wooden moulding or scantling, about twelve cubits long, half a cubit wide, and three fingerbreadths thick, was taken; on its edge was cut a channel a little more than one finger in breadth; having made this groove very straight, smooth, and polished, and having lined it with parchment, also as smooth and polished as possible, we rolled along it a hard, smooth, and very round bronze ball. Having placed this board in a sloping position, by lifting one end some one or two cubits above the other, we rolled the ball, as I was just saying, along the channel, noting, in a manner presently to be described, the time required to make the descent. We repeated this experiment more than once in order to measure the time with an accuracy such that the deviation between two observations never exceeded one tenth of a pulse beat. Having performed this operation and having assured ourselves of its reliability, we now rolled the ball only one quarter the length of the channel; and having measured the time of its descent, we found it precisely one half of the former. Next we tried other distances, comparing the time for the whole length with that for the half, or with that for two thirds, or three fourths, or indeed for any fraction; in such experiments, repeated a full hundred times, we always found that the spaces traversed were to each other as the squares of times, and this was true for all inclinations of the plane, i.e., of the channel, along which we rolled the ball. . . .

For the measurement of time, we employed a large vessel of water placed in an elevated position; to the bottom of this vessel was soldered a pipe of small diameter giving a thin jet of water, which we collected in a small glass during the time of each descent, whether for the whole length of the channel

[4] *Ibid.*, p. 174.

or for a part of its length; the water thus collected was weighed, after each descent, on a very accurate balance; the differences and ratios of these weights gave us the differences and ratios of the times, and this with such accuracy that although the operation was repeated many, many times, there was no appreciable discrepancy in the result.[5]

4. Some Criteria of a Good Hypothesis.   (1) Since the main purpose of a hypothesis is to *explain, bring into order, and summarize a body of facts in the form of a possible law or theory,* the *first* criterion of a good hypothesis is that it be capable of accomplishing this purpose. This is what John Stuart Mill meant when he stated that one condition of a genuinely scientific hypothesis is that it "be of such a nature as to be either proved or disproved by comparison with observed facts." This is the statment of an ideal, however, for it is not always known in advance whether or not an hypothesis can be confirmed or confuted; the rule asserts merely that an hypothesis should be adequate to its purpose and must not raise absurd conjectures which admit of no method of experimental and operational testing.

(2) A corollary to the above is the *second* criterion, that a hypothesis *be so conceived and so formulated as to be susceptible to deductive and mathematical development of its consequences,* so that they may be compared with facts implied by the hypothesis; that is, *it should have predictive power.*   This is especially necessary in hypotheses which cannot be verified directly, as in the illustration quoted from Galileo on the law of falling bodies. Since he could not find any way of testing directly the hypothesis that the velocity of a falling body would vary with the time of its fall, it was necessary to use mathematical deductions which enabled him to assert that, if the hypothesis were true, the distance through which the body would fall should be proportional to the square of the time of its fall. These deductions were then capable of being put to the test directly by experimentation with rolling a ball down an inclined plane.

(3) The *third* criterion of a good hypothesis is that *it must be consistent with the presuppositions, postulates, principles, and already verified facts in the field of investigation.*   Great care is needed in interpreting this rule, since it might seem to inhibit originality and to discourage the use of scientific imagination. Its purpose, however, is to ensure logical and systematic consistency rather than to discourage novelty.

(4) Finally, *adherence to the principle of parsimony is* usually regarded as an important mark of a good hypothesis. This principle

[5] *Ibid.,* pp. 178, 179.

states that economy and simplicity should be observed in the selection of hypotheses, but it requires great care in interpretation. It does not mean that the simplest hypothesis is always the true one, but rather that when there are competing hypotheses, ordinarily *the simplest hypothesis that will account for the facts* should be chosen. For example, I look across the valley on a clear morning as the train comes into view around a bend, and observe a cloud of steam issuing from the engine, and then in a few seconds hear the blast of a whistle. If I am equally ignorant of the principles of steam whistles and light and sound waves, I may believe that the steam left the engine and dispersed in the air before the sound issued from the whistle, as my senses seem to tell me. If I am not ignorant of steam whistles, I cannot accept this hypothesis for it does not account for the production of the sound. A simpler hypothesis which accounts for all the facts is that light waves travel faster than sound waves. While this hypothesis is not simple, in that it rests on certain physical assumptions, it can be illustrated in many analogous cases such as thunder and lightning and artillery fire.

VI. EMPIRICAL VERIFICATION AND CONFIRMATION

Empirical *verification* or *confirmation* is the final stage in the scientific procedure and is the process of testing data, or evidence, and the performing of the necessary operations for comparison of these with hypotheses and theories. The term *verification* has long been used to describe this process, but since the literal meaning of the word is "to make true" or "to prove true," it is perhaps better to use some such word as *confirmation* in those fields where scientific hypotheses are held only provisionally, or with degrees of probability, with no claim to absolute finality. The facts which are found to be in agreement or which converge upon the hypothesis are said to be explained by it. The methods of verification vary with the nature of the field in which the hypothesis is made. In the more exact sciences, experimentation involves the control of conditions so that one or more *variables* may be isolated or inserted at will, and the results observed and recorded. It is a kind of interference with nature in order to force her to reveal secrets which do not lie on the surface, or a sort of speeding up of natural processes for which it would be wasteful of time to wait. In some cases, experiment involves the investigation of evidence from causal sequences, where such methods as those of agreement, difference, and concomitant variations are used. These methods will be discussed later. Experimentation also usually involves the use of instruments and operations which extend the capacity of our senses, and devices of measurement and recording which insure accuracy.

Sometimes it is possible to perform what is known as a *crucial experiment* to decide between rival hypotheses. Abstractly stated, Hypothesis H_1 implies that phenomenon P will occur, while hypothesis H_2 implies that phenomenon P will not occur. An experiment is then performed to test the hypotheses. If phenomenon P occurs, H_1 is accepted and H_2 is rejected.

The now famous experiment by Foucault on the nature of light is a good example of the technique, but the results were not as conclusive as at first believed. Since the time of Newton, the corpuscular theory of light had been accepted, but, by the middle of the nineteenth century, the wave theory challenged it. To decide between the two, Arago suggested that, if the corpuscular theory is correct, the speed of light would increase with the density of the medium, and, if the wave theory is correct, the speed would decrease.

Foucault performed an experiment and showed that the velocity of light was less in water than in air, which result was in favor of the wave theory. However, today the theory most widely accepted accounts for the nature of light as both waves and particles and is known as the theory of "quantum electrodynamics."

In less exact fields such as the historical and social sciences and law, the evidence which confirms hypotheses must be sought in diverse events, facts, and circumstances, which together *converge* to establish proof. The social sciences make much use of statistical methods, involving confirmation with varying degrees of probability. This method is proving successful in the physical sciences, and to some extent in the social sciences wherever quantitative data are sufficient. It is somewhat defective in dealing with qualitative and dynamic materials.

PROBLEMS

1. Invent an example, or recall a case of your own thinking, in which you solved a problem or made a discovery. Show the various steps in the solution, such as observation, analysis, inductions, hypotheses, deductions, verification, and their interrelations.

2. What are some of the requirements of good observation such as that required in a controlled scientific experiment, and what are some important traits in a good scientific observer?

3. What is an hypothesis, and what is its function in scientific method? What are the criteria of a good hypothesis? How are induction and deduction related in the use of hypotheses?

4. Examine Galileo's hypothesis on the laws of falling bodies in the light of the four criteria. Explain in what respects it does or does not meet these criteria?

5. How would you account for the following hypotheses, which at one time were regarded as satisfactory explanations?

(1) The earth is flat, and the sun revolves around it.
(2) Combustion is due to the presence of a principle known as "phlogiston."
(3) "Abiogenesis," or spontaneous generation, accounts for the presence of microorganisms.
(4) The rise and fall of the Nile is due to the action of the sun upon the water.
(5) The fossils found in the earth are evidence of sudden catastrophic events in the past.

6. Marshal the evidence which supports the following hypotheses. Can you suggest a rival hypothesis in each case?

(1) That the first six books of the Old Testament are not of single authorship
(2) That acquired characteristics are not inherited
(3) That the energy of any material system can be neither increased nor decreased
(4) That the bite of the mosquito causes yellow fever
(5) That organic evolution is due to natural selection

7. Why, for the purposes of anthropology, is the classification of races on the basis of such properties as pigmentation, hair structure, shape of nose, and shape of head more important than that of blondes, brunettes, redheads, and nondescripts?

8. What is an analogy, and what is the nature of analogical thinking in science?

9. Give three examples of arguments by analogy which you feel are valid. Give three which you feel are not valid.

10. The following are arguments by analogy. Evaluate each one, and tell why you think it is sound or not sound.

(1) The government of the United States may safely continue to borrow, as long as the government of Great Britian does so.
(2) Because French and Spanish are both derived from Latin, their grammatical structures should be very similar.
(3) The similarity of climate between southern California and southwestern Australia makes it logical to suppose that the two areas could grow very similar crops.
(4) The armies of both Japan and China are Oriental and are largely

copied after those of Western nations; therefore, they are of about the same efficiency.

(5) The success with which our Constitution unified the thirteen original colonies is a powerful argument in favor of a United States of Europe under a similar constitution.

11. In each of the following cases, what scientific method is being used?

(1) The breaking up of the sun's light into its spectroscopic colors
(2) The arrangement of animals or plants in groups such as genus, species, family, etc.
(3) The use of the telescope in astronomy
(4) The testing of materials by the United States Bureau of Standards
(5) The reconstruction of a dinosaur from fragments of bones found in various places
(6) The construction and validation of an intelligence test

12. Look up the experimental evidence which tends to verify Einstein's theory of relativity. Show how these facts are related and how they follow as consequences of the theory.

13. The Fitzgerald contraction theory was proposed to account for the facts discovered in the Michelson experiment, namely, that our velocity through the ether could not be determined by experiments with beams of light. The Fitzgerald hypothesis was that this negative result could be explained if we supposed that motion through the ether resulted in the contraction of every body moving through the ether in the direction of its motion. Why could not this hypothesis be verified?

14. Look up in an encyclopedia or textbook of astronomy or physics the method used by Fizeau in the first laboratory experiment to determine the speed of light. Make a list of the various deductions which were necessary before the final experiment could be made. (There is a good account of this experiment in *Astronomy*, by Skilling and Richardson, pp. 105–7.)

15. Show how observation, hypotheses, deductions, confirmation and analogy would interplay in collecting materials and writing a biography of a person about whom not much information is readily available.

16. Suggest several real or imaginary examples of crucial experiments.

15

Causal Connection
and Methods of
Experimental Inquiry

I. THE CONCEPT OF CAUSAL CONNECTION

We have frequently referred to the purpose of science as that of seeking order in experience and nature. We saw that classification of objects into natural kinds, generalizations such as "heat expands bodies," and hypotheses confirmed by experiments are examples of ordering which enable us not only to understand, but to predict within limits, the behavior of things and events.

The various procedures for discovering causal connections among phenomena are in effect methods of testing causal hypotheses, and hence constitute a very significant aspect of scientific methods. When hypotheses of causal connections have been confirmed, a form of explanation has been achieved. In the concrete sciences, where the sequences and uniformities are specific and repeatable, knowledge of causal connections enables us to predict and control. In the historical and social sciences, where the sequences and uniformities are more complex and less capable of repetition and control, less exactness is to be expected.

The concept of cause and effect is perhaps one of the most familiar, most widely accepted, and yet one of the most controversial concepts in the history of science.   The common-sense notion of cause is doubt-less derived from our everyday experience as agents in getting things done.   If we step on the gas, or the brake, we regard ourselves as the remote cause of the resulting flow of gasoline or of brake fluid, which brings about the immediate or proximate cause of the effect of greater or less speed.   We mean by *cause* in everyday life, very simply, that which makes things happen.

The causal situation involves an *antecedent* and a *consequent*, familiarly called cause and effect, so related that whenever the ante-cedent occurs, the consequent follows as a result.   That is, the cause is an invariable antecedent of the effect.   Stated negatively, no ante-cedent is the cause of a consequent event if in its absence the event occurs, or if in its presence the event fails to occur, or if it varies in a certain manner when the event does not vary in a corresponding manner.

This statement of the causal situation presupposes a certain amount of coherence and interdependence between things and events.   Every causal situation involves a *set of conditions* which must be present if the effect is to occur.   There are two kinds of conditions which should be carefully distinguished, namely, *sufficient conditions* and *necessary conditions*.   A sufficient condition of an event is such that whenever the condition is present the event will occur.   For example, a puncture is a sufficient condition of a flat tire, but it is not a necessary condition because other conditions might also be sufficient; e.g., the air may have escaped through the valve.   It may be symbolized as $p \supset q$.   A necessary condition of an event is such that the event never occurs in the absence of the condition.   For example, a necessary condition of life is air, for only if organisms have a supply of oxygen can they sustain life.   It may be symbolized as $-p \supset -q$ or $q \supset p$.   While this is a necessary condition, it is not sufficient, for, in addition, other conditions are also necessary such as food and water.   A condition is both sufficient and necessary if whenever it is present the event occurs, and whenever it is absent the event does not occur.   For example, after observing the conditions surrounding the threat of inflation in wartime, we might conclude: *If and only if* rigid price control is en-forced will we escape wartime inflation.   Here we have asserted that rigid price control is both the sufficient and the necessary condition of escaping inflation.   Another example is: "If a triangle is equilateral, it is equiangular."   This is symbolized as $p \supset q . -p \supset -q$.   The ideal of science is to discover the sufficient and necessary conditions of all events, but in practice this is almost never achieved, for one can never be sure that for all observed cases some unknown condition may be present or absent.

While it is possible in certain complex situations to make a distinction between *cause* and *condition*, for our purpose it is sufficient to say that the cause is the total set of conditions. Now not all of the conditions surrounding a causal situation may be relevant to our purpose, and some can safely be neglected. On the other hand, cursory investigation is in danger of failing to notice relevant conditions and falls short of discovering causal laws. Common sense often neglects all but the most obvious or most impressive, whereas science in search of the most general laws neglects many minor aspects.

While it is beyond the scope of this work to go into the philosophical controversy over the fundamental nature of causality, it might be of interest to mention briefly two major rival views. The philosopher Hume (1711–76) subjected the notion of causality to an elaborate critical examination, and showed that we have no logical right to use the principle of cause and effect to make inferences from fact to fact and from the present to the future. He rejected both the common-sense idea that there is some kind of a power in objects which, when exerted on other objects, results in causes, as well as the idea of necessity between cause and effect. He held that the reason for our belief in necessary causal connections is the constant repetition we have observed as one thing follows another in our experience. Belief in causality is nothing but a mental habit or custom of expecting to see one event follow another, or of inferring one event from another. Causality is nothing more than the observed uniformity of succession which is projected by us into the nature of things.

In contrast to this view, as we saw in Chapter 13, John Stuart Mill (1806–73) based his theory upon the Law of Universal Causation. For him causal laws are types of invariant relations, which we can rely upon to the extent that we can assume a uniformity of nature, a causal connection among events, and a limit to the possible variety of events. A cause is an unconditional invariant antecedent, and experimental inquiry was the method of discovering these invariant relations between events. For this purpose he formulated five methods of experimental inquiry, namely, *the Method of Agreement, the Method of Difference, the Joint Method of Agreement and Difference, the Method of Concomitant Variations,* and *the Method of Residues.* In this chapter, by example and illustration, we shall seek to make clear how these methods are employed and to point out some of their limitations.

II. THE METHOD OF AGREEMENT[1]

Rule: "If two or more instances of the phenomenon under investigation have only one circumstance in common, the circumstance in which alone all the instances agree, is the cause (or effect) of the given phenomenon."

We may substitute here for the term "phenomenon" any more familiar synonym, such as "occurrence" or "event," and for the rather vague term "circumstance" some such term as "attendant conditions" or "events."

In illustrating these methods symbolically, we shall follow Mill in using capital letters for antecedents and small letters for consequents, thus:

1. Symbolic Illustration.

Instance 1. A B C D followed by t u v w.
Instance 2. A E F G followed by t x y z.
Instance 3. A H I J followed by t q r s.

In conformity with the above rule, "A" is the only event common to the antecedents in the three sets of instances, and "t" is the only event common to the consequents in the three sets. These are the only constants amidst the contrasting variety. Hence we conclude that "A" is the cause of "t." It is obvious that when symbols are used, the situation is over-simplified and artificial. Events in their complex context of nature do not stand out sharply and are not so easily determined as in this illustration, as will appear in the more concrete examples which follow:

2. Concrete Illustration: Determining the Cause of Typhoid Fever.

Suppose that a typhoid epidemic has broken out in a given community, and that the local Board of Health is searching for the cause. On the basis of the accepted principles of medical science, the ultimate cause of typhoid is known to be the introduction of the typhoid bacillus into the body, either from food or water. It is the causal source of the bacilli that is sought. If a number of cases are studied corresponding to the above instances, and if it is found that the groceries are bought in different stores, the milk is bought from different dairies, vegetables are grown in different gardens, but in all cases water consumed came

---

[1] So called because the instances agree in only one respect, i.e., the given effect and its cause.

from a common reservoir, the health authorities would have good grounds for the conclusion that water is the probable source. The concrete factual situation may be combined with the symbolic illustration as follows:

	Water	Groceries	Milk	Vegetables	Typhoid
Instance 1.	A	B	C	D	followed by t u v w.
Instance 2.	A	E	F	G	followed by t x y z.
Instance 3.	A	H	I	J	followed by t q r s.

Hence, "A" is the cause of "t."

In the first place, by way of criticism of the above method, it should be noted that the requirements of the rule, that there should be only one circumstance in common, are impossible of realization. The typhoid victims might have many things in common, such as doing business at the same bank, going to the same theater, and wearing the same make of clothes. If it be objected that these things are irrelevant to the ingestion of the typhoid bacillus, this will be granted, but it should be pointed out that it is not the method itself which provided the knowledge that these circumstances are irrelevant. Thus if the method had been followed slavishly and without previous knowledge, any one of these common factors might be held to be the cause. Furthermore, it is clear that the method will not yield the true cause unless that cause is included among the items listed as antecedents. Mill himself recognized this and said, "If we could be certain of having ascertained all the invariable antecedents, we might be sure that the unconditional invariable antecedent, or cause, must be found somewhere among them."[2] Mill also regarded this method as primarily one of elimination or exclusion of irrelevant factors, as is shown by the following quotation: "Whatever circumstances can be excluded, without prejudice to the phenomenon, or can be absent notwithstanding its presence, is not connected with it in the way of causation."[3] Thus, in the above illustration, we have arrived at the hypothesis that water is the cause of the typhoid fever by reason of having eliminated the other alternatives of groceries, milk, and vegetables on the grounds that they were different in every case, whereas the water was present in all cases. This however does not render the conclusion certain.

The greatest imperfection in this method, which was recognized by Mill, is *the plurality of causes*. This means that a given effect may be

---

[2] J. S. Mill, *A System of Logic* (New York: Harper & Bros., 1887), p. 279.
[3] *Ibid.*, pp. 279, 280.

produced by one cause in one instance, and by another in another instance. Thus it is easily within the realm of possibility that in a typhoid epidemic something other than water might be the source of the bacilli in one or more of the observed instances. According to Mill the following method overcomes this imperfection.

III. THE METHOD OF DIFFERENCE[4]

Rule: "If an instance in which the phenomenon under investigation occurs, and an instance in which it does not occur, have every circumstance in common save one, that one occurring only in the former; the circumstance in which alone the two instances differ, is the effect, or the cause, or an indispensable part of the cause, of the phenomenon."

1. Symbolic Illustration.

Instance 1.　A B C D followed by f g h i.
Instance 2.　　 B C D followed by　g h i.

The phenomenon under investigation is "f." It occurs in the first instance and does not occur in the second. The two instances have everything in common except "A," hence "A" is the cause or an indispensable part of the cause of "f."

2. Concrete Illustration: Discovering the Cause of Yellow Fever.
Major Walter Reed, a United States Army surgeon, headed a commission to study sanitary conditions in Cuba after the Spanish-American War. After some preliminary observations and experimentation with mosquitoes suspected of carrying the infection, a carefully controlled experiment was carried out. Two mosquito-proof compartments were constructed. In one, mosquitoes which had bitten yellow fever patients at a period sufficiently previous to allow the maturity of the parasite were placed. A nonimmune volunteer subject lived for some time in this room and was bitten repeatedly by the mosquitoes. In the other compartment, which contained no mosquitoes, stayed another nonimmune volunteer. The yellow fever was contracted by the subject in the compartment containing mosquitoes and was not contracted by the subject in the room which did not contain them.

---

[4] So called because the instances differ in only one respect, i.e., the given effect and its cause. This method is the epitome of the laboratory experiment, where conditions can be isolated and controlled.

We may now combine the above example with the symbols to make the illustration clearer:

		Insect-			Yellow
Positive	Mos-	proof	Sanitary	Nonimmune	fever
Instances:	quitoes	tent	tent	subjects	↓
	A	B	C	D	followed by f g h i.

		Insect-			
Negative		proof	Sanitary	Nonimmune	
Instances:		tent	tent	subjects	
		B	C	D	followed by g h i.

Thus mosquitoes "A" are causally connected with yellow fever "f."

The Method of Difference is clearly a more truly experimental method, since factors may be introduced or left out at will and the results observed. There is, however, as in the Method of Agreement, difficulty in adhering strictly to the letter of the rule, for no instances can be found which are exactly alike in all circumstances save one. Obviously "all circumstances" should be interpreted to mean "all relevant circumstances," but the Method of Difference itself does not reveal just what a "relevant" circumstance is. In his discussion of the Method of Difference, Mill stated a test or application of it: "But to determine whether this invariable antecedent is a cause, or this invariable consequent an effect, we must be able, in addition, to produce the one by means of the other: or, at least, to obtain . . . an instance in which the effect 'a' has come into existence, with no other change in the preexisting circumstances than the addition of 'A.' "[5] Thus, in the above example, the yellow fever was capable of being produced by the introduction of mosquitoes, with other preexistent circumstances kept as stable as possible. As a process of elimination, this method is guided by the rule that nothing can be the cause of a phenomenon in the presence of which it fails to occur.

IV. THE JOINT METHOD OF AGREEMENT AND DIFFERENCE

Rule: "If two or more instances in which the phenomenon occurs have only one circumstance in common, while two or more instances in which it does not occur have nothing in common save the absence of that circumstance, the circumstance in which alone the two sets of

[5] J. S. Mill, *A System of Logic* (New York: Harper & Bros., 1887), p. 282.

instances differ, is the effect, or the cause, or an indispensable part of the cause, of the phenomenon."[6]

1. Symbolic Illustration.

Positive Instances:	A B C D followed by	p q r s.
	A E F G followed by	p t u v.
	A H I J followed by	p w x y.
Negative: Instances:	B C K followed by	q r o.
	E F L followed by	t u n.
	H I M followed by	w x y.

Hence, "A" is causally related to "p."

2. Concrete Illustration: Determining the Cause of Ptomaine Poisoning.

Suppose that we have a party of six people who eat at a cafeteria and that afterwards three develop ptomaine poisoning. An inquiry is made into the details of their menus, and it is found that every item of their meals differed with the exception of chicken. All of those stricken with the poisoning had eaten this one thing, and only this, in common. According to the Method of Agreement, the chicken would be regarded as the cause of the poisoning. But if we wished to make a check in order to be doubly sure, we would supplement our inquiry by comparing those afflicted with the three who were not afflicted. We find that the negative cases, i.e., those not poisoned, have alone in common the absence of chicken on their menus. Combining the symbols with the concrete illustration, we have the following:

					Ptomaine Poisoning ↓
Positive Instances:	Chicken A	Potatoes B	Bread C	Olives D	followed by p q r s.
	Chicken A	Salad E	Pickles F	Fruit G	followed by p t u v.
	Chicken A	Peas H	Rolls I	Nuts J	followed by p w x y.
Negative Instances:		Potatoes B	Bread C	Steak K	followed by q r o.
		Salad E	Pickles F	Beef L	followed by t u n.
		Peas H	Rolls I	Duck M	followed by w x z.

Hence, chicken "A" is causally related to ptomaine poisoning "p."

It is clear that the Joint Method must be handled with care and

---

[6] In other words, given (1) several positive cases, (2) several negative cases, and (3) one and only one factor that is both (a) present in all positive cases and (b) absent in all negative cases, then that factor is the cause.

discrimination with reference to relevant factors. The strict requirements of the rule, that the negative instances "have nothing in common save the absence of that circumstance," is capable of several interpretations. Using the above illustration as an example, it would be impossible to find a group of three people eating at a cafeteria who had absolutely nothing in common save the absence of chicken from their meal. There are such common factors as the kitchen, the proprietor, the self-service, etc. At the other extreme of absurdity it would be possible to interpret the rule so loosely that we might have included in our antecedents such items as weight, height, complexion, and other factors not in common which would fulfill the strict requirements of the rule but which are obviously irrelevant. Finally, it is possible to interpret the rule, as indeed Mill meant that it should be interpreted, so as to include only factors relevant to the problem, as in this case, items on the menu that could have had some connection with ptomaine poisoning. However, the rule itself does not give us the means of deciding upon and selecting those relevant factors. Thus corrected, the Joint Method is superior to the Method of Agreement alone, and Mill included it because of the shortcomings of that method, but he did not regard it as satisfying all of the conditions of the Method of Difference. He considered it rather, as a double employment of the Method of Agreement, the first set of instances agreeing in the presence of one antecedent, and the second set agreeing in its absence.

V. THE METHOD OF RESIDUES

Rule: "Subduct from any phenomenon such part as is known from previous inductions to be the effect of certain antecedents, and the residue of the phenomenon is the effect of the remaining antecedents."

1. Symbolic Illustration.

A B C D followed by w x y z.
A B C and w x y known by previous inductions to be causally related as antecedents and consequents.

Hence, "D" is causally related to "z."

2. Concrete Illustration: Discovery of the Planet Neptune.
The planet Uranus was discovered in 1781. Between this date and 1820, observations were made and tables constructed of the motions not only of Uranus, but of Jupiter and Saturn as well. Uranus, however, failed to obey the theoretical expectations, misbehaving to an extent greater than could be attributed to errors of observation. This led to the

suggestion that the perturbations of Uranus were at least partly due to some unknown planet.

Two mathematicians, Leverrier in France, and Adams in England, worked on the problem between 1843 and 1846 and, independently and simultaneously, arrived at almost identical conclusions. Leverrier is sometimes erroneously given greater credit, however, for his results were sent to the Berlin observatory, where search was begun immediately. Observations over a period of several nights, with the assistance of some recently compiled star charts, led to the identification of the predicted planet.

The first problem facing the mathematicians had been to account for the discrepancy between the *observed* orbit of Uranus and the *theoretical* orbit, which was based upon calculations of the sun, Jupiter, Saturn, and the other planets, according to the accepted principles of gravity. The mathematical calculation of the influence of these interior bodies accounted for only a part of the deviation of Uranus. When this influence was subducted from the entire deviation, there was left a residue of deviation to be accounted for. This was accounted for by the hypothesis of the existence of an unknown planet.

The second part of the problem was to locate the position of the hypothetical planet so that astronomers might be directed in their search for it. This was accomplished by a series of hypotheses relating to mass and position, upon the basis of which deductions were made concerning the effect of such an hypothetical body upon the orbit of Uranus. Finally the mass and position which would account for the residual perturbations were determined.

We may now combine the symbolic illustration of the method with our concrete case:

Sun	Planets	Satellites	Unknown Planet		Motions of Uranus
A	B	C	D	followed by	w x y z.
					Motions of Uranus (known by previous inductions)
Sun	Planets	Satellites			
A	B	C		followed by	w x y.

Hence, the residual effect in the orbit of Uranus, "z," is caused by the unknown planet, "D," or Neptune.

It should be observed that the Method of Residues is not strictly an inductive method, as was well recognized by Mill. The results are reached, as in the above illustration, by mathematical calculations and deductions. Furthermore, although the initiation of the problem depends upon observation, and final confirmation of the results depends upon previous inductions, the Method of Residues is not a method of experimentation, for the factors cannot be manipulated. It is a variant of the Method of Difference, and was intended by Mill to meet those situations where the Method of Difference could not be applied because of the constancy of certain factors such as gravity. In spite of these limitations it has proved most fertile as a technique, especially in astronomy.

VI. THE METHOD OF CONCOMITANT VARIATIONS

Rule: "Whatever phenomenon varies in any manner whenever another phenomenon varies in some particular manner, is either a cause or an effect of that phenomenon, or is connected with it through some fact of causation."

1. Symbolic Illustration.

$$A \ B \ C \ D_1 \quad \text{followed by} \quad p \ q \ r \ s_1.$$
$$A \ B \ C \ D_2 \quad \text{followed by} \quad p \ q \ r \ s_2.$$
$$A \ B \ C \ D_3 \quad \text{followed by} \quad p \ q \ r \ s_3.$$

As "D" increases, it is followed by an increase in "s"; and as "D" decreases, it is followed by a decrease in "s." Hence, "D" is causally related to "s."

2. Concrete Illustration: The Presence of Microorganisms in Air Dusts.

In 1860 Louis Pasteur was working on experiments to refute the theory of spontaneous generation. He wanted to study the dusts of the air, taken at different levels, with respect to their microorganic contents. He made a trip to the Alps with seventy-three sterile sealed flasks containing a putrescible liquor. Twenty were opened and air admitted in the country at about sea level, eight of which produced microorganisms. Twenty more were opened at the top of a mountain about one-half mile above sea level, and of these only five showed the presence of germs. He then ascended to an even higher elevation, opening twenty more; this time only one was found to contain the growths. He concluded that the minute organisms were not spontaneously generated from the liquid in the flasks but came rather from the dusts of the air, decreasing in quantity in the higher, colder, and more rarefied air of the Alps.[7]

[7] René Vallery-Radot, *The Life of Pasteur* (New York: Doubleday, Doran & Co., 1923), pp. 97, 98.

Combining the symbolism with the concrete illustration, we have the following:

Glass Jar	Liquid	Sealed	Air at Sea Level		Jars with Microorganisms
A	B	C	D_0	followed by	p q r s_8
Glass Jar	Liquid	Sealed	Air at $\frac{1}{2}$ mile		Jars with Microorganisms
A	B	C	$D_{\frac{1}{2}}$	followed by	p q r s_5
Glass Jar	Liquid	Sealed	Air at 1 mile		Jars with Microorganisms
A	B	C	D_1	followed by	p q r s_1

The quantity of "s" is seen to vary in inverse proportion to the quantity "D"; hence, "D" is held to be causally related to "s"; i.e., the altitude, and hence the existing dusts suspended in the air are seen to be causally connected with the presence of microorganisms in the liquids of the flasks.

Mill obviously did not mean by the rule quoted above that whenever covariant relations are observed between phenomena, that one *must* be either the cause or the effect of the other. There are many concomitant relations that are not causal. It is quite true, however, that whenever concomitant variations are observed, such as the tides and the moon, the sun and heat, moisture and vegetation, our suspicion is aroused that there is a probability of a causal relation between them, or between them and some other factor. The method of concomitant variation may then be used by way of introducing variables to determine the existence of causal laws. What we seem to demand in addition to the mere observance of concomitance is an explanation in terms of a law as to why the concomitance exists.

Stated negatively, however, Mill's method is very valuable for the elimination of irrelevant conditions, since no antecedent which varies in a certain manner when the event does not vary in a corresponding manner, or does not vary when the event does, can be said to be the cause of the event.

Concomitant variations are of three kinds: *Strict causal laws*, or invariant and unconditional laws of nature; *functional relations* between variables; and *statistical correlations*.

The notion of functional relations is supplementing or replacing the notion of cause in those sciences where exactness in terms of quantitative measurement is possible. Max Planck defines a physical law as follows: "A physical law is any proposition enunciating a fixed and absolutely valid connection between measurable quantities—a connection which permits us to calculate one of these quantities if the others have been discovered by measurement."[8]

When these measurements are precise the relation between two variables approaches the nature of a mathematical function. A mathematical function may be defined as a measurable variable whose values are determined by one or more other variables. That is, for every determinate value of one variable there is a corresponding determinate value of the other or others. The circumference of a circle is a function of its radius, a person's weight is a function of his diet, the number of tiles on the bathroom floor is a function of the size of the room. We would not say that the length of the radius of a circle was a cause of the circumference, or vice versa, yet we would say that there is a causal relation between diet and weight.

In the formula $y = f(x)$, y is said to be the function of x. The value of y may be calculated when the value of the independent variable x is known. The variable from which the calculation begins is known as the *independent* variable, and the other is called the *dependent* variable. For example, there is a functional relation between the price of wool and the price of men's suits if it can be shown that from the independent variable x, with the value of $1,000 per ton, we can calculate the dependent variable y, the price of men's suits $75.00 apiece. From the observation of this functional relation, we would be justified in the assumption of a causal relation, which on further investigation would be shown to rest on a set of agricultural, economic, and physical laws.

Concomitant variations may also be expressed in statistical correlations and may lead to the discovery of functional relations and causal laws. The presence of statistical correlations does not mean that strict causal laws can be inferred, since there are such things as chance correlations, coincidental and accidental relations. For example, we might find a high correlation between the number and length of the leaves on the trees and the blades of grass on the lawn, but we would not insist that this is a causal relation. But the presence of statistical correlations may lead us to suspect the causal relation and thus provide hypotheses for further testing by means of the various methods suggested in this chapter. Statistical correlations will be treated in Chapter 17.

[8] Reprinted from *The Universe in the Light of Modern Physics* (p. 58) by Max Planck, by permission of W. W. Norton & Company, Inc. Copyright, 1931, by the publishers.

PROBLEMS

1. Invent or recall a number of problems which might be solved by the application of each of Mill's methods.

2. Using the illustration given in Chapter 14 on discovering the source of crab grass in a lawn, indicate which of Mill's methods were employed in the various experiments. What is meant by the "plurality of causes"?

3. Analyze the factors involved in good scholarship in college, such as I.Q., family background, amount of time spent on studies, freedom from worry, scholastic interests, etc., and show how you would go about determining the exact cause.

4. Distinguish between sufficient conditions and necessary conditions, and give examples of each. Give examples of conditions which are both sufficient and necessary.

5. In terms of problem 3, distinguish between necessary and sufficient conditions of good scholarship in college.

6. Show how an understanding of the distinction between sufficient conditions and necessary conditions will help in the understanding and resolution of disputes such as the following:

   (1) We have had a losing football season, so we should fire the coach.
   (2) Mr. President, I deserve a raise in salary, for I have applied myself diligently to my job this last year.
   (3) If the foreign policy of the United States had been more favorable to Chiang Kai-shek, the revolution in China would not have occurred.
   (4) Materialism is the truest explanation of life, since all life has a physicochemical basis.

7. Look up the story of the discovery of Pluto, and indicate by what methods the planet was found.

8. An insurance policy reads as follows: "We-Pay-Nothing Insurance Company insures John Blank against loss resulting directly and independently of all other causes from bodily injuries sustained during the term of this policy." Mr. Blank, the insured, has a very bad heart and, while crossing some slippery pavement on crutches, is struck by an automobile and later pronounced dead by the doctor at the hospital to which he is taken. How would the insurance company determine whether or not the man's death came as a result of bodily injuries "directly and independently of all other causes"?

9. Frazer, in *The Golden Bough*, tells of the practice among certain Australian tribes of knocking out a boy's front teeth as a part of tribal initiation ceremonies. The teeth were then preserved, and it was believed that any injury to them or their capture by the enemy would

bring injury to their previous owner. Criticize this custom, with regard to the causal principles involved.

10. What are the advantages for science of the use of "functional correlation," compared to the formerly more prevalent use of "causal laws"?

11. What is the relation of concomitant variations to causal laws? What is the relation of functional relations and statistical correlations to causal laws?

12. In the following illustrations, are the coincidences causal or accidental?

  (1) All the clocks in a certain town indicate the same time.
  (2) All the privates in a certain company of the army receive the same amount of pay per month.
  (3) The product of 3 and 10 is the same as the product of 6 and 5.
  (4) The stars in the sky appear very close together and are spoken of as a "pair" of stars.
  (5) John is a good trombone player, a fast runner, and a poor student in geometry.
  (6) A man threw a pair of dice five times, and each time the combination of *five* turned up.

13. Analyze the following problems, and indicate which of Mill's methods might best be used in their solution:

  (1) A study of the effect of low economic status upon a group of delinquent children
  (2) A study of the effects of various color environments upon the behavior of rats
  (3) The measurement of the weight of a load of coal in a truck known to weigh one ton
  (4) The determination of the effect of tension upon the pitch of a violin string
  (5) A study of the effect of ultraviolet rays upon the severity of colds

14. In testing whether or not ordinary air contained bacteria, Pasteur exposed a vessel containing sterilized liquid to air which had been heated, and later could find no bacteria in the flask. He then exposed a *similar* vessel to ordinary air which had not been heated, and found that after a day or two a great many bacteria had appeared. Which of Mill's methods was he using?

15. Illustrate the difference between the mechanical pattern of analysis given by Mill and the pattern which must be used in historical and social sciences, by seeking to determine the causes of World War II.

16. Which one of Mill's methods is suggested by the following?

Wednesday night I drank rum and soda; night before last I drank whiskey and soda; last night I drank gin and soda; today I drank brandy and soda. It must have been the soda which gave me such a violent headache.

CAUSAL CONNECTION, EXPERIMENTAL INQUIRY   249

17. Which of Mill's methods does the following study illustrate? What, according to the study, would be held as the cause of the high crime and delinquency rate? What criticisms do you have to offer of the methods and results?

In a certain survey made by sociologists of a group of towns in the central part of the state, it was found that in three towns which had a high crime and delinquency rate the following conditions existed:

Town No. 1: Good schools, mediocre churches, poor recreation program, good police force, heterogeneous population, good economic conditions.

Town No. 2: Good churches, good recreation program, poor police force, homogeneous population, good schools, poor economic conditions.

Town No. 3: No recreational program, mediocre economic conditions, heterogeneous population, poor churches, mediocre police force, good schools.

18. Which of Mill's methods is being used in the first and which in the second phase of the following experiment:

(1) A research worker experimented with the effects of vitamin A on rats. One hundred healthy rats were divided into two groups. Group A was fed on the customary ration, which has maintained them in a normal healthy state. Group B had the major foods containing vitamin A withdrawn from its diet. Within a few weeks, Group B developed severe sinus trouble.

(2) The sinus-infected group was then fed daily rations of cod-liver oil, which is known to contain vitamin A. Within six weeks, the infected rats were restored to normal health.

16

Probability

I. THE GENERAL NATURE OF PROBABILITY

We have already seen that one of the most characteristic features of induction, as opposed to deduction, is that, whereas deductive reasoning from *some* to *all* is a logical fallacy, such reasoning constitutes the fundamental pattern of induction. Since not all of the instances of any complex field can be brought under direct observation, inductive inferences must be of the general form "Some [all observed] S's are P's; therefore, all S's are P's." The word "probable" is derived from the Latin *"probare,"* which means "to try," "to prove," and in popular parlance means that there is more evidence for than against. When degrees of probability are to be calculated or measured, they may be represented as ranging in a continuous series between impossibility, or O, and certainty, or 1. In Chapter 13, we discussed the different kinds of cognitive certainty which are possible in human knowledge. It was indicated that certainty is confined to the relatively narrow fields of immediate sensory experiences and logical consistency. Inductive generalizations from experience, which constitute the great bulk of our claims to knowledge, are only probable, ranging from low probability to high.

As Keynes[1] pointed out, the word "probability" is employed in different senses. It refers, *first,* to the logical relation between two sets of propositions, known as the *probability relation.* *Second,* it is used to refer to the *degrees of rational belief* arising out of knowledge of secondary propositions, which assert the existence of probability relations. *Third,* it refers to the *proposition* which is the object of the

[1] J. M. Keynes, *A Treatise on Probability* (New York: St. Martin's Press, Inc., 1963), pp. 11–12.

probable degree of rational belief. This might be illustrated by the following example, sometimes called "the statistical syllogism":

If we know that, out of 100 people in a room, 75 are blondes, and X is the first person to emerge from the room, the probability is ¾ that X is a blonde.

1. The relation between these sets of propositions is the *probability relation*, corresponding to the implicative relation in deductive arguments.
2. The *degree of rational belief* is indicated by the conclusion; that is, on the basis of the evidence, we have the rational belief that there is a ¾ chance that X is a blonde.
3. The *proposition* "The probability ˙s ¾ that X is a blonde" is what asserts the degree of rational belief, and, therefore, it is this proposition that is probable.

Whenever the phrase "probability of the event" is used in discussions of probability, it is usually a shorthand statement of "the probability of the truth of the proposition which asserts that the event will happen." All claims to knowledge, whether certain or probable, are based upon evidence and are relative to it. The theory and calculus of probabilities are attempts to discover ways to calculate and to measure degrees of tenable knowledge, or degrees of rational belief on the basis of the evidence. It is obvious that in some fields the evidence is of a very objective nature, while in others it is difficult to distinguish objectivity from subjectivity. In practical affairs, as also in law and politics, the desire and necessity for certainty are so strong that there is bound to be great complexity in the evidentiary situation, since it usually includes the factors of objective fact, subjective motives and beliefs, and the practical need for certainty.

Let us take a hypothetical case as an example of this complexity. Suppose the following alibi were presented by a man accused of the crime of robbing a bank:

The day before the crime was committed, a man stopped me on the street and asked me if I would like to make a hundred dollars by acting as his companion on a scientific expedition. Being out of work at the time, I accepted his offer. That night we left on his specially constructed rocket ship, and after several days we arrived on the moon, staying there two days. Since he blindfolded me before taking me to his laboratory, I do not know where it is, nor do I have any idea who he is or where to find him. I cannot imagine how the stolen money came to be in my room.[2]

The first thing to notice is that the entire story could be true; that is, it cannot be ruled out as being *impossible*, even though it is well known that the most advanced scientists and technicians, working at highly competitive speed, have not completed the research and testing

[2] Adapted from a student's paper.

sufficient to enable passengers to land on the moon, to survive, and to return. But, in view of the *objective evidence* presented at the trial— that the money was found in his room, that he had previously been convicted of robbery, and that a floor plan of the robbed bank was found in his possession when he was arrested—would you, if a member of the jury, have the slightest hesitancy in condemning him?

Thousands of people are in prison today who have been legally and properly convicted of crimes which no one can be absolutely certain they committed. But, if we are not certain on the basis of objective and rational evidence, why do we so often act as if we were? The answer is very simple. It is because in practical matters we must come to some conclusion in order to act, and we must act. For example, the jury in the above case had to decide whether the defendant was *guilty* or *not guilty*, and, lacking complete objective evidence, they were forced to risk error in an attempt to reach truth. Indeed, this practical necessity, so to speak, is a recognized principle of jurisprudence, for, as Justice Brandeis pointed out, "in most matters it is more important that the applicable rule of law be settled then that it be settled right."[3]

At the same time, however, we do not feel that our decisions, even though uncertain, are entirely haphazard. We often consider them acceptable if there is slightly more evidence for them than against. This is the popular meaning of probability. But it is obvious that in some cases it is extremely difficult to determine just what "more" evidence is. Anyone who is acquainted with intercollegiate forensics is well aware of the multiplicity of systems used in judging debates. An expression often used by debaters is "Don't worry about your arguments; worry about the judge." By one judge's standards, a certain argument or bit of evidence might be very acceptable, but, by another's, completely ridiculous. And yet, in such cases, it may be impossible to demonstrate an argument objectively, so the conflicting views may be allowed to stand. Consequently, the probability for one judge may be very low, and for another high, on the evidence. While this subjective factor cannot be eliminated entirely, it operates less in those fields where the materials are structured, objective, and public. When evidence of the latter kind is made the premises for probability judgments, predictions can be made with a high degree of probability. Two forms of probability theory, the mathematical and the empirical, or frequency theory, have been of most interest to logicians. We turn now to a discussion of these.

[3] Louis P. Brandeis, opinion in *Burnet* v. *Coronado Oil and Gas Co.*, 285 U.S. 393, 406.

II. MATHEMATICAL PROBABILITY[4]

1. The General Principle. Mathematical probability is purely deductive. This means that the probabilities follow logically from the assumptions, axioms, or postulates used as premises. The primary postulate, sometimes called the "law of chance," may be stated as follows: "The mathematical probability that any event will occur is the ratio of the favorable ways in which the event can occur to the total possible ways, favorable and unfavorable—these being equally possible." The principle may be stated in the formula

$$P = \frac{F}{F + U}$$

where P stands for the probability, F for the favorable alternatives, and U for the unfavorable.

If we analyze this principle, we shall see that three conditions are stated:

1. We must know the *favorable alternatives*, that is, the possible ways in which the desired result can be produced.
2. We must know the *total* number of possible alternatives.
3. We must know that these alternatives are *equally possible*.

The third condition, that the alternatives must be equally possible, is known as the *principle of indifference* and defines what is meant by "equally possible" as follows: "If there is no known reason for predicating of our subject one rather than another of several alternatives, then,

---

[4] The mathematical calculus of probability may be illustrated without reference to concrete *events* but as the *possible combinations of certain numbers*. If we expand the binomial with any desired exponent, we get the same mathematical results as we would from the calculation of the theoretical probabilities of tossing true coins.

For example:

$$(\tfrac{1}{2} + \tfrac{1}{2})^4 = \tfrac{1}{16} + \tfrac{4}{16} + \tfrac{6}{16} + \tfrac{4}{16} + \tfrac{1}{16}$$

If, however, we wish to calculate the probability of actual events as illustrated in the tossing of *four* coins, we assume the three conditions stated above and state our formula as follows:

$$(\tfrac{1}{2}H + \tfrac{1}{2}T)^4 = \tfrac{1}{16}H^4T^0 + \tfrac{4}{16}H^3T^1 + \tfrac{6}{16}H^2T^2 + \tfrac{4}{16}H^1T^3 + \tfrac{1}{16}H^0T^4$$

A clear understanding of the relation between theoretical possibilities and actual probabilities of *events* (as defined on page 251) is necessary if we are to avoid errors and fallacies in trying to apply the calculus of probability to nature, to games of chance, or to any subject matter where the structure of the materials is not determinate, in the sense of conforming to the three postulates given above.

relatively to such knowledge, the assertions of each of these alternatives have an equal probability."[5]

2. Single Independent Events. For example, in predicting the mathematical probability that a tossed coin will come down *heads,* we assume a normal coin and form a fraction the numerator of which is the ways it can come down heads (the favorable ways), which is 1, and the denominator of which is the total number of possible alternatives, which is 2 (i.e., heads and tails), and, if the coin is a true, or normal, coin, we know of no reason why the alternative sides are not equiprobable.   The resulting fraction is, of course, ½.

Again, to find the mathematical probability that a die will turn up 3, we take as our numerator the number of ways it can come up 3, which is 1, and as our denominator the total number of possible alternatives, which is 6.   The probability is ⅙ that the die will turn up 3.

Playing cards present the same, although a little more complex, situation.   The probability that we can pick an ace at random from a full deck of 52 cards is 4/52, for there are 4 aces (i.e., 4 favorable alternatives) and 52 cards in all (i.e., 52 possible alternatives).   This fraction then reduces to 1/13.

There is a distinction between the mathematical probability of an event as here defined and the *odds.*   Odds refers to the ratio between the favorable and unfavorable alternatives, or F/U.   Thus, to find the odds, we subtract the numerator of the probability fraction from the denominator.   For example, knowing that the probability of getting heads on a tossed coin is ½, to find the odds we subtract the 1 from the 2, which yields 1 to 1, or, colloquially, 50–50.   The probability of getting a heart in one draw from a normal pack of playing cards is ¼; so the odds in *favor* are ⅓.   The odds *against* are found by simply reversing the fraction; the odds against getting a heart are 3/1.

In calculating probability is this way, it makes no difference whether we are thinking of tossing one coin twenty-five times or twenty-five coins all at once.   The probabilities of the various possible combinations are the same in either case.

3. Compound Independent Events. By *compound events,* we mean any combination of more than a single event, such as two or more heads in tossing a coin.   By *independence,* it is meant that what happens on the first throw in no way affects what happens on the

[5] Keynes, *op. cit.,* p. 42.

subsequent throws, and vice versa. For this purpose, we use the *product theorem*. We compute the individual probabilities and then multiply them. If we ask what is the probability of getting two heads in tossing a coin twice, we begin by computing the individual probabilities. The probability of a head on the first toss is $\frac{1}{2}$, and that of a head on the second is $\frac{1}{2}$, and the product is $\frac{1}{2} \times \frac{1}{2}$, or $\frac{1}{4}$. This may be simplified further. If we chart the various possibilities when a coin is tossed twice, we have the following: HH HT TH TT, and examination will show that in one case out of the four we have the combination of two heads. Again, if we ask, what is the probability of two 5's in two throws of a die, we find that this is an example of compound independent events. Since the probability of a 5 on each of the two throws is $\frac{1}{6}$, the compound probability is $\frac{1}{6} \times \frac{1}{6}$, or $\frac{1}{36}$. The accompanying chart will enable us to check any combination of two dice thrown simultaneously, or two throws with the same die. The first number in each column will stand for the number on the first die, and the second number in the column for the number on the second:

11	21	31	41	51	61
12	22	32	42	52	62
13	23	33	43	53	63
14	24	34	44	54	64
15	25	35	45	55	65
16	26	36	46	56	66

For example, if we ask what is the probability of getting a total of 7 in tossing two dice, we find by examining the chart that there are 6 ways in which a 7 can appear, and 36 total alternatives, so we have the answer in the fraction $\frac{6}{36}$, or $\frac{1}{6}$.

4. Compound Dependent Events. The formula for determining the probability of compound dependent events is the same as that for independent events, as above, but it must be remembered that, in the case of dependent events, the result of the first event affects the probabilities of those which follow. This is what is meant by the term *dependent*. Thus, if there are 10 beans and 8 peas in a bag, the probability of getting 2 peas in the first two draws from the bag (the product of the individual probabilities) is $\frac{8}{18}$ (the probability in the first draw) times $\frac{7}{17}$ (the probability in the second draw), or $\frac{28}{153}$. This, of course, is based on the assumption that 1 pea has been drawn and not returned when the second draw takes place. Again, the probability of drawing 3 hearts in succession from a pack of playing cards (provided each card drawn is left out) is $\frac{13}{52}$ times $\frac{12}{51}$ times $\frac{11}{50}$—the number of hearts in the deck, as well as the total number of cards, decreasing with each draw. This yields the result of $^{1716}\!/_{132600}$, or approximately $\frac{1}{77}$.

5. Mutually Exclusive Independent Events. In determining the probability of events when an alternative is present, we use the *addition theorem;* that is, the probability of alternative independent events is the *sum* of the separate probabilities. Thus the probability of getting either heads or tails in one toss of a coin is $\frac{1}{2}$ plus $\frac{1}{2}$, or 1 (i.e., certainty). The probability of getting either a 1 or a 2 in one throw of a die is $\frac{1}{6}$ plus $\frac{1}{6}$, or $\frac{1}{3}$.

This rule does not apply to situations where an alternative toss (i.e., an alternative trial) is offered, but only where there is an alternative way of obtaining a favorable result. The probability that a tossed coin will come down heads in *either* the first or second throw is not $\frac{1}{2}$ plus $\frac{1}{2}$. There are two ways of calculating probabilities in problems of this kind. First, we may list the total possibilities as HH HT TH TT, as before. Each of these has the probability of $\frac{1}{4}$, and in three of them the necessary condition, the presence of a head, is satisfied. Hence, the probability of getting at least one head in either the first or second throw is equal to the sum of the separate probabilities, i.e., $\frac{1}{4}$ plus $\frac{1}{4}$ plus $\frac{1}{4}$, or $\frac{3}{4}$.

The second method of calculating the probability of getting at least one head on either the first or second toss (and other problems of the same kind) is as follows: There are only two possibilities: (1) At least one head will appear on two tosses. (2) No heads will appear on two tosses (i.e., this is the nonprobability of getting a head). Since these exhaust the possibilities, the probability that at least one of these will occur is 1, or certainty. Now, if we compute the probability of (2), that is, of getting two tails, we have $\frac{1}{2}$ times $\frac{1}{2}$, or $\frac{1}{4}$, the product of the separate probabilities. Subtracting this $\frac{1}{4}$ from 1, we have $\frac{3}{4}$, which agrees with the previous result.

III. BAYES' THEOREM

In current discussions of probability, a good deal of emphasis is being placed on Bayes' theorem. The Reverend Thomas Bayes (*ca.* 1702–61), a Fellow of the Royal Society, proposed a theorem to account for the probability of what he called "causes." What he obviously meant by "cause" is some antecedent occurrence relevant to the event, the probability of which was to be accounted for. We prefer in this discussion to use the two terms *hypothesis, H,* and *event, E*.

Since Bayes' formula involves an aspect of probability known as *conditional probability*, we shall briefly explain and illustrate this concept. If event B cannot happen unless some other event, A, has happened, or unless some condition has been imposed, then the probability of B must include the probability that the condition A has been met. The conditional probability of the event B, given the observed event A, is symbolized as $P(B \mid A)$. The conditional probability of the event A, given the observed event B, is written $P(A \mid B)$. The following is an example:

Four red balls and 1 blue ball are placed in a vase, and 2 red balls and 3 blue balls are placed in an identical vase. If one of the vases is selected at random and 1 ball withdrawn from it, what is the probability that it will be red?

Since the probabilities are even that either vase will be chosen, the probability is $\frac{1}{2}$ for either vase. On the condition that the first vase is chosen, in view of the fact that there are 4 red balls, out of a total of 5, the probability is $\frac{4}{5}$ for a red ball. On the condition that the second vase is chosen, since there are in it 2 red balls, and a total of 5, the probability is $\frac{2}{5}$. The probability, then, that a red ball from the first vase will be chosen is the product of the two probabilities, $\frac{4}{5}$ times $\frac{1}{2}$, or $\frac{2}{5}$. The probability that a red ball from the second vase will be chosen is $\frac{2}{5}$ times $\frac{1}{2}$, or $\frac{1}{5}$. The conditional probability of drawing a red ball is, then, the sum of the probabilities for the two vases: $(\frac{4}{5} \times \frac{1}{2}) + (\frac{2}{5} \times \frac{1}{2})$, or $\frac{3}{5}$.

In order to use Bayes' formula, the situation must be such that the probability of each alternative hypothesis is not zero, and that the several hypotheses of the sample space constituting the case are exhaustive and disjunctive. Bayes' theorem is of value in revising prior estimates of probability on the basis of new information. It is regarded as of great importance in decision making. The formula is as follows:

$$P(H1 \mid E) = \frac{P(H1) \cdot P(E \mid H1)}{P(H1) \cdot P(E \mid H1) + P(H2) \cdot P(E \mid H2) + \cdots + P(Hn) \cdot P(E \mid Hn)}$$

where H = hypothesis

E = event

$P(H1)$, etc. = the *a priori* probability of $H1$, etc.

$P(H1 \mid E)$ = the *a posteriori* probability of $H1$, given the observed event E

$P(E \mid H1)$, etc. = the probability of E, given $H1$, etc.

The term *a priori* means, "prior to any information yielded by experiment."

The term *a posteriori* means, "based upon experience," or "given the observed event."

The following example is chosen to illustrate Bayes' theorem, because such examples fulfill the requirements mentioned above:

Box No. 1 contained 5 white and 3 black balls; another box, No. 2, contained 4 white and 7 black balls. One ball was transferred from the first to the second box, and then a ball was drawn from the second. If the latter ball was white (the event E), what is the probability that the transferred ball was black? We have here two possible hypotheses: $H1$, that the transferred ball was black, and $H2$, that the transferred ball was white.

The probability that a black ball was transferred from the first to the second box is $\frac{3}{8}$, since there were 3 black balls in this box, and a total of 8. The probability that a white ball was transferred from the first to the second is $\frac{5}{8}$, since there were 5 white balls and a total of 8. The transfer of a ball to the second box produced a total of 12, so the probability of then drawing a white ball from the second box, on the assumption that the transferred ball was black, was $\frac{4}{12}$, and the probability of drawing a white ball from the second box, based on the assumption that the transferred ball was white, was $\frac{5}{12}$.

Hence, the probability that the transferred ball was black, hypothesis 1, given E (the event that the first ball drawn was white), is found by the following Bayes'-theorem formula:

$$P(H1 \mid E) = \frac{P(H1) \cdot P(E \mid H1)}{P(H1) \cdot P(E \mid H1) + P(H2) \cdot P(E \mid H2)}$$
$$= \frac{\frac{3}{8} \cdot \frac{4}{12}}{\frac{3}{8} \cdot \frac{4}{12} + \frac{5}{8} \cdot \frac{5}{12}} = \frac{12}{37}$$

A more practical illustration of Bayes' theorem is as follows:

A dress factory produces 2,000 garments per day—1,000 of model A
400 of model B
600 of model C

The production of model A is 50% of total production.
The production of model B is 20% of total production.
The production of model C is 30% of total production.

A garment drawn at random from a day's production is found to be defective. What is the probability it is model A? B? or C?

Let E be the event that the sample was defective.

Let $H1$ be the hypothesis that the defective item is model A.

Let $H2$ be the hypothesis that the defective item is model B.
Let $H3$ be the hypothesis that the defective item is model C.

$P(E \mid H1) = .03\%$ of model A which failed to pass inspection
$P(E \mid H2) = .02\%$ of model B which failed to pass inspection
$P(E \mid H3) = .01\%$ of model C which failed to pass inspection

By the application of Bayes' theorem, we have the following:

$P(H1 \mid E)$

$$= \frac{P(H1) \cdot P(E \mid H1)}{P(H1) \cdot P(E \mid H1) + P(H2) \cdot P(E \mid H2) + P(H3) \cdot P(E \mid H3)}$$

$$= \frac{(.50 \cdot .03)}{(.50 \cdot .03) + (.20 \cdot .02) + (.30 \cdot .01)} = \frac{.0150}{.0220} = 68\%$$

$P(H2 \mid E)$

$$= \frac{\overset{(.20 \quad \cdot \quad .02)}{P(H2) \cdot P(E \mid H2)}}{\underset{(.50 \quad \cdot \quad .03) \quad + \quad (.20 \quad \cdot \quad .02) \quad + \quad (.30 \quad \cdot \quad .01)}{P(H1) \cdot P(E \mid H1) + P(H2) \cdot P(E \mid H2) + P(H3) \cdot P(E \mid H3)}}$$

$$= \frac{.0040}{.0220} = 18\%$$

$P(H3 \mid E)$

$$= \frac{\overset{(.30 \quad \cdot \quad .01)}{P(H3) \cdot P(E \mid H3)}}{\underset{(.50 \quad \cdot \quad .03) \quad + \quad (.20 \quad \cdot \quad .02) \quad + \quad (.30 \quad . \quad .01)}{P(H1) \cdot P(E \mid H1) + P(H2) \cdot P(E \mid H2) + P(H3) \cdot P(E \mid H3)}}$$

$$= \frac{.0030}{.0220} = 14\%$$

The *a priori* probability that the defective garment was model A is 50%; model B, 20%; and model C, 30%.

The application of Bayes' theorem enables us to revise these probabilities so that the *a posteriori* probabilities are model A, 68%; model B, 18%; and model C, 14%.

IV. EMPIRICAL PROBABILITY: FREQUENCY THEORY

Empirical probability differs from mathematical probability in that, while the latter is purely deductive, empirical probability is based upon experience, upon actual observation of the frequencies of the class of objects or events under investigation.

If we were to experiment by tossing coins or dice, and if we were to tabulate the results, we might find that in 100 trials the empirical results would not correspond, with anywhere near exactness, with the theoretical predictions. This in no way invalidates the mathematical predictions, since they depend upon the postulate of an ideal situation where no particular causes operate to interfere with the principle of indifference, thus rendering the situation capable of deductive treatment. If nature and society were homogeneous in terms of finite alternatives, observed frequencies, and equipossibility, science would approximate a deductive system. The fact that they are not so constitutes the problem of induction and probable inference.

1. Qualitative Empirical Probability. Proceeding from the simple to the complex, we shall begin by discussing qualitative probability judgments which occur frequently in common life and are expressed in popular language. It may be regarded as an indication of caution, perhaps often learned through painful experience with hasty generalizations, that our speech abounds in probability assertions. We say, "It will probably rain," "He will probably be on time," "It is probably John Smith," "It is probably an enemy plane." Such statements are but vague expressions of the fact that the event is a little more likely to occur than not, on the evidence, which may be based either upon past observed instances, upon analogy from similar situations, or upon a complex of background conditions made up of both knowledge and ignorance. All such judgments are relative to this background knowledge, which, together with the observed instances, constitutes the evidence. No event is probable or improbable in iteslf without reference to the evidence. If we know something of the complexion of the Congress of the United States, we can say with some degree of probability that certain types of legislation have a good chance of success. But, if the composition of the Congress changes because of a conservative trend in local and state elections, we have grounds for probability judgments that legislation of this kind will have hard sledding.

A simple form of probability judgment is illustrated by situations in which we are led to expect a certain amount of uniformity in human behavior because of past experience. If we say, "He will probably be on time; he always has been," we are expressing a degree of rational belief in the probability of the event on the basis of repeated instances in the past, the character of the person, and the circumstances. The first two may provide evidence for a high degree of probability, but the complexity of the surrounding conditions may constitute the negative factor and lessen the probability.

The judgment "It is probably an enemy plane" is slightly different in that it may be based not on repeatable instances from the past but on such factors as the relative positions of our own planes, the strength of the enemy, and the estimated value to the enemy of aerial action at such a time and place. The final verification must rest upon direct or indirect perceptual observation.

Such a probability judgment as "It will probably rain" is usually based upon analogy. It is of the general form "Today resembles yesterday with respect to low atmospheric pressure and clouds, which yesterday were accompanied by rain. Hence, today will probably resemble yesterday with respect to rain."

2. Quantitative Empirical Probability. By "quantitative probability" we mean simply that the probability ratio may be expressed in the form of a fraction from observed frequencies. If we recall the pattern for the calculation of mathematical probability, we will remember that the numerator of our fraction consisted of favorable ways, and the denominator of the total possibilities. Now what we need in order to estimate both empirically and quantitatively is just such a fraction, constructed, however, from observed frequencies. It is obvious that in some simple matters we may know in advance the nature and extent of the materials, whereas in more complex matters we may know nothing about the extent of the materials or the nature of the possible alternatives. Let us take examples of each. We shall deal with the latter first. Suppose we have before us a barrel of apples. We do not know how many apples there are, or what kinds. Then let us suppose that we are stimulated to find out by a wager or a guessing game. We begin by drawing out samples of, say, 5 apples at a time. The first sample yields all "Jonathans." Now, not knowing the number in the barrel, we cannot make any exact fraction; hence, we cannot state the probability in any definite form, and any statement we might make on this limited evidence would be of no value. But suppose we continue to draw samples from the barrel in groups of 5 until we have tabulated 100 draws and 500 apples—all "Jonathans." We are now able to say, though not quantitatively, that the probability is higher that all of the apples in the barrel are "Jonathans." As we continue, and near the bottom of the barrel, if we still continue to draw "Jonathans," we are justified in claiming that the probability is higher as we near the bottom of the barrel. On our assumption, however, we do not know how near the bottom we are, and we still cannot state the probability mathematically or quantitatively. Now let us suppose that we do know the number of apples in the barrel before we begin—let us say 600—but we do not know what kinds. If, as before on our first sampling, we draw out 5 "Jonathans," we can now form a fraction and say that the probability is that $5/600$ that all of the apples in the barrel are "Jonathans"—the numerator being the number drawn, and the denominator the total number of alternatives. If we assume that, as the sampling continues, the numerator becomes larger and larger with no exceptions, we are justified in saying that the probability becomes greater until unity, or certainty, is reached.

Now suppose that on the second sampling we find that 2 of the apples are "Delicious," and as the sampling continues to the twentieth sample we have 75 "Jonathans" and 25 "Delicious." We are then able to form the fraction $75/100$ and interpret it as grounds for the statistical generalization that $3/4$ of the apples in the barrel are "Jonathans." Likewise we may, on the evidence, assert that $25/100$, or $1/4$, of the apples in the barrel are "Delicious." But it will be obvious that these generalizations at this stage of the sampling process are not as reliable as they would be at a later stage. What, then, can be said about the probability of the truth of the generalizations themselves? That is, what is the probability of the truth of the assertion "$3/4$ of the apples in the barrel are 'Jonathans' "? This can be estimated by taking as the numerator of the probability fraction the total number drawn, or 100, and taking as the denominator the total number in the barrel, or 600, resulting in $1/6$. As the sampling process continues and the numerator becomes larger, the probability becomes greater and greater that it is a true sample of the whole barrel.

The social sciences and insurance companies make practical use of generalizations from frequencies. The most spectacular example of success in predicting from observed frequencies is found in insurance statistics on life expectancies. For example, let us ask, "What is the probability that a child ten years of age will live to be fifty"? Let us suppose that, upon consulting the mortality tables, we find that, out of a total of 200,000 cases of this class, 140,000 have lived to be fifty. The numerator of the fraction is made up of observed instances favorable to the event, or 140,000. The denominator is made up of the totality of observed instances, or 200,000. The fraction reduces to $7/10$, on the basis of which we may assert that the probability that members of this class (children of ten) will live to be fifty is $7/10$. It should be remembered that any unusual change in the relevant conditions, such as an epidemic, earthquake, war, or famine, will invalidate these results. Furthermore, since the class studied does not include any future cases, it cannot be regarded as a prediction about any individual case. From the viewpoint of the insurance company, it is very valuable to know the frequencies of death, since this information forms the basis of financial success. From the viewpoint of the individual, it cannot have much meaning, and it tells him nothing about how long he will live.

3. Probability and Inductive Generalizations. Inductive generalizations are truth claims for assertions of invariant relations, either positive or negative, in the materials dealt with in the sciences. As we have seen, inductive inferences are of the general form "Some [all observed] S's are P's; hence, all S's are P's." Examples are "All life comes from life," "All magnets will attract iron," "All scholars are introverts," "All water freezes at 32°F." It might well be asked, at the outset, why anyone should raise any question as to the degree of probability of most of these, since most of them have been regarded for many years as invariant laws of nature. How do we know, for example, that the next water we drink will not kill us? Practically, it is only because we have found no cases where pure water has been deadly (and we have been drinking it all our lives), and, arguing from cases in the past to cases in the present and future, i.e., *from some to all*, we proceed to act as though all water is harmless. For practical purposes, it is sufficient to say that our confidence is based upon the fact that such assumptions work. So we may also reason with regard to the above generalizations. In every case where observations have been made (a very large number), the event has occurred, and no negative instances have been observed. This leads to the very natural question "If there are alternatives, why do they not appear"? Since they do not, we begin to suspect that there are none. This would perhaps be the practical answer of almost anyone who might be called upon to defend his belief in such generalizations. But this answer has two defects. It contains certain unexpressed assumptions about the order of nature and at the same time avoids facing certain theoretical difficulties inherent in all generalizations from experience.

Again, we recall that only in the case in which we could observe instances as the result of sampling, and at the same time know the total number of apples in the barrel, were we able to form a probability fraction from which to make estimates of probability. In the case where we knew nothing about the number in the barrel, the denominator of the fraction was always an unknown. Now most of the above generalizations differ from this concrete case, in that they belong to natural systems which may be infinitely complex. If we may suppose that nature is infinitely complex, it is clear that, no matter how many observations were made from samples, the probability would not be increased. Not only have the observations, for example, on magnets attracting iron, been limited in number, they have been limited as to variety of conditions under which the observations were made in a possibly infinite universe—hence, the limited nature of the numerator of our probability fraction. The denominator of our fraction is even more unsatisfactory, since it may represent a possibly infinite number and variety of alternatives. The larger the denominator, the smaller the possibility of making probable inferences, and, without some assumption as to limitations of entities and order in nature, the fraction would read,

$$\frac{\text{Any observed number}}{\text{Unknown}}$$

Keynes sought to overcome this difficulty in inductive probability by means of the *postulate of limited independent qualities,* stated as follows: "Excluding, therefore, the possibility of a plurality of generators, we can justify the method of perfect analogy, and other inductive methods, in so far as they can be made to approximate to this, by means of the assumption that the objects in the field, over which our generalizations extend, do not have an infinite number of independent qualities; that, in other words, their characteristics, however numerous, cohere together in groups of invariable connections, which are finite in number."[6] This postulate, together with that of the *uniformity of nature,* which we have already discussed (page 211), provides the logical grounds for probability judgments based on finite qualities and on relative homogeneity and consistency in their structure and operations. As relatively finite and homogeneous systems become established, the interrelated parts tend to become more and more coherent and mutually self-supporting.

V. SAMPLING

The problem of sampling is central in the attempt to estimate or measure degrees of probability. Since only a limited part of any field in time and space can be observed, inductive inference necessarily must resort to *random* sampling upon which to base probability judgments. The number and nature of the samples, and the methods employed in selecting them, will depend upon the nature of the field under investigation. The term *random sample* is used here in the

[6] *Op. cit.,* p. 256.

technical sense of a crossection representative of the whole group both in quantity and quality. The ideal conditions for securing a representative, or random, sample are fulfilled *when the members of the group to be sampled are limited in number, when the nature of the materials is homogeneous, and where there are certain controls to prevent counting the same sample more than once.*

As we have noticed in our discussion of hypotheses, we very rarely approach any field of investigation without a certain amount of background knowledge of the field. We usually begin in the middle. If we know in advance that our materials are relatively homogeneous in structure, as in chemistry, one sample is as good as many. This sort of material represents the ideal situation for scientific experiment, since certain variables may be introduced at will and the effects noted.

A different problem is presented for sampling in those situations, such as were suggested in the last section, where the field, although known to be relatively homogeneous, is nevertheless practically unlimited in extent. To make generalizations with high probability in the field of magnetism, it would be necessary to take random samples of magnets attracting iron under all possible relevant experimental conditions. Samples may be taken at various places on the surface of the earth, in the earth, in the air, and under the ocean, and the more of these found to be irrelevant, the higher the probability of the generalization. As irrelevant factors are eliminated, the experiments may be confined to the factors found to be most relevant, such as temperature.

Again, in those fields where a great deal of heterogeneity exists, as in the study of populations, we do not need to depend on merely counting heads. We may consult records of vital statistics, census records, and previous studies—all of which may give us a clue to the important types or groups to be included in our sample. The most successful application of this procedure is found in the public-opinion polls. The method of sampling is described here:

The secret of this new type of opinion sampling is not numbers. Statisticians have repeatedly demonstrated that a few thousand voters correctly selected will reflect faithfully the views of an electorate of millions of voters. The secret is in the cross section—in the way voters for the sample are selected. To be a reliable indicator of public opinion the sample must include views of members of all political parties, and of rich and poor, old and young, men and women, farmers and city dwellers, persons of all religious faiths—in short, voters of all types from every state in the land. Moreover the sample must include these types numerically in approximately the same proportion as they exist in the voting population. It must, in effect, select a miniature electorate that is representative of the views of the larger whole.[7]

A similar technique is employed in sampling populations for the purposes of the study of physical, social, or mental traits. For example, if we wished to learn the I.Q.'s of the seventh-grade children in a certain city, we might hesitate to undertake the heavy task of testing the whole group. On the basis of previous knowledge of relevant factors, we would make up a list of characteristics to be included in our sample. These would probably consist of geographical area, economic status, rating of school, and other factors which might be considered on the grounds of local conditions.

In those cases where we do not know anything about the possible homogeneity or heterogeneity of our materials, as in sampling the oranges in a truckload, or the wheat in a bin, the only method is to choose samples from random areas and base our estimates upon a reasonable number of these. If we have a knowledge of agricultural methods, we might suspect a good deal of homogeneity in these cases, but, if heterogeneity appears and increases as we continue to sample, the number of samples must be increased in proportion.

PROBLEMS

1. List three propositions which you feel are absolutely certain, and give your reasons for thinking so.

2. Choose a current political controversy, and, for one side of the question, list arguments which you feel might lead an intelligent observer to favor that side, on a scale of from 1 to 5; then do the same for the opposite view, and state the results in terms of probability on the evidence.

3. Calculate the mathematical probabilities of the following events:

    (1) Five heads in a row in tossing a true coin
    (2) Three heads and a tail, in that order, in tossing four coins
    (3) A total of 7 in throwing a pair of dice
    (4) A total of 4 each time in throwing a pair of dice twice
    (5) Either an ace or the queen of diamonds in drawing from a deck of playing cards
    (6) Three red cards in a row in drawing from a deck of playing cards

4. What is the mathematical probability of getting at least one head in three tosses of a coin?

5. In a bowl there are 14 balls: 4 white balls, 5 black balls, and 5

[7] *The New Science of Public Opinion* (Princeton, N.J.: American Institute of Public Opinion, 1944), p. 1.

red balls. If three are selected at random, what is the probability that those chosen will be

(1) 1 red, 1 black, and 1 white
(2) 3 red balls
(3) 1 white and 2 black

6. A bag contains 3 beans and 2 peas. What are the odds that one can draw out a pea on the first or second draw? (What is drawn on the first draw is not to be returned to the bag.)

7. On the basis of mortality tables which show that 89,368 out of 100,000 children three years of age live to be twenty-one, what is the probability that an individual three years old will not live until his twenty-first birthday?

8. What is the probability of drawing each of the following from a box containing 4 black and 6 white balls:

(1) 2 black balls simultaneously
(2) 3 black balls successively replacing the ball after each draw
(3) 2 black balls and a white ball in one draw of 3 balls

9. On a throw of 2 dice simultaneously, what is the probability for

(1) Either a 7 or an 11
(2) An even number on each die
(3) A total of 5 three times in a row

10. A box contains the following balls:

3 black
1 mottled and red
2 checkered and green
5 checkered and black
2 red, white, and blue
2 striped and green
2 mottled and green

One ball is drawn at a time and returned. What is the probability of drawing

1. A checkered ball
2. A mottled ball
3. A striped ball
4. A black ball
5. A blue ball

11. Give two examples of hypothetical syllogisms in which you think the affirming of the consequent establishes a strong probability of the antecedent.

12. Rank yourself on a scale of from 1 to 5 on some highly controversial issue, letting 5 equal absolute certainty, 4 high certainty, 3 fair certainty, 2 low certainty, and 1 almost no certainty. Then write down five factual statements which you regard as evidence for

your opinion. Have these graded on a scale of from 1 to 5 by a competent person, and correlate the two sets of results.

13. What is the probability that, of 100 people at a party, of whom 25 are redheads, the first person leaving will be a redhead? What are the odds in favor, and against?

14. How would you go about selecting samples upon which to base generalizations in the following cases?

(1) To discover the reasons for nonvoting in your community
(2) To test the generalization that women are more extravagant in buying clothes than men
(3) To determine where to drill for oil in a newly discovered oil area
(4) To discover what is the favorite dance orchestra of a student body

15. Explain the nature of mathematical probability as contrasted with empirical probability, or frequency theory. What is the general rule or principle for calculating mathematical probability?

16. Argue for or against the view that mathematical probability is invalidated by the fact that empirical frequencies may not correspond to it.

17. What is the probability that the thirteenth person who sits down to dinner will be the first of the group to die?

17

Measurement and
Statistical Methods

I. MEASUREMENT

It is not necessary in modern times to emphasize the enormous prestige of measurement in both pure and applied science, nor to stress its importance in prediction and control. If anything, we need to learn caution and reserve in claiming quantitative results in certain fields, when in fact such results do not always warrant our inferences from them.

Counting and measuring are extensions of observational and inductive methods for the purpose of exactness and precision. Because of the great success achieved in developing standards for measuring mass, space, time, motion, temperature, etc. in the physical sciences, great impetus has been given in recent years, since the pioneer work of Binet, to the attempt to develop standards whereby quantitative expression may be given to the many human and social traits, capacities, and achievements. As a result we have today highly developed instruments and techniques in the new sciences of anthropometry and psychometry, and a great mass of experimental data in intelligence and achievement testing.

The belief that "anything that exists can be measured" expresses a laudable faith in scientific technique, but to be completely intelligible it needs amplification and clarification. We do express a kind of measurement in our rather vague value judgments of everyday life in terms of degrees of goodness, badness, hardness, tenderness, whiteness, handsomeness, etc. But is this measurement in the same sense as in the physical sciences? Things, processes, and qualities exist in different degrees of availability to observation and control, and in different degrees of homogeneity and heterogeneity, and measurement means different things when applied to different qualities. It will be our purpose in this section to discuss certain logical considerations relating to the problem of assigning quantitative units to the diversity of qualities in our environment.

1. Counting. The simplest, and perhaps earliest, form of measurement is counting, or simple enumeration of individual units as they are discriminated in perception. It consists of assigning a number unit to each object, person, or element, in a one-to-one correlation which may then be placed in serial order and operated upon by the familiar methods of addition, subtraction, etc. We may assume that in primitive times some rough method of counting was used by the early shepherd, such as correlating a stone with a sheep, and transferring a stone from one pile to another as the sheep passed him. Even at this early stage his method was quite advanced because abstract; that is, he had gone beyond the necessity of having a specific stone stand for a specific sheep. The invention of number was a great step in advance because an abstract mental process was then substituted for the physical operation.

As in classification, so in enumeration, the individual items of a group must be discontinuous or discreet, so that we may know exactly what it is we are counting; that is, the unit of measurement has to be decided upon and carefully defined. If we assume that we are counting "students" in a class and find that we have visitors, or if we are counting "bald-headed people" and cannot distinguish what degree of absence of hair constitutes baldness, we cannot count until we have first made the proper distinctions. It is obvious that the group must be small enough to be countable.

When these conditions are fulfilled and we have counted a limited group, we have introduced a form of ordering which has exactness, neatness, utility, and objectivity. The operations can be repeated and tested by competent observers. The numbers may be manipulated, and group compared with group by means of various statistical methods to be discussed later.

2. Fundamental Measurement: Additive or Extensive Qualities. Why is it that we are able to measure some qualities and not others? Is it some characteristic of the materials, something in the nature of measurement itself, or simply that our techniques have not been developed in certain areas?

In some cases it is a combination of all three, but primarily it is because of the nature of the qualities involved. Because of the nature of the so-called *extensive qualities,* some standards of measurement are very old, such as the balance for measuring weight, the clock for measuring time, and the various systems of measuring length. Methods of measuring velocity, temperature, electrical resistance, and other qualities are more recent. With some of these, such as weight, the method is direct. It consists of an accurately constructed balance and an arbitrarily chosen standard. If, when an object is placed on one end of the beam and the standard on the other, they balance, they are said to be equal. If the standard end goes down, it is said to be heavier, and if it goes up, it is said to be lighter. It can then be said that if X is heavier than Y, and Y than Z, then X is heavier than Z. Also, if X is equal in weight to X^1, and Y is equal in weight to Y^1, X and Y taken together at one end of the scales will balance X^1 and Y^1 at the other. In other words, the quality of weight is additive.

Russell, in his *Principles of Mathematics,* has laid down the rule that strict measurement demands that in some cases the proposition "this magnitude is double that" have an *intrinsic* meaning. In the above case of weight, as we have seen, it does apply. How does it apply to certain other commonly used measurements?

Suppose that we have a group of children and adults assembled with a group of experts in anthropometric, psychometric, and personality measurement for the purpose of finding out what kinds of measurements are objective and can be repeated by other competent testers. Weight, height, chest expansion, head size, hand grip, reaction time, are all measured by well-standardized methods. The units are objective in the sense that they have the same meaning for all. They all conform to the above standard of being additive. It can be demonstrated by a physical operation that A, who weighs 200 pounds, is twice as heavy as B, who weighs 100, or that A is as heavy as B and C, each of whom weighs 100 pounds. It is meaningful to say that this man has a chest measurement twice as large as this child's if the operation of laying a standard tape around the man shows that his girth is 40 inches, and that of the child 20 inches, subject of course to variations due to error.

3. Measurement by Scales: Nonadditive or Intensive Qualities. But now suppose that we wish to proceed to the measurement of other qualities and characteristics such as intelligence, disposition, handsomeness, and such personality traits. These qualities are capable of measurement, but it is measurement in a different sense. It is measurement by ranking on a scale arranged from low to high. From the viewpoint of the exact sciences, this type of measurement might be regarded as quite limited. For the practical purposes of educational adjustment, insight into educational processes, and determination of progress in certain fields, it is quite adequate. Binet recognized the limited nature of the measurement of intelligence when, in 1898, referring to his work in measuring individual differences, he said: "It is not measurement in the physical sense . . . but classification of individuals with reference to others."[1]

The requirement for measurement of this type is simply that the items be capable of arrangement in a scale from low to high. In technical terms, that they have an asymmetrical and transitive relation. By asymmetrical, as indicated in Chapter 12, we mean that, if on our scale A is greater than B, then B is less than A. By transitive relation we mean simply that, if A is greater than B, and B is greater than C, then A is greater than C.

Now, if in our experiment we were to give to our group the standard intelligence tests, the results would conform to the above requirement and we would be able to construct a scale, and to say that one person accomplished more or less in a given time. We might still reserve our judgment as to what is actually measured, and it would be quite meaningless to say that one who stood on the scale at an I.Q. of 100 was twice as intelligent as one who stood at 50, or that the difference between 50 and 75 was the same as the difference between 75 and 100. Neither would this type of measurement be objective in the sense that it is always exactly repeatable under the same conditions by another tester, rendering the same results.

If we try another group of qualities in our measuring experiment, such as handsomeness or beauty, we will find that these too can be placed in a scale from high to low; but we will also doubtless find that this assigning of values is quite arbitrary. This will illustrate the fact that some qualities are more difficult to rate than others. It is true that there are certain standards which are applicable to any art form, such as harmony, proportion, symmetry, etc., but there are so many subtle factors in the human face that objective standards would be rendered almost useless. Such qualities are sometimes called *intensive qualities*, and are nonadditive, that is, they cannot be treated mathematically.

In the measurement of nonadditive qualities we need to beware of the assumption that when we assign numbers to various degrees of a

[1] Quoted by R. Pintner, *Intelligence Testing* (New York: Henry Holt & Co., Inc., 1923), p. 27.

quality, and engage in mathematical operations upon the numbers, we are manipulating the qualities in the same ratio. We must be careful to discriminate between fundamental measurement and measurement that ranks by scale, and not claim for our results more than is warranted by the particular type of measurement utilized.

II. THE USES OF STATISTICS

It will be possible in this chapter to give only the barest outline of the simpler statistical methods and to introduce the student to but a portion of the terminology which he will encounter in reading the literature of testing and measuring. No attempt will be made to deal critically with the numerous technical and controversial aspects of the subject. Materials which will enable the student to follow up the various operations introduced here will be found in works on statistics, some of which have been suggested in the bibliography at the end of this book.

The term "statistics" was first used with reference to bodies of data collected by states, such as population, taxation, mortality, and trade. Statistical methods and operations provide the tools for dealing with quantitative data, and are therefore of the utmost value in the social, biological, and physical sciences as well as in practical and theoretical problems of education, psychology, and accounting. Wherever mass data need to be reduced to meaningful and manageable order and proportions, and expressed in mathematical form, statistical techniques are invaluable. Wherever we must resort to sampling, as we must in studying large populations of any kind, statistical probabilities enable us to determine the probable reliability of our samples.

III. THE FREQUENCY DISTRIBUTION

Let us suppose that as a result of an examination in logic we have the group of scores given in Table II.

As these scores stand, they are quite meaningless, unless, perhaps, by inspection we may discover that they range from 100 down to 45. In order to compare this group with other groups, or in order to determine whether the abilities measured by this test may be in any sense representative of a larger group from which it is a selection, it is necessary that the raw scores be reduced to meaningful order.

The first step is to group the scores into a *frequency distribution*. A class-interval is a simple device for the purpose of collecting groups

Table II

80	57	45	74	76
100	75	63	85	91
75	75	60	85	87
58	85	69	60	73
87	79	80	74	73
80	80	66	72	73
77	87	87	86	70
55	67	78	56	70
75	65	73	78	71
79	77	82	92	71
81	80	74	84	

of scores into neat packages so that they may be more easily handled. A convenient method of determining the size of the class-interval to use is to divide the range by 10 for a maximum interval, and by 20 for a minimum. We may in this case arbitrarily decide to divide it by 10, and since the range is 55, the quotient is 5.5. Since it is easier to use a round number, the class-interval of 5 is selected. The mid-point of each class-interval is the average of the extremes of that interval.

Table III
Frequency Distribution

Class-interval	Mid-point	Tabulation	Frequency
95–100	97.5	/	1
90–94.9	92.5	//	2
85–89.9	87.5	////////	8
80–84.9	82.5	////////	8
75–79.9	77.5	///////////	11
70–74.9	72.5	////////////	12
65–69.9	67.5	////	4
60–64.9	62.5	///	3
55–59.9	57.5	////	4
50–54.9	52.5		0
45–49.9	47.5	/	1
			54

There are many ways of visualizing statistical data so that they may be more easily understood. Some of these are the frequency polygon, the histogram, ogive curve, bar chart, area diagram, etc. For example, the above frequency distribution may be visualized in a frequency polygon as in Figure 3. The horizontal base line represents the mid-point of the scores in class-intervals of 5. The vertical lines represent the number of students, or of scores, which fall in a particular class-interval, at a particular point on the scale.

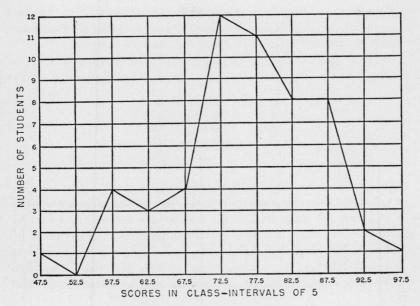

Figure 3. Frequency Polygon

IV. THE NORMAL PROBABILITY CURVE

We saw in the last chapter that, according to a principle sometimes called "the law of normal frequency," it is possible to state mathematically the chances of events happening or not happening, for example, in the tossing of coins or dice. If we toss 4 coins simultaneously, there is the theoretical possibility of 16 different combinations of heads and tails. The probabilities of the different combinations may be charted as follows:

Heads	Tails	Combinations						Favored Ways	Probabilities
4	0	HHHH						1	$\frac{1}{16}$
3	1	HHHT	HHTH	HTHH	THHH			4	$\frac{4}{16}$
2	2	HHTT	HTHT	HTTH	THHT	THTH	TTHH	6	$\frac{6}{16}$
1	3	TTTH	TTHT	THTT	HTTT			4	$\frac{4}{16}$
0	4	TTTT						1	$\frac{1}{16}$

If we tried the experiment of actually tossing 4 coins, we would probably not find in 16 throws that these ideal conditions would be exemplified. We must remember that this is a purely theoretical condition representing the mathematical possibilities. But we have reason to believe that if we continued the process of throwing coins, we ought in the long run to get about the same ratio.

Now if we plot a graph of the above ideal distribution, we will find it falling into the shape of a polygon, but if we may assume a large

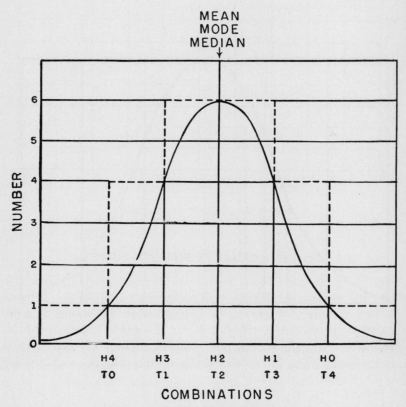

Figure 4.   Normal Probability Curve

number of cases, we will find it approaching the form of a smooth, bell-shaped curve, or normal probability curve, also called normal frequency curve, and curve of error. An example of the normal probability curve is given in Figure 4.

It will be observed that the probability of getting 4 heads or 4 tails is $\frac{1}{16}$ and is represented by the extreme left and right of the curve, while the probability of getting 2 heads and 2 tails is $\frac{6}{16}$, and is the highest, and is represented as the highest point on the curve. This central vertical line of the curve is the *mean,* the *mode,* and the *median,* which are all types of averages or measures of *central tendency,* and which coincide in a perfectly normal distribution. They are used to give a brief picture of the achievement as represented in any group of scores, to compare group with group, and for locating a given score with reference to the average.

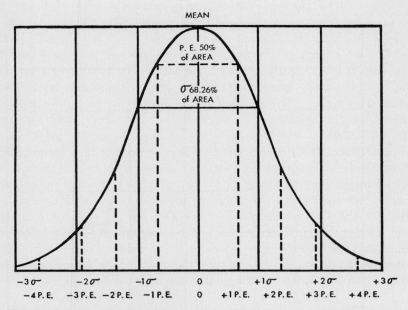

Figure 5. Normal Probability Curve, Illustrating the Nature of the Area Under the Curve in Terms of Standard Deviation and Probable Error

The spread of a set of measures away from the average toward the extremes of the curve is known as *dispersion* or *variability.* In order to interpret the properties of a series of measures, or to compare one series with another, a knowledge of both central tendency and dispersion is necessary.

In the Normal Probability Curve, Figure 5, the area within the solid black line of the curve, the base line, and the ordinates (solid lines) erected at a distance of 1 *standard deviation* or *sigma* plus and minus from the mean includes 68.26 per cent of the cases.

Likewise, in Figure 5, the area within the solid black line of the curve, the base line, and the broken lines of the ordinates erected at a distance of 1 *PE* or *probable error* plus and minus from the mean includes 50 per cent of the cases.

Notice that on each side of the mean, the *Standard Deviation* (sigma) ordinates divide the curve into three equal parts, labeled + and —1 to + and —3. A plus sign means above the mean, and a minus sign below it.

Notice that on each side of the mean, the *Probable Error* (*PE*) ordinates divide the curve into 4½ parts labeled + and —1 to + and —4. A plus sign indicates that the deviation is above the mean, and a minus sign below it.

This ideal curve is taken as the norm or standard by which to compare actual, usually skewed,[2] distributions found in the measurement of the many human, social, and natural traits and occurrences studied in those sciences which utilize statistics. It is also used to determine the reliability of statistical results from empirical frequencies, such as averages, measures of variability, and measures of correlations. The justification of this procedure is that, empirically, natural phenomena, human traits and abilities, and the dynamics of social interaction are found to follow roughly the normal probability curve, and that they tend more and more toward this ideal distribution as the size of the sample increases. It is assumed that the sample gives a clue to the nature of the hypothetical group from which the sample is taken, and the ideal curve provides the standards and suggests the degree of probability of the inferences which may be made from observed samples to the total group which is unobserved.

V. MEASURES OF CENTRAL TENDENCY

1. The Arithmetic Mean or Simple Average. (a) *For a simple ungrouped series.* In this case the formula for the mean is simply

$$M = \frac{\Sigma m}{N}$$

where M = mean
Σ = the sum of
m = the measures
N = the number of items

[2] A skewed distribution is nonsymmetrical, and is the result of extremes either in the higher or lower end of the distribution.

In other words, the numbers or scores are added up and divided by the number of items.

(*b*) *By the "short method."* When the measures are grouped in a frequency distribution as above, it is much easier to find the average by the so-called short method. The formula for this is

$$M = AM + c$$

where M = the mean
    AM = the assumed mean
     c = the correction

The formula for the correction is

$$c = \frac{\Sigma fd}{N} \times i$$

where f = frequency
    d = deviation of class-interval from the interval containing AM
    i = class-interval

In order to illustrate clearly how to find the average by this method, we shall go through the various steps, referring to the frequency distribution in Table IV (page 281).

The steps to be followed are:

1. Guess at the interval which contains the mean. The midpoint of this interval will be regarded as the assumed mean. In the example above, $AM = 72.5$.
2. Indicate the number of units which each class-interval deviates from the assumed mean, designating as positive those which are greater than the assumed mean, and as negative those which are less. This is shown in the column labeled d (deviation).
3. Multiply frequency by deviation, recording signs; this gives the frequency deviation (column fd). Then find the algebraic sum of the fd's. In the example there is a total of 64 positive fd's and a total of 27 negative fd's; $(+64) + (-27) = +37$.
4. Divide the result by the number of measures. This yields (c') in units of step intervals. $37/54 = .685$. Then multiply by the number of units in the class-interval. $.685 \times 5 = 3.4$. This is the correction in score units (c).
5. Add the correction (3.4) to the assumed mean. This yields the mean. $72.5 + 3.4 = 75.9$. The results of this short method may be checked by adding up all of the measures and dividing by the number of items.

2. Weighted Arithmetic Mean. The formula for the weighted mean is

$$WM = \frac{\Sigma mW}{\Sigma W}$$

where m = measures
W = weights

It is used in cases where certain values occur more frequently than others, and where the simple arithmetic mean does not tell the true story of the situation. For example, the average salary in a firm which employs two executives at $10,000 each, and ten other employees at $800 each, if computed on the basis of the simple arithmetic mean would be about $2,333. The weighted mean gives us a much fairer idea of the average salary of the firm, which, computed according to the above formula, would be approximately $1,153. In finding the weighted mean, each item is multiplied by a weight (in this case, the frequency of the occurrence of the item) and the total result is then divided by the sum of the weights, as follows:

m	W	mW
$10,000	2	20,000
10,000	2	20,000
800	10	8,000
800	10	8,000
800	10	8,000
800	10	8,000
800	10	8,000
800	10	8,000
800	10	8,000
800	10	8,000
800	10	8,000
800	10	8,000
$28,000	104	120,000

$$\frac{\Sigma mW}{\Sigma W} = \frac{120,000}{104} = \$1,153.76 \text{ weighted mean}$$

3. The Median. (a) For a simple ungrouped series the median is the middle measure in the series arranged in order of magnitude, or, in other words, that point on a scale on each side of which one half of the measures fall. In an ungrouped series it may be discovered by inspection. The formula is

$$Md = \frac{N + 1}{2}$$

Table IV
Illustration of the Calculation of Mean

Class-interval	Mid-point	f	d	fd	Σfd
95–100	97.5	1	+5	+ 5	
90–94.9	92.5	2	+4	+ 8	
85–89.9	87.5	8	+3	+24	
80–84.9	82.5	8	+2	+16	
75–79.9	77.5	11	+1	+11	+64
70–74.9	72.5	12	0	0	
65–69.9	67.5	4	−1	− 4	
60–64.9	62.5	3	−2	− 6	
55–59.9	57.5	4	−3	−12	
50–54.9	52.5	0	−4	− 0	
45–49.9	47.5	1	−5	− 5	−27
		54			+37

(b) By the "short method," when the measures are grouped in a frequency distribution as above, the formula for computing the median, working up from the bottom, is

$$Md = L + \left(\frac{N/2 - Fl}{fp}\right) i$$

where Md = the median

L = the lower limit of class-interval containing Md

Fl = the sum of the frequencies *lower* than the class-interval containing the Md

fp = the frequency of class-interval containing the Md

i = the class-interval

Applying the formula to the above frequency distribution in Table IV, we take the following steps:

1. Find $N/2$ i.e., one half of the measures, $54/2 = 27$.
2. Find Fl by beginning at the lower end of the f column and adding the measures up to the class-interval which contains the 27th measure. We may assume that the median lies somewhere in the class-interval containing the 27th measure. In the above example, the sum of the measures up to the interval, 75–79 is $1 + 0 + 4 + 3 + 4 + 12$, or 24.
3. Subtract the 24 from one half of the measures. $27 - 24 = 3$. This indicates that 3 more scores are needed from the next interval above to obtain the required 27.
4. fp (the denominator of the formula) the frequency of the class-interval

containing the Md is 11.   Divide the 3 obtained in step 3 by this 11. This means that we must go $\frac{3}{11}$ of the distance into the next class-interval to reach the Md.

5. Multiply the result by the class-interval, which in this case is 5. $\frac{3}{11} \times 5 = 1.36$.

6. Add the result 1.36 to L, the lower limit of the class-interval containing the Md, which is 75; $75 + 1.36$ yields the median 76.4.

4. The Mode.   The mode is simply the value on the scale which occurs most frequently.   In a simple ungrouped series it may be determined by inspection.   The above frequency distribution is multi-modal since several scores appear four or more times.   In a frequency distribution, the so-called "crude mode" is the midpoint of the interval in which the largest number of measures fall.   On the whole it is not a very trustworthy measure since the change of one score in the series changes the mode.

VI. MEASURES OF VARIABILITY

Whereas the various measures of central tendency which we have discussed are expressed as "position on a scale," the measures of variability are expressed as "distance on a scale."   They point out the degree of concentration around, and dispersion away from, the central or average position.   This can be observed by an examination of the normal probability curve (page 277).   Measures of variability are necessary to complete a meaningful picture of a distribution since the average of two groups may be the same, yet they might differ greatly with respect to their scatter above and below the average. Two sets of scores may have the same average, and yet the abilities measured may vary widely, as indicated by a large or small standard deviation or other measure of dispersion.   A knowledge of both central tendency and variability enables us to interpret the importance of unequal scores in such cases where different standards of assigning grades exist.   Two students may get the score of 70 in different classes in the same subject, and wish to compare them.   If the average of one class is 60 with a standard deviation or sigma of 10, a mark of 70 is high.   On the other hand, if the average of the other class is 75 with a sigma of 5, the mark of 70 is low.   The measures of variability are the *range,* the *mean deviation,* the *quartile deviation,* and the *standard deviation.*

1. The Range.   The range is the difference between the smallest and the largest measures in the series, and hence includes all of the measures. It is used when a rough comparison of the variability of two or more groups is desired. In the above example the range is 100–45, or 55. The range is regarded by statisticians as a very unreliable measure of variability since it takes no account of the form of the distribution or the nature or degree of concentration at various points on the scale. It will be observed that the omission of one measure at the low end of the scale will change the range materially. Hence the range should always be stated along with other measures of variability.

2. Mean Deviation, or Average Deviation. The mean or average deviation of a series of items is the arithmetic mean of their deviations from either the median or the mean. In the following illustrative example we shall find the average deviation from the mean. It is used to compare the variability of individuals with the group, or group with group. A small deviation indicates homogeneity of the group, i.e., concentration around the mean, and if large, heterogeneity or spread away from the mean, always relative to the standard of measurement. When the distribution is normal, the MD includes approximately the middle 57 per cent of the cases. The formula is as follows:

$$MD = \frac{\Sigma fd + c'(Fl - Fg)}{N} \times i$$

where fd = the frequency times the deviations disregarding signs, i.e., plus and minus

Fl = the sum of the f's for those intervals whose mid-points are *less* than the mean

Fg = the sum of the f's for those intervals whose mid-points are *greater* than the mean

c' = the correction, which is equal to $\dfrac{\Sigma fd}{N}$

i = the class-interval

In order to demonstrate the new steps, we shall again bring forward the frequency distribution in Table V.

The following steps should be performed:

1. We now know that the mean of this series is 75.9, so we begin our computation from the class-interval 75–79.9.
2. Find the arithmetic sum of the fd's disregarding signs. $fd = 85$.
3. Find the correction (c'), which is the algebraic sum of $+34$ and -51, divided by N or 54, or $-.314$.

4. Find Fl by adding the f's from the bottom up to the interval containing the mean: $1 + 0 + 4 + 3 + 4 + 12 = 24$.

5. Find Fg by adding the f's from the top down to and including the interval containing the mean: $1 + 2 + 8 + 8 + 11 = 30$. Note that the sum of the Fl and Fg equals the total scores.

6. Applying the formula, we have:

$$MD = \frac{85 - .314(24 - 30)}{54} \times 5 = \frac{85 + 1.88}{54} \times 5$$

$$= \frac{86.88}{54} \times 5 = 1.60 \times 5$$

$$= 8 \text{ mean deviation}$$

In a perfectly symmetrical distribution approximately 57 per cent of the cases should fall between the mean of the distribution and the mean deviation plus and minus. In our example where the mean is 75.9 and the mean deviation is 8, it would be written as 75.9 ± 8.

Table V
Illustration of the Calculation of the MD

Class-interval	Mid-point	f	d	fd	fd^2
95–100	97.5	1	+4	+ 4	16
90–94.9	92.5	2	+3	+ 6	18
85–89.9	87.5	8	+2	+16	32
80–84.9	82.5	8	+1	+ 8	8
75–79.9	77.5	11	0	0	0
70–74.9	72.5	12	−1	−12	12
65–69.9	67.5	4	−2	− 8	16
60–64.9	62.5	3	−3	− 9	27
55–59.9	57.5	4	−4	−16	64
50–54.9	52.5	0	−5	− 0	0
45–49.9	47.5	1	−6	− 6	36
		54		85	229

This simply means that the scores deviate 8 points on either side of the mean. On this basis we can say that the area between 67.9 (8 points below the mean) and 83.9 (8 points above the mean) should contain about 57 per cent of the scores. Reference to Table V will show that this percentage is approximated.

3. Quartile Deviation or Semi-interquartile Range. The quartile deviation is one half the distance between the 75th and the 25th percentile points in the distribution. Twenty-five per cent of the scores fall below the first quartile $Q1$, and 75 per cent of the scores lie below $Q3$. $Q1$ and $Q3$ mark off the limits within which fall the middle

50 per cent of the scores. Q is a measure of the closeness with which the measures are grouped around the median. The formula is

$$Q = \frac{Q3 - Q1}{2}$$

Using Table IV as a basis for computation, the following steps are taken:

1. Divide the total number of items by 4. $^{54}\!/_4 = 13.5$.
2. To find $Q1$, begin at the bottom of the frequency and count up to the interval containing the 25th percentile, or 13.5. Since there are 12 measures up to that interval, we need $13.5 - 12$, or 1.5, from the frequency 12 in the class interval 70–74.9.
3. Therefore $Q1$ equals $70 + 1.5/12 \times 5$, or $70 + 0.625$, or 70.62.
4. To find $Q3$, begin at the other end of the frequency and count down to the interval containing 13.5. Since there are 11 measures down to that point, we need $13.5 - 11$, or 2.5, from the frequency 8 in the class-interval 80–84.9.
5. Hence $Q3$ equals $84.9 - 2.5/8 \times 5 = 84.9 - 1.5 = 83.4$.
6. Applying the formula, the Q or quartile deviation is

$$Q = \frac{83.4 - 70.6}{2} = 6.4$$

Q is a measure of score density around the center of a distribution since it measures the average distance of the quartile points from the median. If the scores are closely centered around the median, the Q will be small; if they are widely scattered, the Q will be large. Q has the advantage of not being greatly influenced by extremes in the distribution since it is a measure of the range of the middle 50 per cent of the scores. In our example the difference between $Q3$ or 83.4 and $Q1$ or 70.6 is 12.8. This figure, it would seem, might be taken to represent accurately the range of the middle 50 per cent, but it is customary in statistical procedure to divide this difference by 2 to obtain the *semi-interquartile* range—6.4, in this case.

4. Standard Deviation or Sigma. The standard deviation is a special form of average deviation from the mean, and when laid off on each side of the mean in a symmetrical distribution, includes 68.26 per cent of the cases. The SD is the square root of the mean of the squares of the deviations from the mean. The formula is

$$SD = \sqrt{\frac{\Sigma f d^2}{N} - (c')^2} \times i$$

Again utilizing Table V, we shall illustrate the computation of the standard deviation in the following steps:

1. Multiply each number in the fd column by the corresponding number in the d column, recording these in a new column, fd^2.
2. Add the numbers in the fd^2 column, and divide by N. In Table V, this is $229\!\frac{1}{54}$ or 4.24.
3. Square c', or .314, and subtract from 4.24, i.e., $4.24 - .098 = 4.14$.
4. Find the square root of 4.14, which is 2.03.
5. Multiply this result by the class-interval (i or 5). $2.03 \times 5 = 10.2$, the standard deviation.

The standard deviation is to be interpreted as follows: Since the mean of our distribution is 75.9, and the standard deviation is 10.2, a score of 86.1 (the sum of 75.9 and 10.2) would be represented on the curve as $+1$ sigma above the mean. Likewise a score of 65.7 (the difference between 75.9 and 10.2) would be written -1 sigma below the mean. This means that, between the limits 65.7 and 86.1, approximately 68.26 per cent of the scores, or 37, should lie. An examination of the frequency table will indicate that, between the class-intervals 85–89.9 and 65–69.9, there are 43 scores. Because of the small number of cases and because the distribution is somewhat irregular, this discrepancy is to be expected. An examination of the normal probability curve will show that 3 sigmas plus and minus from the mean include about 99 per cent of the scores.

VII. COEFFICIENT OF CORRELATION

The measures of central tendency and of dispersion are methods of interpreting the properties of single series. The coefficient of correlation, or r, is a measure of functional relationship between variables, or in less technical language, the degree of positive or negative relationship between two sets of measures. It must not be assumed, however, because there is a statistical correlation between two sets of scores that there is necessarily either a causal or functional relationship as well. A perfect positive correlation is expressed as $+1$, a perfect negative correlation as -1, and complete absence of correlation is expressed as 0. Degrees of correlation are indicated by positive and negative decimals between $+1$ and -1. It is quite generally agreed by statisticians that a correlation either plus or minus .30 or below is low, .30 to .49 is moderate, .50 to .69 is significant, and .70 and above is high. In the interests of simplicity we shall illustrate the working out of the coefficient of correlation on two short sets of scores representing achievement in mathematics and logic. We shall use the formula for an ungrouped series of scores, which is as follows:

$$r = \frac{\Sigma \quad xy}{N \quad SDx \quad SDy}$$

Table VI

Illustration of the Calculation of Correlation

Student	Scores in Mathematics	Deviation x	Scores in Logic	Deviation y	x^2	y^2	xy
A	100	+12	96	+17	144	289	+204
B	92	+ 4	95	+16	16	256	+ 64
C	91	+ 3	80	+ 1	9	1	+ 3
D	88	0	80	+ 1	0	1	+ 0
E	88	0	78	− 1	0	1	− 0
F	87	− 1	78	− 1	1	1	+ 1
G	86	− 2	75	− 4	4	16	+ 8
H	85	− 3	75	− 4	9	16	+ 12
I	82	− 6	70	− 9	36	81	+ 54
J	81	− 7	63	−16	49	256	+112
	88 average		79 average		268	918	458

Steps:

1. Find the average of the scores, 88 and 79.
2. Find the deviations from the mean of the x scores and of the y scores.
3. Square each deviation and add up the totals, e.g., 268 and 918.
4. Find the arithmetic mean of these totals, e.g., 26.8 and 91.8.
5. Find the square root of these means, e.g., $\sqrt{26.8} = 5.18$ and $\sqrt{91.8} = 9.58$. It will be observed that the above steps are the steps necessary to find the standard deviations.
6. Multiply the standard deviation of x by the standard deviation of y and multiply the result by the number of measures, e.g., 5.18 × 9.58 × 10 = 496. This is the denominator of the formula.
7. Multiply the deviation of x by the deviation of y and record the result in the column xy. Find the sum of this column, e.g., 458. This is the numerator of the formula.
8. Divide 458 by 496. Then $r = .9$.

VIII. ESTIMATES OF RELIABILITY OF CENTRAL TENDENCY, DISPERSION, AND CORRELATION

In the above computations of central tendency and variability, the purpose has been merely descriptive, and no attempt has been made to generalize beyond the group studied. In statistics, *reliability* is a term used to indicate a standard to which a test or measure must conform. A test or examination is said to be reliable if it measures what it professes to measure consistently and accurately. The question of the reliability of statistical results arises when findings on any given sample are generalized to the larger population of which it is a sample.

In the following discussion of reliability, we shall continue to use the same illustrative examples, but they will now be treated as samples of a larger population of the same or similar kind of students, given the same or similar tests.

1. The Reliability of the Mean in Terms of the Standard Error of the Mean. The formula for the standard error of the mean is

$$SE_M = \frac{SD(\text{dis})}{\sqrt{N}}$$

where $SD(\text{dis})$ = standard deviation of the distribution
N = number of items in the sample

In our distribution, the mean is 75.9; the number of cases, 54; and the standard deviation, 10.2. Working out the formula, we have

$$SE_M = \frac{10.2}{7.36}, \text{ or } 1.38$$

This means that the chances are 68 to 100 that, if additional samples of 54 students each were taken, the "true" mean would lie between 75.9 ± 1.38, or between 77.3 and 75, and that the chances are 99 to 100 that it would lie between $75.9 \pm 3 \times 1.38$, or 72 and 80. Reference again to the normal probability curve (page 277) will show that 3 sigmas plus and minus from the mean include 99 per cent of the cases. To put it another way, it means that chances are 99 to 100 that the obtained average does not deviate from the "true" average more than 3×1.38, or 4.14 points.

2. The Standard Error of the Standard Deviation. The formula is as follows:

$$SE_{sd} = \frac{SD(\text{dis})}{\sqrt{2N}}$$

The standard deviation of our distribution is 10.2. The N is 54; the square root of 54×2, or 108, is 10.4. Hence, 10.2/10.4 is .98. This is written sigma $10.2 \pm .98$. The question is "How reliable is this standard deviation, i.e., how representative of the 'true' sigma if it could be computed on the basis of the 'true' average?" The above formula enables us to say that the chances are 68 in 100 that the obtained sigma 10.2 does not differ from the "true" sigma by more than ±.98 points, and that the chances are 99 in 100 that it does not differ from the "true" sigma by more than 3 × .98, or 2.94. We multiply the obtained result by 3 because 3 sigmas plus and minus from the mean include 99 per cent of the cases.

3. The Standard Error of the Coefficient of Correlation. The formula is

$$SE_r = \frac{1 - r^2}{\sqrt{N}}$$

The correlation found in Table VI is .9, the square of which is .81, which, subtracted from 1, gives us .19 as the numerator. The square root of N, or 10, is 3.16. Hence .19/3.16 = .06, the standard error of r. This is written .9 ± .06 and indicates that it may be expected that 68 out of 100 samples drawn at random from this population will yield estimates which do not differ from the obtained r, or .9 by more than .06.

Some of the pitfalls and fallacies of statistical methods may be found at the end of Chapter 19, on inductive fallacies.

PROBLEMS

1. Using the following set of figures representing daily wages in dollars for employees in a department of an aircraft plant, find the mean, median, and mode by the short method: 7, 8, 9, 11, 10, 6, 5, 13, 14, 10, 12, 10, 8, 7, 6, 13, 14, 13, 12, 12.

2. Find the range, average deviation, and standard deviation of the above set of figures.

3. Suppose it is found that, in a certain campus building, there is a proportional relation between the number of books on the shelves and the number of tiles on the floor. What is the significance of this relationship from the causal or functional viewpoint? Why? What is the significance of the relationship between the number of tiles on the floor and the area of the room in square feet? Why?

4. Read *The New Science of Public Opinion*, published by The American Institute of Public Opinion, Princeton, New Jersey, and explain how the Institute is able to secure representative samples without striving for large numbers in the samples.

5. What is a *normal frequency curve*, and how is it derived? What are its uses in assigning a distribution of grades in large unselected groups? What are the logical objections to its strict application to small selected groups?

6. Find the correlation between the two following sets of scores representing, respectively, scores on a college entrance examination and average college grades over a four-year period.

Student	College Entrance Examination	Average College Grade
A	75	80
B	95	90
C	80	70
D	85	89
E	82	84
F	90	93
G	93	90
H	65	70
I	70	73
J	75	71

7. Find the *standard error of the mean* and the *standard error of the standard deviation* of each set of scores in Problem 6. Find the *standard error of the coefficient of correlation* of the same set of scores.

8. What is the fundamental difference between measurement in the strict sense and ranking on a scale?

9. What is meant by the *unit* of measurement, and why is it considered important in measurement and statistics?

18

Logic and Scientific Methods in Legal Thinking

I. LEGAL THINKING AS APPLIED LOGIC

In bringing our discussion of logic and scientific methods to a conclusion, it is our purpose in this chapter to illustrate the application of certain methods and principles here developed to legal thinking as typical of a phase of human activity which has utilized these principles and methods in an interesting and vital manner. Legal thinking illustrates in a peculiarly practical and concrete way the operation of all of the techniques and methods known in the human search for evidence by which reasoned conclusions regarding matters of fact may be reached.

It is our view that while the case method in legal training is invaluable, it is equally true that knowledge of the principles of logical thinking and scientific methods, which apply to the solution of any kind of problem and to the nature of evidence anywhere, are equally important for the student of law. In this connection we quote from the remarks of Professor Walter W. Cook, who suggests a new approach to the field of legal education: "First and foremost, the members of such a group would need to have and to give to their students a clear conception of what the scientific study of anything involves, and of the available tools for pursuing it in the legal field. This would require them to take account of modern investigations into logical and human reasoning, and to survey in general outline at least, the development of science and scientific method."[1]

The logical processes which go on in our courts, ordinarily known as *judicial proof*, are essentially those of the *inductive-hypothetico-deductive method*. In criminal investigation and trials, they operate, it is true, under great difficulties and limitations, because subject in a peculiar degree to all of the fallacies known to the hazardous search for facts, truth, certainty, or preponderance of evidence in any other field. If we may assume that the purposes of the courts as instruments of the citizens of the modern state are the defense of human rights, the solution of social conflicts, and the establishment of justice, it is easy to understand why they have become vested with great dignity and, at least for the lay mind, clothed with the atmosphere of infallibility. In practice, while they often fall short of both dignity and infallibility, nevertheless it is highly desirable that the greatest possible degree of certainty be attained in the decisions and conclusions upon which the administration of justice is based. In the last analysis this is a question not only of statutes and rules of court procedure, but of the methods employed in the search for factually reliable and logically correct evidence.

But the logical processes of the law are carried on under conditions which make it difficult for the methods desirable for patient research and the calm weighing of evidence to operate. Litigation takes place in the heat of controversy. Passions and prejudices often predominate. Individuals are fighting for their own advantage whether right or wrong, and tend to rationalize their desires. Testimony is likely to be subject to many of the errors known to human observation, perception, memory, and reporting. Since the juries are laymen, there is a temptation on the part of attorneys to take advantage of the art of persuasion and to induce psychological assent rather than rational and logical conviction. The natural ambiguities of language, when rules, principles, and statutes are greatly condensed, provide pitfalls for judge, jury, and lawyers. The danger of irrelevancy, hasty generalization, selection of evidence, defects in observation, confusion of authority with evidence, failure to distinguish probability from certainty, are a few of the many logical hazards of judicial proof. The justification for this unavoidable human situation is of course the long established belief that out of the clash of opposing wills the truth is likely to emerge.

[1] "Scientific Method and The Law," *American Bar Association Journal*, XIII (June, 1927), pp. 303–309.

Furthermore, the work of the courts is always carried on in an area between a set of relatively fixed principles, rules of procedure, and precedents, on the one hand, and a rapidly changing body of experience on the other. Each new case is individual, and even though it may be subsumed under a certain rule of law, statute, principle, or precedent, the question as to whether or not it is to be so subsumed must be determined in the light of the novel factors in the case.

II. DEDUCTION AND INDUCTION IN LEGAL THINKING

Much of the law is necessarily stated in the form of generalizations in the interest of economy of effort. Rules of law have been developed to guide procedure and admissibility of evidence. Principles and precedents are appealed to in seeking guidance from the wisdom of the past. It is natural that in certain schools of jurisprudence, rules and precedents come to be regarded as fixed and self-evident principles. On the other hand, it is desirable that there be a great deal of freedom and discretion in interpreting principles in their application to novel situations. A controversy has raged in the realm of the philosophy of law over this point comparable to that between rationalists and empiricists in philosophy. The controversy has reached about the same solution in law as in philosophy. It is now clearly seen that while principles and precedents are necessary and important, they must be progressively modified in the light of empirical evidence which could not have been anticipated by the general principle. It is also recognized that both deductive and inductive inferences are necessary in the solution of complex legal problems as hypotheses are set up and either verified or refuted. In some cases one type of inference may be a little more prominent than the other.

In simple cases where the statute, principle, or rule of law is clear and unambiguous, it may constitute the major premise of the syllogism. The specific case, and the process of establishing it as fact, is inductive or empirical, and constitutes the minor premise. When the minor is established as fact, the conclusion follows deductively from the premises. For example:

> Statute: Any person under the age of 16 who shall have in his possession any pistol, revolver, or other firearms, of a size which may be concealed, without license, shall be guilty of a
> (Major premise)   misdemeanor.
> Fact: John Smith, who is under 16, has in his possession such a
> (Minor premise)   weapon, without license.
> (Conclusion)   Hence, John Smith is guilty of a misdemeanor.

Or we may take as an example the application of a rule of evidence to a particular piece of testimony:

> Rule: No assertion offered as testimony can be received unless it
> is or has been open to test by cross-examination, or an
> (Major premise)   opportunity therefor.
> Fact: The witness for this piece of testimony is not present, and
> (Minor premise)   has not been cross-examined.
> (Conclusion)   Hence, this piece of evidence is inadmissible.

But the criticism may be justly made that these cases are trivial and obvious, and as we have pointed out in previous contexts, the deductions are made almost intuitively. Of much wider application to a dynamic situation and to concrete bodies of experience is the hypothetical form of deduction. This is the general form of a great deal of legal thinking in the detection of crime, in defense against false accusations, and in the establishment of alibis. If the police are called to a certain house to investigate a murder and proceed to hold everybody present at the time of the crime, they are reasoning from the hypothetical major premise, if X and Y and Z were present at the time of the crime, they could have committed it. If, however, after investigation they find that the murder was committed in an upstairs room, and X is a cripple confined to a wheel chair on the lower floor, they might reason hypothetically:

> If the murder was committed upstairs, it must have been done by some-
> one able to get upstairs.
> X is not able to get upstairs.
> Hence, X did not commit the murder.

And so in the same way either Y or Z or both might be eliminated and the field of possible suspects narrowed. W, who may also be a suspect, but who was not on the premises at the time of the crime, has an alibi which may be stated hypothetically:

> If W was not on the premises at the time of the crime, he did not com-
> mit the murder.
> W was in the village at the time of the crime.
> Hence, W did not commit the murder.

Or again, when the circumstances are not so simple and the conclusion cannot be established by the affirmation of the antecedent, or the denial of the consequent, the argument may be stated so that the affirmation of the consequent will yield some weight of evidence, although formally invalid. The general form of the argument is as follows:

If W committed the crime, then the circumstances c_1, c_2, etc., should be observed.
Circumstances c_1, c_2, etc., are observed.
Hence, W committed the crime.

The conclusion is of course only probable on this evidence, and while it may contribute very little toward establishing guilt, nevertheless when taken together with additional evidence based on further deductions and well-established factual minor premises it lends its cumulative weight to the final solution.

It is the establishment of the truth of minor premises in all of these examples which calls for great skill in inductive inference, involving, as it does, empirical observation, identification, causal analysis, generalization, and verification. With the development of new laboratory techniques, these operations have attained a high degree of exactness where concrete materials are involved.

III. THE ROLE OF EVIDENCE IN JUDICIAL PROOF

1. Testimonial, or Direct, Evidence. Testimonial evidence consists of any assertion offered by an individual in support of any fact-in-issue. It is based upon direct personal observation and firsthand knowledge, not hearsay. There are certain rules designed to protect the integrity of the court both with reference to competence of witnesses to give testimony, and admissibility of evidence. Testimonial evidence may also be offered in support of circumstantial evidence. For example, testimonial evidence of the first kind might be illustrated by the assertion of a witness that he saw a man entering an upstairs window of a certain house where it later appeared a robbery had been committed. Testimonial evidence in support of circumstantial evidence would be exemplified by the testimony of a pawnbroker who had bought a watch from the accused the week following the robbery. Expert testimony would be a combination of both testimonial and circumstantial evidence, and owing to the development of technical scientific research, has come into great prominence in recent times. Identification of a certain substance under the microscope or by means of chemical analysis, or the establishment of the fact that a particular bullet was fired from a certain gun are examples. Testimonial evidence is open to all of the weaknesses and defects of human observation, perception, memory, and reporting. Notorious cases of misplaced justice due to "psychological inability" to give reliable testimony have led to a reexamination of the relative importance of testimonial evidence and circumstantial evidence. The relative merits of the two will be discussed later. Cross-examination of the witness is the guarantee that these above-mentioned defects may not pass unchallenged. It is usually accepted as a general principle, based upon psychological knowledge of human nature, that when testimony is given which goes against the interests of the witness, the witness being aware of this fact, it may be regarded as sound, for there is no normal motive for the witness to lie in order to injure his own interests.

2. Circumstantial, or Indirect, Evidence. Circumstantial evidence may be defined as evidence from related circumstances, events, objects, and facts, of a nontestimonial character from which inferences to the fact-in-issue may be drawn. What is behind the generally accepted belief that circumstantial evidence is usually of a low order, as expressed in the derogatory term "merely circumstantial"? Is it not because the term "circumstantial" is ambiguous? There are different degrees of relevancy and concreteness in the circumstances surrounding a crime. When the term "merely" is applied, it carries the significance of an incidental rather than an essential relationship to the main event, but because of the peculiar and perhaps accidental combination of circumstances may appear to point to a conclusion bearing upon the fact-in-issue. Poor circumstantial evidence is thus often relied upon because of the absence of other conclusive evidence, and because the known circumstances have in the past usually been associated with similar situations.

On the other hand, circumstantial evidence may be of a very conclusive nature when the "circumstances" are concrete objects in relation to other objects, and verified facts in relation to other facts not capable of otherwise being accounted for. Stolen goods found on the person or property of the accused, fingerprints found on the furniture in the room which has been robbed, or marks on the rifled desk identical with those which might be made by a blunt instrument proved to be part of his tool kit—these are "circumstances" that bear such a close causal connection with the crime itself that they demand to be "explained away" if they are not to be taken as conclusive. When a combination of circumstances consisting of such objects, facts, and concrete events as these is established by experts, this kind of circumstantial evidence is of a high order.

Reasoning from circumstantial evidence is often regarded as a sort of analogical reasoning, where from similarities in certain particulars, similarities in other particulars are inferred. Certain objects or events observed in the new case are suspected of being related to others because of certain similarities in this situation to some other previously and better known situation, or again, certain similarities are observed between this accused person and the hypothetical guilty person.

As has already been pointed out, the soundness of an analogy depends upon whether the resemblances and connections are superficial, or whether they are of a fundamental and systematic character enabling us to infer with high probability from observed similarities to other hidden characteristics. When used with care, analogies are very fruitful in suggesting possible hypotheses for testing by means of the convergence of evidence.

Ordinarily no one bit of circumstantial evidence is sufficient to warrant an inference capable of establishing proof, but an accumulation of resemblances, or convergence of evidence, both circumstantial and testimonial, leads to an inference with increasing degrees of probability.

It is an interesting question in legal thinking and criminal investigation as to which of the two kinds of evidence is more reliable. Developments in the field of technological and scientific research, such as ballistics, microscopy, chemical analysis, and toxicology render circumstantial evidence of this nature more reliable. Moreover, recent developments in the field of "witness psychology" lead to the conclusion that the ability of the average witness to observe, remember, and report accurately under stress is limited. Harry Söderman and J. J. O'Connell commented as follows on this point:

> Unfortunately, modern witness psychology does not yet offer means of directly testing the credibility of testimony. It lacks precision and method, in spite of worthwhile attempts on the part of such learned men as Binet, Gross, Stein, Lipmann, Gorphe, Locard, and others. It does not, therefore, lead to definite ways of achieving certainty. At the same time, witness psychology has through the gathering of many experiences concerning the weakness of human testimony been of invaluable service in criminology. It shows clearly that only evidence of a technical nature has absolute value as proof.[2]

While the question of the absolute superiority of one kind of evidence over another cannot be determined, it would perhaps be a reasonable conclusion to say that if the choice is between reliable testimonial evidence versus doubtful circumstantial evidence, or between doubtful testimonial evidence and reliable circumstantial, the choice will always be in favor of that which is reliable, provided that reliability can be determined.

[2] *Modern Criminal Investigation* (New York: Funk & Wagnalls Co., 1936), p. 13.

The Convergence of Testimonial and Circumstantial Evidence. As indicated above, it is the convergence of testimonial and circumstantial evidence, one leading into and supporting the other, that leads to conclusive evidence or proof. The following example is given by Wigmore:[3]

The respective kinds of evidence are symbolized by C and T; F is the fact-in-issue consisting of F^1 (forcible entry) and F^2 (taking goods).

On a prosecution of D (defendant) for burglary, an inmate of the house, P (plaintiff), testifies (T^1) that he saw D, an intruder, in the bedroom taking jewelry (F^2); another, Q, testifies (T^2) that he saw D jumping out through the window (C^1); a bystander, R, testifies (T^3) that he saw D later picking broken glass out of his hand (C^2); a policeman, S, testifies (T^4) that he later found jewelry in D's trunk (C^3) and the inmate, P, testifies (T^5) that the jewelry found is the jewelry that was in the room (C^3).

Here the fact of D's jumping hurriedly out of the window (C^1) is circumstantial evidence that he had entered forcibly (F^1); C^1 is evidenced testimonially by T^2, the witness who saw him, and circumstantially by the broken glass in his hand (C^2), which in turn is evidenced testimonially by the witness who saw him (T^3). Then the taking of the jewelry (F^2) is evidenced testimonially by the witness who saw him (T^1), and circumstantially by the finding of the jewelry in his trunk (C^3), which in turn is evidenced testimonially by the combined testimony of the policeman who found it (T^4) and the inmate who identified it (T^5). Thus, the testimonial and the circumstantial evidence are related in separate but converging series. Arranging these pieces of evidence in logical order, they assemble as follows:

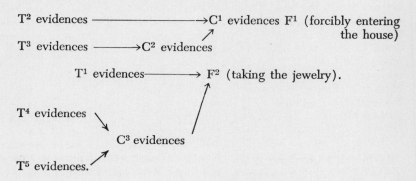

PROBLEMS

1. Analyze the following cases, setting forth briefly the main facts in the case, the main question before the court, the rule of law governing the case, the decision of the court, and the reasons for the de-

[3] J. H. Wigmore, *A Student's Textbook of the Law of Evidence* (New York: The Foundation Press, Inc., 1935), pp. 40, 41.

cision. Put the final reasoning of the court into the form of a syllogism, showing major and minor premises and conclusion.

(1) *Roth* v. *United States of America* (UNITED STATES SUPREME COURT REPORTS, Vol. I, Second Series, 1957)

The constitutionality of a criminal obscenity statute is the question in
each of these cases (Roth, N.Y.; Alberts, Calif.). In Roth, the primary
constitutional question is whether the federal obscenity statute violates the
provision of the First Amendment that "Congress shall make no law . . .
abridging the freedom of speech, or the press. . . ."

Other constitutional questions are: whether these statutes violate due
processes, because too vague to support conviction for crime; whether
power to punish speech and press offensive to decency and morality is in the
States alone, so that the federal obscenity statute violates the Ninth and
Tenth Amendments. . . .

Roth conducted a business in New York in the publication and sale of
books, photographs and magazines. He used circulars and advertizing matter
to solicit sales. He was convicted by a jury in the District Court for the
Southern District of New York upon four counts of a 26 count indictment
charging him with mailing obscene circulars and advertizing, and an obscene
book, in violation of the federal obscenity statute. His conviction was
affirmed by the Court of Appeals for the Second Circuit. We granted
certiorari.[4] [Brief history of laws relating to obscenity.]

In the light of this history it is apparent that the unconditional phrasing
of the First Amendment was not intended to protect every utterance. This
phrasing did not prevent this Court from concluding that libelous utterances
are not within the area of constitutionally protected speech. [Cases cited.]
At the time of the adoption of the First Amendment, obscenity law was not as
fully developed as libel law, but there is sufficiently contemporaneous evidence to show that obscenity, too, was outside the protection intended for
speech and press . . . . All ideas having even the slightest redeeming social
importance—unorthodox ideas, controversial ideas, even ideas hateful to the
prevailing climate of opinion—have the full protection of the guaranties, unless excludable because they encroach upon the limited area of more important interests. But implicit in the history of the First Amendment is the
rejection of obscenity as utterly without redeeming social importance. . . .

There are certain well-defined and narrowly limited classes of speech, the
prevention and punishment of which have never been thought to raise any
constitutional problem. These include the lewd and obscene . . . . It has
been well observed that such utterances are no essential part of any exposition
of ideas, and are of such slight social value as a step to truth that any benefit
that may be derived from them is clearly outweighed by the social interest in
order and morality. . . .

It is strenuously argued that these obscenity statutes offend the constitutional guaranties because they punish incitation to impure sexual
thoughts, not shown to be related to any overt antisocial conduct which is or

---

[4] The name of a writ of review or inquiry.

may be incited in the persons stimulated to such *thoughts*. In Roth the trial judge instructed the jury: "The words 'obscene, lewd and lascivious' as used in the law, signify that form of immorality which has relation to sexual impurity and has a tendency to excite lustful thoughts."

The fundamental freedoms of speech and press have contributed greatly to the development and well-being of our free society and are indispensable to its continued growth. Ceaseless vigilance is the watchword to prevent their erosion by the Congress or by the States.

The door barring federal and state intrusion into the area cannot be left ajar; it must be kept tightly closed and opened only the slightest crack necessary to prevent encroachment upon more important interests. It is therefore vital that the standards for judging obscenity safeguard the protection of freedom of speech and press for material which does not treat sex in a manner appealing to prurient interest. . . .

In summary, then, we hold that these statutes, applied according to the proper standard for judging obscenity, do not afford constitutional safeguards against convictions based upon protected material, or fail to give men in acting adequate notice of what is prohibited. Roth's argument that the federal obscenity statute unconstitutionally encroaches upon the powers reserved by the Ninth and Tenth Amendments to the states and the people to punish speech and press where offensive to decency and morality is hinged upon his contention that obscenity is expression not excepted from the sweep of the proviso of the First Amendment that "Congress shall make no law . . . abridging the freedom of speech, or of the press . . ." That argument falls in light of our holding that obscenity is not expression protected by the First Amendment. We therefore hold that the federal obscenity statute punishing the use of the mails for obscene material is a proper exercise of the postal power delegated to Congress by Art. 1, Sec. 8. [Cases cited.] The Judgments are affirmed.

(2) *New York Times Co.* v. *L. B. Sullivan* et al. (UNITED STATES SUPREME COURT REPORTS, Vol. II, Second Series, 1964)

The present action for libel was brought in the Circuit Court of Montgomery, Alabama, by a city commissioner of public affairs whose duties included the supervision of the police department; the action was brought against *The New York Times* for the publication of a paid advertisement describing the maltreatment in the city of negro students protesting segregation, and against four individuals whose names, among others, appeared in the advertisement. The jury awarded plaintiff damages of $500,000 against all defendants, and the judgment on the verdict was affirmed by the Supreme Court of Alabama on the grounds that the statements in the advertisement were libelous *per se*, false, and not privileged, and that the evidence showed malice on the part of the newspaper; the defendants' constitutional objections were rejected on the ground that the First Amendment does not protect libelous publications.

On writ of *certiorari*, the Supreme Court of the United States reversed the judgment below and remanded the case to the Alabama Supreme Court.

In an opinion by Brennan, J., expressing the views of six members of the court, it was held that (1) the rule of law applied by the Alabama courts was constitutionally deficient for failure to provide the safeguards for freedom of speech and press that are required by the constitutional guaranty in a libel action brought by a public official against critics of his official conduct, and in particular, a failure to provide a qualified privilege for honest misstatement of fact, defeasible only upon a showing of actual malice; and (2) under the proper standards the evidence presented in the case was constitutionally insufficient to support the judgment for the plaintiff.

The concurring opinions expressed the view that the constitutional guaranty of free speech and press affords the defendants an absolute, unconditional privilege to publish their criticism of official conduct. Respondent's complaint alleged that he had been libeled by statements in a full-page advertisement that was carried in *The New York Times* on March 29, 1960 entitled "Heed Their Rising Voices," the advertisement began by stating that "As the whole world knows by now, thousands of southern negro students are engaged in widespread non-violent demonstrations in positive affirmation of the right to live in human dignity as guaranteed by the United States Constitution and the Bill of Rights." It went on to charge that "in their efforts to uphold these guarantees, they are being met by an unprecedented wave of terror by those who would deny and negate that document which the whole world looks upon as setting the pattern for modern freedom." Succeeding paragraphs purported to illustrate the "wave of terror" by describing certain alleged events. . . . The text appeared over the names of 64 persons, many widely known for their activities in public affairs, religion, trade unions and the performing arts. . . .

Of the ten paragraphs of text in the advertisement, the third and a portion of the sixth were the basis of respondent's claim of libel. They read as follows: Third paragraph: "In Montgomery, Alabama, after students sang 'My Country 'Tis of Thee,' on the State Capitol steps their leaders were expelled from school, and truckloads of police armed with shotguns and tear-gas ringed the Alabama State College Campus. When the entire student body protested to state authorities by refusing to re-register, their dining hall was padlocked in an attempt to starve them into submission."

Sixth paragraph: "Again and again the southern violators have answered Dr. King's peaceful protests with intimidation and violence. They have bombed his home almost killing his wife and child. They have assaulted his person. They have arrested him seven times—for speeding, loitering, and similar offenses. And now they have charged him with perjury,—a *felony*, under which they could imprison him for ten years."

Although neither of these statements mentions respondent by name, he contended that the word "police" in the third paragraph referred to him as the Montgomery Commissioner who supervised the police department, so that he was being accused of "ringing" the campus with police. He further claimed that the paragraph would be read as imputing to the police, and hence to him, the padlocking of the dining hall in order to starve the students into submission. As to the sixth paragraph, he contended that since arrests are ordinarily made by the police, the statement "They have arrested [Dr. King] seven times" would be read as referring to him.

It is uncontroverted that some of the statements made in the two paragraphs were not accurate descriptions of events which occurred in Montgomery. . . .

On the premise that the charges in the sixth paragraph could be read as referring to him, respondent was allowed to prove that he had not participated in the events described. . . .

The cost of the advertisement was $4800, and it was published by The Times upon an order from a New York advertising agency acting for the signatory committee. . . .

The general proposition that freedom of expression upon public questions is secured by the First Amendment has long been settled by our decisions. The constitutional safeguard, we have said, "was fashioned to secure unfettered interchange of ideas for the bringing about of political and social changes desired by the people." . . .

Thus we consider this case against the background of a profound national commitment to the principle that debate on public issues should be uninhibited, robust, and wide open, and that it may well include vehement, caustic, and sometimes unpleasantly sharp attacks on government and public officials. The present advertisement as an expression of grievance and protest on one of the major public issues of our time, would seem clearly to qualify for the constitutional protection. The question is whether it forfeits that protection by the falsity of some of its factual statements and by the alleged defamation of respondent. . . .

We hold today that the Constitution delimits a State's power to award damages for libel in actions brought by public officials against critics of their official conduct. Since this is such an action, the rule requiring proof of actual malice is applicable. The Judgment of the Supreme Court of Alabama is reversed and the case is remanded to that Court for further proceedings not inconsistent with this opinion. Reversed and remanded.

(3) *Estes* v. *Texas* (UNITED STATES SUPREME COURT REPORTS, Vol. XIV, Second Series, 1965)

The question presented here is whether the petitioner, who stands convicted in the District Court for the Seventh Judicial District of Texas at Tyler for swindling, was deprived of his right under the Fourteenth Amendment to due process by the televising and broadcasting of his trial. Both the trial court and the Texas Court of Criminal Appeals found against the petitioner. We hold to the contrary and reverse his conviction. . . .

Petitioner's case was originally called for trial on September 24, 1962 in Smith county after a change of venue from Reeves county, some 50 miles west. Massive pretrial publicity totaling eleven volumes of press clippings, which are on file with the clerk, had given it national notoriety. At that time a defense motion to prevent telecasting, broadcasting by radio and news photography and a defense motion for continuance were presented, and after a two day hearing the former was denied and the latter granted.

These initial hearings were carried live by both radio and television and news photography was permitted throughout. The video-tapes of these hearings clearly illustrate that the picture presented was not one of that

judicial serenity and calm to which petitioner was entitled.   Indeed, at least
twelve cameramen were engaged in the courtroom throughout the hearing
taking motion and still pictures and televising the proceedings.   Cables and
wires were snaked across the courtroom floor, three microphones were on the
judge's bench and others were beamed at the jury box and the counsel table.

It is contended that this two-day pretrial hearing cannot be considered in
determining the question before us.   We cannot agree.   Pretrial can create
a major problem for the defendant in a criminal case.   Indeed, it may be
more harmful than publicity during the trial for it may well set the community opinion as to guilt or innocence.   Though the September hearings
dealt with motions to prohibit television coverage, and to postpone the trial,
they are unquestionably relevant to the issue before us.   All of this two-day
affair was highly publicized and could only have impressed those present, and
also the community at large, with the notorious character of the petitioner
as well as the proceeding.   The trial witnesses present at the hearing, as well
as the original jury panel, were undoubtedly made aware of the peculiar public
importance of the case by the press and television coverage being provided,
and by the fact that they themselves were being televised live and their
pictures rebroadcast on the evening show.

When the case was called for trial on October 22 the scene had been altered.
A booth had been constructed at the back of the courtroom which was painted
to blend with the permanent structure of the room.   It had an aperture to
allow the léns of the cameras an unrestricted view of the courtroom.   All
television cameras and newsreel photographers were restricted to the area of
the booth when shooting film or telecasting.   Because of continual objection,
the rules governing live telecasting, as well as radio and still photos, were
changed as the exigencies of the situation seemed to require.   As a result,
live telecasting was prohibited during a great portion of the actual trial.
Only the opening* and closing arguments of the State, the return of the
jury's verdict and its receipt by the trial judge were carried live with
sound. . . .

We start with the proposition that it is a "public trial" that the Sixth
Amendment guarantees to the "accused."   The purpose of the requirement
of a public trial was to guarantee that the accused would be fairly dealt with
and not unjustly condemned. . . .   It is said however, that the freedoms
granted in the First Amendment extend a right to the news media to televise
from the courtroom, and that to refuse to honor this privilege is to discriminate between the newspapers and television.   This is a misconception
of the rights of the press. . . .

The State, however, says that the use of television in the instant case was
"without injustice to the person immediately concerned," basing its position
on the fact that the petitioner has established no isolatable prejudice and
that this must be shown in order to invalidate a conviction in these circumstances.   The State paints too broadly in this contention, for this Court itself has found instances in which a showing of actual prejudice is not a pre-
requisite to reversal.   This is such a case.

* Due to mechanical difficulty there was no picture during the opening
argument.

As has been said, the chief function of our judicial machinery is to ascertain the truth. The use of television, however, cannot be said to contribute materially to this objective. Rather its use amounts to the injection of an irrelevant factor into court proceedings. In addition, experience teaches that there are numerous situations in which it might cause actual unfairness—some so subtle as to defy detection by the accused or control by the judge. We enumerate some in summary:

1. The potential impact of television on juries is perhaps of the greatest significance. They are the nerve center of the fact finding process. . . .
2. The quality of the testimony in criminal trials will often be impaired. The impact upon a witness of the knowledge that he is being viewed by a vast audience is simply incalculable. . . .
3. A major aspect of the problem is the additional responsibility the presence of television places on the trial judge. His job is to make certain that the accused receives a fair trial. This most difficult task requires his undivided attention. Still when television comes into the courtroom he must also supervise it. . . .
4. Finally, we cannot ignore the impact of courtroom television on the defendant. Its presence is a form of mental—if not physical—harassment, resembling a police line up or the third degree. . . .

It is said that the ever advancing techniques of public communication and the adjustment of the public to its presence may bring about a change in the effect of telecasting upon the fairness of criminal trials. But we are not dealing here with future developments in the field of electronics. Our judgment cannot be rested on the hypothesis of tomorrow but must take the facts as they are presented today. The Judgment is therefore reversed.

2. State the *probandum,* the evidentiary facts for prosecution and defense, the nature of the expert knowledge of drugs involved, and the basis for alibi in the following case. Show the evidence and line of reasoning leading to acquittal or proof of guilt.

A woman who had a violent disposition and was subject to attacks of hysteria accused her husband of having attempted to poison her. As proof of her charge, she produced a white powder, which, she alleged, he had put into her food. The powder was found to be white arsenic, and the food was found to contain a fatal quantity of that poison. The husband was immediately arrested and confined in prison pending investigation (December 31). He denied that he had ever put any arsenic into her food. The woman was perfectly well for eight days but on the ninth day became very violent and did many eccentric things. On the next day, she died (assume this date to be January 10), and examination of the body showed that arsenic had been the cause of her death.[5]

3. Using the method given by Wigmore in the body of the chapter, analyze and diagram the convergence of circumstantial and testimonial

[5] Cited in J. H. Wigmore, *The Science of Judicial Proof* (3d ed.; Boston: Little, Brown & Co., 1937), pp. 68–69.

evidence in the solution of a crime in one of your favorite mystery stories.

4. Analyze and report on a case in which circumstantial evidence, and one in which testimonial evidence, led to false conviction for a crime.

5. In view of the different kinds of inference and methods of securing evidence studied in this chapter, how would you classify and illustrate the methods used to solve the following problems?

(1) A detective is seeking to determine whether a dead man was murdered, committed suicide, died a natural death, or died as the result of an accident.

(2) A judge, in rendering a decision on a case, cites precedent from past cases to support his own conclusions.

(3) A statute is applied to a specific case when the facts in the case have been established.

(4) A court is examining and sifting circumstantial and testimonial evidence in the case of an automobile accident in which the defendant is accused of running into the plaintiff's car, and of failing to yield right-of-way at an intersection.

(5) A man, accused of assault and battery at a certain time and place, establishes an alibi.

6. In Felix Frankfurter's study of *The Case of Sacco and Vanzetti*,[6] Chapters 2 and 3, what is meant by the terms *psychologically impossible* and *consciousness of guilt*, and what part did these concepts play in this famous trial?

[6] Boston: Little, Brown & Co., 1927.

19

Fallacies of Induction
and Scientific Methods

In our discussion of induction and scientific methods we have referred only incidentally to the errors, fallacies, and defects of the methods to which we are liable. We shall now sum up and illustrate the more important of the so-called inductive fallacies, although the list is in no sense complete, and may overlap in many instances the semantic, and material fallacies discussed in Chapter 5. Since the truth of a proposition cannot be determined aside from its intelligibility, and since to a large extent language is the tool of communication in science as in everyday life, *ambiguities of language* must be regarded as a perennial source of error in scientific methods. For a fuller discussion of the relation of logic to language see Chapter 2.

I. INDIVIDUAL PREJUDICES AND PREPOSSESSIONS

While a complete discussion of the errors and fallacies due to individual prejudices and prepossessions belongs more to psychology than to logic, it is important to realize that this hazard to objectivity stands ever in the background in scientific methods. We can do no better by way of emphasizing this source of error than to quote from the Aphorisims of Francis Bacon under the head, "The Idols of the Cave."

The Idols of the Cave are the idols of the individual man. For every one (besides the errors common to human nature in general) has a cave or den of his own, which refracts and discolors the light of nature; owing either to

306

his own proper and peculiar nature; or to his education and conversation with others; or to the reading of books, and the authority of those whom he esteems and admires; or to the differences of impressions, accordingly as they take place in a mind preoccupied and predisposed or in a mind indifferent and settled; or the like. So that the spirit of man (according as it is meted out to different individuals) is in fact a thing variable and full of perturbation, and governed as it were by chance. Whence it was well observed by Heraclitus that men look for sciences in their own lesser worlds, and not in the greater or common world.

The idols of the cave take their rise in the peculiar constitution, mental or bodily, of each individual; and also in education, habit, and accident. Of this kind there is a great number and variety; but I will instance those the pointing out of which contains the most important caution, and which have most effect in disturbing the clearness of the understanding.

Men become attached to certain particular sciences and speculations, either because they fancy themselves the authors and inventors thereof, or because they have bestowed the greatest pains upon them and become most habituated to them. But men of this kind, if they betake themselves to philosophy and contemplations of a general character, distort and color them in obedience to their former fancies; . . .[1]

Bacon was here making a generalization about mankind as a whole. Perhaps to be quite just we should distinguish between the undisciplined mind and the carefully trained scientific mind. While it is quite obvious that these personal factors are likely to influence any scientist or research worker in any field, to some extent, in his choice of a science, his choice of a problem, his selection of materials in a given research, and his choice between rival hypotheses, they are perhaps more dangerous to the worker in the social sciences. Here the materials are less specific, more heterogeneous and more subject to influences created by the spirit of the times, or the mental weather, especially in such fields as economics, politics, race, religion, and morals.

II. FALLACIES OF OBSERVATION

Since inductive inferences are made upon the basis of observations of data as evidence, we must next examine the fallacies which occur in observation.

1. Incomplete Observation. Incomplete observation consists in overlooking or neglecting either instances or related circumstances which should be observed. It is not unrelated to the previous discussion of prejudice, since the commonest form of this fallacy is the

---

[1] *Bacon Selections,* ed. Matthew T. McClure, The Modern Student's Library (New York: Charles Scribner's Sons, 1926), pp. 289, 295.

selection of positive instances and the neglect of negative ones due to some form of special interest, inattention, bias, or selective memory.

Darwin recognized the importance of the selective tendency of memory when he wrote in his autobiography: "I had also during many years, followed a golden rule—namely, whenever a published fact, a new observation or thought came across me, which was opposed to my general results, to make a memorandum of it without fail and at once; for I had found by experience that such facts and thoughts were far more apt to escape from the memory than favorable ones."[2]

People who believe themselves in possession of powers of prediction are prone to this fallacy, due to the fact that they remember and record only those instances where their predictions have been fulfilled, and fail to note the many which are unfulfilled. It is for the same reason a source of superstitions, irrational belief in predictions from astrology, fortune telling, and dreams.

2. Inaccurate Observation. The reasons for inaccurate observation are often classified as *physical, physiological,* and *psychological.* Physical factors are those which have to do with the medium in which or by which observations are made. Such physical conditions as darkness, fog, and haze affect observation. Where instruments are used, a defect in the mechanism may distort the results. The chief *physiological* factors affecting observation are abnormality or limitations of sense organs, and fatigue. *Psychological* factors, in addition to those already mentioned under "incomplete observation," which affect accuracy of observation, are emotion, imagination, and misplaced attention. The chief source of inaccurate observation is, however, found in the confusion of what is actually observed with inferences which are made from the observations. This error is not unrelated to incomplete observation because if the observations had been more complete they might not have led to incorrect inferences. The history of science is replete with notable examples of common-sense observations and inferences which have later been contradicted by more correct observations and inferences based upon a more complete consideration of relevant facts. The belief that the earth is flat, is at the center of the solar system, and that the sun revolves around it is the most familiar example.

In the sciences where conditions of experiment and observation are under control, many of the above errors of observation may be allowed

[2] Charles Darwin, *Life and Letters of Charles Darwin* (New York: Appleton-Century-Crofts, Inc., 1896), I, p. 71.

for or eliminated. In daily life and in the courts, however, where we must depend upon testimony based upon casual observation, recorded in memory and reproduced under conditions unfavorable to objectivity, incredulity and cross-examination are the best safeguards of truth.

In order further to illustrate the unreliability of ordinary observation, we quote from a famous experiment recorded by Münsterberg.

There was, two years ago in Göttingen, a meeting of a scientific association, made up of jurists, psychologists, and physicians, all, therefore, men well trained in careful observation. Somewhere in the same street there was that evening a public festival of the carnival. Suddenly, in the midst of the scholarly meeting, the doors open, a clown in highly colored costume rushes in in mad excitement, and a negro with a revolver in hand follows him. In the middle of the hall first the one, then the other, shouts wild phrases; then the one falls to the ground, the other jumps on him; then a shot, and suddenly both are out of the room. The whole affair took less than twenty seconds. All were completely taken by surprise, and no one, with the exception of the President, had the slightest idea that every word and action had been rehearsed beforehand, and that photographs had been taken of the scene. It seemed most natural that the President should beg the members to write down individually an exact report, inasmuch as he felt sure that the matter would come before the courts. Of the forty reports handed in, there was only one whose omissions were calculated as amounting to less than twenty per cent of the characteristic facts; fourteen had twenty to forty per cent of the facts omitted; twelve omitted forty to fifty per cent, and thirteen still more than fifty per cent. But besides the omissions there were only six among the forty which did not contain positively wrong statements; in twenty-four papers up to ten per cent of the statements were free inventions and in ten answers—that is, in one fourth of the papers—more than ten per cent of the statements were absolutely false, in spite of the fact that they all came from scientifically trained observers. Only four persons, for instance, among forty noticed that the Negro had nothing on his head; the others gave him a derby or high hat, and so on. In addition to this, a red suit, a brown one, a striped one, a coffee-colored jacket, shirt sleeves, and similar costumes were invented for him. He wore in reality white trousers and a black jacket with a large red necktie. The scientific commission which reported the details of the inquiry came to the general statement that the majority of the observers omitted or falsified about half of the processes which occurred completely in their field of vision.[3]

III. FALLACIES OF CLASSIFICATION

1. Incomplete Classification. This fallacy is a simple breach of the rule that a classification should be *exhaustive*. This is, of course, an

[3] From *On the Witness Stand* (pp. 51–53) by Hugo Münsterberg, copyright 1913 by Doubleday & Company, Inc., New York.

ideal which is never completely realized, since a classification of natural objects can never achieve absolute completeness. The fallacy consists of making a scientific classification into species, subspecies, etc., and leaving out certain species or subspecies known to exist, so that the sum of the subordinate classes does not equal the genus. For example, if we classify mammals, and leave out the whale because it has many of the characteristics of the fish, we would commit this fallacy.

2. Overlapping Classification. This fallacy is a violation of an obvious requirement that a classification should be such that the subclasses should be *mutually exclusive*. An example would be the classification of public schools, colleges, universities, and professional schools as making up the genus educational institutions.

3. Cross-classification. If the requirement of classification, namely, that a classification should be *based upon a single principle*, is disregarded, this fallacy results. If we classify drama, poetry, essay, fiction, and entertainment as covering the field of literature, we have a cross-classification, since we have utilized both the principle of literary form, and the principle of purpose in the classification.

IV. FALLACIES IN THE USE OF HYPOTHESES

1. Improbable Hypotheses. In Chapter 14 we discussed four criteria of a good hypothesis. Since it is desirable that there should be the greatest freedom in the making of hypotheses, and since it is often the case that hypotheses seemingly absurd, and seemingly inconsistent with the known facts in the field, have led to important discoveries, it is well not to regard the breach of all of these guiding principles as fallacies. There is one rule, however, which if violated leads to a stalemate and therefore constitutes a fallacy. It is that *an hypothesis should be of such a nature that its consequences may be deduced, in order to be confirmed or refuted.* If it cannot be so formulated, it is highly improbable that it will account for the facts. For example, the hypothesis that the suspected occupant of a certain house is a ghost is impossible of confirmation by any means known to science, and hence is not very useful as an hypothesis.

2. Hypothesis "Contrary to Fact." It is a harmless form of speculation to form an hypothesis as to what would have happened if something other than what did happen had happened. However, if this is used as an argument to prove something, it constitutes a fallacy. For example, if we argue, not as a matter of probability but as a certainty, that, if the United States had joined the League of Nations, World War II would not have occurred, or if a different political party had come to power, an economic crisis would have been avoided, we are liable to this fallacy.

V. FALLACIES INCIDENT TO THE DETERMINATION OF CAUSES

1. *Post Hoc Ergo Propter Hoc* (After that, therefore, caused by that). This is the common fallacy of concluding without sufficient investigation that because two events stand in temporal succession they are therefore related. If a cold develops after sitting near a draught, or if we have a headache after a motorbus ride, we often without further investigation or thought attribute the indisposition to the immediately preceding event. This is one explanation of the origin of such superstitious beliefs as that it is unlucky to walk under a ladder, to see a black cat cross the road, and to engage in activities connected with the number thirteen.

2. Insufficient Analysis and Enumeration of Antecedents. Since the dangers and weaknesses of Mill's causal methods have been discussed in some detail in Chapter 15, we shall not go into detail here. The correct employment of the *method of agreement* presupposes, as we have seen, an exhaustive enumeration of the antecedents, and an elimination of all irrelevant factors. If this is not the case, we are likely to conclude that some common circumstance is the cause when it is not.

3. Insufficient Analysis and Enumeration of Differences. Failure to take account of the many differences which may be present when positive instances and negative instances are compared results in an error in the use of the *method of difference*. For example, the difference between a living man and a certain dead one lying on the floor with a bullet through him is that one has the bullet hole in his body and the other hasn't, whereupon it might be concluded, and in some cases accurately, that the bullet is the cause of his death. Actually, further analysis and investigation may show that he died of fright, heart failure, or as the result of hitting his head on a brick when he fell.

4. Accidental, Temporal, or Partial Concomitance. Since the essential principle of the *method of concomitant variations* is the concomitant increase and decrease between the related factors, it is easy to fall into the error of mistaking accidental, temporal, and partial concomitance for causal or functional relations. For example, a fallacy would be committed if a superintendent of an airplane factory, noticing that production greatly increased during the period covered by the waxing of the moon and decreased during its waning, were to conclude without further investigation that a causal relation existed between the two factors.

5. Confusion of Condition and Cause. In Chapter 15 a distinction between *cause* and *condition* was suggested. By "cause" we ordinarily mean some specific event which brings about another specific event called the effect. But every cause-effect relation has a set of related conditions under which it takes place, and in the absence of which it would not occur. The cause may be thought of as that which produces the effect, whereas the condition is a part of the cause and provides the opportunity for the operation of the cause. To confuse the cause and condition or to regard them as identical is a fallacy. For example, it is often argued that the cause of the economic prosperity of a country is its specific form of government, when the form of government may have merely provided the opportunity for prosperity, as might be shown in many cases of other countries with similar forms of government which do not have similar national resources and lack prosperity. An individual who has the disadvantages of a poverty-stricken childhood and who has turned to crime might argue that poverty was the cause of his downfall, whereas poverty may have merely provided the conditions favorable to crime.

6. Confusion of Cause and Reciprocal Relation. In the cause-effect relation, influences which mutually affect each other are called "reciprocals." Education and eugenics are reciprocal in producing a sound, intelligent, educated, and effective population. If one of these is taken in isolation as the sole cause of human well-being, or its neglect as the sole cause of deterioration, a fallacy results. Partisans of heredity versus environmental factors who would argue that one or the other is *exclusively* capable of explaining the facts of mature development are confusing cause and reciprocal relation.

7. Confusion of Sufficient and Necessary Conditions. As we have seen, a proposition p may be said to be a *sufficient* condition for another proposition q when the assertion "p implies q" is true. A proposition p states a *necessary* condition of another proposition q if "not-p implies not-q" is true. In other words, "Whenever p is true, q is true" asserts that a sufficient condition exists and "Only when p is true, q is true" asserts that a necessary condition exists. When these are confused a fallacy results. For example, having a good football coach is a necessary condition for a winning team, but not sufficient, since so many other factors enter in, such as team spirit, ability of players, school support, leadership qualities of the captain, etc. The support of a foreign government by a friendly ally may be a necessary condition for the survival of that government against an internal revolution, but it may not in any sense be sufficient.

VI. HASTY GENERALIZATION

This is the simple fallacy of inferring more than the evidence warrants, or drawing conclusions about *all cases* when only *some cases* have been observed or have been observed inadequately. Such everyday statements as "all ministers' sons are rascals," "all lawyers are liars," and "all Turks are treacherous" are examples. In science the generalization is never hasty in this sense, but any conclusion on insufficient supporting data is a case in point. In medical diagnosis it is likely to occur from insufficient examination of the specific case of disease. In statistics it occurs because conclusions are based on wrongly selected or too limited samples.

VII. FALSE ANALOGY

This is a very ancient form of fallacious thinking, and is closely connected with homeopathic or imitative magic in primitive tribes. The principle behind it is that things which resemble each other in some respect are the same in others as well. It is a false analogy to reason that because Roy and Tom both have the good qualities of even temper and intelligence, Tom will be honest and thrifty because Roy also has these qualities.

VIII. STATISTICAL FALLACIES

1. Unrepresentative Sampling. The major fallacy in the use of statistics is a form of hasty generalization due to unrepresentative sampling. An obvious example would be to ask the next five people you see what their opinion is on a certain controversial question, and to assume that this sample is representative of the community. The polling of public opinion through the mails by utilizing telephone subscribers lists or *Who's Who* lists is an example of this fallacy inasmuch as these lists are economically and culturally selective and not representative of the total population. It is avoided by a careful method of selecting a cross section which includes different geographical, economic, sex, age, cultural, and political factors.

2. Application of Results Derived from Group Phenomena to Individual Cases. This fallacy is not likely to be committed by anyone familiar with statistical methods, but it is a very common misinterpretation of statistics by the layman. It is illustrated by the example of a man who prepared to die on a certain date because his insurance company had informed him what his "life expectancy" was.

3. Failure To State the Reliability of Results. Failure to state the reliability of such statistical results as averages, deviations, and correlations tends to suggest to the uninitiated the false assumption that statistical results are both reliable and certain. What they really claim is a certain degree of probability within a certain margin of error, and in scientific studies this is usually precisely stated.

4. Fallacy of Chance Correlation. This is the statistical fallacy of assuming that, because a statistical correlation may appear between two groups of phenomena, the factual basis for an actual correlation exists in the phenomena themselves rather than in the statistical procedure. The number of stones in each tier of the Pyramid of Cheops may coincide with the number of years between wars, but no connection can be reasonably inferred.

PROBLEMS

1. Detect and describe the nature of the fallacy or fallacies implicit in the following quotations:

(1) "It has well been answered by him who was shown in a temple the votive tablets suspended by such as had escaped the peril of shipwreck, and was pressed as to whether he would then recognize the power of the gods, by an inquiry, 'But where are the portraits of those who have perished in spite of their vows?' "—Francis Bacon

(2) "We know that individuality springs from these two sources [heredity and development]. . . . Is heredity more important than development, or vice versa? Watson and the behaviorists proclaim that education and environment are capable of giving human beings any desired form. Geneticists believe, on the contrary, that heredity imposes on man like ancient fate, and that the salvation of the race lies not in education but in eugenics."[4]

(3) "A Better Business Bureau reports the case of a man to whom an astrologer offered to send a horoscope . . . after stating that the year would be one of vast importance to him and predicting an im-

[4] Alexis Carrel, *Man the Unknown* (New York: Harper & Bros., 1935), p. 251.

provement in his financial condition and a greater and happier future.

"These predictions, according to the astrologer, were based upon an individual study of the man's birthday horoscope. The astrologer asked $2.00 for further information. The astrologer has not received the remittance. The man to whom he addressed the letter has been dead for a year."—*M.L.C.U. Call*

2. According to the following account of the investigation of the famous medium Eusapia, given by Jastrow, what fallacy accounted for her ability to convince eyewitnesses that she had supernormal powers, and what scientific method was employed to discredit them?

"To prove an unknown force, all that is necessary is to slip away the left foot, make the right foot serve to keep contact with one foot of each 'control,' and to apply said agile and versatile left member to the leg of the table. . . . To fortify the conclusion, a second séance was arranged (Eusapia being ignorant of the outcome of the first) at which there were no concealed observers, and at which the usual phenomena took place so long as the 'controls' exercised such lax guardianship as the amateur commands. But upon signal, the control was made real and effective; and the result was decisive. From that moment on, nothing happened. The medium grew excited and irritable, complained of the holding which was in reality gentle but properly directed, tried again and again to throw the observers off their guard, but all to no avail. Expert control stopped the phenomena under the precise conditions under which a half hour before, with complacent and ordinary control, they had occurred in profusion. The 'forces' required the use of Eusapia's hands and feet."[5]

3. What fallacies are present in the following?

(1) I overheard a student who took a certain course last year say that he "got by" without reading the textbook, so I can do the same this year.

(2) A doctor diagnosed a case of rash on a patient's face as follows: "You have changed your cosmetics; it always acts this way when you change your cosmetics."

(3) If I had only taken the advice of my dear friend Smith, my life would not now be in the terrible mess it is.

(4) According to the insurance statistics based upon mortality tables, my life expectancy is twenty years. Therefore: (a) I shall die twenty years from now. (b) The same mortality rate will continue for the next twenty years.

(5) Human beings, on the whole, fall into a normal distribution or biological curve with reference to I.Q. I therefore assume that the I.Q. of this class of juniors and seniors in an elective course will conform to the normal distribution curve.

[5] Joseph Jastrow, *The Psychology of Conviction* (Boston: Houghton Mifflin Co., 1918), pp. 107–110.

(6) Go to Dr. X and ask him for some of this medicine; it will cure your cough because it cured mine.

4. A man bought two apples from the same box and ate one of them unpeeled. Inside of an hour he was seized by an attack of nausea and vomited. He recovered in about two days. He then wanted to test whether or not it was the apple which made him sick.

(1) What fallacy might be committed by assuming without further investigation that the apple caused his illness?
(2) What scientific method might he have employed to make the test without running the risk of another case of poisoning?
(3) What does it indicate regarding his belief in the probability that it was the apple which caused the illness, that he peeled the second one?

5. What fallacies are illustrated in the following account?

A man who had just arrived in a foreign city without much knowledge of the language or merchandising, wishing to send some wine to a fellow passenger at the dock, was looking for a wine store. He saw some wine bottles in the window of a large building and went in to purchase some wine. He found that it was the headquarters of the Board of Trade, devoted to the display of the products of the colonies, of which wine was one.

6. Discuss pro and con the following viewpoints regarding the differences and similarities of the natural sciences and the social sciences.

(1) Whether one is observational purely and the other purely experimental
(2) Whether we can measure precisely in the physical sciences and not at all in the social sciences
(3) Whether it is desirable and how far possible for the social sciences to adopt and repeat the methods of the physical sciences
(4) Whether the differences in these two great branches of science are determined mostly by the nature of the materials with which they deal and the consequent methods that must be employed, or by the human and social attitudes toward the results of research in these fields

7. In the report of the experiment on observation by Münsterberg in this chapter, why do you suppose the members of the conference (well trained in observing) made such a poor showing in describing the events which occurred?

APPENDIXES

A

The Genealogical
Tree of Logic

The chart on page 320, *The Genealogical Tree of Logic,* presents the history of logic graphically, from the Greeks to the present. If the tree be imagined as a three-dimensional living thing instead of a drawing on a plane surface, the inductive and deductive sides, instead of being at opposite poles, come together into a living whole. The roots of the tree growing from Greek soil represent in their beginnings the main logical tendencies, deductive and inductive, which have persisted throughout with some variations in the modern and recent periods. The medieval period is represented as the trunk of the tree, carrying forward the two main streams, with emphasis on the deductive side. In this period was revived the problem of the status of universals which became known as the Realistic-Nominalistic controversy. The modern period is marked by a consolidation of the inductive-deductive methods into the main body of the logic of the sciences, and at the same time has been fertile in the production of offshoots from the parent trunk in the nature of improvements and developments of the traditional logic. The recent period is represented by the sturdy trunk and limbs of a well-developed tree, not yet fully grown.

The five branches and the main trunk of the tree symbolize the six main schools of logic today, namely: (1) The Logic of Science, (2) Aristotelian or Traditional Logic, (3) Symbolic Logic, (4) Epistemological Logic, (5) Multivalued Logic, and (6) Pragmatic Logic with its two subdivisions, Voluntarism and Instrumentalism.

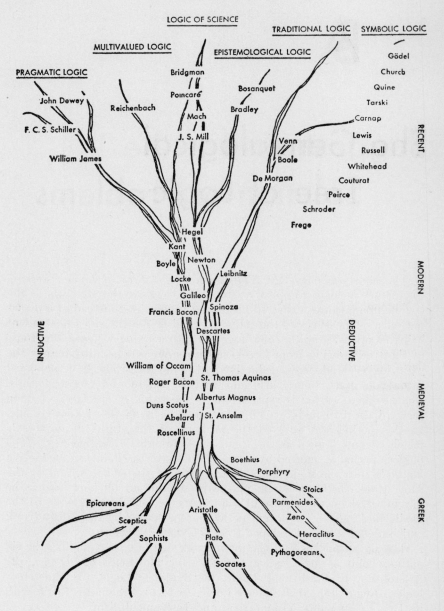

Figure 6. The Genealogical Tree of Logic

B

Suggestions for the Solution of Problems

CHAPTER 1

Problem II:2. If there are only 400 brands of stockings, each one of the first 400 girls could be wearing a different kind. If the next 400 repeated the process, at least 2 girls would be wearing the same kind. There would then be 200 girls left, and, no matter what kind they wore, there would be at least 3 girls wearing stockings of the same make.

Problem III:4.

$$24 = \text{Mary's present age}$$
Let $x = $ Ann's present age and Mary's former age
Let $y = $ interval of time elapsed, and difference between the two girl's ages
$x - y = $ Ann's former age
$$24 = 2(x - y) \qquad y = x - 12$$
$$x + y = 24 \qquad y = 24 - x$$
$$x - 12 = 24 - x$$
$$2x = 36$$
$$x = 18 \text{ (Ann's present age)}$$

Problem III:8. Since the number of amoebae doubles every minute, and the bowl is full in 40 minutes, it must have been half full in 39 minutes.

Problem III:9. There are two solutions to this problem.
First solution:

Let A, B, and C symbolize the three men, respectively.
If A is a nobleman, he told the truth, saying, "I am a nobleman."
If A is a huntsman, he must have lied and said, "I am a nobleman."

321

Hence, in either case, one said, "I am a nobleman." For this solution, then, we shall make the hypothesis that A is a nobleman.

If B is a nobleman, he told the truth in saying, "He says he's a nobleman."

If B is a huntsman, he lied in saying, "He says he's a nobleman," which we already know to be true; hence, it must have been said by a nobleman. B therefore must be a nobleman.

If C is a nobleman, he told the truth in saying, "He's not a nobleman, he's a huntsman," which we assume to be true; hence, it would not have been said by a nobleman.

If C is a huntsman, he lied in saying, "He's not a nobleman, he's a huntsman," which on our assumption is untrue and could be said only by a huntsman.

Conclusion: A and B are noblemen and C is a huntsman.

Second solution: Begin with the hypothesis that A is a huntsman, and proceed in the same manner as before.

Conclusion: A is a huntsman, and B and C are noblemen.

Problem III:13. This is an example of a paradox, or meaningless statement involving a contradiction. Thus, if the barber shaves himself, then he is shaved by the barber and so does not shave himself, which is a contradiction. If the barber does not shave himself, then he is shaved by the barber and so does shave himself, which is a contradiction.

CHAPTER 2

The student will be able to work out the answers to these problems after reading the chapter.

CHAPTER 3

Problem 1. For the distinction between connotation and denotation, see the text.

If we make a series of five terms—*human being, westerner, American, citizen of the United States, native of California*—we observe that the denotation of *human being* includes the denotation of all which come under it and, hence, is the broadest in scope. The denotation of *native of California* is the narrowest. Inversely, the connotation of *native of California* includes that of all of the others. This applies only to certain series of terms.

Problem 7.

(1) " 'Man' is a featherless biped" is defective as a definition because it lacks sufficient differentiae to distinguish man from other bipeds.

(2) " 'Prejudice' is being down on what you are not up on" is a literary definition which is amusing but makes no pretense of being logically exact.

(3) " 'Glass' is something you can see through" is vague both as to genus ("something") and differentia, which does not distinguish it from other transparent objects.

(4) " 'It' [life] is a tale/Told by an idiot, full of sound and fury,/ Signifying nothing" is another literary expression, not seeking to give the essence of "life" but giving rather accidents (in the Aristotelian sense) from a pessimistic viewpoint.

(5) " 'Biology' is the science of life" is an etymological definition, *bios* (life) $+$ *logos* (science of), and is quite adequate for nontechnical purposes.

CHAPTER 4

Problem 2. On the basis of the principle of function, we might divide a city lot into house, garden, roads and walks, garage, swimming pool, and playground. On the basis of the principle of groundcovering, it might be concrete foundations, grass, bricks, tile, flowers, trees, and fences.

Problem 4. Fallacy of cross division is introduced by dividing *army*, on the basis of the principle of method of fighting, into artillery, infantry, flying corps, engineers, signal corps, and medical corps, and then introducing another principle such as rank, with subdivisions of officers and enlisted personnel.

Fallacy of incomplete division is due to omitting any one important subdivision such as infantry.

Fallacy of overlapping species is due to failure to make the subclasses mutually exclusive, for example, artillery, infantry, etc., and reserves and state guards.

CHAPTER 5

Problem III:5. Material fallacy of *ad hominem*.

Problem III:8. This is a fallacy of composition, which is due to arguing from *each* to *all*. The "all" of the major premise must be understood distributively as "each" in order to make sense. In the minor, however, the "all" refers to the angles collectively—hence, the fallacy.

Problem III:14. This is the fallacy of division, arguing from the whole to the part.

Problem III:23. This is the fallacy of accident, and is due to arguing from what is essentially true of water under normal conditions to what is true under accidental conditions such as elevation above and depression below sea level.

Problem III:30. This is the fallacy of begging the question, or *petitio principii*.

Problem III:34. This is the fallacy of *argumentum ad verecundiam,* or the appeal to the authority of great names.

CHAPTER 6

Problem 5. (1) A, (2) A, (3) I, (4) I, (5) O, (6) E, (7) A.

Problem 7. In every case, the A proposition resulting from the reduction of an exceptive term, such as *only* or *none but,* has the position of the original subject and predicate reversed.

(1) E, A; (2) I, O; (3) O; (4) E, A; (5) E, A; (6) E, A; (7) E, A; (8) I, O; (9) E, A; (10) E, A.

CHAPTER 7

Problem 4.

(1) The contradictory O: Some politicians are not opportunists.
(2) The contradictory E: No poets are engineers.
(3) The contradictory I: Some lions are invertebrates.
(4) The contradictory A: All tigers are gentle.

Problem 8.

(1) Converse: Some criminals are bootleggers.
    Obverse: No bootleggers are non-criminals.
(2) Converse: No good general is a rash man.
    Obverse: All rash men are non-good (poor) generals.
(3) Converse: No elements are compounds.
    Obverse: All compounds are non-elements.
(4) Converse: Some snobs are men.
    Obverse: Some men are not non-snobs.
(5) Converse: Some of those who must be punished are those who are guilty.
    Obverse: None of those who are guilty are those who must be non-punished.

CHAPTER 8

Problem 1.

(1) No mortal man can perform miracles.
    The President of the United States is a mortal man.
    Hence, the President of the United States cannot perform miracles.

Problem 3:(1). "Only churches have cross-crowned spires" is ambiguous and may be reduced to either

(a) I. "Some churches have cross-crowned spires," in which case the syllogism contains the fallacy of undistributed middle.
    Or

(b) E. "No non-churches have cross-crowned spires," in which case we have introduced the fallacy of four terms by changing churches to non-churches, and we have also the fallacy of drawing an affirmative conclusion from one negative premise.

Or

(c) A. "All buildings having cross-crowned spires are churches." This syllogism is valid.

Problem 3:(4). If we can assume that all of the terms in this syllogism are unambiguous, then formally the argument is a valid EAE in the first figure. The strange conclusion, which we know to be false, may lead us to suspect that one or more of our premises are false. The major premise is false and, hence, yields a false conclusion.

Problem 4:(6). All of the propositions in this argument contain the exceptive term *unless* and, hence, must be reduced to the standard form as follows:

A.   All cases of having a picnic are cases of missing the concert.
E.   No cases of unclear weather are cases of having a picnic.
A.   Hence, all cases of unclear weather are cases of missing the concert.

The argument is invalid—AEA first figure—since we have an affirmative conclusion from a negative premise.

Problem 5:(1). In order to test a syllogism, one should arrange it in logical order of premises first and conclusion last. It is essential to be able to detect which proposition constitutes the conclusion. Such words as "because" and "since" are used to introduce premises, and such words as "so," "hence," and "therefore" are used to introduce conclusions. The full argument is "All believers of this doctrine are heretics. You are not a believer of this doctrine; so you are not a heretic." This commits the fallacy of *illicit major*.

Problem 5:(6). We must determine exactly what the statement "The blinds are always closed when he is away" means. It does not mean "All cases of the blinds's being closed are cases of our neighbor's being away," but it does mean "All cases of our neighbor's being away are cases of closed blinds." The minor premise is "This is a case of closed blinds"; the conclusion is "This is a case of our neighbor's being away." The fallacy of *undistributed middle* is present.

Problem 6:(3). Most of these syllogisms from Lewis Carroll involve a knowledge and use of both immediate and mediate inference. In the syllogism

All philosophers are logical.
An illogical man is obstinate.
Hence, some obstinate persons are not philosophers.

notice that there are four terms: *philosophers, logical, illogical,* and *obstinate persons.* In order to eliminate one term, we obvert "All philosophers are logical" into "No philosophers are illogical"; then the argument is valid, mood EAO, fourth figure.

Problem 7:(3).

Complete justice presupposes a knowledge of all the facts in the case.
A drama critic has necessarily a meager knowledge of the facts.
Therefore, in the strictest sense, we cannot expect complete justice in dramatic criticism.

CHAPTER 9

Problem 5:(4). $[-(p \cdot q)-q] \supset p$

p	q	$-(p \cdot q)$ (premise)	$-q$ (premise)	p (conclusion)
T	T	F	F	T
F	T	T	F	F
T	F	T	T	T
F	F	T	T	F

In the last row, the premises are true and the conclusion false—hence, invalid.   (Denies one disjunct.)

Problem 7. This problem employs the method of hypotheses. It assumes normal perception and ability to follow the directions. It is obvious that none of the candidates can see her own forehead; hence, the answer must be deduced.

A can see that both B's and C's marks are black. A forms the hypothesis "My mark is white" and then reasons, "If my mark is white, what will happen?" B would deduce that C was tapping because of B's black mark, and C would deduce that B was tapping because of C's black mark, and one or both would stand up. Since they do not stand up, what follows? The complete argument is stated as follows in the form of a hypothetical syllogism:

If my mark were white, either B or C would stand up.
Neither B nor C does stand up.
Hence, my mark must be non-white (black).

Problem 8:(5). Fallacy of affirming the consequent in the minor and affirming the antecedent in the conclusion.

Problem 9:(2). Fallacy of affirming one alternative in the minor and denying the other in the conclusion when the alternatives are not exclusive.

Problem 10:(3). This is a valid disjunctive argument. Since one disjunct has been affirmed, the other must logically be denied.

Problem 11:(2). This dilemma can be met by a counterdilemma as follows:

If I tell the truth, the gods will love me, and, if I tell lies, men will love me.
But I must either tell the truth or tell lies.
Hence, in either case I will be loved.

Problem 11:(6). This is a complex constructive dilemma of the form $[(p \supset q) . (r \supset s)] . (p \lor r) \supset (q \lor s)$. It may be attacked by escaping between the horns. Note that the alternatives of the minor premise are not exclusive; that is, we do not have to devote attention exclusively to the Far East or to Europe.

CHAPTER 10

Problem I:4.

1.	$W \supset M$	Pr.
2.	$M \supset D$	Pr.
3.	$W \lor C$	Pr.
4.	$-D$	Pr. $/ \therefore C$ (conclusion)
5.	$W \supset D$	1, 2, H.S.
6.	$-W$	4, 5, M.T.
7.	C	3, 6, A.A.

Problem II:12.

1.	$P \supset N$	Pr.
2.	$N \supset H$	Pr.
3.	$H \supset S$	Pr.
4.	$-S$	Pr.
5.	$P \lor M$	Pr. $/ \therefore M$ (conclusion)
6.	$P \supset H$	1, 2, H.S.
7.	$P \supset S$	6, 3, H.S.
8.	$-P$	7, 4, M.T.
9.	M	8, 5, A.A.

Problem II:28.

1.	$E \lor (F \supset H)$	Pr.
2.	$-(E \lor H)$	Pr. $/ \therefore -F$ (conclusion)
3.	$-E . -H$	2, De M
4.	$-E$	3, Simp.
5.	$-H$	3, Simp.
6.	$--E \lor (F \supset H)$	1, D.N.
7.	$-E \supset (F \supset H)$	6, Impl.
8.	$F \supset H$	4, 7, M.P.
9.	$-H \supset -F$	8, Cont.
10.	$-F$	5, 9, M.P.

Problem II:32.

1. $M \supset H$ Pr.
2. $H \supset S$ Pr.
3. $M \vee E$ Pr.
4. $-S$ Pr. $/ \therefore E$ (conclusion)
5. $M \supset S$ 1, 2, H.S.
6. $-M$ 4, 5, M.T.
7. E 3, 6, A.A.

CHAPTER 11

Problem II:(2).

1. $(x) (Fx \supset Mx)$ Pr.
2. $(\exists x) (Ox) . (Fx)$ Pr. $/ \therefore (\exists x) (Ox) . (Mx)$ (conclusion)
3. $Oa . Fa$ 2, E.I.
4. $Fa \supset Ma$ 1, U.I.
5. $Fa . Oa$ 3, Comm.
6. Fa 5, Simp.
7. Ma 4, 6, M.P.
8. Oa 3, Simp.
9. $Oa . Ma$ 8, 7, Conj.
10. $(\exists x) (Ox) . (Mx)$ 9, E.G.

Problem III:(8).

1. $(\exists x) (Bx . Sx)$ Pr.
2. $(x) (Sx \supset Rx)$ Pr.
3. $(x) (Rx \supset -Gx)$ Pr. $/ \therefore (\exists x) (Bx . -Gx)$ (conclusion)
4. $Ba . Sa$ 1, E.I.
5. $Sa \supset Ra$ 2, U.I.
6. $Ra \supset -Ga$ 3, U.I.
7. $Sa . Ba$ 4, Comm.
8. Ba 4, Simp.
9. Sa 7, Simp.
10. Ra 5, 9, M.P.
11. $-Ga$ 6, 10, M.P.
12. $Ba . -Ga$ 8, 11, Conj.
13. $(\exists x) (Bx . -Gx)$ 12, E.G.

CHAPTER 12

Problem 2. Notice the rules for the progressive sorites: (1) Only the last premise can be negative. (2) Only the first premise can be particular.

(1) Illustration of the fallacy of *illicit major* introduced by making one premise other than the last negative.

No A is B.
All B is C.

All C is D.
All D is E.
No A is E.

According to the rules of the syllogism, if one premise is negative, the conclusion must be negative. Notice that the predicate of the conclusion, the major term E, is distributed, whereas it is undistributed in the premises. If the last premise were negative (No D is E), the E would be distributed, and no fallacy would result.

(2) Illustration of the fallacy of *undistributed middle* introduced by making particular a premise other than the first.

All A is B.
All B is C.
All C is D.
Some D is E.
Hence, some A is E.

According to the rules of the syllogism, if one premise is particular, the conclusion must be particular. Notice that the term D in the last two premises is undistributed so that it refers only to an indefinite part of the class of D's; hence, only an indefinite part of the D is in E, and it need not be the part which contains the A. Hence the conclusion, "Some A is E," does not follow. These fallacies can be illustrated further by the Euler Diagrams.

Problem 3:(2). This is an enthymeme of the first order, since the major premise is suppressed. The conclusion, "There must be a sadistic streak in this man," is deduced from the single minor premise, "He takes pleasure in punishing his dog." But the deduction is not complete until the major premise is explicitly stated: "Anyone who takes pleasure in punishing his dog has a sadistic streak in him."

Problem 5:(4). We recognize this as a relational argument, and the relation as that of the time relation "before." If we know something about the nature of time relations, we know that the relation is transitive, and the argument is valid. Symbolically: a R b, b R c; hence, a R c.

Problem 5:(10). "Agrees with" is a psychological relation which is subject to variation and differences of degree. It is neither transitive nor intransitive, but nontransitive. The conclusion, therefore, may or may not follow, depending on the individual case. The argument is invalid.

CHAPTER 13

Problem 1. The purpose of this problem is to call attention to the differences in nature and degrees of complexity of the materials with

which the sciences deal, and hence degrees of difficulty in verification
of various kinds of propositions and hypotheses.

(1) Propositions (5), (8), and (10) are concrete and relatively simple
and are verified by the simple operations of testing, measuring, and counting.

(2) Propositions (1) and (7) are more difficult to verify, in that technical
training and technical laboratory equipment are necessary.

(3) Propositions (2) and (6) are historical propositions and are verified
or refuted by reference to competent historical authorities. Proposition (3)
is somewhat more complex. The date of the birth of Washington according
to the Julian calendar was February 11, 1732. The Gregorian calendar,
adopted by English-speaking peoples in 1752, advanced the calendar ten
days; hence, February 11 became February 22.

(4) Propositions (4), (9), and (11) are value judgments and are verified
or refuted pragmatically in a social context. They are less objectively
verifiable than the others.

Problem 7:(1). A clinical or statistical study of human traits such
as intelligence, temperament, aesthetic appreciation, etc., which are
known to vary widely, would become more accurate with an increase
in the number of cases studied, up to a certain point. In a study of
materials known to be homogeneous, such as the composition of certain
chemicals or of certain manufactured goods turned off the assembly
line, the validity would not be improved by a large number of samples.

Problem 8. This difference of opinion on the nature of science on
the part of eminent logicians is largely a matter of difference in
emphasis. Those sciences which deal with measurable quantities and
seek to formulate general laws of nature in terms of mathematics are
necessarily abstract and general. In this, Russell is correct. Schiller's
view is correct in regard to the example cited. Another good example
would be in medicine, where knowledge of general laws is used to treat
specific cases of disease, but the specific case may be unique.

CHAPTER 14

Problem 5:(1). Primitive cosmology was based upon common-
sense observation with a very limited perspective, and, from this
viewpoint, the earth appears to be flat and the sun appears to revolve
around it.

Problem 5:(3). This was due to careless observation, lack of facili-
ties for observation, and lack of controlled experiments providing any
contrary evidence prior to the controlled experiments of Pasteur.

Problem 5:(5). The theory of special creation accepted on biblical
authority did not provide for a sufficient lapse of time for minute
geological changes to lay down strata and preserve deposits of organisms little by little.

Problem 10:(1). While there are certain positive analogies between the two governments to justify many similarities in policy, these similarities do not necessarily extend to economic factors, which are very complex and which might quite properly lead to quite different economic policies.

Problem 10:(5). This is generally considered a good analogy. The negative factors are the differences in historical background, and greater complexity in the political, economic, and cultural conditions.

Problem 11:(1). Observation, induction, hypothesis, deduction, experimentation.

Problem 11:(5). Observation, classification, induction, evolutionary hypothesis, comparative method, deduction, agreement, and difference.

CHAPTER 15

Problem 2. The method of agreement was tried, and, if all of the boxes had agreed in growing crab grass, the only constant factor, fertilizer, might have been held as the source. Their negative agreement, however, was almost as valuable, since it proved that fertilizer was not the source. The method of difference was used in experimenting with different boxes under different conditions. This method was also used in comparing results on front and back lawns.

Problem 12:(1). This is a causal and mathematical relationship, if the number is large; if there are only a few, it might be accidental.

Problem 12:(6). Since the probability of this happening is so low (1/59,049), we would be justified in suspecting some causal factor such as loaded dice. If we know that the dice are not loaded, it would then be explained as an event which according to the probability calculus should happen only once in 59,049 series of throws.

Problem 13:(1). The method of agreement should first be tried. If a high correlation is found to exist between delinquency and low economic status, we would be justified in assuming a causal factor. The method of concomitant variations might reveal a scale of decreasing delinquency with improvement in economic status. The method of difference should be employed in further studying a group of nondelinquent children in comparison with the delinquent group.

Problem 13:(5). The methods of agreement, difference, and concomitant variations might all be profitably employed on this problem.

CHAPTER 16

Problem 3:(1). Since the probability of getting a head in one toss is $\frac{1}{2}$, then, applying the rule, we have $(\frac{1}{2})^5$, or $\frac{1}{32}$.

Problem 3:(2). $(\frac{1}{2})^4$, or $\frac{1}{16}$. To illustrate this, we might chart all 16 possible combinations (see page 275) and notice that this order, HHHT, appears once among the 16.

Problem 3:(3). A 7 can come up in any one of six ways: 1-6, 2-5, 3-4, 4-3, 5-2, 6-1. Since there are 36 possible combinations of two dice, the probability ratio is $\frac{6}{36}$, or $\frac{1}{6}$.

Problem 3:(4). A 4 can come up in any one of three ways: 1-3, 2-2, 3-1. The ratio for a 4 is, then, $\frac{3}{36}$, or $\frac{1}{12}$, and, for two 4's in two throws, it would be $\frac{1}{12} \times \frac{1}{12}$, or $\frac{1}{144}$.

Problem 3:(5). There are 4 aces and 1 queen of diamonds, making a total of 5 favorable alternatives. Since there are 52 possible alternatives in all, the ratio is $\frac{5}{52}$.

Problem 3:(6). Since there are 26 red cards, the probability for the first draw will be $\frac{26}{52}$. On the second draw, there will be only 25 red cards, and, on the third draw, only 24. The total formula is $\frac{26}{52} \times \frac{25}{51} \times \frac{24}{50}$, or 15,600/132,600, or $\frac{2}{17}$.

Problem 7. On the basis of these mortality figures, the probability that a three-year-old will live to be twenty-one is about $\frac{9}{10}$; hence, the probability that he will not live to be twenty-one is about $\frac{1}{10}$.

Problem 13. Since the favorable alternatives are 25 and the total possibilities 100, the probability is $\frac{1}{4}$. The odds are $\frac{1}{3}$ in favor and $\frac{3}{1}$ against.

CHAPTER 17

Problem 1. Formula for mean:

$$M = AM + \frac{\Sigma fd}{N} \times i$$

Class interval	Midpoint	Tabulation	Frequency	Deviation	fd
14–13	13.5	/////	5	+2	+10
12–11	11.5	////	4	+1	+ 4
10–9	9.5	////	4		
8–7	7.5	////	4	−1	− 4
6–5	5.5	///	3	−2	− 6
					+14
					−10
					+ 4

Solving the formula, $\frac{4}{20} \times 2 = \frac{8}{20}$ or $\frac{2}{5}$ or .4. Choose the midpoint 9.5 as assumed mean. The correction is .4. Hence 9.5 + .4

Problem 1:(1).   Bacon was here pointing to the human tendencies to observe only positive cases and to neglect the negative instances. If conclusions are based only on positive cases when equally balanced by negative ones, it is obvious that the generalizations will be erroneous because of this selective factor in the inductions.

Problem 3:(1).   This contains the hidden assumption that all of the factors making for scholarship are the same in the two students, which is very doubtful.

Problem 3:(2).   This is a hasty generalization made, no doubt, upon the basis of wide experience in quick diagnosis but open to the objection that this case may be an exception.

Problem 3:(3).   Hypothesis contrary to fact.

Problem 3:(4).   (a) The incorrect application of statistical mass data to individual cases. (b) A prediction about the future which is almost certainly incorrect. Judging from trends, and barring catastrophes, the mortality rate will probably decrease. Whether this rate of decrease will be high or low can be predicted only from trends in the past and present.

CHAPTER 18

Problem 1:(3). *Estes v. Texas.* The argument may be summed up in the following syllogism:

The function of our judicial machinery is to ascertain the truth.

The use of television in the courtroom, because it has a deleterious impact on juries, testimony, witnesses, trial judge, and defendant, tends to obscure the truth.

Hence, the use of television in the courtroom does not contribute to the main objective of our judicial machinery.

Problem 5:(11). Testimonial and circumstantial evidence, laboratory tests and ballistics, hypotheses, inductions and deductions, and the methods of agreement and difference.

Problem 5:(2). Inductions, deductions, and the method of authority.

Problem 5:(3). Deduction.

Problem 5:(4). Measurement of skid marks on the pavement, observation of damage to cars, relative positions of cars at and after col-

lision, and convergence or nonconvergence of testimonial and circumstantial evidence.

Problem 5:(5). Testimonial and factual evidence establishing the fact that he was elsewhere at the time of the crime. If this is established, the conclusion follows deductively that he could not have committed it.

CHAPTER 19

APPENDIXES

C

Glossary of Logical Terms

A fortiori: With greater force; all the more. Said of a conclusion which, as compared with some other, is even more certain or necessary.

"A" PROPOSITION: A universal affirmative proposition. It is of the form, "All S's are P's," and asserts that all of the subject is included in the predicate class. Thus, the subject is distributed, but the predicate is undistributed.

ABSTRACT: Considered apart from any application to a particular object.

ACCIDENT: A nonessential quality or state of something; e.g., the color of an automobile, for the automobile would still be an automobile if its color were changed. Opposed to an essential characteristic, such as the ability of an automobile to run under its own power.

ADDITIVE QUALITIES: Qualities capable of being measured and treated quantitatively by means of the mathematical operations of addition, multiplication, and subtraction; also called extensive magnitudes.

AGREEMENT, METHOD OF: One of Mill's canons: "If two or more instances of the phenomenon under investigation have only one circumstance in common, the circumstances in which alone all the instances agree is the cause (or effect) of the given phenomenon."

ALTERNATIVE: Each of the possibilities enumerated by an alternative proposition.

ALTERNATIVE PROPOSITION: A proposition (characterized by the "either . . . or . . ." construction) which states that all of the possibilities it enumerates (its alternatives) may be true, but that *all* cannot be false for *at least one must be true.*

ALTERNATIVE SYLLOGISM: An argument made up of an alternative major premise, a categorical minor premise, and a categorical con-

335

clusion. The minor premise *denies* all but one of the alternatives in the major, and the conclusion *affirms* the remaining alternative.

AMBIGUOUS: Having a double meaning; capable of being understood in either of two or more possible senses.

AMPHIBOLY: Ambiguity in the *structure* of a sentence or proposition. Also, the phrase or proposition containing such ambiguity.

ANALOGY: A form of inference in which it is reasoned that if two (or more) things agree with one another in one or more respects, they will (probably) agree in yet other respects.

ANALYTICAL PROPOSITION: A proposition, the predicate of which is implied by the subject, and hence simply analyzes, draws out, or defines the subject, for example, "A square is an equilateral parallelogram having four right angles."

ANTECEDENT: The first part of a hypothetical proposition, stating the condition from which the consequent would follow. For example, in the hypothetical proposition, "If he goes, he will be sorry." "If he goes" is the antecedent or condition.

ANTILOGY: A contradiction in terms or ideas.

ANTINOMY: The mutual contradiction of two principles or inferences resting on premises of equal validity.

A posteriori: Based upon experience.

A priori: Independent of experience, in the sense of not being derived from experience nor explained by experience.

ARGUMENT: A reason or reasons offered in proof; reasoning. Discourse designed to convince or persuade.

Argumentum ad baculum: Literally, argument to the big stick; resort to force. This type of argument is quite obviously nonlogical.

Argumentum ad hominem: Literally, argument to the man; an argument directed at one's prejudices rather than at one's intellect. Also, an argument based upon irrelevant circumstances relating to one's opponent, as when a lawyer points out in court that the defendant has committed past crimes not related to the one in question.

Argumentum ad ignorantiam: Literally, argument to ignorance. It is a fallacy of irrelevancy and is committed when one claims that his opponent's inability to *disprove* a contention *is proof* that the contention is true.

Argumentum ad misericordiam: Appeal to pity. A fallacy of irrelevancy.

Argumentum ad populum: Literally, argument to the people. It is another of the fallacies of irrelevancy and is committed when one attempts to sway an audience by appealing to popular feeling or sentimental weakness. It is a common fallacy of the propagandist and demagogue.

Argumentum ad rem: An argument to the point, i.e., a relevant argument as distinguished from such evasions as *argumentum ad hominem,* etc.

Argumentum ad verecundiam: Appeal to reverence or authority. It is a fallacy of irrelevancy and is committed when one uses respected men as authorities in fields other than those in which they are expert, as when Darwin, a biologist, is cited as an authority in a discussion of religion.

Argumentum a fortiori: An argument from analogy which shows that the proposition advanced is more admissible than one previously conceded by an opponent.

ASYMMETRY: The property of any relation which, if it holds between A and B, cannot possibly hold between B and A, as, "Henry is the father of George" (George cannot possibly be the father of Henry).

AXIOM: A proposition, often seemingly self-evident, which is accepted without question as true for the purpose of further reasoning within a system.

BAYES' THEOREM: A theorem in probability theory, proposed by Thomas Bayes (1702–61), enabling us to revise prior estimates of probability in the light of new information.

BICONDITIONAL PROPOSITION: A proposition of the form "p if and only if q," $(p \supset q) \cdot (q \supset p)$.

BOUND VARIABLE: A variable which is governed by a quantifier in a quantificational formula.

CATEGORICAL PROPOSITION: The simplest form of assertion or denial, consisting of a *subject* about which something is asserted, and a *predicate,* that which is asserted about the subject, joined by a *copula,* which is some form of the verb "be." Also, a proposition stated without qualification.

CATEGORICAL SYLLOGISM: A syllogism made up of three categorical propositions.

CENTRAL TENDENCY: In statistics, the tendency of a frequency distribution of measures to pile up in the center toward a central value such as the mean, median, and mode.

CIRCULAR DEFINITION: A definition which contains in the *definiens,* directly or indirectly, the subject being defined.

CIRCUMSTANTIAL EVIDENCE: Evidence that tends to prove a fact in issue by proving circumstances which afford a basis for a reasonable inference of the occurrence of the fact.

CLASSIFICATION: (a) *Natural.* Classification based upon the natural structures of the materials classified. (b) *Artificial.* Classification which is guided by some human purpose, such as convenience. (c) *Diagnostic.* Classification in a growing dynamic field not susceptible of purely natural or artificial classification.

COMPLEX DILEMMA: An argument in which the hypothetical proposi-‌tions of the major premise have different antecedents *and* different consequents.

COMPLEX QUESTION, FALLACY OF: A fallacy resulting from the presence of a hidden assumption in a question, so that a single answer in-volves a double admission.

COMPOSITION, FALLACY OF: Taking distributively in one part of an argument words or terms which in other parts of the argument are taken compositely or collectively. It sometimes takes the form of assuming that what is true or false of the parts, taken by them-selves, is true or false of the whole.

COMPOUND PROPOSITION: A proposition whose parts are themselves propositions, for example, "The axle broke and the car stopped."

CONCLUSION: A proposition which is claimed to follow as a result of the logical relationship to accepted premises; the third proposition of the syllogism (its subject is the minor term and its predicate is the major term).

CONCOMITANT VARIATIONS, METHOD OF: One of Mill's canons: "What-ever phenomenon varies in any manner whenever another phe-nomenon varies in some particular manner, is either a cause or an effect of that phenomenon, or is connected with it through some fact of causation."

CONFIRMATION: The act of supporting a proposition or hypothesis by evidence of varying degrees of probability.

CONJUNCTIVE PROPOSITION: A proposition made up of two categorical propositions which are joined by "and." For example, "It is a cold winter in California, *and* it is not a good winter for fruit."

CONNOTATION: Meaning; the sum of the qualities implied by a term, or essential to the thing named; intension; signification.

CONSEQUENT: The second part of a hypothetical proposition, i.e., the part which follows the condition named by the antecedent. For example, in the hypothetical proposition "If it snows, the crops will fail," "the crops will fail" is the consequent.

CONTRADICTION: A proposition that is necessarily false by reason of its truth-functional form. Also, the relation of opposition between two propositions such that, if one is true, the other must necessarily be false, and, if one is false, the other must necessarily be true.

CONTRADICTION, LAW OF: One of the so-called Laws of Thought. Given a class A, A cannot be both A and non-A at the same time. Symbolically: $A\bar{A} = 0$, i.e., the A which is non-A equals zero.

CONTRADICTORY: Two propositions are said to be contradictory (and each is said to be the contradictory of the other) when if p is true, q is false, and if p is false, q is true. In the traditional square of opposition, A and O are contradictories, and E and I are contra-dictories also.

CONTRAPOSITION: The process of immediate inference in which the contradictory of the original predicate becomes the subject of the inferred proposition. The simple rule of contraposition is to follow three steps: *obvert, convert* (this yields the partial contrapositive), and *obvert* (this yields the full contrapositive).

CONTRARY: Two propositions are said to be contrary (and each is said to be the contrary of the other) when if p is true, q must be false, and if q is true, p must be false. However, if one is known to be false, the truth or falsity of the other remains undetermined. In the traditional square of opposition, A and E propositions are contraries.

CONVERSION: The changing of the position of the subject and predicate with the retention of the original meaning.

COPULA: A form of the verb "be" used to join the subject and predicate of a categorical proposition.

CORRELATION: A statistical process, symbolized by r, whereby two or more measurements of a series are described in terms of relations between them as, for example, the relation between the length and width of a group of leaves.

COUNTERDILEMMA: A dilemma used as a rebuttal or defense against a previous dilemma already put forth by one's opponent.

CRUCIAL EXPERIMENT: An experiment which decisively eliminates one of two contrary hypotheses when it is assumed that both are plausible and one is true. Either H_1 or H_2 is true, and H_1 implies P, while H_2 implies not-P. Thus, if phenomenon P is observed, then, H_2 is false; therefore, H_1 is accepted as true.

DEDUCTION: The methods of correct reasoning from premises to conclusions. It is often called the method of formal proof as contrasted with induction, the method of discovery.

DEFINIENDUM: The term, concept, or thing being defined.

DEFINIENS: The sentence or proposition explaining the meaning of a term, concept or thing.

DEFINITION: Explanation of the meaning or meanings of a word. (For kinds of definition and the rules of definition see Chapter 3).

DENOTATION: The aggregate or class of individuals or instances falling under a conception or named by a term.

DICHOTOMY: Division of a class into two subclasses, especially two opposed by contradiction, as *white* and *not white*.

Dictum de omni et nullo: Whatever is affirmed or denied of an entire class denoted by a general term may be affirmed or denied of any member of the class.

DIFFERENCE, METHOD OF: One of Mill's canons: "If an instance in which the phenomenon under investigation occurs, and an instance in which it does not occur, have every circumstance in common save one, that one occurring only in the former; the circumstance in which alone the two instances differ, is the effect, or the cause, or an indispensable part of the cause, of the phenomenon."

DIFFERENTIA: In definition, the characteristics of the thing defined which distinguish it from other members of its genus or class.

DILEMMA: The dilemma is an argument, the major premise of which contains two hypothetical propositions conjunctively affirmed, and the minor of which is an alternative proposition, either affirming the antecedents, or denying the consequents of the major premise; the conclusion may be either categorical or alternative.

DISJUNCT: Each of the possibilities enumerated in a disjunctive proposition.

DISJUNCTIVE PROPOSITION: A proposition (of the "not both . . . and . . ." construction) which states that all of the possibilities it enumerates (its disjuncts) may be false, but that all cannot be true for *at least one must be false.*

DISJUNCTIVE SYLLOGISM: An argument made up of a disjunctive major premise, a categorical minor premise, and a categorical conclusion. The minor premise *affirms* all but one of the disjuncts of the disjunctive proposition in the major, and the conclusion *denies* the remaining disjunct.

DISPERSION: In statistics, the measures of the degree of concentration around, and variability from the central or average position, such as, average deviation, standard deviation, etc.

DISTRIBUTED: Said of terms when they refer to *all* of the members of a class, i.e., when they have the widest possible extension or denotation.

DISTRIBUTION: The degree of the denotation or extension of a term.

DIVISION, FALLACY OF: A semantic fallacy (the converse of the fallacy of composition) which consists of using a term in one part of an argument in a collective sense which in another part is used distributively, or of arguing that what is true of the whole is true of its parts.

"E" PROPOSITION: A universal negative proposition. It is of the form "No A's are B's" and excludes all of the subject class from the predicate class. Thus, both subject and predicate are distributed.

EDUCTION: A form of immediate inference in which the inferred proposition is either the converse, obverse, contrapositive, or inverse of the original.

ENTHYMEME: An argument which suppresses either premise or conclusion.

EQUIVALENCE: Two propositions are said to be equivalent if, and only if, they assert the same values of truth or falsity.

EQUIVOCATION: A semantic fallacy by which a word or phrase is used in a double sense, especially when used with intent to deceive.

ESCAPE BETWEEN THE HORNS: A method of defense against the dilemma, consisting of the detection of a fallacy of imperfect disjunction in the minor premise, or of showing that the alternatives in the minor premise are not exhaustive.

ESSENCE: That without which a thing would not be what it is.

EVIDENCE: Any accepted or acceptable fact which is considered as supporting the truth of a given proposition.

EXCEPTIVE PROPOSITION: A proposition containing such an expression as "except," "unless," or "all but." It may be reduced to a categorical proposition as in the following example: "All of the books except those on the shelf are fiction" becomes "All books not on the shelf are fiction."

EXCLUDED MIDDLE, LAW OF: One of the traditional laws of thought. It asserts that given the class A, everything must be either A or non-A.

Ex hypothesi: To reason from what is granted, i.e., "from the hypothesis."

EXISTENTIAL: Said of propositions when they directly assert the existence of their subjects.

EXISTENTIAL GENERALIZATION, E.G.: The rule of inference that, if a given individual is such and such, then some individual is such and such.

EXISTENTIAL INSTANTIATION, E.I.: The rule of inference that from any existential quantification we may infer any instance of it, provided the name being introduced has no prior occurrence in the deduction.

EXISTENTIAL QUANTIFIER: The notation ($\exists$) where any variable such as x may be supplied prefixing a formula containing that variable. $(\exists x)$ Px corresponds to "There is at least one x, such that x is a P."

EXTENSION: Denotation.

FACT: An indubitable truth of actuality; a brute event; synonymous with actual event.

FALLACY: Any reasoning failing to satisfy the conditions of logical proof or violating the laws of valid argument.

FALSE ANALOGY, FALLACY OF: Arguing that because two things are alike in some respects they are therefore alike in other respects in which, as a matter of fact, they are not.

FICTION: A term without denotation, as for example, the "average man" of a group.

FIGURES OF THE SYLLOGISM: The four possible arrangements of the middle term in the categorical syllogism.

FORM: The structure or manner in which a proposition is made or an argument arranged, as contrasted with the "matter" of the proposition or argument.

FREE VARIABLE: A variable which is not governed by a quantifier in a quantificational formula.

FREQUENCY DISTRIBUTION: The frequency with which the measures or scores are distributed throughout the group, as shown by tabulation in frequency tables.

GENERALIZATION: An argument from particular instances; a proposition resting on such an argument.

GENERAL TERM: One which names a class, e.g., *horse, dog, man.*

GENUS: A class of objects divided into several subordinate species.

HASTY GENERALIZATION, FALLACY OF: Drawing a conclusion from too few instances, or with a degree of certainty which goes beyond the evidence for it.

HYPOTHESIS: A tentative theory or supposition provisionally adopted to explain certain facts and to guide in the investigation of others; something assumed or conceded merely for the purposes of argument.

HYPOTHETICAL PROPOSITION: A proposition of the form "If *p*, then *q*," "If *p*" being the antecedent or condition, "then *q*" being the consequent. Also called implicative or conditional proposition.

HYPOTHETICAL SYLLOGISM: (1) The mixed hypothetical syllogism consists of a hypothetical major premise, a categorical minor premise (which either affirms the antecedent or denies the consequent of the major), and a categorical conclusion (which either affirms the consequent or denies the antecedent, depending upon the action of the minor). (2) In the *pure* hypothetical syllogism the action is exactly the same except that the minor premise and the conclusion are hypothetical, not categorical.

"I" PROPOSITION: A particular affirmative proposition. It is of the form "Some S's are P's" and asserts that some of the subject class is in the predicate class. Both subject and predicate are undistributed.

IDENTITY, LAW OF: One of the traditional laws of thought, asserting that a thing is equal to (i.e., *identical* with) itself. It is variously rendered as "A is A," "x = x," "*p* implies *p*" ("$p \supset p$"), etc.

IDOLS: Erroneous and misleading elements of experience, as described by Francis Bacon.

IDOLS OF THE CAVE: Errors peculiar to the person, such as individual prejudices and mental defects.

IDOLS OF THE MARKET PLACE: Weaknesses and faults in language as a means of communication of thought.

IDOLS OF THE THEATER: Errors arising from the dogmas of philosophical systems, and wrong laws of demonstration, which are really but stage plays.

IDOLS OF THE TRIBE: Errors which have their foundation in the understanding of the human race itself.

IMPLICATION: The logical relation between premises and conclusion in a categorical syllogism. The relation between two propositions, p and q, when if p is true, q is true (rendered by the symbol $\supset$).

INDUCTION: The method of arriving at general conclusions of varying degrees of probability on the basis of factual evidence. As contrasted with the method of formal proof (deduction), it is often designated the method of discovery.

INFER: To draw a conclusion from facts or premises.

INFERENCE: The act of drawing a conclusion from premises or data. That which is inferred.

INTENSION: Connotation; the attributes or qualities comprehended in a term.

INTRANSITIVITY: The property of any relation between terms when, if the relation is known to exist between A and B and between B and C, it cannot possibly hold between A and C. Thus, the relation "mother of" is intransitive, for if Mary is the mother of Alice and Alice is the mother of Jane, Mary cannot possibly be the mother of Jane.

INVERSION: The process of immediate inference in which the contradictory of the original proposition's subject becomes the subject of the inverse.

Ipse dixit: A dogmatic statement supposed to be accepted on authority, without proof.

JOINT METHOD OF AGREEMENT AND DIFFERENCE: One of Mill's canons: "If two or more instances in which the phenomenon occurs have only one circumstance in common, while two or more instances in which it does not occur have nothing in common save the absence of that circumstance, the circumstance in which alone the two sets of instances differ, is the effect, or the cause, or an indispensable part of the cause, of the phenomenon."

JUDGMENT: The mental act of accepting or rejecting, affirming or denying. It is the simplest unit of significant expression of opinion, taste, or knowledge, sometimes treated as synonymous with *proposition*.

JUDICIAL PROOF: Evidence, tests, or operations tending to establish fact or truth in the administration of justice.

LARGE NUMBERS, LAW OF: The principle that, if an event has the ideal probability p, then, the greater the number of actual trials, the closer the proportion grows in fact to p.

LAWS OF THOUGHT: The principles of identity, contradiction, and excluded middle, held to be fundamental presuppositions of reasoning according to Aristotle.

LIMITED INDEPENDENT QUALITIES: A principle or postulate suggested by J. M. Keynes, to the effect that the number of varieties in the universe is finite.

LOGICAL CONSTANT: Symbols which have a fixed and constant meaning, such as symbols for negation, alteration, implication, conjunction, and equivalence.

MAJOR PREMISE: In the categorical syllogism, the premise which contains the major term together with the middle term.

MAJOR TERM: In the categorical syllogism, the term that is the predicate of the conclusion (also found in the major premise along with the middle term).

MATTER: As contrasted with form, the actual material dealt with in a proposition or argument. Also, the truth or falsity of such a proposition or argument.

MEAN: The simple average (the sum of the measures divided by the number of items).

MEAN, WEIGHTED: A modified average.

$$\text{Formula:} \quad WM = \frac{\Sigma m W}{\Sigma W}$$

MEDIAN: The point in a group of measures below which and above which may be found an equal number of the measures.

MIDDLE TERM: In the categorical syllogism, the term common to both the major and minor premise, but not found in the conclusion.

MINOR PREMISE: The second premise of the syllogism. In the categorical syllogism it consists of the middle and minor terms.

MINOR TERM: In the categorical syllogism, the subject of the conclusion also found in the minor premise, together with the middle term.

MODE: The value on the scale which occurs most frequently in a simple ungrouped series of measures.

Modus ponens: To affirm the conclusion by affirming the antecedent. $(p \supset q) \cdot p \supset q$.

Modus tollens: To deny the conclusion by denying the consequent. $(p \supset q) \cdot -q \supset -p$.

MOODS OF THE SYLLOGISM: The 64 possible different combinations of A, E, I, and O propositions in the categorical syllogism.

NECESSARY CONDITION: If all cases of A are cases of B, then B is said to be a necessary condition of A, e.g., being in motion (B) is a necessary condition of being a planet (A).

NONADDITIVE QUALITIES: Qualities which are measured by being placed on a scale from high to low. They may be equal to, greater than, or less than other similar qualities. Also called intensive magnitudes.

Non sequitur: The name applied to any process of drawing a conclusion for which there are no logical grounds.

NORMAL PROBABILITY CURVE: Sometimes called "normal curve of error." In a distribution resulting from the purely mathematical probabilities, the curve is perfectly symmetrical and ideal. In a distribution based upon empirical results, the curve is usually skewed.

"O" PROPOSITION: A particular negative proposition, of the form "Some S's are not P's." The subject is undistributed; the predicate is distributed.

OBVERSION: A form of immediate inference in which the quality of the proposition is changed from affirmative to negative or from negative to affirmative, and the predicate of the original proposition is contradicted.

OCCAM'S RAZOR: The law of parsimony, enunciated by William of Occam. It is stated *"Entia non sunt multiplicanda praeter necessitatem"* ("Entities ought not to be multiplied beyond necessity"). Thus, if two explanations are equally acceptable, the simpler of the two should be chosen.

ODDS: The ratio between favorable and unfavorable alternatives in the probability calculus. Formula: f/u.

Onus probandi: The burden of proof.

OPPOSITION: Relations between propositions, such as, contrary, contradictory, privative, and relative.

OSTENSIVE DEFINITION: Definition by pointing.

PARADOX: A proposition or assertion contrary to the generally accepted belief, for which the evidence is as good as the evidence for the generally accepted belief.

PARALOGISM: A fallacious argument; a formal error in reasoning.

PARTICULAR PROPOSITION: An I or O proposition; a proposition whose subject is undistributed.

PATHETIC FALLACY: Ascribing human feelings and emotions to nature.

Petitio principii: The fallacy of assuming in one of the premises the thing to be proved.

Post hoc ergo propter hoc: Literally, After that, hence caused by that. The fallacy of assuming that because two events stand in temporal succession they are therefore causally related.

POSTULATES: A proposition assumed or enunciated without proof.

PREDICABLES: The five most general attributes involved in logical division and predication, namely, genus, species, difference, property, and accident.

PREDICATE: The third part of the categorical proposition, e.g., that which is asserted or denied about the subject.

PREMISE (OR PREMISS): A proposition constituting the data or grounds of any argument. Either of the first two propositions of a syllogism.

PRINCIPLE OF PARSIMONY: Sometimes called Occam's Razor. In attempting to explain anything, the least possible number of assumptions should be made which will account for the facts.

PROBABILITY: Empirical probability is an approximation to fact or truth, relative to the weight of evidence. Mathematical probability is the ratio or number of possible favorable outcomes of an occurrence to the total number of possible outcomes, these being "equally possible."

$$\text{Formula:} \quad \frac{f}{f + u}.$$

PROBABLE ERROR: A measure of distance along the base line of a normal curve; when laid off on both sides of the mean, it includes half of the scores.

Probandum: That which is to be tested or proved.

PROBATIVE: Affording evidence or truth.

PROOF: Deductively valid argument resulting from the observation of logical rules. Inductively, proof is the adequate reason or reasons for holding to the truth or probability of a proposition on the basis of evidence.

PROPOSITION: A logical assertion. The simplest logical unit.

PROPOSITIONAL FUNCTION: An expression containing one or more variables.

PROTOCOL STATEMENT: Sometimes called basic sentences. Statements in which the results of observations are formulated which furnish the basis for confirmation of propositions or hypotheses.

QUALITY (OF PROPOSITIONS): Whether affirmative or negative.

QUANTIFICATION: The operation of symbolizing such words as "some," "all," and "no," for the purpose of carrying out inferences.

QUANTIFIER: Words such as "all," "no," "none," or "some" which make the quantity of subject terms explicit and indicate distribution.

QUANTITY (OF PROPOSITIONS): Fullness or extent of denotation, i.e., whether or not distributed.

QUESTION-BEGGING EPITHET: An adjective which ascribes a quality, attribute, or property whose presence is under dispute or investigation.

RANDOM SAMPLE: A fair or representative sample or selection.

REBUTTAL: Argument by counter dilemma.

Reductio ad adsurdum: Reduction to absurdity as a means of disproof; (e.g., if A implies B and B is absurd, then A is absurd).

REFERENT: The object referred to by a symbol or word.

REFUTE: To disprove and overthrow by argument, evidence, or proof; to prove to be false or erroneous.

RELATION: Any of a number of logical structures by which two or more terms may be associated, e.g., bigger than, equal to, brother of, etc.

RELEVANCE: The property of bearing upon or applying to the case in hand; pertinence.

RELIABILITY: In statistics a term used to indicate a standard to which
a test or measure must conform. A test is said to be reliable if it
measures what it professes to measure accurately. The reliability
of samples is tested by such measures as standard error and probable error.

RESIDUES, METHOD OF: One of Mill's canons: "Subduct from any phenomenon such part as is known by previous inductions to be the
effect of certain antecedents, and the residue of the phenomenon is
the effect of the remaining antecedents."

SAMPLING: The process and technique of selecting instances representative of a whole group.

SELECTED INSTANCES: The fallacy of generalizing from unrepresentative instances.

SEMANTICS (OR SEMASIOLOGY): The science of the meanings of words
and symbols; specifically, the relation between symbols and referents.

SIGN: A mark or indication by which anything is made known.

SIMPLE DILEMMA: One in which the consequents or antecedents of both
hypothetical propositions of the major premise are the same.

SINGULAR PROPOSITION: One whose subject is a singular term.

SINGULAR TERM: One which names a class having only one member.

SOPHISTRY: Captious or fallacious reasoning, particularly if the inten-
tion is to deceive.

SORITES: A chain argument in the form of a polysyllogism of which
only the final conclusion is expressed.

SPECIAL PLEADING: In equity practice, a special answer showing cause
why the suit should be either dismissed, delayed, or barred.

STANDARD DEVIATION: A statistical measurement of dispersion.

$$\text{Formula:}\quad \sigma = \sqrt{\frac{\Sigma FD^2}{N} - (c')^2} \times \text{step interval.}$$

STANDARD ERROR: A measure of reliability in statistics.

STIPULATION: In semantics, the process of assigning meanings to words.

SUBALTERN: Particular, with reference to a related universal. See
subimplication.

SUBCONTRARY: The propositions p and q are subcontraries when if p
is false q is true, and if q is false p is true, while both may be true.
In the traditional square of opposition, I and O are subcontraries.

SUBIMPLICATION: A proposition q stands in relation of subimplication
to p when from the truth of q nothing can be inferred regarding the
truth value of p, but if q is false, p is also false. In the traditional
square of opposition, I and O propositions stand in the relation of
subimplication to A and E propositions, respectively.

SUBJECT: The first of the three parts of the categorical proposition; the term about which the predicate asserts something.

SUFFICIENT CONDITION: If all cases of A are cases of B, A is a sufficient condition of B; e.g., a running motor (A) is a sufficient condition of igniting fuel (B).

SUPERIMPLICATION: A proposition p stands in the relation of super-implication to q when from the truth of p the truth of q follows. In the square of opposition, A and E propositions stand in the relation of superimplication to I and O propositions, respectively.

SYLLOGISM: Defined by Aristotle as "discourse in which certain things being posited, something else than what is posited necessarily follows merely from them." The syllogism is made up of three propositions: the major premise, the minor premise, and the conclusion.

SYMBOL: A conventional sign by which a term or property is abbreviated or represented.

SYMMETRY: A property of any relation between terms when, if the relation holds between A and B, it holds between B and A. Thus, the relation "married to" is symmetrical, for, if John is married to Joan, Joan is married to John.

SYNTHETIC PROPOSITION: One in which the predicate asserts something of the subject which is not discoverable by the nature of the subject itself. Opposed to analytical proposition, or definition.

TAKE BY THE HORNS: A method of defense against dilemma consisting of the detection of a fallacy of the consequent not following from the antecedent in either or both parts of the major premise.

TAUTOLOGY: A proposition that is necessarily true by virtue of its truth-functional form.

THEOREM: A proposition in a deductive system implicit in the primitive notions and postulates of the system.

THEORY: A verified hypothesis applicable to many related phenomena.

TRANSITIVITY: A property of any relation when, if the relation holds between A and B and between B and C, it also holds between A and C. Thus, the relation "greater than" is transitive, for, if A is greater than B and B is greater than C, then A is greater than C.

TRUTH-FUNCTIONAL PROPOSITION: A proposition is truth-functional if its truth value is uniquely determined by (i.e., is a function of) the truth values of other propositions, as are the component propositions in a conjunction.

TRUTH TABLE: A truth table is a technique in symbolic logic for exhibiting the truth values of compound propositions through an exhaustive portrayal of all of the possible truth values of their simple components.

UNDISTRIBUTED: Not fully denotative or extended; denoting only part of a class.

UNIVERSAL GENERALIZATION, U.G.: The rule of inference which allows us to argue from any arbitrarily selected individual to the universal class, provided names introduced through the use of existential instantiation are excluded.

UNIVERSAL INSTANTIATION, U.I.: The rule of inference which enables us to say that, from a universal quantification, we may validly infer any instance of it.

UNIVERSAL QUANTIFIER: The notation ( ), where any variable such as "x" may be supplied, prefixing a formula containing that variable. For instance, (x) Px corresponds to "For every value of x, x is a P."

UNIVERSAL PROPOSITION: An A or E proposition, i.e., one whose subject is distributed.

UNIVERSE OF DISCOURSE: A context of thought; a department of knowledge.

UNIVOCAL: Having only one meaning; not equivocal or ambiguous.

VAGUENESS: A characteristic of terms which have no precise application in a given context.

VALIDITY: The central problem of deduction, involving the question of whether or not the premises imply the conclusion. In testing, a test is valid if it measures what it professes to measure.

VARIABLE: A magnitude which has different values under different conditions, as opposed to *constant*.

VERIFICATION: The process of showing that a proposition is true. Confirmation of an hypothesis by showing that its predictions agree with the facts.

VICIOUS CIRCLE: The fallacy of proving a proposition by one or more other propositions which themselves rest on it for proof.

D

Classification of Formal, Semantic, Material, and Inductive Fallacies

1. FORMAL FALLACIES

A. Fallacies of immediate inference
    (1) False conversion
    (2) False obversion
B. Fallacies of division
    (1) Cross division
    (2) Incomplete division
    (3) Overlapping division
C. Fallacies of the categorical syllogism: mediate inference
    (1) Four terms of ambiguous middle
    (2) Undistributed middle
    (3) Illicit major
    (4) Illicit minor
    (5) Two negative premises
    (6) Affirmative conclusion from a negative premise
    (7) Negative conclusion from two affirmative premises
    (8) Two particular premises
    (9) The existential fallacy
D. Fallacies of the hypothetical syllogism
    (1) Affirming the consequent
    (2) Denying the antecedent
E. Fallacy of the alternative syllogism
    (1) Affirming one alternate

350

F. Fallacy of the disjunctive syllogism
   (1) Denying one disjunct
G. Dilemmatic fallacies
   (1) Consequents do not follow from antecedents in the major premise
   (2) Imperfect disjunction in the minor premise
   (3) Conclusion capable of rebuttal by a counterdilemma

2. RELATIONAL FALLACIES

A. When only one relation is used in the premises:
   Failure to use transitive relations throughout the argument
B. When more than one relation is used in the premises:
   Failure to eliminate, combine, or substitute relations correctly in the conclusion

3. FALLACIES OF AMBIGUITY, OR SEMANTIC FALLACIES

A. Fallacy of equivocation
B. Fallacy of amphiboly
C. Fallacy of composition
D. Fallacy of division
E. Fallacy of accent

4. MATERIAL FALLACIES

A. Fallacy of accident
B. Converse fallacy of accident
C. Fallacies of irrelevancy
   (1) *Argumentum ad hominem* (directed toward the man)
   (2) *Argumentum ad populum* (appeal to the crowd)
   (3) *Argumentum ad misericordiam* (appeal to pity)
   (4) *Argumentum ad verecundiam* (appeal to authority and reverence)
   (5) *Argumentum ad ignorantiam* (appeal to ignorance)
   (6) *Argumentum ad baculum* (appeal to force)
   (7) *Non sequitur*
D. Fallacies of unwarranted assumption
   (1) Begging the question, or *petitio principii*
   (2) Arguing in a circle
   (3) Question-begging epithets
   (4) False cause
   (5) Complex question or many questions

5. INDUCTIVE FALLACIES

A. Individual prejudices and prepossessions
B. Fallacies of observation
   (1) Incomplete observation
   (2) Inaccurate observation
C. Fallacies of classification
   (1) Incomplete classification
   (2) Overlapping classification
   (3) Cross-classification
D. Fallacies in the use of hypotheses
   (1) Improbable hypotheses
   (2) Hypothesis "contrary to fact"
E. Fallacies incident to the determination of causes
   (1) *Post hoc ergo propter hoc*
   (2) Insufficient analysis and enumeration of antecedents
   (3) Insufficient analysis and enumeration of differences
   (4) Accidental, temporal, or partial concomitance
   (5) Confusion of condition and cause
   (6) Confusion of cause and reciprocal relation
   (7) Confusion of sufficient and necessary condition
F. Hasty generalization
G. False analogy
H. Statistical fallacies
   (1) Unrepresentative sampling
   (2) Application of results derived from group phenomena to individual cases
   (3) Failure to state the reliability of results
   (4) Fallacy of chance correlation

E

Selected Bibliography

A. SEMANTICS

CARNAP, R. *Introduction to Semantics.* Cambridge, Mass.: Harvard University Press, 1942.

———. *The Logical Syntax of Language.* New York: Harcourt, Brace & World, Inc., 1937.

CHASE, S. *The Tyranny of Words.* New York: Harcourt, Brace & World, Inc., 1938.

———. *Power of Words.* New York: Harcourt, Brace & World, Inc., 1954.

GOMPERZ, H. "The Meanings of 'Meaning,'" *Philosophy of Science,* Vol. VIII (1941), No. 2.

GREENOUGH, J. B., and KITTRIDGE, G. L. *Words and Their Ways in English Speech.* New York: The Macmillan Co., 1906.

HAYAKAWA, S. I. *Language in Action.* New York: Harcourt, Brace & World, Inc., 1941.

———. *Language in Thought and Action.* New York: Harcourt, Brace & World, Inc., 1949.

JESPERSON, O. *Language.* London: George Allen & Unwin, 1922.

KORZYBSKI, A. *Science and Sanity.* 2d ed. New York: The International Non-Aristotelian Library Publishing Co., 1941.

LINSKY, LEONARD (ed.). *Semantics and the Philosophy of Language.* Urbana: University of Illinois Press, 1952.

MACKAYE, J. *The Logic of Language.* Hanover; N.H.: Dartmouth Publications, 1939.

MARTIN, R. M. *Truth and Denotation.* Chicago: University of Chicago Press, 1958.

MORRIS, C. W. "Foundations of the Theory of Signs," *International Encyclopedia of Unified Science,* Vol. I (1947), No. 2.

———. *Signs, Language and Behavior.* Englewood Cliffs, N.J.: Prentice-Hall, Inc., 1946.

OGDEN, C. K., and RICHARDS, I. A. *The Meaning of Meaning.* New York: Harcourt, Brace & World, Inc., 1948.

PARTRIDGE, E. *Words, Words, Words.* London: Methuen & Co., Ltd., 1933.

QUINE, W. V. O. *Word and Object.* New York: John Wiley & Sons, Inc., 1960.

ROBINSON, R. *Definition.* Fair Lawn, N.J.: Oxford University Press, 1950.

RUSSELL, B. *An Inquiry into Meaning and Truth.* London: George Allen & Unwin, 1948.

SIDGWICK, A. *The Use of Words in Reasoning.* London: Adam & Charles
    Black, Lt., 1901.
STERN, G. "Meaning and Change of Meaning," *Arsskrift* (Götsborgs Hogskolas),
    Vol. XXXVIII (1932).
TARSKI, ALFRED. *Logic, Semantics, Mathematics.* Fair Lawn, N.J.: Oxford
    University Press, 1956.
WALPOLE, H. *Semantics.* New York: W. W. Norton & Co., Inc., 1951.
WEEKLEY, E. *The Romance of Words.* 4th ed. London: John Murray Pub-
    lishers, Ltd., 1925.

B. SYMBOLIC LOGIC

AMBROSE, A., and LAZEROWITZ, M. *Fundamentals of Symbolic Logic.* 2d ed.
    New York: Holt, Rinehart & Winston, Inc., 1962.
BASSON, A. H., and O'CONNOR, D. J. *Introduction to Symbolic Logic.* New
    York: The Free Press of Glencoe, Inc., 1960.
BOOLE, G. *An Investigation of the Laws of Thought.* 2d ed. New York: Dover
    Publications, Inc., 1951.
————. *The Mathematical Analysis of Logic.* Oxford, England: Basil Blackwell
    & Mott, Ltd., 1948.
CARNAP, R. "Foundations of Logic and Mathematics," *International Encyclo-
    pedia of Unified Science,* Vol. I (1947), No. 3.
————. *Introduction to Symbolic Logic and Its Applications.* New York:
    Dover Publications, Inc., 1958.
CHURCH, A. *Introduction to Mathematical Logic.* Princeton, N.J.: Princeton
    University Press, 1956.
CHURCHMAN, C. W. *Elements of Logic and Formal Science.* Philadelphia:
    J. B. Lippincott Co., 1940.
COOLEY, J. C. *A Primer of Formal Logic.* New York: The Macmillan Co., 1942.
COPI, I. *Symbolic Logic.* 3d ed. New York: The Macmillan Co., 1967.
COUTURAT, L. *The Algebra of Logic.* La Salle, Ill.: The Open Court Publishing
    Co., 1914.
DE MORGAN, A. *Formal Logic.* La Salle, Ill.: The Open Court Publishing Co.,
    1926.
DICKOFF, J., and JAMES, PATRICIA. *Symbolic Logic and Language* (a programmed
    text). New York: McGraw-Hill Book Co., Inc., 1965.
FARIS, J. A. *Truth-functional Logic.* New York: The Free Press of Glencoe,
    Inc., 1962.
————. *Quantification Theory.* New York: Dover Publications, Inc., 1964.
FITCH, F. B. *Symbolic Logic: An Introduction.* New York: The Ronald Press
    Co., 1952.
HALBERSTADT, W. H. *An Introduction to Modern Logic.* New York: Harper
    & Row, 1960.
KALISH, D., and MONTAGUE, R. *Logic Techniques of Formal Reasoning.* New
    York: Harcourt, Brace & World, Inc., 1964.
LANGER, S. K. *An Introduction to Symbolic Logic.* 2d ed. New York: Dover
    Publications, Inc., 1953.
LEE, HAROLD N. *Symbolic Logic.* New York: Random House, Inc., 1961.
LEWIS, C. I. *Survey of Symbolic Logic.* 2d ed. New York: Dover Publications,
    Inc., 1960.
————, and LANGFORD, C. H. *Symbolic Logic.* 2d ed. New York: Dover Publica-
    tions, Inc., 1959.
QUINE, W. V. O. *Elementary Logic.* Rev. ed. Cambridge, Mass.: Harvard
    University Press, 1966.

————. *Mathematical Logic*. 2d ed. Cambridge, Mass.: Harvard University Press, 1951.

————. *Methods of Logic*. 2d ed. New York: Holt, Rinehart & Winston, Inc., 1959.

REICHENBACH, H. *Elements of Symbolic Logic*. 2d ed. New York: The Free Press of Glencoe, Inc., 1966.

ROSENBLOOM, P. C. *The Elements of Mathematical Logic*. New York: Dover Publications, Inc., 1950.

SMITH, H. B. *Logic as the Art of Symbols*. New York: F. S. Crofts & Co., 1933.

STRAWSON, P. F. *Introduction to Logical Theory*. New York: John Wiley & Sons, Inc., 1952.

SUPPES, P., and HILL, S. *First Course in Mathematical Logic*. 2d ed. Boston: Ginn & Co., 1966.

TARSKI, A. *Introduction to Logic*. 3d ed. Fair Lawn, N.J.: Oxford University Press, 1965.

VENN, J. *Symbolic Logic*. 2d ed. London: The Macmillan Co., Ltd., 1894.

WHITEHEAD, A. N., and RUSSELL, B. *Principia Mathematica*. 2d ed. London: Cambridge University Press, 1950.

C. SCIENTIFIC METHOD

BALLENTINE, W. G. *Logic of Science*. New York: Thomas Y. Crowell Co., 1933.

BARKER, S. F. *Induction and Hypotheses*. Ithica, N.Y.: Cornell University Press, 1957.

BENJAMIN, A. C. *The Logical Structure of Science*. London. Routledge & Kegan Paul, Ltd., 1936.

BRAITHWAITE, R. B. *Scientific Explanation*. New York: Harper & Row, 1953.

BRIDGMAN, P. W. *The Logic of Modern Physics*. New York: The Macmillan Co., 1927.

BROAD, C. C. *Scientific Thought*. 2d ed. Ames, Iowa: Littlefield, Adams & Co., 1959.

CAMPBELL, N. *What Is Science?* New York: Dover Publications, Inc., 1952.

CARMICHAEL, R. D. *The Logic of Discovery*. La Salle, Ill.: The Open Court Publishing Co., 1930.

DE SANTILLANA, G., and ZILSEL, E. "The Development of Rationalism and Empiricism," *International Encyclopedia of Unified Science*, Vol. II (1947), No. 8.

HEMPEL, CARL G. *Aspects of Scientific Explanation*. New York: The Free Press of Glencoe, Inc., 1965.

JEFFREYS, H. *Scientific Inference*. 2d ed. London: Cambridge University Press, 1957.

JEVONS, W. S. *The Principles of Science*. Rev. ed. New York: Dover Publications, Inc., 1958.

KEMENY, J. G. *A Philosopher Looks at Science*. Princeton, N.J.: D. Van Nostrand Co., Inc., 1959.

LENZEN, V. F. "Procedures of Empirical Science," *International Encyclopedia of Unified Science*, Vol. I (1948), No. 5.

MADDEN, E. H. *Structure of Scientific Thought*. Boston: Houghton Mifflin Co., 1960.

NAGEL, E. *The Structure of Science*. New York: Harcourt, Brace & World, Inc., 1961.

NORTHROP, F. S. C. *The Logic of the Sciences and the Humanities*. New York: The Macmillan Co., 1947.

POINCARÉ, H. *Science and Hypothesis.* New York: Dover Publications, Inc., 1952.

POPPER, K. R. *The Logic of Scientific Discovery.* London: Hutchinson & Co., Ltd., 1959.

RITCHIE, A. D. *Scientific Method.* New York: Harcourt, Brace & World, Inc., 1923.

SINGER, C. F. (ed.). *Studies in the History and Methodology of Science.* Vols. I (1917), II (1921).

SMART, H. R. *The Logic of Science.* New York: Appleton-Century-Crofts, Inc., 1931.

WILLIAMS, D. C. *The Ground of Induction.* Cambridge, Mass.: Harvard University Press, 1947.

WILSON, E. B. *An Introduction to Scientific Research.* New York: McGraw-Hill Book Co., Inc., 1952.

WOLF, A. *Essentials of Scientific Method.* London: George Allen & Unwin, 1928.

WRIGHT, G. H. *The Logical Problem of Induction.* 2d ed. Oxford, England: Basil Blackwell & Mott, Ltd., 1957.

————. *A Treatise on Induction and Probability.* London: Routledge & Kegan Paul, Ltd., 1951.

WRIGHT, HELEN, and RAPPORT, SAMUEL. *Great Adventures in Science.* New York: Harper & Row, 1956.

D. PROBABILITY AND STATISTICS

ADLER, IRVING. *Probability and Statistics for Everyman.* Rev. ed. New York: The John Day Co., 1963.

BOREL, E. F. E. J. *Elements of the Theory of Probability.* Englewood Cliffs, N.J.: Prentice-Hall, Inc., 1965.

CROXTON, F. E., and COWDEN, D. J. *Applied General Statistics.* 3d ed. Englewood Cliffs, N.J. Prentice-Hall, Inc., 1960.

DAY, JOHN P. *Inductive Probability.* New York: Humanities Press, Inc., 1961.

FELLER, W. *An Introduction to Probability Theory and Its Applications.* 3d ed. New York: John Wiley & Sons, Inc., 1966.

FREEMAN, L. C. *Elementary Applied Statistics.* New York: John Wiley & Sons, Inc., 1965.

FREYER, H. C. *Elements of Statistics.* New York: John Wiley & Sons, Inc., 1954.

FRY, T. C. *Probability and Its Engineering Uses.* Rev. ed. Princeton, N.J.: D. Van Nostrand Co., Inc., 1965.

GARRETT, H. E. *Statistics in Psychology and Education.* 5th ed. New York: David McKay Co., Inc., 1958.

GOLDBERG, SAMUEL. *Probability: An Introduction.* Englewood Cliffs, N.J.: Prentice-Hall, Inc., 1960.

GRAY, C. T., and VOTAW, D. F. *Statistics Applied to Education and Psychology.* New York: The Ronald Press Co., 1939.

GUILFORD, J. P. *Psychometric Methods.* New York: McGraw-Hill Book Co., Inc., 1936.

————. *Fundamental Statistics in Psychology and Education.* 4th ed. New York: McGraw-Hill Book Co., Inc., 1965.

HAMMOND, K. R., and HOUSEHOLDER, J. E. *Introduction to the Statistical Method.* New York: Alfred A. Knopf, Inc., 1964.

KELLEY, TRUMAN L. *Fundamentals of Statistics.* Cambridge, Mass.: Harvard University Press, 1947.

KEYNES, J. M. *A Treatise on Probability.* New York: St. Martin's Press, Inc., 1963.

KNEALE, W. C. *Probability and Induction.* Fair Lawn, N.J.: Oxford University Press, 1949.

LEVIN, R. I., and KIRKPATRICK, G. A. *Quantitative Approaches to Management.* New York: McGraw-Hill Book Co., Inc., 1965.

LINDLEY, DENNIS U. *Introduction to Probability and Statistics from a Bayesian Viewpoint.* London: Cambridge University Press, 1965.

LINDGREN B. W., and McELRATH G. W. *Introduction to Probability and Statistics.* 2d ed. New York: The Macmillan Co., 1966.

MOOD, ALEXANDER M. *Introduction to the Theory of Statistics.* New York: McGraw-Hill Book Co., Inc., 1950.

NAGEL, E. "Principles of the Theory of Probability," *International Encyclopedia of Unified Science,* Vol. I (1947), No. 6.

PARRATT, LYMAN G. *Probability and Experimental Errors in Science.* New York: John Wiley & Sons, Inc., 1961.

PEARSON, FRANK A., and BENNETT, K. R. *Statistical Methods.* New York: John Wiley & Sons, Inc., 1942.

SMITH, G. E. *A Simplified Guide in Statistics.* 3d ed. New York: Holt, Rinehart & Winston, Inc., 1962.

STANLEY, J. C. *Measurement in Today's Schools.* 4th ed. Englewood Cliffs, N.J.: Prentice-Hall, Inc., 1964.

THORP, E. O. *Elementary Probability.* New York: John Wiley & Sons, Inc., 1966

WERT, J. E., NEIDT, C. O., and AHMANN, J. S. *Statistical Methods in Educational and Psychological Research.* New York: Appleton-Century-Crofts, Inc., 1954.

YOUNG, R. K., and VELDMAN, D. J. *Introductory Statistics for the Behavioral Sciences.* New York: Holt, Rinehart & Winston, Inc., 1965.

E. LOGIC AND LAW

BAADE, H. W. (ed.). *Jurimetrics.* New York: Basic Books, Inc., 1963.

BAKER, NEWMAN F., and INBAU, FRED E. "The Scientific Detection of Crime," *Minnesota Law Review,* Vol. XVII (1933), 602.

BODENHEIMER, E. "Law and Scientific Method," *Chapter 17 in Jurisprudence.* Cambridge, Mass.: Harvard University Press, 1962.

COOK, W. E. "Legal Logic," *Columbia Law Review,* Vol. XXXI (January, 1931), 108–15.

———. "Scientific Method and the Law," *American Bar Association Journal,* June 13, 1927.

DEWEY, JOHN. "Logical Method and Law," *Cornell Law Quarterly,* Vol. X (December, 1924), 17–27.

FRANKFURTER, F. *The Case of Sacco and Vanzetti.* Boston: Little, Brown & Co., 1927.

LEVI, EDWARD H. *An Introduction to Legal Reasoning.* Chicago: University of Chicago Press, 1963.

LEVY, B. H. *Cardozo and the Frontiers of Legal Thinking.* Fair Lawn, N.J.: Oxford University Press, 1938.

McCORMICK, CHARLES T. *Handbook of the Law of Evidence.* St. Paul: West Publishing Co., 1954.

MAYER, MARTIN. "Justice, the Law, and the Lawyers," *Saturday Evening Post,* February 26, 1966, pp. 36 ff.

MORRIS, C. *How Lawyers Think*. Cambridge, Mass.: Harvard University Press, 1937.

MUNSTERBERG, H. *On the Witness Stand*. New York: Clark Boardman Co., Ltd., 1927.

RADIN, M. *Law as Logic and Experience*. New Haven: Yale University Press, 1940.

ROONEY, M. T. "Law and the New Logic," *Proceedings of the American Catholic Philosophical Association*, 1940.

TURNER, R. F. *Forensic Science and Laboratory Techniques*. Springfield, Ill.: Charles C Thomas, 1949.

WASSERSTROM, R. A. *The Judicial Decision*. Stanford, Calif.: Stanford University Press, 1961.

WELLMAN, F. L. *The Art of Cross Examination*. 4th ed. New York: The Macmillan Co., 1945.

WIGMORE, J. H. *The Science of Judicial Proof*. 3d ed. Boston: Little, Brown & Co., 1937.

———. *The Student's Textbook of the Law of Evidence*. New York: Foundation Press, Inc., 1935.

Index

S